THE NEW EU COMPETITION LAW

This book provides the first comprehensive account of the New EU Competition Law: an emerging understanding of the discipline that breaks from the consensus of the early 2000s and that ventures into uncharted territories. Competition law has undergone fundamental transformations in the past decade, from the rise and fall of the 'effects-based approach' to the challenge of Big Tech and the growing interaction with intellectual property. Making sense of these changes and fully grasping their implications can be difficult.

The book discusses the shift from traditional enforcement in the industrial era to the sort of intervention that a knowledge-based economy demands. It presents the changes that the field is undergoing (policy priorities, relationship with regulation and intangible assets, move away from efficiency and consumer welfare) and illustrates them by reference to the most significant developments.

The analysis includes an up-to-date evaluation of the Digital Markets Act and addresses the application of EU competition law to key areas, including energy, pharma, telecommunications and online platforms.

Conceived as a 'modular' book, practitioners and advanced students will find it useful as a map to navigate the underlying trends and as an in-depth dissection of the key case law and administrative practice of the past decade.

Online resources to accompany this book are available at www.bloomsburyonlineresources.com/the-new-eu-competition-law. If you experience any problems, please contact Bloomsbury at: onlineresources@bloomsbury.com

The New EU Competition Law

Pablo Ibáñez Colomo

·HART·
OXFORD · LONDON · NEW YORK · NEW DELHI · SYDNEY

HART PUBLISHING

Bloomsbury Publishing Plc

Kemp House, Chawley Park, Cumnor Hill, Oxford, OX2 9PH, UK

1385 Broadway, New York, NY 10018, USA

29 Earlsfort Terrace, Dublin 2, Ireland

HART PUBLISHING, the Hart/Stag logo, BLOOMSBURY and the Diana logo are trademarks of Bloomsbury Publishing Plc

First published in Great Britain 2023

Copyright © Pablo Ibáñez Colomo, 2023

Pablo Ibáñez Colomo has asserted his right under the Copyright, Designs and Patents Act 1988 to be identified as Author of this work.

All rights reserved. No part of this publication may be reproduced or transmitted in any form or by any means, electronic or mechanical, including photocopying, recording, or any information storage or retrieval system, without prior permission in writing from the publishers.

While every care has been taken to ensure the accuracy of this work, no responsibility for loss or damage occasioned to any person acting or refraining from action as a result of any statement in it can be accepted by the authors, editors or publishers.

All UK Government legislation and other public sector information used in the work is Crown Copyright ©. All House of Lords and House of Commons information used in the work is Parliamentary Copyright ©. This information is reused under the terms of the Open Government Licence v3.0 (http://www.nationalarchives.gov.uk/doc/open-government-licence/version/3) except where otherwise stated.

All Eur-lex material used in the work is © European Union, http://eur-lex.europa.eu/, 1998–2023.

A catalogue record for this book is available from the British Library.

A catalogue record for this book is available from the Library of Congress.

Library of Congress Control Number: 2023947604

ISBN:	HB:	978-1-50996-710-0
	ePDF:	978-1-78225-915-2
	ePub:	978-1-78225-914-5

Typeset by Compuscript Ltd, Shannon

To find out more about our authors and books visit www.hartpublishing.co.uk. Here you will find extracts, author information, details of forthcoming events and the option to sign up for our newsletters.

ACKNOWLEDGEMENTS

As academics, we often take pride in delivering 'research-led' teaching. As I understand the term, it is intended to signal that we ask our students to work on academic material as if they were scholars in the making, not just consumers of bite-size pieces of information. What we often fail to acknowledge – and we should – is how much our research is teaching-led. There is a great deal of truth in the claim that we do not really understand an issue until we are asked to lecture on it. The classroom is the ideal space to test the most effective way to convey complex concepts. The ideas with which we toy in our head and the patterns that we spot are not easy to turn into an intelligible framework. It takes time and energy. Conversations with advanced students are an indispensable part of the gestation process, and definitely the most rewarding one.

This book is inseparable from my teaching. I see it as the companion of an LLM seminar I have delivered at LSE Law School for a decade (*Competition Law: Challenges and Prospects*, which was then split into *Competition Law, Technology and Intellectual Property* and the *Law and Economics of Network Industries*). This module was designed with the explicit purpose of exposing students to the frontiers of knowledge in the field. Competition law has changed so much in the past two decades that I felt that the available materials did not do the ongoing substantive and intellectual transformations justice. Showing students what was going on and equipping them for their professional lives required a new vocabulary and a new conceptualisation of the behaviour of key institutional players.

My first debt of gratitude therefore goes to the LLM candidates with whom I shared these ideas. The immense fortune of teaching at LSE Law School is that students love being exposed to the uncharted territory of emerging developments in a sui generis area of the law. I distinctly remember a comment in a teaching evaluation, where a student praised the course precisely because it was so difficult (which, if you ask me, is pretty much the best feedback one can hope to receive as a lecturer). Of the dozens of excellent students that I have had over the years, I have to single out Ioanna Kladi. In the last stages of the project, she assisted with the revision and the preparation of the manuscript. When doing so, she displayed remarkable intellectual maturity, good judgement and attention to detail. All these qualities will no doubt allow her to excel in the career she chooses to pursue.

LSE Law School is a vibrant environment not just because of its students, but because of the top scholars that I am fortunate enough to call my colleagues. Since joining the School in September 2010, I have always been convinced that its secret lies in the senior academics, who are invariably rigorous and original thinkers from whom one always learns something. Two of these scholars, Niamh Moloney and David Kershaw, led the Law School when this book was written. I am very grateful to them for creating the conditions within which junior colleagues can flourish and learn from one another. Eduardo Baistrocchi has followed the evolution of the project from the early stages and was always willing to share his thoughts. His devotion to ideas and his energy are, as anyone who knows him is aware, contagious. Niamh Dunne and Andriani Kalintiri taught the module with me at various points in time; they deserve a shout-out for that and for being all-round wonderful colleagues.

Other academics and practitioners have provided invaluable input at various stages of the process. Every conversation with Heike Schweitzer is memorable, and her insights on several aspects of the book improved it significantly. I have to thank Christian Ahlborn, Rafael Allendesalazar, Or Brook, Jorge Contreras, Adrien de Hautecloque, Alexandre de Streel, Mark English, Carla Farinhas, Martin Husovec, Robin Jacob, Thorsten Käseberg, William Leslie, Orla Lynskey, Stavros Makris, Luke McDonagh, Igor Nikolic, Luminita Olteanu, Jorge Padilla and Ryan Stones for sharing their expertise and for providing comments on several chapters. I definitely have to thank Alfonso Lamadrid de Pablo, too, even though he never gets to read any of my books (no matter how passionately I talk about them over the phone). Many of the ideas expressed here were first sketched in our blog (which was then neglected to complete these pages).

I am immensely lucky to have bumped into Sinéad Moloney and Roberta Bassi. Sinéad felt there was a potentially good project on the back of some half-baked ideas and two pages outlining how I intended to structure them. This was sufficient for her to offer a contract, which I took a while to honour – in my defence, there was so much going on that finding the right time was not an easy task. Roberta took over the project and the impetus she provided was absolutely crucial in the last year. The faith she placed in it was pivotal to its completion (her patience was pivotal, too). Publishers make a big difference, and it is not by chance that Hart has become the natural home for some of the most ambitious scholarly ventures.

This book was conceived and shaped as I was building my life with Alicia. The two processes happened at the same time, and I find it hard to disentangle one from the other. Some pages were written right before our weekly visits to Sazzy & Fran, some right in the middle of a messy renovation. I may or may not have drafted a few passages in a café in Florence while Alicia was visiting the Duomo; and I definitely spent time on the book when we should have been hiking, travelling or just enjoying some time together. She must be incredibly patient, you may be thinking. She is. And she is also loving and supportive. This book is dedicated to her.

NOTE ON RECENT DEVELOPMENTS

This book, and the data that supports the findings, reflects the law as it stood on 30 April 2023. I was under no illusion that the book would be fully up to date by the time of publication. Given the fast-paced nature of the field, the only fully updated competition law book is the one that never comes out. It was therefore inevitable that some important developments would take place between the submission of the manuscript and its release. Instead of delaying the launch date, I thought I would add a short note commenting on (some of) these developments. Conveniently, all of them appear to confirm the main theses underpinning the book and exemplify the trends and patterns it describes (including the use of competition law as regulation, the rejection of formalism by the Court of Justice[1] and the reorientation of the Commission's resources to digital markets).

It makes sense to say a word about some developments. Chapters 3, 4 and 7 discuss at some length the Guidelines on horizontal co-operation agreements. On 1 June 2023, the European Commission announced the release of a new version of this instrument.[2] The aspects addressed in the book – and in particular the legal treatment of standardisation agreements – do not change fundamentally from the previous one. Just like its predecessor, the 2023 Guidelines provided for a detailed ex ante regulatory regime applying to the activities of standard development organisations. On 14 June, the Commission launched a Statement of Objections in the *Google – Adtech and Data-related practices*, which is already mentioned in Chapter 8.[3] This Statement of Objections not only confirms the rise of 'market-shaping' enforcement in digital markets, but shows how EU competition law increasingly aims at restructuring industries (and not simply conduct). In its press release, the Commission hints, in fact, at the adoption of a structural remedy. Finally, on 4 July, the Court of Justice delivered its preliminary ruling in *Meta v Bundeskartellamt*.[4] Just like the precedents discussed in the book, the judgment confirmed that a breach of a sector-specific regime can amount to a breach of Article 102 TFEU. More importantly, it went to show how closely intertwined EU competition law and economic regulation have become in the new era.

---

[1] Case C-211/22 *Super Bock Bebidas, SA and others v Commission*, EU:C:2023:529.
[2] European Commission, 'Antitrust: Commission adopts new Horizontal Block Exemption Regulations and Horizontal Guidelines' IP/23/2990 (Brussels, 1 June 2023).
[3] European Commission, 'Antitrust: Commission sends Statement of Objections to Google over abusive practices in online advertising technology' IP/23/3207 (Brussels, 14 June 2023).
[4] Case C-252/21 *Meta Platforms Inc. and others v Bundeskartellamt*, EU:C:2023:537.

CONTENTS

Acknowledgements .... *v*
Note on Recent Developments .... *vii*
List of Figures and Tables .... *xiii*
Table of Cases .... *xv*
Table of Legislation .... *xxv*

Introduction 1
   1. EU Competition Law and Policy: A Moving Target 1
   2. Law, Policy and Institutions under Regulation 1/2003 2
   3. Structure and Design of the Book 5
   4. Hallmarks of the New EU Competition Law 6

PART I
MAPPING THE TRANSFORMATION

1. The Changing Face of Enforcement under Regulation 1/2003 13
   1. The Rise of 'Market-shaping' Enforcement 13
   2. 'Market-shaping' Enforcement in Practice 21
   3. The Decline of 'Law-driven' Enforcement 26
   4. Explaining the Shifts in Enforcement: An Economic Perspective 31
   5. Explaining the Shifts in Enforcement: A Legal and Institutional Perspective 37
   6. Implications for Law and Policy-making 40

2. The Rise and Decline of the 'More Economics-based Approach' 46
   1. The Path to the 'More Economics-based Approach' 46
   2. The Emergence of the 'Brussels Consensus' 50
   3. The Consolidation of the 'More Economics-based Approach' in the Case Law 56
   4. Why the Tide Turned: The Latent, the Old and the New Debates 62
   5. Towards a New Consensus? 68

3. Competition Law and Economic Regulation 73
   1. The Overlapping Application of Competition Law and Regulation 73
   2. Competition Law as a Safety Net: The Auxiliary Role of Articles 101 and 102 TFEU 82

x   *Contents*

    3. Competition Law as a Gap-filling Instrument 86
    4. Competition Law as a Means to Rectify Regulation 91
    5. Competition Law and the 'Expectation of Regulation' 97

4. **Competition Law and Intangible Property** 100
    1. The Features of Intangible Property: Public and Private
       Responses 100
    2. The Complex Relationship between Competition Law
       and Intellectual Property 103
    3. The Deferential Approach to Intangible Property 111
    4. The Decline of the Deferential Approach 118

5. **The DMA as the Expression (and Endgame) of the**
   New Competition Law 124
    1. The DMA as the Endgame of the New EU Competition Law 124
    2. From a Law-driven Process to Policy-driven Outcomes 129
    3. From Exclusion to Restructuring and Redistribution..............................133
    4. The Shift in the Centre of Gravity of Enforcement 140
    5. A 'Third Way' to Promote Dynamic Competition 143
    6. The End of Competition Law or a New Relationship
       with Regulation? 147

PART II
CASE STUDIES

6. **Energy and Telecommunications** 153
    1. Competition Law in the Telecommunications and
       Energy Sectors 153
    2. Autonomous Forms of Abuse in Regulated Markets:
       'Margin Squeeze' and Beyond 163
    3. The Expansion of Existing Doctrines and the Creation of
       New Ones 172
    4. Exploring the Limits of Market Restructuring 181
    5. Analysis: Expansion, Fragmentation, Symbiosis 187

7. **Patents and Copyright** 194
    1. Intellectual Property and its Discontents 194
    2. Standards and Standard Development 198
    3. Intellectual Property and the Regulation of Medicines 207
    4. Copyright Harmonisation via Competition Law Enforcement?
       The *Pay-TV* Saga 219
    5. Conclusions 231

Contents

8. Digital Markets 232
    1. Competition Law in Digital Markets: Product Design and Business Models 232
    2. When Competition Law Interferes with Product Design and Business Models 239
    3. How EU Competition Law Deals with Product Design and Business Model Issues 246
    4. Pro-competitive Gains and Competition on the Merits 250
    5. The Indispensability Condition in Digital Markets 254
    6. The Assessment of Anticompetitive Effects in Digital Markets 260
    7. The Administration of Principles-based Remedies in Digital Markets 266
    8. Conclusions 269

Conclusions 271
    1. The New EU Competition Law in a Changing Landscape 271
    2. Expansion 273
    3. Fragmentation 275
    4. Blending with Economic Regulation 277
    5. Epilogue: Towards the Demise of Articles 101 and 102 TFEU? 278

Bibliography 279
Index 289

LIST OF FIGURES AND TABLES

Figure 1.1	Enforcement variables	15
Figure 1.2	Detection-deterrence enforcement	16
Figure 1.3	Trade-enabling enforcement	17
Figure 1.4	Market-protecting enforcement	17
Figure 1.5	Market-shaping enforcement	18
Figure 1.6	Enforcement paradigms in the EU system	19
Figure 1.7	Remedies in EU competition law	24
Figure 1.8	Evolution of fines under Regulation 1/2003	31
Table 1.1	Commission decisions involving the administration of proactive obligations under Regulation (EC) 1/2003	42
Figure 2.1	The 'Brussels consensus'	56
Figure 2.2	The emerging consensus	72
Figure 3.1	Substantive and temporal overlaps	75
Figure 3.2	'Expectation of regulation'	76
Figure 3.3	Partial overlap and complementarity	77
Figure 4.1	The deferential approach and the specific subject-matter of a patent	113
Figure 5.1	Changing the operation of the gatekeeper's core segment via interoperability	137
Figures 5.2.1 and 5.2.2	Opening up layers within the ecosystem	138
Figure 5.3	The DMA as a tool to promote innovation	147
Table 5.1	A taxonomy of regulatory obligations under the DMA	149
Table 6.1	Energy and telecommunications decisions adopted under Regulation (EC) 1/2003	192
Figure 7.1	Reverse payment settlements as a context-dependent exercise	214
Figure 7.2	Approaches to the assessment of potential competition	214
Figures 8.1.1 and 8.1.2	Two options to access Android	237
Figure 8.2	Product design and the level of horizontal and vertical integration	240
Figures 8.3.1 and 8.3.2	Product design and the choice between closed and open (modular) layers	241
Figure 8.4	Product design and interoperability	241

TABLE OF CASES

Case law

Judgments of the Court of Justice (EU)

56/65 *Société Technique Minière v Maschinenbau Ulm GmbH*,
   EU:C:1966:38 .... 58, 116,
   248, 262–63
56 and 58/64 (joined) *Établissements Consten S.à.R.L. and
   Grundig-Verkaufs-GmbH v Commission of the European
   Economic Community*, EU:C:1966:41 .... 15, 58, 79,
   111, 176, 196
6/72 *Europemballage Corporation and Continental Can Company Inc.
   v Commission*, ECLI:EU:C:1973:22 182
6/73 and 7/73 (joined) *Istituto Chemioterapico Italiano S.p.A.
   and Commercial Solvents Corporation v Commission*,
   EU:C:1974:18 .... 80, 183, 257
15/74 *Centrafarm BV and Adriaan de Peijper v Sterling Drug Inc*,
   EU:C:1974:114 112–13
26/75 *General Motors Continental NV v Commission*, EU:C:1975:150 176
26/76 *Metro SB-Großmärkte GmbH & Co. KG v Commission*,
   EU:C:1977:167 .... 32, 250, 254
27/76 *United Brands Company and United Brands Continentaal BV
   v Commission*, EU:C:1978:22 176
85/76 *Hoffmann-La Roche & Co. AG v Commission*, EU:C:1979:36 48
62/79 *SA Compagnie générale pour la diffusion de la télévision,
   Coditel, and others v Ciné Vog Films and others*, EU:C:1980:84 .... 121, 220
268/78 *L.C. Nungesser KG and Kurt Eisele v Commission*,
   EU:C:1982:211 .... 79, 106–07, 109,
   117, 249–50
262/81 *Coditel SA, Compagnie générale pour la diffusion de la
   télévision, and others v Ciné-Vog Films SA and others*,
   EU:C:1982:334 .... 79, 103, 113–14,
   121, 225–26
322/81 *NV Nederlandsche Banden Industrie Michelin v Commission*,
   EU:C:1983:313 251
35/83 *BAT Cigaretten-Fabriken GmbH v Commission*, EU:C:1985:32 .... 115, 211
243/83 *SA Binon & Cie v SA Agence et messageries de la presse*,
   EU:C:1985:284 16

42/84 *Remia BV and others v Commission*, EU:C:1985:327..........102, 117, 147, 248
311/84 *Centre belge d'études de marché – Télémarketing (CBEM)
v SA Compagnie luxembourgeoise de télédiffusion (CLT)
and Information publicité Benelux (IPB)*, EU:C:1985:394........................ 256–57
161/84 *Pronuptia de Paris GmbH v Pronuptia de Paris Irmgard
Schillgallis*, EU:C:1986:41 .... 103, 117,
250, 254
27/87 *SPRL Louis Erauw-Jacquery v La Hesbignonne SC*, EU:C:1988:183...........114
395/87 *Ministère public v Jean-Louis Tournier*, EU:C:1989:319...............................35
110/88, 241/88 and 242/88 *François Lucazeau and others v
Société des Auteurs, Compositeurs et Editeurs de Musique
(SACEM) and others*, EU:C:1989:326 35
C-62/86 *AKZO Chemie BV v Commission*, EU:C:1991:286...................................253
C-234/89 *Stergios Delimitis v Henninger Bräu AG*, EU:C:1991:91 48
C-89/85, C-104/85, C-114/85, C-116/85, C-117/85 and C-125/85
to C-129/85 (joined) *A. Ahlström Osakeyhtiö and others
v Commission*, EU:C:1993:120...33
C-9/93 *IHT Internationale Heiztechnik GmbH and Uwe Danzinger
v Ideal-Standard GmbH and Wabco Standard GmbH*, EU:C:1994:261 211
C-241/91 P and C-242/91 P (joined) *Radio Telefis Eireann (RTE)
and Independent Television Publications Ltd (ITP) v Commission,*
EU:C:1995:98 .... 22, 24, 79, 94,
105, 111–12, 115–16,
120, 141–42, 147,
164, 172, 196, 202–04,
231, 246, 250, 252, 255
C-7/95, *John Deere Ltd v Commission*, EU:C:1998:256 248
C-7/97 *Oscar Bronner GmbH & Co. KG v Mediaprint Zeitungs- und
Zeitschriftenverlag GmbH & Co. KG and others*, EU:C:1998:569 ...... 22, 84, 158,
165, 257, 259, 273
C-344/98 *Masterfoods Ltd v HB Ice Cream Ltd*, EU:C:2000:689 227
C-322/01 *Deutscher Apothekerverband eV v 0800 DocMorris NV
and Jacques Waterval*, EU:C:2003:664 74
C-2/01 P and C-3/01 P (joined) *Bundesverband der Arzneimittel-
Importeure eV and Commission v Bayer AG*, EU:C:2004:2 74
C-418/01 *IMS Health GmbH & Co. OHG v NDC Health
GmbH & Co. KG*, EU:C:2004:257.. 22, 79, 105,
108, 115, 147,
196, 202, 251
C-552/03 P *Unilever Bestfoods (Ireland) Ltd v Commission*,
EU:C:2006:607 256
C-238/05 *Asnef-Equifax, Servicios de Información sobre Solvencia
y Crédito, SL and Administración del Estado v Asociación
de Usuarios de Servicios Bancarios*, EU:C:2006:734...248

Table of Cases   xvii

C-95/04 P *British Airways plc v Commission*, EU:C:2007:166 60
C-468/06 to C-478/06 (joined) *Sot. Lélos kai Sia EE and Others v GlaxoSmithKline AEVE Farmakeftikon Proïonton, formerly Glaxowellcome AEVE*, EU:C:2008:504 176
C-501/06 P, C-513/06 P, C-515/06 P and C-519/06 P (joined) *GlaxoSmithKline Services Unlimited v Commission*, EU:C:2009:610 .... 17, 74
C-441/07 P *Commission v Alrosa Company Ltd*, EU:C:2010:377 .... 29, 163
C-280/08 P *Deutsche Telekom AG v Commission*, EU:C:2010:603 .... 61, 78, 84, 156–58, 167–68
C-108/09 *Ker-Optika bt v ÀNTSZ Dél-dunántúli Regionális Intézete*, EU:C:2010:725 74
C-52/09 *Konkurrensverket v TeliaSonera Sverige AB*, EU:C:2011:83 ..... 55, 156, 258
C-403/08 and C-429/08 (joined) *Football Association Premier League Ltd and Others v QC Leisure and Others and Karen Murphy v Media Protection Services Ltd*, EU:C:2011:631 .... 121, 222, 250
C-226/11 *Expedia Inc. v Autorité de la concurrence and Others*, EU:C:2012:795 86
C-209/10 *Post Danmark A/S v Konkurrencerådet*, EU:C:2012:172 .... 34, 57, 60, 264
C-295/12 P *Telefónica SA and Telefónica de España SAU v Commission*, EU:C:2014:2062 168
C-67/13 P *Groupement des cartes bancaires (CB) v European Commission*, EU:C:2014:2204 .... 59, 98
C-170/13 *Huawei Technologies Co. Ltd v ZTE Corp. and ZTE Deutschland GmbH*, EU:C:2015:477 .... 95, 204
C-23/14 *Post Danmark A/S v Konkurrencerådet*, EU:C:2015:651 .... 60–61, 248, 251
C-373/14 P *Toshiba Corporation v Commission*, EU:C:2016:26 212
C-413/14 P *Intel Corp. v Commission*, EU:C:2017:700 .... 173, 250
C-525/16 *MEO – Serviços de Comunicações e Multimédia SA v Autoridade da Concorrência*, EU:C:2018:270 264
C-307/18 *Generics (UK) Ltd and Others v Competition and Markets Authority*, EU:C:2020:52 .... 58, 62, 71, 111–12, 217–18, 231, 248, 250, 253, 263
C-228/18 *Gazdasági Versenyhivatal v Budapest Bank Nyrt. and others*, EU:C:2020:265 .... 59, 116, 248
C-567/18 *Coty Germany GmbH v Amazon Services Europe Sàrl and Others*, EU:C:2020:267 102
C-132/19 P *Groupe Canal + SA v Commission*, EU:C:2020:1007 .... 29, 122, 226, 228
C-165/19 P *Slovak Telekom, a.s. v Commission*, EU:C:2021:239 .... 76, 105, 141, 156, 169, 203, 246–47

C-182/21 Nokia Technologies Oy v Daimler AG, EU:C:2021:575 206
C-117/20 bpost SA v Autorité belge de la concurrence, EU:C:2022:202 .... 79, 172
C-377/20 Servizio Elettrico Nazionale SpA and Others v Autorità Garante
    della Concorrenza e del Mercato and Others, EU:C:2022:379................ 60, 187
C-680/20 Unilever Italia Mkt. Operations Srl v Autorità Garante della
    Concorrenza e del Mercato, EU:C:2023:33 85
C-48/22 P Google LLC and Alphabet, Inc. v Commission, pending......................236
C-738/22 P Google LLC and Alphabet, Inc. v Commission, pending 239

Judgments of the General Court (EU)

T-111/96 ITT Promedia NV v Commission, EU:T:1998:183 .... 197, 201–03
T-374/94, T-375/94, T-384/94 and T-388/94 (joined) European
    Night Services Ltd and others v Commission, EU:T:1998:198 248
T-184/01 R IMS Health Inc. v Commission, EU:T:2001:259 120
T-342/99 Airtours plc v Commission, EU:T:2002:146 48–50
T-65/98 Van den Bergh Foods Ltd v Commission, EU:T:2003:281 48
T-203/01 Manufacture française des pneumatiques Michelin
    v Commission, EU:T:2003:250 47
T-219/99 British Airways plc v Commission, EU:T:2003:343 47
T-87/05 EDP – Energias de Portugal, SA v Commission, EU:T:2005:333 96
T-170/06 Alrosa Company Ltd v Commission, EU:T:2007:220 186
T-201/04 Microsoft Corporation v Commission, EU:T:2007:289 .... 94, 117,
    120–21, 123, 147,
    238, 245, 256, 266
T-271/03 Deutsche Telekom AG v Commission, EU:T:2008:101 79
T-111/08, MasterCard, Inc. and MasterCard Europe v Commission,
    EU:T:2012:260 98
T-167/08 Microsoft Corp. v Commission, EU:T:2012:323 267
T-360/09 E.ON Ruhrgas AG and E.ON AG v Commission, EU:T:2012:332 212
T-119/09 Protégé International Ltd v Commission, EU:T:2012:421 .... 197, 201
T-76/14 Morningstar, Inc. v Commission, EU:T:2016:481 29
T-814/17 Lietuvos geležinkeliai AB v Commission, EU:T:2020:545 189
T-612/17 Google LLC and Alphabet, Inc. v Commission, EU:T:2021:763 ....236, 251,
    253–54,
    258, 262
T-286/09 RENV Intel Corporation Inc. v Commission, EU:T:2022:19 .... 61, 64
T-604/18 Google LLC and Alphabet, Inc. v Commission, EU:T:2022:541 ... 239, 244,
    262, 266

Opinions of Advocates General (Court of Justice)

Opinion of AG Reischl in Case C-262/81 Coditel SA, Compagnie générale
    pour la diffusion de la télévision, and others v Ciné-Vog Films SA
    and others, EU:C:1982:290 103

Opinion of AG Mischo in Case 27/87 *SPRL Louis Erauw-Jacquery v La Hesbignonne SC*, EU:C:1987:538 114
Opinion of AG Gulmann in Joined Cases C-241/91 P and C-242/91 P *Radio Telefís Eireann (RTE) and Independent Television Publications Ltd (ITP) v Commission*, EU:C:1994:210 111
Opinion of AG Jacobs in Case C-7/97 *Oscar Bronner GmbH & Co. KG v Mediaprint Zeitungs- und Zeitschriftenverlag GmbH & Co. KG and others*, EU:C:1998:264 .... 105, 170, 247
Opinion of AG Mazák in Case C-52/09 *Konkurrensverket v TeliaSonera Sverige AB*, EU:C:2010:483 165
Opinion of AG Saugmandsgaard Øe in Cases C-152/19 P and C-165/19 P *Deutsche Telekom AG and Slovak Telekom a.s.*, EU:C:2020:678 169–70

Case law from other courts, tribunals and authorities

Pacific Bell Telephone Co. v. linkLine Communications, Inc., 555 U.S. 438 (2009) 165
FTC v Actavis, Inc., 570 U.S. 136 (2013) 209
Paroxetine (Case CE-9531/11) Decision of the Competition and Markets Authority of 12 February 2016 209
Streetmap.EU Ltd v Google Inc. & Ors [2016] EWHC 253 (Ch) 254
Unwired Planet International Ltd v Huawei Technologies Co. Ltd & Anor [2017] EWHC 711 (Pat). 205
Unwired Planet International Ltd & Anor v Huawei Technologies (UK) Co Ltd & Anor [2020] UKSC 37 205
Décision 20-MC-01 of 9 April 2020 concerning the request for interim measures brought by Syndicat des éditeurs de la presse magazine, l'Alliance de la presse d'information générale e.a. et l'Agence France-Presse 90
CA Paris, pôle 5 ch. 7, 19 January 2023, n 21/15387 (Google LLC and others) 90

Administrative practice

Decisions of the European Commission

D.R.U.-Blondel (Case IV/A-03036) Commission Decision of 8 July 1965 26
Hummel-Isbecque (Case IV/A-02702) Commission Decision of 17 September 1965 26
Maison Jallatte S.A.-Hans Voss KG and, Maison Jallatte S.A.-S.A. Ets Vandeputte (Case IV/A-22491) Commission Decision of 17 December 1965 26
A.C.E.C. – Berliet (Case IV/26045) Commission Decision of 17 July 1968 26

Convention chaufourniers (Case IV/242-295) Commission Decision
of 5 May 1969...32
Dyestuffs (Case IV/26.267) Commission Decision of 24 July 1969.......................32
S.A. des pneumatiques Dunlop – S.A. Pirelli France (Case IV/24.471)
Commission Decision of 5 December 1969...32
Omega (Case IV/10.498, 11.546, 12.992, 17.394, 17.395, 17.971, 18.772,
18.888 and ex 3.213) Commission Decision 70/488/EEC of
28 October 1970..27
FN-CF (Case IV/26 624) Commission Decision of 28 May 1971...........................26
Europemballage Corporation (Case IV/26811) Commission Decision
of 9 December 1971...182
Vereeniging van Cementhandelaren (Case IV/324) Commission Decision
of 16 December 1971..32
Henkel/Colgate (Case IV/26917) Commission Decision of 23 December 1971........26
Nederlandse Cement- Handelmaatschappij NV (Case IV/595)
Commission Decision of 23 December 1971...32
Davidson Rubber Co. (Case IV/17.545, 6.964, 26.858, 26.890,
18.673 and 17.448) Commission Decision 9 June 1972............................... 26, 32
ZOJA/CSC – ICI (Case IV/26.911) Commission Decision
of 14 December 1972..32
Kali und Salz/Kali Chemie (Case IV/795) Commission Decision
of 21 December 1973..32
General Motors Continental (Case IV/28.851) Commission Decision
of 19 December 1974..32
SABA (Case IV/847) Commission Decision of 15 December 1975.......................27
Junghans (Case IV/5715) Commission Decision of 21 December 1976...............27
Breeders' rights – maize seed (Case IV/28.824) Commission Decision
of 21 September 1978... 26, 249
ECS/AKZO (Case IV/30.698) Commission Decision of 14 December 1985............34
Magill TV Guide/ITP, BBC and RTE (Case IV/31.851) Commission
Decision of 21 December 1988..94
Van den Bergh Foods Limited (Case Nos IV/34.073, IV/34.395
and IV/35.436) Commission Decision of 11 March 1998..................................33
Michelin (Case COMP/E-2/36.041/PO) Commission Decision
2002/405/EC of 20 June 2001...48
NDC Health/IMS Health: Interim measures (Case COMP/D3.38.044)
Commission Decision of 3 July 2001..120
Deutsche Telekom AG (Case COMP/C-1/37.451, 37.578, 37.579)
Commission Decision of 21 May 2003...153, 171–72
Wanadoo Interactive (Case COMP/38.233) Commission Decision
of 16 July 2003..153
Joint selling of the commercial rights of the UEFA Champions League
(Case COMP/C.2-37.398) Commission Decision of 23 July 2003....................22

Microsoft (Case COMP/C-3/37.792) Commission Decision of
   24 May 2004 .... 94, 120, 238
Joint selling of the media rights to the German Bundesliga (Case
   COMP/C.2/37.214) Commission Decision of 19 January 2005 22
AstraZeneca (Case COMP/A. 37.507/F3) Commission Decision of
   15 June 2005 .... 89, 207
De Beers (Case COMP/B-2/38.381) Commission Decision of
   22 February 2006 22
Joint selling of the media rights to the FA Premier League
   (Case COMP/38.173) Commission Decision of 22 March 2006 .... 22, 45, 80
Wanadoo España vs. Telefónica (Case COMP/38.784) Commission
   Decision of 4 July 2007 .... 30, 153
DaimlerChrysler (Case COMP/E-2/39.140) Commission Decision of
   13 September 2007 .... 25, 45
Fiat (Case COMP/E-2/39.141) Commission Decision of
   13 September 2007 .... 25, 45
Opel (Case COMP/E-2/39.143) Commission Decision of
   13 September 2007 .... 25, 44
Toyota (Case COMP/E-2/39.142) Commission Decision of
   13 September 2007 .... 25, 44
Distrigaz (Case COMP/B-1/37966) Commission Decision of
   11 October 2007 .... 25, 44, 193
MasterCard, EuroCommerce and Commercial Cards (Cases COMP/34.579,
   COMP/36.518 and COMP/38.580) Commission Decision of
   19 December 2007 98
German Electricity Wholesale Market (Case COMP/39388)
   and German Electricity Balancing Market (Case COMP/39389),
   Commission Decision of 26 November 2008 .... 22, 25, 44, 159,
                                                                                                  177–81, 183–86, 193,
                                                                                                  227, 229, 271, 274
RWE Gas Foreclosure (Case COMP/39.402) Commission Decision
   of 18 March 2009 .... 25, 44, 193
Intel (Case COMP/C-3/37.990) Commission Decision of 13 May 2009 .... 34, 50,
                                                                                                  55, 64
Gaz de France (Case COMP/39.316) Commission Decision of
   3 December 2009 .... 25, 173
Long-term contracts France (Case COMP/39.386) Commission
   Decision of 17 March 2010 25
Swedish Interconnectors (Case 39351) Commission Decision of
   14 April 2010 .... 23–25, 44,
                                                                                                  159, 178–80,
                                                                                                  187, 192, 271
E.ON Gas (Case COMP/39.317) Commission Decision of 4 May 2010 .... 25, 44, 192

BA/AA/IB (Case COMP/39.596) Commission Decision of 14 July 2010 .... 29, 44
ENI (Case COMP/39.315) Commission Decision of 29 September 2010..... 24–25,
43, 159, 173,
179–80, 183,
185, 188, 192,
229, 274
Intel/McAfee (Case No COMP/M.5984) Commission Decision of
26 January 2011 243
Telekomunikacja Polska (Case COMP/39.525) Commission
Decision of 22 June 2011.. 30, 153, 192
IBM Maintenance Services (Case COMP/C-3/39692) Commission
Decision of 13 December 2011... 22, 43
Reuters Instrument Codes (Case AT.39654) Commission Decision
of 20 December 2012 .... 21, 43
CEZ (Case AT.39727) Commission Decision of 10 April 2013.............. 43, 183, 192
Continental/United/Lufthansa/Air Canada (Case COMP/AT.39595)
Commission Decision of 23 May 2013... 29, 43
Fentanyl (Case AT.39685) Commission Decision of 10 December 2013............209
Lundbeck (Case COMP/AT.39226) Commission Decision of
19 June 2013 .... 112, 209–10, 215,
217–18, 231
Samsung – Enforcement of UMTS Standard Essential Patents
(Case AT.39939) Commission Decision of 29 April 2014 ....23, 43, 203–04
Motorola – Enforcement of Standard Essential Patents
(Case AT.39985) Commission Decision of 29 April 2014 ....203–04, 231
Perindopril (Servier) (Case AT.39612) Commission Decision
of 9 July 2014...209
Slovak Telekom (Case AT.39523) Commission Decision of
15 October 2014 .... 30, 83, 153,
168, 172, 192
Air France/KLM/Alitalia/Delta (Case AT.39964) Commission
Decision of 12 May 2015 .... 29, 43
BEH Electricity (Case AT.39767) Commission Decision of
10 December 2015.. 24, 43, 159,
176, 183–84,
188, 192, 275
Container Shipping (Case AT.39850) Commission Decision of
7 July 2016 ....23–24, 43
CDS Information Market (Case AT.39745) Commission Decision
of 20 July 2016 .... 22, 24, 43
Cross-border access to pay-TV (Case AT.40023) Commission
Decision of 26 July 2016 ....23, 42, 122, 226,
230, 272, 275

ARA Foreclosure (Case AT.39759) Commission Decision of
  20 September 2016 .... 30, 42, 232
Google – Google Search (Shopping) (Case AT.39740) Commission
  Decision of 27 June 2017 .... 14, 24–25, 30–31,
  37, 42, 98–99, 232–35,
  234, 239, 246–47, 250,
  255, 259, 264–65,
  268, 272, 274
Baltic Rail (Case AT.39813) Commission Decision of 2 October 2017 .... 42, 189
Car battery recycling (Case AT.40018) Commission Decision of
  8 December 2017 33
Upstream Gas Supplies in Central and Eastern Europe
  (Case AT.39816) Commission Decision of 24 May 2018 .... 42, 159, 192
Liberty Global/Ziggo (Case M.7000) Commission Decision of
  30 May 2018 77
Google Android (Case AT.40099) Commission Decision of
  18 July 2018 .... 14, 24, 31, 37,
  42, 98, 232–33,
  236–39, 260–62,
  264–66, 272
DE/DK Interconnector (Case AT.40461) Commission Decision
  of 7 December 2018 .... 42, 176, 192
Guess (Case AT.40428) Commission Decision of 17 December 2018 .... 30, 230
Google Search (AdSense) (Case AT.40411) Commission Decision
  of 20 March 2019 .... 14, 31, 232,
  272–74
Mastercard II (Case AT.40049) Commission Decision of 29 April 2019;
  and *Visa MIF* (Case AT.39398) Commission Decision of
  29 April 2019 .... 43, 99
Character merchandise (Case AT.40432) Commission Decision of
  9 July 2019 230
Cephalon (Case AT.39686) Commission Decision of 26 November 2020 209
Amazon Marketplace and Amazon Buy Box (Case AT.40462 – AT.40703)
  Commission Decision of 20 December 2022 .... 14, 42,
  123, 270

TABLE OF LEGISLATION

Primary EU legislation

Charter of Fundamental Rights of the European Union [2012]
OJ C326/391 197

Secondary EU legislation

Regulation No 17: First Regulation implementing Articles 85 and 86
of the Treaty [1962] OJ 13/204 .... 2, 21, 271
Regulation No 19/65/EEC of 2 March of the Council on application
of Article 85 (3) of the Treaty to certain categories of agreements
and concerted practices [1965] OJ 36/533 .... 18, 160–61
Commission Regulation (EEC) No. 1984/83 of 22 June 1983 on the
application of Article 85(3) of the Treaty to categories of exclusive
purchasing agreements [1983] OJ L173/5 47
Council Directive 93/83/EEC of 27 September 1993 on the coordination
of certain rules concerning copyright and rights related to copyright
applicable to satellite broadcasting and cable retransmission [1993]
OJ L248/15 .... 95, 221
Council Regulation (EC) No 2100/94 of 27 July 1994 on Community
plant variety rights [1994] OJ L227/1 114
Commission Regulation (EC) No 2790/1999 of 22 December 1999
on the application of Article 81(3) of the Treaty to categories
of vertical agreements and concerted practices [1999] OJ L336/21 49
Directive (EC) 2001/29 of the European Parliament and of the
Council of 22 May 2001 on the harmonisation of certain
aspects of copyright and related rights in the information
society [2001] OJ L167/10 .... 101, 220, 230
Council Regulation (EC) No 6/2002 of 12 December 2001 on
Community designs [2002] OJ L3/1 194
Council Regulation (EC) No 1/2003 of 16 December 2002
on the implementation of the rules on competition laid
down in Articles 81 and 82 of the Treaty [2003] OJ L1/1 .... 2, 20, 161,
227, 232, 271

Council Regulation (EC) 139/2004 of 20 January 2004 on the control of concentrations between undertakings [2004] OJ L24/1 49

Directive (EC) 2006/116 of the European Parliament and of the Council of 12 December 2006 on the term of protection of copyright and certain related rights [2006] OJ L372/12 101

Regulation (EC) No 469/2009 of the European Parliament and of the Council of 6 May 2009 concerning the supplementary protection certificate for medicinal products (Codified version) [2009] OJ L152/1 207

Regulation (EC) No 713/2009 of the European Parliament and of the Council of 13 July 2009 establishing an Agency for the Cooperation of Energy Regulators [2009] OJ L211/1 153

Regulation (EC) No 714/2009 of the European Parliament and of the Council of 13 July 2009 on conditions for access to the network for cross-border exchanges in electricity and repealing Regulation (EC) No 1228/2003 [2009] OJ L211/15 153

Directive 2009/72/EC of the European Parliament and of the Council of 13 July 2009 concerning common rules for the internal market in electricity and repealing Directive 2003/54/EC [2009] OJ L211/55 153

Commission Regulation (EU) No 316/2014 of 21 March 2014 on the application of Article 101(3) of the Treaty on the Functioning of the European Union to categories of technology transfer agreements [2014] OJ L93/17 .... 109, 224

Regulation (EU) 2015/751 of the European Parliament and of the Council of 29 April 2015 on interchange fees for card-based payment transactions [2015] OJ L 123/1 .... 77, 98

Regulation (EU) 2017/1001 of the European Parliament and of the Council of 14 June 2017 on the European Union trade mark [2017] OJ L154/1 .... 101, 194

Regulation (EU) 2017/1128 of the European Parliament and of the Council of 14 June 2017 on cross-border portability of online content services in the internal market [2017] OJ L168/1 223

Directive (EU) 2018/1972 of the European Parliament and the Council of 11 December 2018 establishing the European Electronic Communications Code [2018] OJ L321/36 .... 3, 75, 125, 185, 278

Directive (EU) 2019/692 of the European Parliament and of the Council of 17 April 2019 amending Directive 2009/73/EC concerning common rules for the internal market in natural gas [2019] OJ L117/1 125

Directive (EU) 2019/790 of the European Parliament and of the Council of 17 April 2019 on copyright and related rights in the Digital Single Market and amending Directives 96/9/EC and 2001/29/EC [2019] OJ L 130/92 90

Directive (EU) 2019/944 of the European Parliament and of the Council
of 5 June 2019 on common rules for the internal market for
electricity and amending Directive 2012/27/EU [2019]
OJ L158/125 .... 3, 93–94,
125, 153, 185
Regulation (EU) 2022/612 of the European Parliament and of the
Council of 6 April 2022 on roaming on public mobile
communications networks within the Union (recast) [2022]
OJ L115/1 220
Commission Regulation (EU) 2022/720 of 10 May 2022 on the
application of Article 101(3) of the Treaty on the Functioning
of the European Union to categories of vertical agreements
and concerted practices [2022] OJ L134/4 224
Regulation (EU) 2022/1925 of the European Parliament and of the
Council of 14 September 2022 on contestable and fair markets
in the digital sector and amending Directives (EU) 2019/1937
and (EU) 2020/1828 (Digital Markets Act) [2022] OJ L265/1 ..... 3, 76, 124, 277

Other

Proposal for a Regulation of the European Parliament and the Council on
standard essential patents and amending Regulation (EU)2017/1001
COM(2023) 232 final 194–95

Commission

Guidelines

Commission, 'Guidelines on the application of EEC competition rules
in the telecommunications sector' [1991] OJ C233/2 161
Commission, 'Guidelines on vertical restraints' [2000] OJ C291/1 48
Commission, 'Guidelines on the assessment of horizontal mergers
under the Council Regulation on the control of concentrations
between undertakings' [2004] OJ C31/5 .... 34, 49
Commission, 'Guidelines on the application of Article 81(3)
of the Treaty' [2004] C101/97 104
Commission, 'Guidelines on the assessment of non-horizontal
mergers under the Council Regulation on the control of
concentrations between undertakings' [2008] OJ C265/6 .... 49, 178, 254
Commission, 'Guidelines on the applicability of Article 101 of the
Treaty on the Functioning of the European Union to horizontal
co-operation agreements' [2011] OJ C11/1 .... 18, 80, 198
Commission, 'Guidelines on the application of Article 101 of the
Treaty on the Functioning of the European Union to technology
transfer agreements' [2014] OJ C89/3 .... 18, 102, 208

xxviii *Table of Legislation*

Commission, 'Guidelines on vertical restraints' [2022] OJ C248/1 .... 18, 224, 237
Commission, 'Framework for State aid for research and development
  and innovation' [2022] OJ C414/1 101

Other documents published in the OJ

Commission, Notice on exclusive dealing contracts with commercial
  agents [1962] OJ 139/2921 39
Commission, Notice on patent licensing agreements [1962] OJ 139/2922 39
Commission, Notice on the application of the competition rules to
  access agreements in the telecommunications sector [1998] OJ C265/2 161
Commission, White Paper on modernisation of the rules implementing
  Articles 85 and 86 of the EC Treaty [1999] OJ C132/1 21
Commission, 'Guidance on the Commission's enforcement priorities
  in applying Article 82 of the EC Treaty to abusive exclusionary
  conduct by dominant undertakings' (Communication) [2009]
  OJ C45/7 .... 7, 39, 49, 165
Commission, Communication from the Commission published
  pursuant to Article 27(4) of Council Regulation (EC) No 1/2003
  in Case AT.39740 – Google (Communication) [2013] OJ C120/22 31
Commission, 'Notice on informal guidance relating to novel or
  unresolved questions concerning Articles 101 and 102 of the
  Treaty on the Functioning of the European Union that arise
  in individual cases (guidance letters)' [2022] OJ C381/9....................................28

Other Commission documents

Commission, 'Inquiry pursuant to Article 17 of Regulation
  (EC) No 1/2003 into the European gas and electricity sectors
  (Final Report)' COM(2006) 851 final... 87, 161, 271
Commission, 'Pharmaceutical Sector Inquiry (Final Report)'
  SEC(2009) 952 final 207–09
Commission, 'Executive Summary of the Pharmaceutical Sector
  Inquiry Report' COM(2009) 351 final 87, 89
Commission, 'Preliminary Report on the E-commerce Sector Inquiry'
  SWD(2016) 312 final 220
Commission, 'Report from the Commission on the first short-term
  review of the Geo-blocking Regulation' COM(2020) 766 final 223
Commission, 'Sector inquiry into consumer Internet of Things
  (Final Report)' SWD(2022) 10 final 206
Draft Guidelines on the applicability of Article 101 of the Treaty
  on the Functioning of the European Union to horizontal
  co-operation agreements C(2022) 1159 final. 18, 80, 198

Introduction

1. EU Competition Law and Policy: A Moving Target

EU competition law and policy are subject to constant change.[1] To those immersed in the discipline, this sentence reads like a statement of the obvious. However, they – judges, civil servants, practitioners, academics – tend to underestimate the rate and scale of the perpetual transformation of the field. This is so because incremental refinements are relatively modest in and of themselves. It is only when one takes some distance from the day-to-day application of the law, or when one attempts to look at the bigger picture over a longer period of time, that the magnitude of the shifts becomes apparent. The reference texts of yore – think of Korah's Little Yellow Book[2] and Waelbroeck's and Frignani's contribution to the *Commentaire Mégret*[3] – resemble little today's treatises and textbooks. The tone and substance of the debates are so different that they make one wonder whether they truly deal with the same discipline.

Taking perspective helps one realise, among other things, that many discussions that seem to have been with us for a long time are relatively recent. For instance, reverse payment settlements were so new in the mid-2000s that it took the European Commission (hereinafter, the 'Commission') several years to make sense of the potential concerns to which they may give rise and to formulate its policy.[4] Similarly, 'margin squeeze' conduct was little more than an academic curiosity before the turn of the century. The toolkit – that is, Articles 101 and 102 TFEU – has remained unchanged for over 60 years. The landscape to which it applies has not. Just like the rest of the legal system, EU competition law has adapted to changes in the economy, including the growing importance of intangible assets, the liberalisation of network industries and the rise of Big Tech.

---

[1] So much so, in fact, that finding a cut-off date for this project turned out to be a difficult task. The book, including the figures and charts supporting the findings, reflects developments until 30 April 2023. Where some new developments seemed imminent, a reference to them has been made if deemed relevant.

[2] Valentine Korah, *An Introductory Guide to EC Competition Law and Practice* (Hart Publishing 2007).

[3] Michel Waelbroeck and Aldo Frignani, *Commentaire J. Mégret: le droit de la CE, vol 4. Concurrence* (Éditions de l'Université de Bruxelles 1998).

[4] Danish Competition Authority 'Press Release: Investigation of Lundbeck – Council Meeting' (Copenhagen, 28 January 2004), as cited in Michael Clancy, Damien Geradin and Andrew Lazerow, 'Reverse-payment patent settlements in the pharmaceutical industry: An analysis of US antitrust law and EU competition law' (2014) 59 Antitrust Bulletin 153. For an extensive discussion, see Chapter 7, where these materials are cited.

This book provides an account of the transformations that EU competition policy has undergone since the entry into force of Regulation 1/2003.[5] As the title suggests, the mutations described in the chapters that follow have led to the emergence of a new EU competition law that departs in several key respects from the traditional understanding of the discipline. The ambition of the account is to complement both textbooks and individual articles. It seeks to complement textbooks (and treatises) in the sense that it focuses on the factors driving change and does not ambition to provide an overarching framework capturing the accumulated body of knowledge. It places the emphasis, in other words, on the moving object – what is new – and on what marks a break from past practices. It seeks to complement articles, on the other hand, by offering a perspective that is both panoramic and specific on recent and ongoing developments. Because it is not limited by the usual space constraints of law reviews, this monograph can examine a number of substantive issues in detail while simultaneously discussing the underlying trends.

2. Law, Policy and Institutions under Regulation 1/2003

2.1. Scope of the Project

It makes sense to define the boundaries and ambitions of the project at the outset. From an institutional perspective, the book focuses on the Commission's administrative action since the adoption of Regulation 1/2003. This choice leaves outside of its scope a significant fraction of the enforcement that has taken place over the past two decades. In the current landscape, and just as the EU legislature intended, most decisions are adopted by national competition authorities, not the Commission.[6] There are, however, powerful reasons to focus on the latter's activity. By design, Regulation 1/2003 placed the Commission at the apex of the enforcement regime. Under this system, it enjoys greater leeway to define its administrative priorities. In spite of the decentralising ambition of the legislation, moreover, it is entrusted with ensuring the uniform application of Articles 101 and 102 TFEU across the EU. The purpose of the book, against this background, is to discuss how the Commission has made use of its powers as a *primus inter pares* among competition authorities, once liberated from the burdens and constraints imposed by Regulation 17.[7]

---

[5] Council Regulation (EC) No 1/2003 of 16 December 2002 on the implementation of the rules on competition laid down in Articles 81 and 82 of the Treaty [2003] OJ L1/1.
[6] Wouter P.J. Wils, 'Ten Years of Regulation 1/2003: A Retrospective' (2013) 4 Journal of European Competition Law & Practice 293.
[7] Regulation No 17: First Regulation implementing Articles 85 and 86 of the Treaty [1962] OJ 13/204 (no longer in force).

From a substantive perspective, second, the scope of the book is confined to Articles 101 and 102 TFEU. This choice follows logically the focus on Regulation 1/2003. Merger control is relevant only at the margins. It is mentioned, for instance, when discussing the rise of the 'more economics-based approach' or when addressing the boundaries between the behavioural and the structural. Economic regulation – and in particular sector-specific regimes in the telecommunications,[8] energy,[9] and digital[10] industries – plays a more prominent role in the book. These regimes are relevant in two main respects. First, they overlap in substance with Articles 101 and 102 TFEU. As a result of this interaction, they may influence the interpretation of these two provisions. Second, intervention under Articles 101 and 102 TFEU is occasionally the prelude to the adoption of formal regulation. The Digital Markets Act, on which Chapter 5 focuses, encapsulates the trends of enforcement of the past two decades.

2.2. Policy-making Through Law

Competition policy, as formulated by the Commission, must be implemented through law, and must remain within the limits allowed by the relevant provisions. Law constrains policy-making in a number of respects. To begin with, intervention under Articles 101 and 102 TFEU demands evidence of a behavioural trigger (an agreement or a unilateral practice implemented by a dominant firm). Thus, the mere fact that the market structure does not allow for competition to emerge or be sustained does not warrant administrative action. In addition, a claimant or authority would need to show, in accordance with the principles laid down in the case law, that the practice under examination has either the object or effect of restricting competition. In the same vein, an infringement would have to be established, case-by-case, in relation to every practice. Finally, remedial intervention would need to keep proportion with the breach.

When seeking to attain its policy goals, the Commission's administrative practice since the adoption of Regulation 1/2003 has regularly tested the substantive and institutional boundaries of its powers. For instance, some of its decisions appear to suggest that anticompetitive market structures can sometimes justify, in and of themselves, intervention under Article 102 TFEU. Other decisions seemingly challenge the very operation of the intellectual property system, as opposed to the exercise of the right as such. The Commission has also made a creative use of

---

[8] Directive (EU) 2018/1972 of the European Parliament and the Council of 11 December 2018 establishing the European Electronic Communications Code [2018] OJ L321/36.

[9] Directive (EU) 2019/944 of the European Parliament and of the Council of 5 June 2019 on common rules for the internal market for electricity and amending Directive 2012/27/EU [2019] OJ L158/125.

[10] Regulation (EU) 2022/1925 of the European Parliament and of the Council of 14 September 2022 on contestable and fair markets in the digital sector and amending Directives (EU) 2019/1937 and (EU) 2020/1828 (Digital Markets Act) [2022] OJ L265/1.

the instruments it can deploy to maximise the reach of its policy goals. Generally speaking, the authority's practice of the past 20 years owes much to commitments decisions adopted pursuant to Article 9 of Regulation 1/2003. Sector inquiries conducted in accordance with Article 17 have also been central to enforcement in specific areas, in particular energy.

This interaction between law and policy-making is one of the central themes of the book. The analysis considers the shifts in policy-making that have taken place under the existing enforcement regime, how these shifts have explored the outer boundaries of the system and the techniques on which the Commission has relied to do so. The picture that emerges is one that is consistent with the aspirations of Regulation 1/2003. As the authority sitting at the top of the system, the Commission has chosen to focus on the cases and industries raising the most complex and novel issues, thereby leaving other matters to national courts and authorities. This policy choice has occasionally resulted in the introduction of new legal doctrines and the reinterpretation of existing ones. It has also led to the introduction of ambitious remedies, which have sometimes led to the fundamental restructuring of the relevant markets.

2.3. Policy-making and the Limits of Competition Law Institutions

The debate around ambitious remedies has both a legal dimension (that is, whether intervention was necessary and proportionate to bring the infringement to an end) and an institutional one. As explained in detail in Chapter 1, dealing with the most challenging cases exposes the competition law system to the limits of what it can effectively administer and achieve. Some of the Commission's policy priorities of the past two decades require it to adopt a role akin to that of a utilities regulator. These remedies – which are termed 'proactive' in the book – are much more demanding for competition authorities than the administration of cease-and-desist orders. They are difficult to design and implement in practice. It is sufficient to think of the complexities associated with the imposition of an *ex novo* access obligation or with mandating a divestiture. What is more, they tend to demand more resources insofar as compliance is likely to require monitoring on a continuous basis (as opposed to a one-off intervention).

The institutional limits of the competition law system feature prominently in the chapters that follow, and in various guises. Some of the case studies expose these limits and provide concrete illustrations showing that the enforcement apparatus was not designed to administer proactive remedies on a systematic basis. In some instances, such remedies have failed to attain the desired results; in other instances, legal uncertainty has followed. In the same vein, the institutional constraints of the system are central to the understanding of the relationship between competition law and economic regulation and of the various ways in which they interact with one another. They explain why and when sector-specific regimes are enacted, and the various roles Articles 101 and 102 TFEU can play in regulated markets.

3. Structure and Design of the Book

3.1. Structure of the Book

The book is structured in two parts. The first part provides an overview of the transformations of competition policy since the adoption of Regulation 1/2003. It explains, first, the sort of cases that the Commission has prioritised under the current regime. It considers, second, the sources of legitimacy of policy-making. In this regard, it places a particular emphasis on the influence of economic analysis and on how emerging ideas are having an impact on its influence (as well as the substantive interpretation of the provisions). Chapters 3 and 4 ponder the consequences of contemporary policy-making on the relationship between competition law and economic regulation (which by definition becomes more frequent, if not symbiotic) and on the way Articles 101 and 102 TFEU deal with intangible assets (in particular when protected by intellectual property rights). Finally, Chapter 5 is devoted to the Digital Markets Act, which is presented as an encapsulation of the trends underpinning the new EU competition law.

The second part of the book illustrates the main ideas introduced in the first by reference to several case studies in three broad areas of enforcement. The first set of case studies addresses the application of Articles 101 and 102 TFEU in the energy and telecommunications industries. More precisely, the chapter explains how competition law enforcement accompanied and supported the liberalisation of network industries. These cases, most of which were decided over a decade ago, signal the direction of the new competition law. The second set of case studies concerns the changing relationship with intellectual property. In the areas of patent and copyright, Articles 101 and 102 TFEU have been relied upon by the Commission to correct some aspects of the operation of national regimes. The third chapter deals with the enforcement of the two provisions – in particular the latter – in digital markets.

3.2. Design of the Book

There is a conscious choice behind the design of the book. As much as the author would like it to be the case, monographs are rarely ever read cover to cover. It is typically one aspect or the other that will – hopefully – be read in detail and checked again occasionally. Different bits will interest different readers. While there is a theme underpinning the whole book, the monograph has been conceived so that individual chapters can be read as stand-alone pieces. Readers interested in the relationship between competition law and intellectual property or in the application of Article 102 TFEU to digital platforms, for instance, would be able to focus on the dedicated chapter alone, without the need to turn to other parts of the book for context. The modular aspect of the book would ensure that the new editions – which will hopefully follow this one – can incorporate chapters illustrating the transformation of EU competition law and policy in a seamless way.

4. Hallmarks of the New EU Competition Law

4.1. The Recalibration of Competition Policy under Regulation 1/2003

4.1.1. The Rise of 'Market-shaping' Enforcement

The behaviour of the Commission following the adoption of Regulation 1/2003 is consistent with the vision underpinning the regime. To begin with, the authority's enforcement priorities were redefined and focused on the most egregious breaches of Articles 101 and 102 TFEU, on the one hand, and on the most complex and demanding cases, on the other. The latter stand apart from the typical competition law scenario in that they demand the administration of proactive obligations. The Commission has adopted a role akin to that of a utilities regulator far more frequently under the current regime than it did under Regulation 17. What was a rare occurrence has become a central aspect of policy-making in the new institutional landscape. In fact, enforcement in certain industries – including energy and digital – is dominated by (structural and behavioural) intervention aimed at restructuring markets.

The rise of 'market-shaping' enforcement can be explained, in part, by the greater leeway allowed to the Commission under Regulation 1/2003. It is not the only factor at play, however. Market restructuring is also a response by the Commission to the specific challenges raised by the features of the industries that it has chosen to prioritise. Traditional competition law enforcement applied in oligopolistic markets, where one-off remedial intervention by means of a cease-and-desist order is effective. By contrast, a number of segments in the energy, telecommunications and digital industries have a marked tendency towards monopoly. In such markets, proactive intervention is likely to become a necessity if competition law enforcement is to achieve its aims. Where there is a market segment that does not support rivalry, it may only be possible to preserve competition on adjacent markets by means of access duties, strict non-discrimination obligations and, in some cases, an outright divestiture.

4.1.2. The Decline of 'Law-driven' Enforcement

The second major trend in policy-making that has followed the adoption of Regulation 1/2003 is the decline of 'law-driven' enforcement. In the formative years of EU competition law, a significant fraction of the Commission's activity was devoted to the clarification of the substantive scope of Articles 101 and 102 TFEU. Under the current regime, there has been a marked shift towards 'policy-driven' enforcement, that is, towards administrative action aimed at attaining the authority's policy goals, rather than defining the boundaries of intervention. The shift is epitomised by the prominent role of commitments decisions adopted in accordance with Article 9 of Regulation 1/2003. These decisions allow the Commission to reach a negotiated outcome without engaging with the substance of Articles 101 and 102 TFEU. A substantial fraction of cases – in particular those demanding proactive intervention – has been closed pursuant to the commitments route. This procedural path has empowered the Commission to explore the outer boundaries of existing legal doctrines and test new ones and to do so, by and large, in the shadow of the law.[11]

4.1.3. The Rise and Decline of the 'More Economics-based Approach'

In the early 2000s, economic analysis was perceived as a major constraint on the Commission's discretion. What came to be known as the 'more economics-based approach' was a response to a crisis of legitimacy in the system. EU competition policy, critics argued, had become difficult to predict and lacked a clear sense of direction. Starting with distribution agreements, the Commission progressively changed its approach to enforcement and sought to bring it in line with the mainstream consensus. So central was the transformation to policy-making that the 'more economics-based approach' became closely associated with the modernisation brought about by Regulation 1/2003. The process symbolically culminated with the adoption of the so-called Guidance Paper, in which the Commission laid down its enforcement priorities in relation to exclusionary conduct.[12] The 'more economics-based approach' represents an approach to enforcement that is relatively modest and that values, above all, reliance on the best available expertise and the process through which decisions are adopted.

One would have been forgiven for thinking that, by the late 2000s, EU competition policy had reached its own 'end of history'. It did not take long after the

---

[11] Expression borrowed from Robert H Mnookin and Lewis Kornhauser, 'Bargaining in the Shadow of the Law: The Case of Divorce' (1979) 88 Yale Law Journal 950.

[12] Guidance on the Commission's enforcement priorities in applying Article 82 of the EC Treaty to abusive exclusionary conduct by dominant undertakings [2009] OJ C45/7.

adoption of the Guidance Paper, however, to see a change in approach to economic analysis. The progressive rise of Big Tech, and the realignment that came with it, led to the redefinition of enforcement priorities. If the Commission had valued predictable and cautious intervention until the early 2010s, emerging attitudes favoured swift and decisive action and emphasised the risks of underenforcement. In the new landscape, the legitimacy of the competition law system depends, first and foremost, on its ability to attain the policy outcomes that are sought. Thus, if the existing tools are unable to achieve the desired results, they are to be revisited to ease policy-making.

4.2. Consequences of the Recalibration of Competition Policy

4.2.1. Testing the Outer Limits of Competition Law

As already suggested above, one of the consequences of the rise of 'market-shaping' and the decline of 'law-driven' enforcement is that the outer boundaries of Articles 101 and 102 TFEU are tested more frequently than in the past. The phenomenon is manifested, first and foremost, in the way the scope of the relevant provisions is interpreted. It is sufficient to mention some examples. For instance, some Commission decisions have suggested that dominant firms may have a duty not just to deal with third parties (as some well-established precedents suggest), but to expand capacity to ensure rivals can compete on the relevant market. Other decisions imply a duty to deal on non-discriminatory terms and conditions and, more generally, the existence of a principle of equal treatment in the context of Article 102 TFEU. The boundaries of the discipline are also explored, second, in the design and administration of remedies. In some instances (and in particular where the parties reach a negotiated outcome with the Commission), the measures imposed appear to venture beyond what was strictly necessary to bring the alleged infringement to an end.

4.2.2. A New Relationship with Economic Regulation and Intellectual Property

The recalibration of competition policy is also manifested in the relationship of Articles 101 and 102 TFEU with economic regulation and intellectual property. The prevailing approach to enforcement has two important consequences. First, proactive intervention often mimics the operation of formal sector-specific regimes, such as those applying in the energy and telecommunications industries. Where Articles 101 and 102 TFEU overlap in substance – totally or partially – with such regimes, they may fulfil three main roles. They may act as a safety net preserving the goals of sector-specific regulation. Alternatively, they may fill gaps in the regimes; or rectify them if they are not judged to lead to optimal outcomes. A second consequence of the new EU competition law is the change in attitude vis-à-vis intellectual property systems. Over the past two decades, enforcement has become less deferential to such systems, thereby questioning some of the core aspects of their operation.

PART I

Mapping the Transformation

1
The Changing Face of Enforcement under Regulation 1/2003

1. The Rise of 'Market-shaping' Enforcement

1.1. Varieties of Competition Policy[1]

EU competition policy is implemented through law, which inevitably constrains the nature and range of cases an administrative agency can investigate. Despite this fact, Articles 101 and 102 TFEU can adapt seamlessly to a wide variety of industries, practices and, ultimately, policy choices. Authorities, both national and supranational, have considerable leeway to set – again, within the boundaries defined by law – their enforcement priorities. The discretion to decide how to make use of their limited resources means that EU competition policy can be shaped in virtually countless ways. Articles 101 and 102 TFEU provide the basis for a broad range of regimes, which may differ significantly from one another. An authority may choose to focus on, say, distribution agreements between supermarket chains and their suppliers; another, on unilateral practices in the electricity and gas sectors.

A look at EU competition law and its evolution exemplifies the extent to which the discipline supports different policy options – or, if one prefers, varieties of enforcement. The practices and sectors to which the European Commission (hereinafter, the 'Commission') has devoted its resources have changed over the years. Agreements partitioning national markets were at the heart of its enforcement efforts in the early days – when the creation of the 'common market' was the clear priority of EU (or EEC) institutions (and the project of European integration at large).[2] These priorities changed over time. With the rise of the 'more economics-based approach', the Commission reoriented a significant fraction of

---

[1] Some of the categories, statistics (updated to April 2023 where necessary) and vocabulary used in Section 1 of this Chapter are drawn from Pablo Ibáñez Colomo and Andriani Kalintiri, 'The Evolution of EU Antitrust Policy: 1966–2017' (2020) 83 Modern Law Review 321. My co-author has expressly consented to their re-use.

[2] Ibid. It provides data showing that 'trade-enabling' enforcement, which captures these cases, represented a significant fraction of all decisions adopted by the Commission up until 2004.

its capacity towards liberalised industries[3] and the fight against cartels.[4] More recently, the centre of policy-making shifted decisively towards Big Tech.[5]

Prioritising some practices and/or industries over others has consequences for the authority and the competition law system. A regime that favours the fight against cartels is fundamentally different from one that devotes its resources to, say, network industries and digital markets. Each variety of enforcement places distinct demands on the institutional apparatus, which needs to adjust accordingly. The main challenge for an authority that chooses to focus on cartel activity, for instance, is to detect and deter conduct that is known to be both illegal and harmful. By contrast, enforcing competition law provisions in digital markets gives rise to challenges of a different nature, namely drawing the line, case by case, between pro- and anticompetitive conduct and designing appropriate remedies that effectively address the concerns identified.

The function of a competition agency changes depending on the direction of policy and the nature of the cases it chooses to prioritise. Some choices – in particular the fight against cartels – require that the authority embrace a role akin to that of a criminal prosecutor. It would be in charge of uncovering concealed practices, bringing infringements to an end and imposing penalties that signal to stakeholders the seriousness and consequences of the breach. This policy priority would make it necessary to adapt the institutional apparatus to cases that are essentially 'fact-intensive' in nature. The authority would have to allocate its resources accordingly. For instance, detecting behaviour conducted in secret demands developing the capacity and intelligence to carry out investigations, gather the necessary information and design appropriate sanctions. It might also require an authority to introduce mechanisms to settle infringements with firms participating in cartel activity.

At the other end of the spectrum, there are policy choices that place competition authorities in a position that is not fundamentally different from that of a utilities regulator. When Articles 101 and 102 TFEU are enforced in the telecommunications, energy and digital industries, market intervention may involve mandating shared access to an input or infrastructure, defining the terms and conditions on which transactions are to be conducted and, in some instances, asking firms to alter the design of their products and/or their business model. Typically, these obligations cannot be implemented on a one-off basis and are complex to set

---

[3] Ibid 367.

[4] Ibid. 'Detection-deterrence' enforcement rose significantly after 2004, with cartel decisions representing an overwhelming majority of decisions establishing an infringement and a substantial fraction overall. An updated look at the figures (until April 2023) does not paint a different picture, in spite of the relative decline of cartel enforcement. On the said relative decline, see the statistics provided in https://competition-policy.ec.europa.eu/system/files/2022-11/cartels_cases_statistics.pdf.

[5] The shift is marked by the adoption of three infringement decisions against *Google – Google Search (Shopping)* (Case AT.39740) Commission Decision of 27 June 2017; *Google Android* (Case AT.40099) Commission Decision of 18 July 2018; and *Google Search (AdSense)* (Case AT.40411) Commission Decision of 20 March 2019 – and one against *Amazon: Amazon Marketplace* (Case AT.40462) and *Amazon Buy Box* (Case AT.40703) Commission Decision of 20 December 2022.

up and keep in place. The authority's limited resources need to be re-allocated to address these challenges effectively. Officials would need to develop the necessary expertise to craft these proactive obligations, to adjust them to economic and technological change and to monitor compliance over time.

1.2. Enforcement Paradigms in EU Competition Law

Figure 1.1 Enforcement variables

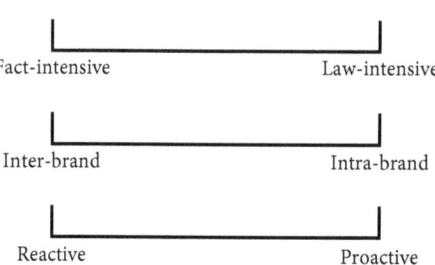

It is useful to present, systematically, the policy paradigms from which the Commission may choose (and, in the same vein, the different roles it may need to adopt when applying Articles 101 and 102 TFEU). A first step to make sense of the various paradigms, and understand how they differ from one another, is to think of each of them as a composite of three variables, depicted in Figure 1.1. The first variable of policy-making concerns the centre of gravity of the investigation. More precisely, it has to do with whether the inquiry is primarily about establishing the facts to the requisite legal standard (that is, whether intervention is 'fact-intensive' in nature) or whether it hinges on the lawfulness of the practice instead (that is, whether action is 'law-intensive'). 'Fact-intensive' investigations are those where the prima facie status of the behaviour is uncontroversial. The difficulty, from the perspective of an authority, is to provide convincing evidence that the said practice has been implemented. 'Law-intensive' cases, by contrast, are those where the relevant facts are typically available to the authority and where the challenge is to determine whether or not they amount to an infringement in the relevant economic and legal context.

The second variable relates to the dimension of competition at stake in the case: 'inter-brand' or 'intra-brand'. Competition is generally associated with the former. It is the only relevant dimension in some jurisdictions. In the EU system, however, the Court of Justice (hereinafter, the 'Court') has consistently held that the latter is also protected under Articles 101 and 102 TFEU.[6] 'Intra-brand'

---

[6] Joined Cases 56 and 58/64 *Établissements Consten S.à.R.L. and Grundig-Verkaufs-GmbH v Commission*, EU:C:1966:41, 339.

competition is at stake when a firm relies on third parties for licensing and distribution purposes. It is the dimension of rivalry that exists, for instance, between the licensees of the same technology, or the retailers of the same product. Conduct that may restrict 'intra-brand' competition includes clauses that limit the territory into which a distributor or licensee may offer a product[7] and those whereby the supplier or licensor prescribes the price at which the said product is to be sold.[8]

The third variable has to do with the nature of remedial action, that is, with the sort of measures that are required to bring an infringement effectively to an end. One may distinguish, in this regard, between intervention of a proactive and a reactive nature. The latter is the sort of measure with which competition law enforcement is associated. A reactive measure is a negative obligation (that is, a cease-and-desist order) that can be administered on a one-off basis. Proactive remedies, on the other hand, entail the administration of positive duties, which can be either behavioural or structural. The quintessential example of proactive intervention of the former type is a duty to deal on regulated terms and conditions. As explained in detail below, these measures are more complex to design, implement and monitor than those of a reactive nature. A structural measure, in turn, is one leading to a divestiture.

Figure 1.2 Detection-deterrence enforcement

Enforcement paradigm	Detection-deterrence		
Enforcement variables	Fact-intensive	Inter-brand competition	Reactive intervention
Role of the authority	Criminal prosecutor		

These three variables can be combined in several ways. Each of these combinations leads to an enforcement paradigm. The first paradigm can be labelled 'detection-deterrence'. It is depicted in Figure 1.2. This policy model focuses on practices that are deemed to be always, or almost always, harmful to inter-brand competition (and are thus 'fact-intensive' in nature). Cartels are the example that comes to mind immediately when thinking about this paradigm. Since the legal status of cartels is not disputed and is well known to stakeholders, the primary challenge for an authority is to detect the conduct (which is concealed from enforcers in the vast majority of cases), establish the facts to the requisite legal standard and, finally, deter other firms from engaging in it (typically by

---

[7] As in *Consten-Grundig* (n 6).
[8] Case 243/83 *SA Binon & Cie v SA Agence et messageries de la presse*, EU:C:1985:284.

imposing large fines). The implementation of remedies, on the other hand, does not give rise to any particular challenges. Firms taking part in these practices will be required to bring the infringement to an end and refrain from engaging in similar conduct in the future.

Figure 1.3 Trade-enabling enforcement

Enforcement paradigm	Trade-enabling		
Enforcement variables	Fact-intensive	Intra-brand competition	Reactive intervention
Role of the authority	Criminal prosecutor		

In the EU, a second policy paradigm ('trade-enabling' enforcement, seen in Figure 1.3) revolves around practices aimed at partitioning the internal market, and in particular agreements that provide for export prohibitions and/or absolute territorial protection.[9] These practices are similar to cartels in that their prima facie legal status is clear. Therefore, cases typically revolve around establishing the relevant facts to the requisite legal standard. Intervention to bring the infringement to an end is also reactive in nature: it simply involves ordering the firms to cease the conduct. These practices differ from cartels in that they relate to intra-brand competition. The fundamental ambition behind this policy paradigm, which is specific to the EU legal order, is to ensure that firms to not re-erect the very borders that the EEC Treaty was designed to bring down.[10]

Figure 1.4 Market-protecting enforcement

Enforcement paradigm	Market-protecting		
Enforcement variables	Law-intensive	Inter/Intra-brand competition	Reactive intervention
Role of the authority	Umpire		

---

[9] As in *Consten-Grundig* (n 6), which provided for absolute territorial protection to the distributor. For an example of an agreement limiting cross-border trade, see Joined Cases C-501/06 P, C-513/06 P, C-515/06 P and C-519/06 P *GlaxoSmithKline Services Unlimited v Commission*, EU:C:2009:610.

[10] *Consten-Grundig* (n 6), 34: '[...] The Treaty, whose preamble and content aim at abolishing the barriers between States, and which in several provisions gives evidence of a stern attitude with regard to their reappearance, could not allow undertakings to reconstruct such barriers [...]'.

The third policy paradigm ('market-protecting' enforcement, seen in Figure 1.4) differs from the above two in that investigations do not revolve around establishing the facts to the requisite legal standard. The facts underlying the case are typically available to the authority and tend not to necessitate an in-depth inquiry. The focus relates instead to whether the conduct under consideration amounts to an infringement. Practices falling within this category are, accordingly, 'law-intensive'. Their legal status depends on the specific circumstances in which they are implemented. This paradigm encompasses, for instance, the majority of vertical restraints. Most of these agreements are not deemed anticompetitive by their very nature. Thus, whether or not they are restrictive of competition necessitates a context-specific evaluation of their actual or potential impact.

This policy model is implemented by means of individual decisions, in addition to delegated legislation (namely Block Exemption Regulations[11]) and soft law instruments (and in particular Guidelines[12]). A look at these instruments shows that the fundamental goal of this variety of enforcement is to protect the competitive process by preserving firms' ability and incentive to rival one another. This aim is also reflected in the nature of the remedies through which infringements are brought to an end. Very much like 'detection-deterrence' and 'trade-enabling' policies, this paradigm can be effectively implemented by means of remedies of a reactive nature (which involve, as mentioned above, negative duties that can be implemented on a one-off basis).

Figure 1.5 Market-shaping enforcement

Enforcement paradigm	Market-shaping		
Enforcement variables	Typically law-intensive	Typically inter-brand competition	Proactive intervention
Role of the authority	Utilities regulator		

The fourth and final policy paradigm ('market-shaping' enforcement, depicted in Figure 1.5) differs from the preceding three in the reach and consequences of

---

[11] Pursuant to Article 103 TFEU, the Commission may be empowered by the Council to adopt regulations declaring that Article 101 TFEU is inapplicable to some categories of agreements. The enabling instrument is Regulation No 19/65/EEC of 2 March of the Council on application of Article 85(3) of the Treaty to certain categories of agreements and concerted practices [1965] OJ 36/533.

[12] See in particular the Guidelines on the applicability of Article 101 of the Treaty on the Functioning of the European Union to horizontal co-operation agreements [2011] OJ C11/1 (and the Draft Guidelines on the applicability of Article 101 of the Treaty on the Functioning of the European Union to horizontal co-operation agreements C(2022) 1159 final); Guidelines on the application of Article 101 of the Treaty on the Functioning of the European Union to technology transfer agreements [2014] OJ C89/3; and Guidelines on vertical restraints [2022] OJ C248/1.

intervention. The fundamental divergence vis-à-vis the preceding models has to do with the nature of remedial action. Instead of the one-off, reactive measures described above, 'market-shaping' enforcement resorts to obligations of a different nature, which can be labelled proactive. As already suggested above, such proactive measures may be behavioural or structural. Behavioural remedies of this nature comprise positive obligations that require monitoring, such as a duty to give access to an input on fair, reasonable and non-discriminatory terms and conditions. They also comprise structural interventions, such as a duty to divest certain activities within the value chain (think of an obligation to sell an infrastructure to a third party).

Given the nature and scale of intervention, 'market-shaping' action is by definition more ambitious and far-reaching than the preceding three policy models. The goal is not simply to preserve the competitive process, but to alter the operation of the process itself. In concrete terms, 'market-shaping' intervention may lead to the change of a firm's business model (if that firm is required to monetise its assets by means of licensing an input to third party rivals on a downstream market, as opposed to sales to end-users). It may also lead to the redesign of products (if a firm is required to ensure that they are interoperable with complements produced by third parties). For the same reason, it is a paradigm that entails greater risks for an authority. Altering how markets operate, whether by means of structural or behavioural remedies, is more demanding and prone to errors than simply requiring that an infringement be brought to an end. As a result, intervention may fail or may yield unintended consequences.

Figure 1.6 Enforcement paradigms in the EU system

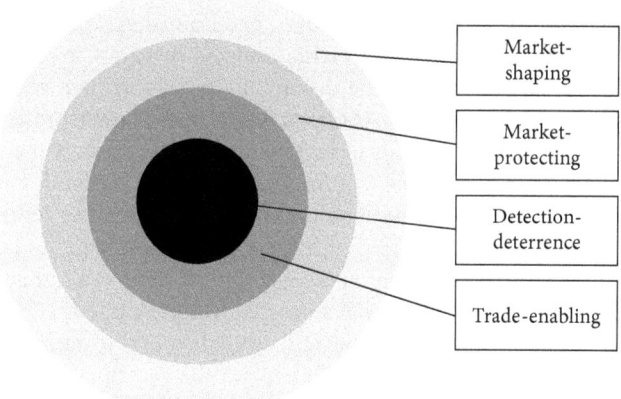

It is useful to think of these four policy paradigms as concentric circles, as seen in Figure 1.6. 'Detection-deterrence' enforcement can be seen as the core of an authority's mission. It deals with the most egregious and harmful infringements and requires the Commission to adopt a role akin to that of a criminal prosecutor. This is also true of the second concentric circle, which is made up of 'trade-enabling' enforcement. In the EU legal order, conduct aimed at restricting cross-border trade is treated in a similar way cartels are. As a result, this paradigm demands enforcement action of the same (criminal-like) nature. The role of the Commission changes under the third model, 'market-protecting'. In this context, a competition authority acts as an umpire that intervenes at the margins and provides clarity about which behaviour is lawful.

As seen in the figure, 'market-shaping' policy-making leads to intervention at or near the outer boundary of the EU competition law system. For the reasons discussed above, the demands placed on authorities under this enforcement paradigm are akin to the demands placed on agencies in charge of the regulation of network industries, such as telecommunications or energy. The Commission would no longer act as a mere umpire, insofar as its 'market-shaping' decisions have an impact on the operation of the relevant market: for instance, they might inject rivalry, if a duty to deal is imposed on a vertically-integrated firm; or may lead to a reallocation of rents, if the enforcement has an impact on the prices at which a firm may sell its products. From a legal standpoint, moreover, 'market-shaping' intervention often ventures into the limits of what Articles 101 and 102 TFEU permit.

1.3. EU Competition Policy under Regulation 1/2003[13]

It is rarely ever the case that an authority applies competition law provisions in accordance with a single paradigm (say, 'detection-deterrence' or 'trade-enabling' enforcement). Policy-making combines, to a greater or lesser degree, all four paradigms. Thus, the question is not so much which paradigm is applied but which 'policy-mix' an authority chooses; and how its priorities evolve. When applied to the Commission's activity, this exercise reveals a marked shift over time.[14] In the formative years of the discipline, its enforcement efforts focused on the middle circles (namely the 'trade-enabling' and 'market-protecting' paradigms). This focus is not difficult to rationalise. At the time, it made sense to contribute, first, to building the 'common market' and, second, to providing legal certainty to businesses. One should not forget, in the latter regard, that EU competition policy was introduced at a time when there was no 'competition culture' in the European continent and stakeholders needed a framework and a clear delineation of what was allowed and what was prohibited.[15]

Over the decades, enforcement moved simultaneously towards the core and the outermost varieties. Two factors can explain the centripetal and centrifugal shifts in policy-making. The rise of 'detection-deterrence', and in particular the

---

[13] Council Regulation (EC) No 1/2003 of 16 December 2002 on the implementation of the rules on competition laid down in Articles 81 and 82 of the Treaty [2003] OJ L1/1.
[14] Ibáñez Colomo and Kalintiri (n 1).
[15] Wouter PJ Wils, 'The Reform of Competition Law Enforcement – Will it Work?', in Dermot Cahill (ed), *The Modernisation of EU Competition Law Enforcement in the EU* (Cambridge University Press 2004).

fight against cartels, gained in prominence from the mid-1990s. This shift to the core can be easily rationalised as a drive to refocus enforcement resources towards the most harmful breaches, from an economic perspective, of EU competition law.[16] It is an expression of the broader 'modernisation'[17] trend, of which Regulation 1/2003 was a part. The rise of 'market-shaping' enforcement, on the other hand, looks like an attempt to direct efforts towards the most challenging cases, at the frontier of law and policy-making. This shift towards the outer boundaries is consistent with the institutional structure created by virtue of the Regulation. As discussed at length below, the regime was designed to free up enforcement resources and give the Commission more leeway to decide the cases on which to focus.

2. 'Market-shaping' Enforcement in Practice

'Market-shaping' enforcement is central to contemporary EU competition policy. The Commission has adopted, in around 25 per cent of cases since the mid-2000s,[18] a role akin to that of a utilities regulator. The rise of this paradigm has had two main consequences in practice. First, it has led to more frequent reliance on, and experimentation with, proactive remedies. The sort of measures that were exceptional under Regulation 17[19] are now at the heart of the system. A second observable consequence has to do with the way in which policy is conducted. The Commission's administrative practice over the past two decades suggests that 'market-shaping' enforcement appears to take place in clusters. At any given point in time, the Commission's efforts in this sense have focused on a sector and/or activity, leading to a string of decisions addressing a narrow set of issues.

2.1. A Taxonomy of Proactive Remedies

'Market-shaping' action by the Commission since the adoption of Regulation 1/2003 has often been far-reaching and transformative. It has resulted, inter alia, in vertically-integrated firms being ordered to share an input or infrastructure with third parties;[20] in the alteration of the terms and conditions under which goods and services are supplied to customers (including a duty to deal on fair,

---

[16] This point is addressed at length in Chapter 2.
[17] White Paper on modernisation of the rules implementing Articles 85 and 86 of the EC Treaty [1999] OJ C132/1.
[18] Ibáñez Colomo and Kalintiri (n 1). An updated analysis paints a similar picture. In the period between January 2018 and March 2023, 'market-shaping' enforcement has featured in the majority of non-cartel cases decided by the Commission. See Table 1.1 for an exhaustive picture.
[19] Regulation No 17: First Regulation implementing Articles 85 and 86 of the Treaty [1962] OJ 13/204.
[20] See for instance *Reuters Instrument Codes* (Case AT.39654) Commission Decision of 20 December 2012.

reasonable and non-discriminatory conditions, or, hereinafter, 'FRAND'[21]); and the re-arrangement of value chains (for instance, by ordering that firms stop obtaining their supplies from a particular provider[22]). Occasionally, intervention has led to the structural separation of different activities across the value chain (for instance, the separation of the generation and the transmission of electricity[23]).

Two decades of 'market-shaping' (or, if one prefers, regulatory-like) enforcement show that there is a recurrent subset of behavioural and structural remedies on which this paradigm relies. The discussion that follows makes it necessary to provide an exhaustive taxonomy of these measures. To begin with, proactive policy-making may lead to the imposition of behavioural obligations that amount, directly or indirectly, to a duty to deal on regulated terms and conditions. This remedy is associated with landmarks like *Bronner*,[24] *IMS Health*,[25] and *Magill*.[26] It has featured prominently in the Commission's practice since the adoption of Regulation 1/2003. In *CDS – Information Market*, for instance, the parties agreed to license to third parties their intellectual property and data on FRAND terms and conditions.[27] Similarly, in *IBM – Maintenance Services*, the firm's spare parts and information were made available to independent mainframe maintainers on the same basis.[28]

Second, 'market-shaping' enforcement may lead to the reconfiguration of the terms and conditions under which products are supplied and/or acquired on the relevant markets. By doing so, remedial action alters the operation of the relevant market, in particular by injecting rivalry (within a segment where perhaps no rivalry existed). A salient example of this form of intervention is *FA Premier League*,[29] which is a milestone in a broader saga of cases interfering with the conditions under which premium television rights are licensed to broadcasters.[30] In that case, the Commission brought its investigation to an end after the Premier League accepted, inter alia, to license its rights in several packages and to ensure that no single broadcaster would be in a position to acquire all packages (the so-called 'single-buyer rule').[31]

---

[21] See for instance *CDS Information Market* (Case AT.39745) Commission Decision of 20 July 2016.
[22] *De Beers* (Case COMP/B-2/38.381) Commission Decision of 22 February 2006.
[23] *German Electricity Wholesale Market* (Case COMP/39388) and *German Electricity Balancing Market* (Case COMP/39389) Commission Decision of 26 November 2008.
[24] Case C-7/97 *Oscar Bronner GmbH & Co. KG v Mediaprint Zeitungs- und Zeitschriftenverlag GmbH & Co. KG and others*, EU:C:1998:569, para 41.
[25] Case C-418/01 *IMS Health GmbH & Co. OHG v NDC Health GmbH & Co. KG*, EU:C:2004:257.
[26] Joined Cases C-241/91 P and C-242/91 P *Radio Telefis Eireann (RTE) and Independent Television Publications Ltd (ITP) v Commission*, EU:C:1995:98 ('*Magill*').
[27] *CDS Information Market* (n 21).
[28] *IBM Maintenance Services* (Case COMP/C-3/39692) Commission Decision of 13 December 2011.
[29] *Joint selling of the media rights to the FA Premier League* (Case COMP/38.173) Commission Decision of 22 March 2006.
[30] See in this sense *Joint selling of the commercial rights of the UEFA Champions League* (Case COMP/C.2-37.398) Commission Decision of 23 July 2003; and *Joint selling of the media rights to the German Bundesliga* (Case COMP/C.2/37.214) Commission Decision of 19 January 2005.
[31] *FA Premier League* (n 29), para 32 ('[…] no one buyer would be able to buy all of the rights […]').

Similar examples of market restructuring can be found in other industries. In *Swedish Interconnectors*,[32] the Commission had expressed concerns about the manner in which the electricity transmission operator in Sweden dealt with congestion in the system – namely by restricting the cross-border trade of electricity. The commitments addressing these concerns resulted in the restructuring of the transmission system in the country, which was divided into several bidding zones that would tackle congestion in a way that would not limit exports to other Member States.[33] In *Container Shipping*, intervention by the Commission led to a fundamental change to the manner in which rivals in an industry went about dealing with customers (and more precisely about the manner in which prices were communicated to them).[34]

It makes sense to mention, in addition, how this form of action under Articles 101 and 102 TFEU has had an impact on the exploitation of intellectual property rights. In a saga of cases pertaining to the licensing of the so-called Standard Essential Patents ('SEPs'),[35] the Commission interfered with the exercise of intellectual property rights and with the remedies on which right holders can rely. More precisely, the authority sought to limit the instances in which patentees can use injunctions against third parties.[36] In *Cross-border access to pay-TV*, in turn, the Commission expressed concerns about clauses limiting the ability of copyright licensees to offer the relevant content outside the territory covered by the agreement.[37] Intervention in these cases amounted, in effect, to limiting the exercise of their copyright by licensors. In fact, the latter accepted not to take action against breaches by licensees.[38]

Third, 'market-shaping' intervention occasionally leads to the redesign of products and/or the alteration of the business model through which a firm monetises its assets. For instance, a vertically-integrated operator that sells finished goods to final consumers may be required to offer individual components separately. Similarly, a firm may be required to alter its products so that

---

[32] *Swedish Interconnectors* (Case 39351) Commission Decision of 14 April 2010.

[33] Ibid, para 47: 'According to the commitments offered by SvK on 4 September 2009 to meet the Commission's competition concerns SvK will subdivide the Swedish transmission system into two or more bidding zones and operate the Swedish transmission system on that basis by 1 July 2011 at the latest […]').

[34] *Container Shipping* (Case AT.39850) Commission Decision of 7 July 2016.

[35] *Samsung – Enforcement of UMTS Standard Essential Patents* (Case AT.39939) Commission Decision of 29 April 2014.

[36] Ibid, para 76: 'Samsung committed not to seek injunctive relief before any court or tribunal in the EEA for infringement of its SEPs (including all existing and future SEPs) reading on a standard ("Mobile Standard") implemented in smartphones and tablets ("Mobile SEPs") against a potential licensee that, within 30 days of receipt of an invitation to negotiate, agrees to, and complies with, a certain licensing framework ("Licensing Framework") for the determination of FRAND terms and conditions'.

[37] *Cross-border access to pay-TV* (Case AT.40023) Commission Decision of 26 July 2016, para 46.

[38] Ibid, para 56: 'Second, Paramount would not: (a) seek to enforce or initiate proceedings before a court or tribunal for the violation of a Broadcaster Obligation in an existing pay-TV output licence agreement; […]'.

they are interoperable with rivals' complements. Examples drawn from digital industries illustrate this manifestation of proactive intervention. In *Google Shopping*, the Commission expressed concerns about the fact that the firm had reserved a feature of its search engine for itself.[39] The remedies bringing the infringement to an end led to a redesign of its product in a way that rivals would have access to the said feature on non-discriminatory terms and conditions.[40] In *Android*, the Commission challenged the very mechanisms through which the dominant firm monetised its assets (namely advertising, and this through the combination of applications that generate revenue and others that do not).[41]

Finally, there is intervention that seeks to change the features and operation of the relevant markets by mandating that a firm sell part of its assets to a third party. Structural remedies of this nature have been applied in the energy sector. In *German Electricity Balancing Market*, for instance, the Commission expressed concerns about the fact that E.On, a vertically-integrated firm, was favouring its upstream division and discriminating against third party suppliers of balancing electricity.[42] In the authority's view, the concerns related to the very market structure, that is, the fact that E.On both generated and transmitted electricity. By the same token, the proceedings were closed once the firm agreed to sell its transmission division to a third party.[43] A similar outcome was reached in *ENI*. In that case, the Commission argued that vertical integration reduced the firm's incentives to expand the capacity of its pipelines, as doing so would improve the position of its downstream rivals.[44]

Figure 1.7 Remedies in EU competition law

Remedy	Nature	Example
Obligation to deal	Behavioural	*Magill, Microsoft, CDS*
Reconfiguration of the terms and conditions of supply/purchase	Behavioural	*Container Shipping, Rambus, Standard & Poor's*
Alterations to the design of a product and/or a business model	Behavioural	*Commercial Solvents, Google Shopping, Google Android*
Market restructuring	Behavioural or structural	*Swedish Interconnectors, BEH Electricity, Gazprom*
Divestiture	Structural	*E.On, ENI*

---

[39] *Google Shopping* (n 5).
[40] Ibid, para 699.
[41] *Android* (n 5).
[42] Ibid, paras 50–55.
[43] Ibid, paras 69–75.
[44] *ENI* (Case COMP/39.315) Commission Decision of 29 September 2010.

2.2. The Clustering of Enforcement Around Sectors and Issues

An overview of the Commission activity since the adoption of Regulation 1/2003 reveals that 'market-shaping' intervention has been accompanied by a parallel phenomenon, which is the clustering of enforcement, at a given point in time, around industries and/or practices. Cases that lead to the administration of proactive remedies rarely come as isolated investigations. The experience of the past two decades shows that the Commission tends to adopt a string of decisions addressing the same (or similar) behaviour in a particular sector. The phenomenon is so pronounced that it is possible to identify a number of clusters on which non-cartel enforcement has focused since 2004. The industries prioritised by the Commission are, in chronological order, the following: airlines, automobile, energy, financial services and digital markets. In addition, the licensing of intangible property (including intellectual property) has featured at various stages over the period.[45]

It is sufficient to mention some examples to show the extent to which enforcement tends to be concentrated in time. As far as the automobile industry is concerned, the Commission adopted four decisions – each addressed to an individual manufacturer – in September 2007.[46] The application of Article 102 TFEU in the energy sector was also relatively concentrated in time: between October 2007 and September 2010, the Commission adopted eight decisions against incumbents in the electricity and gas industries.[47] Some cases would follow in subsequent years, addressing similar conduct.[48] As already mentioned, the focus on digital industries, in turn, becomes apparent following the Commission decision in *Google Shopping* in June 2017.[49] This case was followed by a string of investigations, some of which are still pending at the time of writing.

Clustering, as a phenomenon, concerns not only the industries, but also the substantive issues underpinning the investigations. Each family of cases deals with similar – if not identical – concerns and seeks to achieve the same policy objectives. The cluster applying to the automobile industry, for instance, focused on access by independent third parties to the technical information required to offer

---

[45] See the Table provided at the end of this chapter.

[46] *DaimlerChrysler* (Case COMP/E-2/39.140) Commission Decision of 13 September 2007; *Fiat* (Case COMP/E-2/39.141) Commission Decision of 13 September 2007; *Opel* (Case COMP/E-2/39.143) Commission Decision of 13 September 2007; and *Toyota* (Case COMP/E-2/39.142); Commission Decision of 13 September 2007.

[47] *Distrigaz* (Case COMP/B-1/37966) Commission Decision of 11 October 2007; *German Electricity Wholesale Market* and *German Electricity Balancing Market* (n 23); *RWE Gas Foreclosure* (Case COMP/39.402) Commission Decision of 18 March 2009; *Gaz de France* (Case COMP/39.316) Commission Decision of 3 December 2009; *Long-term contracts France* (Case COMP/39.386) Commission Decision of 17 March 2010; and *Swedish Interconnectors* (n 32); *E.ON Gas* (Case COMP/39.317) Commission Decision of 4 May 2010; and *ENI* (n 44).

[48] See Chapter 6.

[49] *Google Shopping* (n 5).

repair services to end-users.[50] Enforcement in the gas and electricity sectors, in turn, primarily sought to address the effects of the legacy market structures resulting from decades of exclusive rights.[51] Similarly, the two fundamental aims of 'market-shaping' activity in digital markets are the reallocation of rents and the restructuring of markets around bottleneck segments to ensure that they remain competitive.[52]

3. The Decline of 'Law-driven' Enforcement

3.1. The Rise of 'Policy-driven' Enforcement

The clustering of cases around certain sectors and issues is a manifestation of a broader phenomenon. Under Regulation 1/2003, enforcement at the EU level has become increasingly shaped by policy (that is, by the policy outcomes sought). By the same token, 'law-driven' action has significantly declined. Shedding light on the meaning and scope of Articles 101 and 102 TFEU through the case-by-case application of the law has become less central to the Commission's mission. The shift away from 'law-driven' enforcement represents a break from prior administrative practice. When Regulation 17 was in force, the Commission regularly selected cases with the goal of delineating, in an incremental manner, the boundaries of Articles 101 and 102 TFEU. Providing legal certainty to stakeholders by signalling its interpretation of competition law provisions was at the heart of administrative action under the former regime.

Just to mention some examples of 'law-driven' enforcement under Regulation 17, the Commission adopted a series of individual decisions clarifying the legal status of practices such as research and development agreements,[53] technology licensing[54] and vertical restraints, including exclusive[55] and selective

---

[50] European Commission, 'Antitrust: Commission ensures carmakers give independent garages access to repair information' IP/07/1332 (Brussels, 14 September 2007): 'The European Commission has adopted four decisions that legally bind DaimlerChrysler, Toyota, General Motors and Fiat to commitments to provide technical information about car repairs to all independent garages in the EU. [...] The commitments were given after a Commission investigation found that inadequate access to the full range of technical information could drive independent repairers from the market and that the agreements between the carmakers and their authorised repairers would therefore infringe EC Treaty rules on restrictive business practices (Article [101]) [...]'.
[51] See Chapter 6 for an extensive discussion.
[52] See Chapter 8 for an extensive discussion.
[53] *A.C.E.C. – Berliet* (Case IV/26045) Commission Decision of 17 July 1968; *FN-CF* (Case IV/26 624) Commission Decision of 28 May 1971; and *Henkel/Colgate* Commission Decision of 23 December 1971.
[54] *Davidson Rubber Co.* (Case IV/17.545, 6.964, 26.858, 26.890, 18.673 and 17.448) Commission Decision 9 June 1972; and *Breeders' rights – maize seed* (Case IV/28.824) Commission Decision of 21 September 1978.
[55] *Maison Jallatte S.A.-Hans Voss KG* and, *Maison Jallatte S.A.–S.A. Ets Vandeputte* (Case IV/A-22491) Commission Decision of 17 December 1965; *Hummel-Isbecque* (Case IV/A-02702) Commission Decision of 17 September 1965; and *D.R.U.-Blondel* (Case IV/A-03036) Commission Decision of 8 July 1965.

distribution.[56] Often (in fact, more often than not), these 'law-driven' decisions did not declare an infringement and did not impose penalties on the firms. Instead, the Commission either concluded that the practice in question did not amount to a breach of the relevant provision (that is, a 'negative clearance' decision[57]) or that the conditions for an exemption under Article 101(3) TFEU were fulfilled.[58] Even when an infringement was declared, the focus was on interpreting the law, as opposed to imposing a fine and deterring other stakeholders from engaging in similar conduct.

Since the adoption of Regulation 1/2003, by contrast, the Commission's enforcement efforts have been driven, to a significant extent, by the outcomes sought, rather than by the interpretation of the underlying legal provisions. This phenomenon is manifested not only in the clustering effect already discussed. The decline of 'law-driven' enforcement is also apparent, first, when one considers the instruments that the Commission has favoured to formulate policy under the regime. Current legislation provides for a menu of individual decisions from which it can choose. Of these, the authority has expressed a preference for those that do not require it to interpret the scope of Articles 101 and 102 TFEU. The observed decline of 'law-driven' policy-making is also apparent, second, if one pays attention to the level of fines imposed by the Commission. These two aspects are examined in turn.

3.2. 'Policy-driven' Enforcement in Practice: Commitments Decisions

When Regulation 17 was in force, 'law-making' activity was assisted by three instruments that expressly addressed the meaning and scope of Articles 101 and (in some cases) 102 TFEU. First, and most obviously, the Commission was empowered to adopt decisions establishing an infringement of either or both of these provisions. Second, and as already pointed out, it could also issue two types of decisions declaring the absence of a breach: negative clearances and exemptions. Pursuant to the first (negative clearance), it could conclude that there were no grounds for action under Article 101 and/or 102 TFEU. In accordance with the second, the Commission was empowered to decide that an agreement restricting competition within the meaning of Article 101(1) TFEU fell outside the scope of the prohibition insofar as it fulfilled the conditions for an exemption laid down in the third paragraph.

---

[56] *Omega* (Case IV/10.498, 11.546, 12.992, 17.394, 17.395, 17.971, 18.772, 18.888 and ex 3.213) Commission Decision 70/488/EEC of 28 October 1970; *Junghans* (Case IV/5715) Commission Decision of 21 December 1976; and *SABA* (Case IV/847) Commission Decision of 15 December 1975.
[57] Article 2 of Regulation 17 (n 19).
[58] Ibid, Article 6.

In principle, Regulation 1/2003 provides for a substitute for both negative clearance and exemption decisions. Article 10 empowers the Commission to adopt a 'finding of inapplicability', whereby it declares either that Article 101 or 102 TFEU have not been infringed, or that the conditions set out in Article 101(3) TFEU are fulfilled in the specific circumstances of the case.[59] However, these decisions have not been the Commission's instrument of choice under Regulation 1/2003. In fact, the authority has not adopted a single finding of inapplicability decision at the time of writing (and this after two decades under the enforcement regime).[60] The same is true of comparable informal instruments, such as comfort letters, which have only been issued in exceptional circumstances.[61]

In practice, negative clearance and exemption decisions have been replaced, by and large, by the so-called 'commitments decisions', adopted in accordance with Article 9 of Regulation 1/2003.[62] These decisions differ from a 'finding of inapplicability' in that they do not declare whether Article 101 and/or 102 TFEU have been infringed. They do not provide a binding interpretation of EU competition law provisions, either. The substantive analysis under Article 9 is confined to a preliminary assessment in which the Commission outlines the potential concerns expressed to the undertakings involved in the investigation. The formal purpose of these decisions is to make the commitments offered by the parties binding upon them. Once the commitments are accepted, the case is no longer an enforcement priority for the Commission, which closes its probe with no fines. Article 9 provided a structure and a legal basis for the institutionalisation of what was an informal but long-standing practice under Regulation 17.[63]

It is not difficult to understand, against this background, why these instruments are preferred when enforcement is driven by policy, as opposed to law. They allow the Commission to minimise legal constraints when defining and implementing

---

[59] Article 10 of Regulation 1/2003 (n 13). The Preamble clarifies, in Recital 14, that finding of inapplicability decisions are justified '[i]n exceptional cases where the public interest of the [Union] so requires', and this 'with a view to clarifying the law and ensuring its consistent application throughout the [Union], in particular with regard to new types of agreements or practices that have not been settled in the existing case-law and administrative practice'.

[60] Commission Notice on informal guidance relating to novel or unresolved questions concerning Articles 101 and 102 of the Treaty on the Functioning of the European Union that arise in individual cases (guidance letters) [2022] OJ C381/9. For a discussion of the issue, see also Richard Whish, 'Reflections on Regulation 1/2003, declarations of inapplicability and informal guidance' (2022) 2 Concurrences 2.

[61] In particular, the Commission adopted comfort letters in the context of the COVID pandemic. See European Commission, 'Comfort letter: coordination in the pharmaceutical industry to increase production and to improve supply of urgently needed critical hospital medicines to treat COVID-19 patients' (Brussels, 8 April 2020); European Commission, 'Comfort letter: cooperation at a Matchmaking Event – Towards COVID-19 vaccines upscale production' (Brussels, 25 March 2021).

[62] Article 9 of Regulation 1/2003 (n 13). See Recital 13, where it is explained that 'the Commission should be able to adopt decisions which make those commitments binding on the undertakings concerned' and that '[c]ommitment decisions should find that there are no longer grounds for action by the Commission without concluding whether or not there has been or still is an infringement'.

[63] Wouter PJ Wils, 'Settlements of EU Antitrust Investigations: Commitment Decisions Under Article 9 of Regulation No 1/2003' (2006) 29 World Competition 345.

its priorities. To the extent that commitments decisions are the result of a negotiated procedure, it is an avenue through which untested interpretations of EU competition law provisions can be relied upon. For the same reason, it is unlikely to see these acts challenged before the EU courts, in particular by the undertakings offering concessions themselves.[64] What is more, the Court confirmed in *Alrosa* that, as an expression of the Commission's discretion in the definition of competition policy, Article 9 decisions are subject to limited judicial review, and thus controlled only for manifest errors of assessment.[65]

The dominance of commitment decisions following the adoption of Regulation 1/2003 has been widely discussed by commentators.[66] The centrality of this instrument is particularly apparent in 'law-intensive' cases. For a long period under the new regime, a substantial fraction of non-cartel investigations were closed following the commitments offered by the parties.[67] The pattern is particularly apparent when one considers some of the clusters identified above. The string of cases in the energy sector decided between 2007 and 2010, all of which had a significant impact on the structure and operation of gas and electricity markets, was addressed by means of commitments and without a formal interpretation of EU competition law provisions.[68] The same can be said of the investigations, just to mention two examples, into the automobile[69] and airline[70] industries.

'Policy-driven' enforcement continues to dominate the Commission's activity and approach to the application of Articles 101 and 102 TFEU. Over time, however, the prominence of commitment decisions in its practice declined to some extent.[71] As a result, the Commission has resorted to other instruments. Of these, settlements have acquired a major role.[72] This instrument, whereby firms

---

[64] Commitments decisions have only been challenged on three occasions since their introduction. See Case C-441/07 P *Commission v Alrosa Company Ltd*, EU:C:2010:377; Case T-76/14 *Morningstar, Inc. v Commission*, EU:T:2016:481; and Case C-132/19 P *Groupe Canal + SA v Commission*, EU:C:2020:1007.

[65] *Alrosa* (n 64), paras 42 and 67.

[66] The literature is very abundant. Some notable contributions include Wils (n 63); John Temple Lang, 'Commitment decisions and settlements with antitrust authorities and private parties under European antitrust law' (2006) 32 Annual proceedings of the Fordham Corporate Law Institute 265; Heike Schweitzer, 'Commitment Decisions under Art. 9 of Regulation 1/2003: The Developing EC Practice and Case Law' in Claus-Dieter Ehlermann, Mel Marquis (eds), *European Competition Law Annual 2008 – Antitrust Settlements under EC Competition Law* (Hart Publishing 2010); Florian Wagner-von Papp, 'Best and Even Better Practices in Commitment Procedures after *Alrosa*: The Dangers of Abandoning the "Struggle for Competition Law"' (2012) 49 Common Market Law Review 929; and Niamh Dunne, 'Commitment Decisions in EU Competition Law' (2014) 10 Journal of Competition Law & Economics 399.

[67] Ibáñez Colomo and Kalintiri (n 1).

[68] See above n 47.

[69] See above n 46.

[70] *BA/AA/IB* (Case COMP/39.596) Commission Decision of 14 July 2010; *Continental/United/Lufthansa/Air Canada* (Case COMP/AT.39595) Commission Decision of 23 May 2013; and *Air France/KLM/Alitalia/Delta* (Case AT.39964) Commission Decision of 12 May 2015.

[71] Wouter PJ Wils, 'Ten years of commitment decisions under Article 9 of Regulation 1/2003: Too much of a good thing?' (New Frontiers of Antitrust, Paris, 15 June 2015).

[72] Niamh Dunne, 'From Coercion to Cooperation: Settlements within EU Competition Law' (2019) LSE Legal Studies Working Paper 14/2019, available at https://ssrn.com/abstract=3481419.

acknowledge the infringement in exchange for a reduction of the fine, was initially conceived for cartels, but has progressively expanded to quintessentially 'law-intensive' cases addressing issues such as a refusal to deal[73] or vertical restraints.[74] Settlements do not exist as stand-alone instruments in the EU competition law regime. Formally speaking, they are decisions establishing an infringement in accordance with Article 7 of Regulation 1/2003. In substance, however, their operation may not be fundamentally different from commitments. In particular, the underlying decision is unlikely to be challenged before the General Court.[75]

3.3. 'Policy-driven' Enforcement in Practice: Fines

Fines are a powerful means to express policy choices. They signal that a particular practice is an enforcement priority and/or a particularly serious infringement. They also act as a deterrent vis-à-vis stakeholders. In the early days of Regulation 1/2003, penalties were used primarily in 'fact-intensive' investigations. In fact, the stark increase in the level of fines in cartel cases is one of the most recognisable hallmarks of the reorientation of the Commission's enforcement priorities since 2004.[76] In 'law-intensive' cases, by contrast, fines were initially relied upon sparingly. During the first decade of Regulation 1/2003, they were imposed mostly in investigations involving incumbents in the network industries, in particular telecommunications.[77] The limited use of fines in this area of enforcement is primarily explained by the rise of 'commitments decisions', which rule them out by design.

As far as 'law-intensive' cases are concerned, fines gained in prominence as an instrument of policy-making when digital markets became a priority for the Commission. The novelty of the legal issues raised by online platforms' activities and the market power enjoyed by Big Tech appear to explain this shift. Thus, instead of bringing its investigations to an end by means of commitments decisions, the Commission chose to establish an infringement, assorted with fines. The level of penalties, in some landmark cases, even exceeded that of cartel cases. The *Google Shopping* case illustrates, better than any other, the shift in approach. In 2013 and 2014, the Commission came close to accepting commitments from the firm.[78]

---

[73] See for instance *ARA Foreclosure* (Case AT.39759) Commission Decision of 20 September 2016.
[74] See for instance *Guess* (Case AT.40428) Commission Decision of 17 December 2018.
[75] Dunne (n 72).
[76] For a complete statistical overview since 1990, see https://competition-policy.ec.europa.eu/cartels/statistics_en.
[77] *Wanadoo España v Telefónica* (Case COMP/38.784) Commission Decision of 4 July 2007; *Telekomunikacja Polska* (COMP/39.525) Commission Decision of 22 June 2011; and *Slovak Telekom* (Case AT.39523) Commission Decision of 15 October 2014.
[78] European Commission, 'Antitrust: Commission seeks feedback on commitments offered by Google to address competition concerns' IP/13/371 (Brussels, 25 April 2013). See also Andrew Leyden and Maurits Dolmans, 'The Google Commitments: Now with a Cherry on Top' (2014) 5 Journal of European Competition Law & Practice 253.

In fact, it went as far as to 'market-test' the obligations among stakeholders.[79] Eventually, however, the case was closed with a finding of infringement and a (record at the time) EUR 2.42 billion fine.[80] Google was fined again in 2018 (with EUR 4.34 billion)[81] and 2019 (EUR 1.49 billion).[82]

Figure 1.8 Evolution of fines under Regulation 1/2003

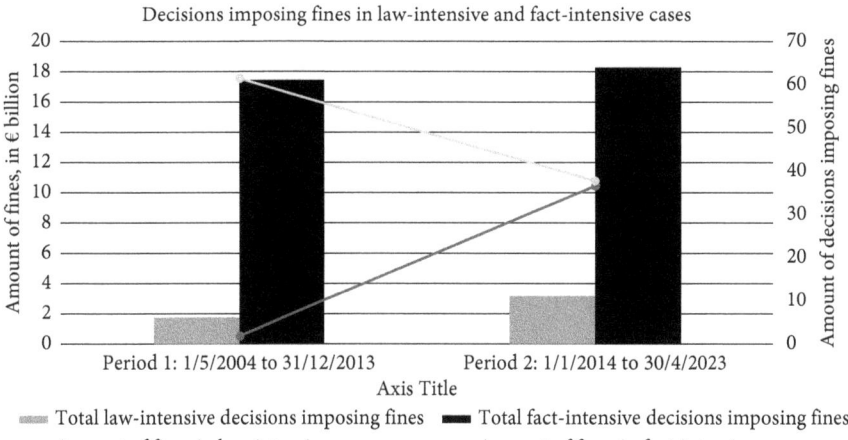

4. Explaining the Shifts in Enforcement: An Economic Perspective

4.1. Traditional Competition Law as a Creature of the Industrial Era

Competition law, as traditionally understood, is a creature of the industrial era. This point is obvious in a sense: the rise in concentration during the nineteenth and twentieth centuries was one of the fundamental factors behind the very emergence of the discipline in North America and Europe.[83] The creation of an antitrust regime as a mechanism to address the power wielded by private firms and its impact on society is well documented.[84] The point is also true in another sense, more relevant for the discussion that follows. Competition law, as developed

---

[79] Communication from the Commission published pursuant to Article 27(4) of Council Regulation (EC) No 1/2003 in Case AT.39740 – *Google* [2013] OJ C120/22.
[80] *Google Shopping* (n 5).
[81] *Android* (n 5).
[82] *AdSense* (n 5).
[83] Herbert Hovenkamp, 'The Invention of Antitrust' (2022) 96 Southern California Law Review 131.
[84] Ibid, 141–142, for an analysis of the historical evidence.

over the years, was designed to deal with the market structure that epitomises the industrial era: the oligopoly. The industries to which Articles 101 and 102 TFEU applied during the formative years of the discipline typically displayed a tendency towards the emergence of a few large players. Car manufacturing (and associated activities),[85] chemicals[86] and cement[87] are examples that come to mind immediately.

The rise of oligopolistic structures was – and is – seen as problematic insofar as firms in concentrated markets enjoy significant market power vis-à-vis suppliers and customers. They may not have a strong incentive to compete with one another; and they may even be naturally inclined to collude. Competition law offered an expert and structured response to these concerns. The discipline provides the tools to deal with practices that have the object and/or the effect of either eliminating firms' incentive (that is, collusion and concentration) and ability to compete (that is, exclusionary conduct). Against this background, the fundamental goal of competition law in the industrial era is to ensure that the degree of rivalry allowed by a given oligopolistic structure can be maintained. Put differently, the logic of this iteration of the discipline is to preserve what has been labelled 'workable competition'.[88] Thus, if the relevant market is structurally suited for four players, each with a significant degree of market power, Articles 101 and 102 TFEU will be enforced to ensure that these firms have the means to compete with one another and that they have more to gain from rivalling each other than from refraining to do so.

This understanding of the discipline sees a relatively modest role for it in the economy. Competition law would not seek to re-engineer market structures and increase the degree of rivalry faced by firms. The point of intervention in the oligopoly era is instead to make the most, for as long as possible, of the existing structures, which are taken as given. The goal of enforcement, in other words, is to preserve rivalry, rather than optimise the operation of the relevant market. For instance, it was soon understood, on both sides of the Atlantic, that ex post enforcement could not do much to address tacit collusion (that is, with instances where the absence of effective competition is attributable to the features of the

---

[85] Some emblematic examples from the formative period include *S.A. des pneumatiques Dunlop – S.A. Pirelli France* (Case IV/24.471) Commission Decision of 5 December 1969; *Davidson Rubber Co.* (n 52); *General Motors Continental* (Case IV/28.851) Commission Decision of 19 December 1974.

[86] Some emblematic examples from the formative period include *Dyestuffs* (Case IV/26.267) Commission Decision of 24 July 1969; *ZOJA/CSC – ICI* (Case IV/26.911) Commission Decision of 14 December 1972; *Kali und Salz/Kali Chemie* (Case IV/795) Commission Decision of 21 December 1973.

[87] Some emblematic examples from the formative period include *Convention chaufourniers* (Case IV/242-295) Commission Decision of 5 May 1969; *Vereeniging van Cementhandelaren* (Case IV/324) Commission Decision of 16 December 1971; and *Nederlandse Cement- Handelmaatschappij NV* (Case IV/595) Commission Decision of 23 December 1971.

[88] Case 26/76, *Metro SB-Großmärkte GmbH & Co. KG v Commission*, EU:C:1977:167, para 20, where the notion of 'workable competition' is defined as '[…] the degree of competition necessary to ensure the observance of the basic requirements and the attainment of the objectives of the Treaty, in particular the creation of a single market achieving conditions similar to those of a domestic market […]'.

relevant market, rather than firm behaviour).[89] Similarly, this is an approach that avoids dictating how firms are to compete with one another (for instance, by setting the prices they should charge for their products or by defining the terms and conditions under which they should deal with customers and suppliers).[90]

Summing up, the traditional expression of competition law that developed during the industrial era was, by and large, deferential to market processes. Intervention would only come into play at the margin, against certain practices that are inherently inimical to a system based on undistorted competition and against other conduct where it has the potential to harm the competitive process in the specific context in which it is implemented. The relative modesty of this approach to competition law is reflected in the nature of the remedies imposed. Deferential market intervention is essentially reactive and proscriptive in nature. Accordingly, it takes the form of negative obligations that can be administered on a one-off basis (and which can be possibly assorted with an obligation to refrain from engaging in similar conduct in the future).

It makes sense to mention some examples to illustrate these ideas. Remedial action in a cartel case amounts, in essence, to declaring the infringement and to ordering cartel members to refrain from engaging in similar conduct in the future.[91] In non-cartel horizontal arrangements, in turn, intervention will also take the form of a negative obligation. A joint purchasing agreement, for instance, may be found to infringe Article 101 TFEU. In such an instance, the firms may be requested to cease and desist the implementation of the practice – if it has already been put into effect – or to refrain from doing so. The same remedy would be relevant in the context of a vertical agreement. If an exclusive dealing clause is found to be likely to foreclose actual or potential rivals, for instance, the supplier may be required not to introduce single-branding obligations (or any other arrangements having an equivalent object and/or effect) in its agreements with distributors.[92]

This understanding of competition law encompasses the three first paradigms discussed above, namely 'detection-deterrence', 'trade-enabling' and

---

[89] Joined Cases C-89/85, C-104/85, C-114/85, C-116/85, C-117/85 and C-125/85 to C-129/85 A. Ahlström Osakeyhtiö and others v Commission, EU:C:1993:120. See René Joliet, 'La notion de pratique concertée et l'arrêt ICI dans une perspective comparative' (1974) 10 Cahiers de droit européen 251; and Donald Turner, 'The Definition of Agreement Under the Sherman Act: Conscious Parallelism and Refusals to Deal' (1962) 75 Harvard Law Review 655.
[90] It is well documented that the Commission has been relatively reluctant to enforce Article 102 TFEU in relation to exploitative conduct. For an overview, see Marco Botta 'Exploitative abuse: recent trends and comparative perspectives', in Pinar Akman, Or Brook and Konstantinos Stylianou (eds), *Research Handbook on Abuse of Dominance and Monopolization* (Edward Elgar 2023).
[91] For an example that follows the canonical structure of cartel decisions, see *Car battery recycling* (Case AT.40018) Commission Decision of 8 December 2017. The decision establishes the infringement (Article 1), imposes a fine on the cartel participants (Article 2) and, in Article 3, requires the parties to bring the infringement to an end and to refrain from engaging in it in the future.
[92] See for instance Articles 4 and 5 of *Van den Bergh Foods Limited* (Case Nos IV/34.073, IV/34.395 and IV/35.436) Commission Decision of 11 March 1998.

'market-protecting' enforcement. What all these paradigms have in common is indeed the fact that effective intervention (to the extent that it is necessary) can take the form of a negative, one-off, obligation. More often than not, action relating to the first two paradigms ('detection-deterrence' and 'trade-enabling' enforcement) relates to conduct that is considered to be inherently inimical to the competitive process (in particular cartels and practices aimed at restricting cross-border trade). As a result, intervention tends to be retrospective: decisions will often be adopted when the conduct has ceased and thus its primary aim would be to signal to stakeholders the seriousness of the breach.

As far as the 'market-protecting' paradigm is concerned, the approach to intervention described above is perhaps best exemplified by Block Exemption Regulations. These legislative instruments, in their different incarnations, invariably provide for a catalogue of hardcore restrictions (some having the effect of excluding the whole agreement from the benefit of the exemption, others merely excluding a particular clause). The purpose of these negative obligations is to identify the instances where the agreement is likely to restrict competition.[93] The conclusions are not different when one considers 'market-protecting' intervention under Article 102 TFEU. Effective enforcement in a predatory pricing or an exclusive dealing case, for instance, takes the form of a duty to cease the conduct and/or refrain from engaging in it.[94]

4.2. The Limits of Traditional Enforcement

There are limits to the application of competition law in the form of a negative obligation administered on a one-off basis. This manifestation of enforcement may not be workable where the discipline applies outside oligopolistic market structures. It has long been understood that competition law cannot change the tendency of an industry towards concentration. Thus, if a given market is not structurally suited for rivalry, the enforcement of Articles 101 and 102 TFEU cannot and will not prevent the emergence of a monopoly. This idea is arguably best captured in *Post Danmark I*, where the Court held that the departure of rivals that are less efficient than the dominant firm is a natural manifestation of the competitive process and, as such, beyond reproach.[95] In the field of merger control, a merger – even a merger to monopoly – will not lead to intervention where the anticompetitive effects would have occurred in any event.[96]

---

[93] Guidelines on vertical restraints (n 12), para 179. See also Joanna Goyder, 'Cet Obscur Objet: Object Restrictions in Vertical Agreements' (2011) 4 Journal of European Competition Law & Practice 327.

[94] Article 3 of *ECS/AKZO* (Case IV/30.698) Commission Decision of 14 December 1985; and Article 3 of *Intel* (Case COMP/C-3/37.990) Commission Decision of 13 May 2009.

[95] Case C-209/10 *Post Danmark A/S v Konkurrencerådet*, EU:C:2012:172, para 22.

[96] Guidelines on the assessment of horizontal mergers under the Council Regulation on the control of concentrations between undertakings [2004] OJ C31/5, paras 89-91, which deal with the 'failing firm

Where a segment of the value chain is structurally unsuited for rivalry (that is, where it is, or displays a tendency towards, monopoly), reactive enforcement may not be a workable remedy to preserve competition in adjacent markets. In other words, the sort of intervention that is characteristic of the industrial era is unlikely to be effective in this context. In presence of a bottleneck, bringing an infringement to an end may require, instead, the sort of 'market-shaping' remedies discussed in Section 2. One should note, in addition, that these are the very market features (a monopoly in a position to extract supracompetitive rents) in which competition authorities are likely to be invited to deal with exploitative conduct. Action against such conduct is another form of proactive intervention that agencies tend to avoid.

Relatively early examples of the application of competition law in bottleneck segments come from collecting societies of copyright and related rights.[97] Given the nature of the activity and the services provided, these societies tend to be structured around monopolies. It is therefore not surprising that there have been recurrent claims that they abuse their dominant position vis-à-vis their members (such as authors and performers) and users (such as broadcasters and night clubs). The concerns considered by the Court of Justice in cases like *Tournier* did not relate to the exclusion of rival collecting societies, but to the unfair and/or discriminatory nature of their practices.[98] In this sense, competition law was relied upon not to preserve the market structure, but to prevent the exploitation by the bottleneck operator of its market power.

The limits of traditional enforcement also become apparent when one considers exclusionary conduct. Consider the paradigmatic example of a refusal to deal by a vertically-integrated dominant firm. Suppose that this firm controls an infrastructure that is indispensable for would-be rivals to operate on a downstream market. To the extent that the infrastructure in question cannot be replicated (that is, has a natural tendency to monopoly), traditional (reactive, one-off) intervention would fail to preserve competition on the relevant downstream market. Instead, it would be necessary for a court or authority to demand shared access to the infrastructure and to monitor compliance with this duty over time. Alternatively, a court (or authority) could demand the structural separation of the upstream and downstream activities. Effective enforcement, in other words, would need to replicate the logic and operation of telecommunications and energy regulation.

---

defence' (that is, instances in which any anticompetitive effects would not be attributable to the merger, but to the inevitable departure of one of the parties from the market).

[97] Case 395/87 *Ministère public v Jean-Louis Tournier*, EU:C:1989:319; and Joined Cases 110/88, 241/88 and 242/88 *François Lucazeau and others v Société des Auteurs, Compositeurs et Editeurs de Musique (SACEM) and others*, EU:C:1989:326. On the bottleneck nature of these markets, see Christian Handke and Ruth Towse, 'Economics of Copyright Collecting Societies' (2007) 38 International Review of Intellectual Property and Competition Law 937.

[98] *Tournier* (n 97), para 7.

4.3. Network Industries and Digital Markets: The Boundaries of Competition Law

The limits of traditional competition law have become apparent in two contexts: the liberalisation of network industries and the rise of Big Tech. Network industries such as telecommunications, energy, rail and postal services are – or at least used to be – structured around a bottleneck (that is, an activity with natural monopoly features). As a result, the provision of goods and services upstream and/or downstream of the bottleneck relies on access to an infrastructure that has high and persistent barriers to entry. This is true, for instance, of the 'last mile' of the telecommunications infrastructure[99] and of the transmission and distribution of electricity.[100] The implication of this feature is that protecting effective competition on the relevant adjacent markets demands the imposition of positive obligations, as well as the setting up of an institutional apparatus aimed at monitoring compliance.

More often than not, these positive obligations are imposed by virtue of sector-specific regulation mandating shared access to the bottleneck segment. Where there is a regulatory framework in place, competition law does not need to engage in 'market-shaping' intervention. In such circumstances, Articles 101 and 102 TFEU can fulfil an auxiliary role and come into play as a 'safety net' where the sector-specific regime fails to deliver. These issues are considered in Chapters 3 and 6. In the absence of sector-specific measures, on the other hand, 'market-shaping' enforcement becomes indispensable. Proactive intervention would also be necessary where the competition authority concludes that existing sector-specific measures do not go far enough in preserving effective competition in the markets adjacent to the bottleneck.

The challenges that the Commission encountered when enforcing competition law in recently liberalised industries emerged again when its priorities shifted to digital markets. There are segments in the digital arena that, just like the last mile of the telecommunications infrastructure, present bottleneck features.[101] As discussed at length in Chapter 5, positions of substantial market power are not infrequent in digital ecosystems. The tendency is attributed to the interplay of large returns to scale in the industry and to network effects.[102] The rise of Windows as the de facto standard operating system illustrates how these factors can, in some circumstances, lead to the emergence of monopolies or quasi-monopolies.[103] The rise of Google and Amazon are other examples that come to mind immediately.

---

[99] Jean-Jacques Laffont and Jean Tirole, *Competition in Telecommunications* (MIT Press 1999).
[100] Jean-Michel Glachant, Paul L Joskow and Michael G Pollitt, *Handbook on Electricity Markets* (Edward Elgar 2021).
[101] Jacques Crémer, Yves-Alexandre de Montjoye and Heike Schweitzer, *Competition Policy for the Digital Era* (2019), available at https://ec.europa.eu/competition/publications/reports/kd0419345enn.pdf.
[102] Ibid, 19–20.
[103] Michael L Katz and Carl Shapiro, 'Systems Competition and Network Effects' (1994) 8 Journal of Economic Perspectives 93.

The application of competition law in digital markets was characterised, until recently, by the absence of a dedicated regulatory apparatus. As a result, the enforcement of Article 101 and 102 TFEU required the administration of the sort of proactive measures described in Section 2. It has been explained above that intervention in *Google Shopping* led to the regulation of the terms and conditions under which the search engine had to provide shared access to one of its features.[104] In order to comply with the non-discrimination duty imposed in the decision, the dominant firm had to alter the design of its product. Similarly, in *Android*, the Commission challenged Google's very business model.[105] As will be discussed at length in Chapter 8, these two decisions exposed the challenges that the system faces when administering remedies of this nature.

5. Explaining the Shifts in Enforcement: A Legal and Institutional Perspective

5.1. Regulation 1/2003

The parallel shifts towards 'market-shaping' and 'policy-driven' enforcement are not just the product of the economic features of the industries to which Articles 101 and 102 TFEU apply. These trends cannot be fully grasped without considering the legal and institutional changes introduced and enabled by Regulation 1/2003. It makes sense to present systematically the choices made by the legislature to understand how they are conducive to the observed evolution. Regulation 1/2003 was expressly designed to maximise the Commission's leeway to shape policy and to minimise any factors constraining its ability to define its enforcement priorities. It did so in two ways. First, by expanding the authority's discretion. Second, by introducing alternative enforcement avenues.

One of the most notable features of Regulation 1/2003 is that there are no circumstances under which the Commission can be compelled to adopt a decision or provide an interpretation of Articles 101 and 102 TFEU, whether formally or informally. It is for the authority to exercise its judgment about how best to make use of its limited resources. For instance, firms are not entitled to a 'finding of inapplicability' within the meaning of Article 10 of the Regulation or to a comfort letter addressing the status of their practices. The Commission may conclude that it is in the public interest to offer guidance about the scope of Article 101 or 102 TFEU, in particular in relation to new practices for which there are no precedents.[106] However, it is under no obligation to do so (and, as pointed

---

[104] *Google Shopping* (n 5), para 699.
[105] *Android* (n 5).
[106] Recital 14 of Regulation 1/2003 (n 13) and above Section 3.2.

out above, has never done so). This institutional setup contrasts with the logic and operation of Regulation 17, which put notifications by undertakings (and the resulting dialogue with undertakings, both formally and informally) at the heart of the regime.

Regulation 1/2003 was also designed to discharge the Commission of part of its enforcement burden. The keystone of the regime is the elimination of its exclusive power to apply Article 101(3) TFEU (at the time, Article 81(3) EC), which dispenses it from the need to deal with individual notifications. Abolishing the Commission's exemption monopoly paved the way for the decentralisation in the enforcement of Articles 101 and 102 TFEU. In this sense, Regulation 1/2003 created the conditions for national courts and authorities to become major actors in the system. National courts are now entitled to apply Article 101 TFEU in full (and thus verify whether the conditions of an exemption are met in a given case).[107] Authorities, in turn, enjoy many of the powers that the Commission itself has (including the adoption of infringement and commitments decisions), which they exercise in coordination with the latter.[108]

In this institutional landscape, the Commission is no longer the (virtually) sole enforcer of Articles 101 and 102 TFEU. Rather, it is *primus inter pares* within a network of authorities and courts. With the multiplication of enforcement avenues, the Commission can focus on a narrow set of priorities without affecting the effectiveness of EU competition policy. In the same vein, Regulation 1/2003 allows it to intervene in some cases as a guide or coordinator, as opposed to an authority *sensu stricto*. It can intervene as an *amicus curiae* in proceedings before national courts,[109] and can be consulted by national authorities.[110] As a result, it can take action to ensure consistency in the application of Articles 101 and 102 TFEU in a manner that is less taxing on its own resources and on its discretion to define policy.

The choices made in Regulation 1/2003 also help explain some of the aspects of enforcement identified above, and in particular the rise of commitments in the system. As already pointed out, Article 9 decisions have become the privileged instrument to deal with 'law-intensive' cases. This development is not surprising if one considers that the institutional framework, as a whole, was expressly conceived to expand the space within which the Commission can exercise its discretion and to ensure that its ability to do so would be relatively unconstrained. The authority has simply made the most effective use, from its perspective, of the possibilities made available to it under the regime. In a decentralised system, moreover, the need to interpret Articles 101 and 102 TFEU is far less pressing. The Commission can therefore choose to leave some matters to national courts and authorities.

---

[107] Ibid, Article 6.
[108] Ibid, Article 5.
[109] Ibid, Article 15(3).
[110] Ibid, Article 11(5).

5.2. The Rise of Guidelines and Other Soft Law Instruments

The past two decades have seen the stark rise of soft law instruments. Commission Guidelines now cover vast swathes of EU competition policy, including horizontal cooperation agreements,[111] vertical restraints[112] and technology transfer agreements.[113] In 2009, the authority issued a Guidance on its priorities when enforcing Article 102 TFEU.[114] While they have been a feature of the legal and institutional landscape since the early days of the discipline,[115] soft law instruments have become considerably more numerous and complex – at least insofar as they cover more issues and at greater length – since 2004.[116] Following the adoption of Regulation 1/2003, the position expressed by the Commission in its Guidelines is the primary – if not the only – port of call for a number of 'law-intensive' matters.

Guidelines and similar notices have been instrumental to the shift towards 'market-shaping' and 'policy-driven' enforcement. They are a complement to the rest of the institutional changes introduced under the regime, in the sense that they facilitate the decentralised application of Articles 101 and 102 TFEU and allow the Commission to focus on other practices and sectors in its case-by-case practice. Soft law instruments provide valuable orientation to national courts and authorities in relation to some practices and issues where case-by-case enforcement is lacking. Just to mention some examples, only in soft law instrument would a national court be able to get an idea of the instances when, in the Commission's view, a resale price maintenance agreement is likely to meet the conditions of Article 101(3) TFEU,[117] or the circumstances under which a research and development agreement is likely to give rise to concerns.[118]

These examples show that soft law instruments have taken over at least some of the functions that individual decisions used to fulfil under Regulation 17. Certain aspects of 'law-driven' enforcement, in other words, have been replaced by other expressions of policy-making. The trend is particularly marked in relation to the 'market-protecting' paradigm (which, as discussed above, deals with 'law-intensive' matters that demand the administration of reactive remedies). This variety of enforcement, which dominated the landscape under Regulation 17, has now been relegated behind 'market-shaping' and 'detection-deterrence' action. It would appear that the Commission has a preference for hinting at its

---

[111] Guidelines on horizontal cooperation agreements (n 12).
[112] Guidelines on vertical restraints (n 12).
[113] Guidelines on technology transfer agreements (n 12).
[114] Guidance on the Commission's enforcement priorities in applying Article 82 of the EC Treaty to abusive exclusionary conduct by dominant undertakings [2009] OJ C45/7.
[115] For the earliest examples, see Notice on exclusive agency contracts made with commercial agents [1962] OJ 2921; and Notice on patent licensing agreements [1962] OJ 2922.
[116] For an empirical analysis, see Ibáñez Colomo and Kalintiri (n 1), 43, which reveals a very substantial rise in the number and complexity of soft law instruments.
[117] Guidelines on vertical restraints (n 12), paras 197–201.
[118] Guidelines on horizontal cooperation agreements (n 12), paras 111–149.

interpretation of 'market-protecting' matters in the context of soft law instruments. It is an approach to policy-making that is consistent with the pre-eminence of commitments decisions in the system.

Remarkably, the Commission's preference for soft law instruments – as opposed to a 'finding of inapplicability' or an infringement decision – has also been displayed in relation to novel legal issues. In the years and decades that followed the adoption of Regulation 1/2003, some points of law for which there were no precedents inevitably came to the fore. In many instances, the Commission chose to address them in its various sets of Guidelines, even when there was a real risk of legal fragmentation. For instance, the status of cooperation agreements aimed at promoting sustainability goals has given rise to much commentary in the past years.[119] It has been argued, inter alia, that the absence of clear guidance has a chilling effect on potentially pro-competitive arrangements, and that the interpretation of Article 101(3) TFEU should be tweaked.[120] In spite of this uncertainty, and even though some competition authorities have taken steps to provide clarity on the issue, the Commission chose to deal with it only in the context of its review of the Guidelines on horizontal cooperation agreements.[121]

6. Implications for Law and Policy-making

6.1. Summary

The adoption of Regulation 1/2003 has had a dual effect on the Commission's activity. First, the regime has seen the rise of 'market-shaping' and 'detection-deterrence' intervention and the relative decline of 'trade-enabling' and 'market-protecting' enforcement. The observed shift reflects the move towards 'policy-driven' and away from 'law-driven' action, at least by means of case-by-case, incremental decision-making. The new incarnation of enforcement epitomises the end of the formative period in EU competition law. The Commission no longer sees the clarification of the scope of Articles 101 and 102 TFEU as a priority. With a competition culture firmly in place, administrative action at the EU level now focuses on the most egregious breaches ('detection-deterrence') and the most challenging ('market-shaping') investigations. This shift is eased by the very institutional structure put

---

[119] Simon Holmes, 'Climate change, sustainability, and competition law' (2020) 8 Journal of Antitrust Enforcement 354.

[120] Maurits Dolmans, 'Sustainable Competition Policy' (2020), available at https://ssrn.com/abstract=3608023; and Anna Gerbrandy, 'Solving a Sustainability-Deficit in European Competition Law' (2017) 40 World Competition 539.

[121] Alexandra Badea and others, 'Competition Policy in Support of Europe's Green Ambition' Competition Policy Brief (September 2021), available at https://ec.europa.eu/competition-policy/publications_en.

in place by Regulation 1/2003. By design, the current system gives considerable leeway to shape policy. It also provides for a set of instruments, such as commitments decisions, that allow the Commission to minimise the constraints to which administrative action is subject.

The growing importance of proactive remedies in policy-making is not capricious. It is a function of, and a necessary adjustment to, the features of the industries to which the Commission has chosen to devote its resources. What network industries – such as telecommunications and energy – and digital markets have in common is that some activities tend to revolve around a bottleneck (that is, a segment of the value chain with a tendency towards monopoly). In such markets, the reactive remedies of the oligopoly era are often ineffective. An abusive refusal to supply an input, for instance, can only be meaningfully addressed by means of an obligation to deal with would-be competitors or, alternatively, by means of a structural separation of the upstream and the downstream activities.

6.2. Testing the Boundaries of Law and Policy-making

'Market-shaping' intervention pushes administrative action towards the outer boundaries of Articles 101 and 102 TFEU. An analysis of the Commission's practice shows that this policy paradigm regularly tests the limits of existing legal doctrines. In some instances, proactive enforcement amounts to questioning the prevailing market structures, as opposed to a behaviour. For example, an investigation may challenge a firm's dominant position (which is not prohibited, in and of itself, under Article 102 TFEU), not the abuse thereof. In other instances, administrative action may not be obvious to reconcile with the relevant case law. Proactive intervention, because of its intrusive and transformative nature, has traditionally been confined by the Court to exceptional circumstances. In this sense, the case law constrains the reach of 'market-shaping' enforcement. It is not surprising that, in the new reality, the Commission has regularly sought to revisit and reinterpret the relevant legal precedents.

Even leaving legal considerations aside, 'market-shaping' enforcement is a challenge for the system. As already mentioned, proactive action puts competition authorities in a position that is not fundamentally different from that of a telecommunications or energy regulator. The administration of remedies such as a duty to deal or a divestiture is demanding in a way that traditional enforcement is not. The design, implementation and monitoring of proactive enforcement necessitates the expertise and the resources with which sectoral agencies are equipped but competition authorities, including the Commission, are not. To the extent that this is the case, 'market-shaping' enforcement exposes the competition law system to the limits of what it can meaningfully and realistically achieve.

Table 1.1 Commission decisions involving the administration of proactive obligations under Regulation (EC) 1/2003

Case	Name	Provision	Type of proactive intervention
40703	Amazon – Buy Box	102	Alterations to the design of a product
40305	Network sharing – Czech Republic	101	Alterations to the design of a product
40511	Insurance Ireland: Insurance claims database and conditions of access	101	Reconfiguration of the terms and conditions of supply
40394	Aspen	102	Reconfiguration of the terms and conditions of supply
40335	Romanian Gas Interconnectors (Transgaz)	102	Reconfiguration of the terms and conditions of supply
40134	AB InBev beer trade restrictions	102	Alterations to the design of a product
39849	BEH Gas	102	Reconfiguration of the terms and conditions of supply
40461	DK/DE Interconnector (TenneT)	102	Obligation to deal
40099	Google Android	102	Market restructuring Obligation to deal
39816	Upstream gas supplies in Central and Eastern Europe	102	Alterations to a business model
39813	Baltic Rail	102	Market restructuring Reconfiguration of the terms and conditions of supply
39740	Google Search (Shopping)	102	Alteration to the design of a product
39759	ARA Foreclosure	102	Alteration to the design of a product
40023	Cross-border access to pay-TV	101	Divestiture
			Market restructuring

Implications for Law and Policy-making 43

39745	CDS – Information market	101/102	Obligation to deal
39850	Container Shipping	101	Reconfiguration of the terms and conditions of supply
39767	BEH Electricity	102	Market restructuring
39964	AF-KL/DL/AZ	101	Reconfiguration of the terms and conditions of supply
39939	Samsung – Enforcement of UMTS standard essential patents	102	Reconfiguration of the terms and conditions of supply
39398	Visa MIF	101	Reconfiguration of the terms and conditions of supply
40049	Mastercard II (the inter-regional interchange fees leg)	101	Reconfiguration of the terms and conditions of supply
39678	Deutsche Bahn I	102	Reconfiguration of the terms and conditions of supply
39731	Deutsche Bahn II	102	Reconfiguration of the terms and conditions of supply
39595	Continental/United/Lufthansa/Air Canada	101	Market restructuring
			Reconfiguration of the terms and conditions of supply
39727	CEZ	102	Market restructuring.
39230	Rio Tinto Alcan	101/102	Reconfiguration of the terms and conditions of supply
39654	Reuters Instrument Codes (RICs)	102	Reconfiguration of the terms and conditions of supply
39692	IBM – Maintenance services	102	Obligation to deal
			Reconfiguration of the terms and conditions of supply
39592	Standard and Poor's	102	Reconfiguration of the terms and conditions of supply
39315	ENI	102	Divestiture

(continued)

Table 1.1 (Continued)

Case	Name	Provision	Type of proactive intervention
39596	BA/AA/IB	101	Market restructuring Reconfiguration of the terms and conditions of supply
39317	E.On gas foreclosure	102	Market restructuring
39351	Swedish Interconnectors	102	Market restructuring
39386	Long term electricity contracts in France	102	Market restructuring Reconfiguration of the terms and conditions of supply
39530	Microsoft (Tying)	102	Alteration to the design of a product
38636	Rambus	102	Reconfiguration of the terms and conditions of supply
39316	GDF foreclosure	102	Market restructuring
39416	Ship Classification	101	Reconfiguration of the terms and conditions of supply
39402	RWE gas foreclosure	102	Divestiture
39388	German electricity wholesale market	102	Divestiture
39399	German electricity balancing market	102	Divestiture
37966	Distrigaz	102	Market restructuring Reconfiguration of the terms and conditions of access
39143	Opel – Access to technical information	101	Obligation to deal Reconfiguration of the terms and conditions of supply
39142	Toyota Motor Europe – Access to technical information	101	Obligation to deal Reconfiguration of the terms and conditions of supply

39141	*Fiat – Access to technical information*	101	Obligation to deal
			Reconfiguration of the terms and conditions of supply
39140	*DaimlerChrysler – Access to technical information*	101	Obligation to deal
			Reconfiguration of the terms and conditions of supply
38173	*FA Premier League*	101	Reconfiguration of the terms and conditions of supply
38381	*Alrosa*	102	Reconfiguration of the terms and conditions of supply
37214	*DFB*	101	Reconfiguration of the terms and conditions of supply

2

The Rise and Decline of the 'More Economics-based Approach'

1. The Path to the 'More Economics-based Approach'

Entire libraries have been written about the 'more economics-based approach' (or 'more economic approach') to EU competition law enforcement.[1] The expression captures the shift in policy-making that took place from the 1990s to the mid-2000s. Because the process started more than two decades ago and because it was so transformational, memories of the old days have faded. The circumstances in which the approach was introduced and the shortcomings it addressed have been, by and large, forgotten. The fundamental problems with EU competition policy in the late 1980s and early 1990s did not relate exclusively (arguably, not even primarily) to the fact that it was not sufficiently informed by economic analysis. Reading the leading commentators of the time suggests that the trouble with enforcement was, first and foremost, that it was inconsistent and did not have a coherent theoretical basis.[2] As the European Commission's (hereinafter, the 'Commission') very reaction to the process shows, the 'more economics-approach' was introduced to steer policy and to assist law-making, not to impose a particular welfare standard.

When leading authors like Korah claimed that policy lacked a clear sense of direction, they meant that the discipline did not have either the means or the methodology to prioritise cases in a systematic and meaningful way. In other words, it was not always obvious to discern what the point of the EU competition law system was, and how it went about achieving its goals. Against this background, economic analysis provided a benchmark against which to make

---

[1] Some of the most notable contributions to the topic include Christian Ahlborn and Jorge Padilla, 'From Fairness to Welfare: Implications for the Assessment of Unilateral Conduct under EC Competition Law', in Claus-Dieter Ehlermann and Mel Marquis (eds), *European Competition Law Annual 2007: A Reformed Approach to Article 82 EC* (Hart Publishing 2008); Josef Drexl, Wolfgang Kerber and Rupprecht Podszun, *Competition Policy and the Economic Approach Foundations and Limitations* (Edward Elgar 2011); Bruce Wardaugh, *Competition, Effects and Predictability: Rule of Law and the Economic Approach to Competition* (Hart Publishing 2020); and Anne C Witt, *The More Economic Approach to EU Antitrust Law* (Hart Publishing 2016).

[2] See in particular Valentine Korah, 'EEC Competition Policy – Legal Form or Economic Efficiency' (1986) 39 Current Legal Problems 85.

and assess policy. As emphasised by Neven, Seabright and Papandropoulos at the time, the enforcement of EU competition rules by the Commission was simultaneously too restrictive and too lenient, at least when examined through formal lenses.[3] The authority was strict vis-à-vis some practices with little or no impact on society and consumers, whereas the most harmful conduct – namely cartel arrangements – was not prioritised.

The legal treatment of vertical restraints, which marks the shift in policy, comes across as the obvious starting point to illustrate these ideas. Distribution agreements were subject to regulation detailing the sort of behaviour in which suppliers and resellers could engage and that from which they had to refrain.[4] As noted then by lawyers and economists, the policy of the time was unduly strict vis-à-vis some practices for no reason other than the fact that they limited contractual freedom.[5] Seen through the lenses of formal economic analysis, the approach favoured by the Commission not only lacked a sense of direction but was counterproductive: it prohibited conduct that could have injected competition in the relevant markets. Conversely, behaviour with the potential to harm the competitive process was treated with relative leniency or was not prioritised. Arguably, the fundamental flaw of enforcement in those days was that it failed to acknowledge that context is crucial when determining whether or not a vertical restraint (and, indeed, most agreements) are restrictive of competition.

The enforcement of Article 102 TFEU was no different. The absence of direction became particularly apparent in the aftermath of two General Court judgments, *Michelin II*[6] and *British Airways*.[7] Economists like Motta (who went on to become Chief Competition Economist at DG Comp) critically dissected the first of these cases.[8] As is true of vertical restraints, the practices at stake in *Michelin II* and *British Airways* – conditional rebate schemes – do not necessarily have an anticompetitive object, and do not invariably lead to foreclosure. In fact, they can be (and often are) a healthy expression of competition on the merits. Again, whether or not intervention is justified is primarily contingent on the specific circumstances of the case. In particular, it is necessary to consider whether the available evidence is consistent with the exclusion of rivals and whether the practice can be plausibly explained on other, pro-competitive, grounds.[9]

---

[3] Damien Neven, Pénélope Papandropoulos and Paul Seabright (eds), *Trawling for Minnows: European Competition Policy and Agreements Between Firms* (Centre for Economic Policy Research 1998).

[4] See, for an example of this approach, Commission Regulation (EEC) No. 1984/83 of 22 June 1983 on the application of Article 85(3) of the Treaty to categories of exclusive purchasing agreements [1983] OJ L173/5.

[5] Barry Hawk, 'System failure: Vertical restraints and EC competition law' (1995) 32 Common Market Law Review 973.

[6] Case T-203/01 *Manufacture française des pneumatiques Michelin v Commission*, EU:T:2003:250.

[7] Case T-219/99 *British Airways plc v Commission*, EU:T:2003:343.

[8] Massimo Motta, 'Michelin II: The Treatment of Rebates' in Bruce Lyons (ed), *Cases in European Competition Policy: The Economic Analysis* (Cambridge University Press 2009).

[9] This position was articulated in EAGCP, 'An economic approach to Article 82' (July 2005), available at http://ec.europa.eu/dgs/competition/economist/eagcp_july_21_05.pdf.

These two Article 102 TFEU cases show, first, the extent to which administrative action lacked clear boundaries and was as such difficult to anticipate. The finding of abuse in *Michelin II* and *British Airways* was based on a legal doctrine that was originally conceived to apply to exclusivity obligations and loyalty rebates.[10] Under the *Hoffmann-La Roche* case law, these two schemes were categorised as abusive regardless of the context and irrespective of their effects. Over time, the scope of the doctrine expanded to cover other practices, including rebates conditional on the volume supplied (as in *Michelin II*).[11] When this point was reached, it became clear that the Commission did not follow a discernible approach to draw the line between pro-competitive and abusive behaviour. Accordingly, virtually any practice implemented by a dominant firm was liable to be deemed abusive, even when there were precedents suggesting the opposite and even when the relevant context suggested that they were harmless.

Second, *Michelin II* and *British Airways* reveal inconsistencies in policy-making. When the Commission started the investigation that would lead to *Michelin II*, it had already reframed its approach to vertical restraints. In the context of Article 101 TFEU, the authority had already accepted that exclusive dealing and other obligations having an equivalent object or effect (including conditional rebates) demand a case-by-case analysis of their actual or potential impact on competition.[12] These practices, in other words, were not treated as presumptive infringements under that provision. In the context of Article 102 TFEU, by contrast, the Commission continued to prioritise cases where the available evidence suggested that exclusionary effects were unlikely.[13] The coexistence of these two approaches – one contextual, one not – was difficult to rationalise. The conflict between both became dramatically apparent in the *Van den Bergh Foods* case, which was based on the joint application of Articles 101 and 102 TFEU.[14]

Finally, *Airtours* is often mentioned as another landmark in the journey towards the 'more economics-based approach'. It is a useful example in that it exposes, from a different angle, the need for a shift in policy. In this merger case, the Commission declared the incompatibility of a transaction with the internal market, based on the fact that it would lead to the strengthening of a collective dominant position.[15] The Commission's interpretation of the notion of collective dominance was controversial for two main reasons. First, it had defined it in a way that disregarded the mainstream consensus. The authority's approach departed from the economic concept of tacit collusion and was not constrained

---

[10] Case 85/76 *Hoffmann-La Roche & Co. AG v Commission*, EU:C:1979:36.
[11] *Michelin II* (n 6), paras 82–95.
[12] Case C-234/89 *Stergios Delimitis v Henninger Bräu AG*, EU:C:1991:91. See also the 2000 version of the Guidelines on vertical restraints (no longer in force), which refers expressly to rebate schemes (Guidelines on vertical restraints [2000] OJ C291/1, para 152; no longer in force).
[13] See in this sense the evidence provided by Motta (n 8) and *Michelin* (Case COMP/E-2/36.041/PO) Commission Decision of 20 June 2001.
[14] Case T-65/98 *Van den Bergh Foods Ltd v Commission*, EU:T:2003:281.
[15] Case T-342/99 *Airtours plc v Commission*, EU:T:2002:146.

by the boundaries that would logically derive from it.[16] Second, the authority's legal understanding of the notion of collective dominance gave it, in effect, the discretion to decide which horizontal mergers to prohibit and which mergers to allow. As pointed out by experts at the time, the Commission crafted a test that would never fail to be established in practice.[17] As a result, it would not have been possible to anticipate administrative action.

The Commission addressed what can be termed a legitimacy crisis in competition policy by adjusting the substantive and institutional dimensions of the system. From a substantive standpoint, the 1999 Vertical Block Exemption Regulation,[18] together with the accompanying Guidelines,[19] heralded a new era, at least in two fundamental ways. First, general policy positions are outlined in advance and at length, thereby constraining the Commission's own discretion and giving stakeholders the ability to anticipate administrative action. Second, the new approach to vertical restraints is made to revolve around the degree of market power enjoyed by the parties to the agreement (as opposed to the formal aspects of the restraints). This same approach was followed in the field of merger control. In the aftermath of the *Airtours* judgment, and following the adoption of Regulation 139/2004,[20] the Commission restructured its policy towards mergers to bring it in line with the expert consensus. Accordingly, the inquiry would revolve around whether the concentration can be expected to lead to coordinated or non-coordinated effects. This policy was made explicit in two sets of Guidelines that sought to capture the prevailing economic ideas of the time.[21]

The process was symbolically culminated with the adoption of the Guidance Paper on exclusionary abuses (hereinafter, the 'Guidance Paper').[22] According to the principles underpinning this instrument, potentially abusive practices are to be prioritised by the Commission based on their capacity to produce anti-competitive effects. In this sense, it acknowledges that the majority of conduct has ambivalent effects on competition, depending on the relevant economic and legal context. The Guidance Paper also included a range of methodologies to evaluate, by proxy, the impact of potential abuses on the market(s) where they are implemented. Of these, the so-called 'as efficient competitor' test (introduced

---

[16] Juan Briones and Jorge Padilla, 'The Complex Landscape of Oligopolies under EU Competition Policy – Is Collective Dominance Ripe for Guidelines?' (2001) 24 World Competition 307, 309–310.

[17] Ibid, 310–311.

[18] Commission Regulation (EC) No 2790/1999 of 22 December 1999 on the application of Article 81(3) of the Treaty to categories of vertical agreements and concerted practices [1999] OJ L336/21.

[19] Guidelines on vertical restraints (n 12).

[20] Council Regulation (EC) 139/2004 of 20 January 2004 on the control of concentrations between undertakings [2004] OJ L24/1.

[21] Guidelines on the assessment of horizontal mergers under the Council Regulation on the control of concentrations between undertakings [2004] OJ C31/5 and Guidelines on the assessment of non-horizontal mergers under the Council Regulation on the control of concentrations between undertakings [2008] OJ C265/6.

[22] Guidance on the Commission's enforcement priorities in applying Article 82 of the EC Treaty to abusive exclusionary conduct by dominant undertakings [2009] OJ C45/7.

to ascertain the exclusionary potential of conditional rebate schemes) has come to be seen as the epitome of the 'more economics-based approach'.[23]

From an institutional standpoint, the setup of DG Comp was changed to ensure that its policy would follow the mainstream consensus among economists. In the aftermath of the annulment of three decisions in the area of merger control – including *Airtours* – Commissioner Monti announced the creation of the office of the Chief Competition Economist.[24] The Office was conceived as a team of experts that would provide independent advice on the methodological aspects of the cases considered by individual teams and to the overall design of DG Comp's policy. In addition to heading an in-house team, the Chief Competition Economist would be in charge of the coordination of the Economic Advisory Group on Competition Policy, a discussion forum of leading academics and sharing views on various Commission initiatives.[25] For instance, the Group produced a report on exclusionary abuses that kickstarted the process that would lead to the adoption of the Guidance Paper.[26]

2. The Emergence of the 'Brussels Consensus'

2.1. Introduction

At some point, during the early to mid-2000s, it looked as if the 'more economics-based approach' captured the views of a clear majority of lawyers and economists working on European competition law matters. Enforcers and practitioners advising private firms had come to share, it seemed, a common understanding of what makes good policy and how to attain it. If there were dissenting views, one would have been forgiven for thinking that they represented those of a shrinking minority. The unequivocal impression at the time was that EU competition policy was reaching its own end of history. From the perspective of the proponents of the approach, the European system was about to attain a stage of development that would make for better, more focused and more predictable enforcement – and this, on a lasting basis. It is in this context that Ahlborn and Padilla coined the term 'Brussels consensus'.[27]

---

[23] Ibid, paras 37–45. For an application of the test, see *Intel* (Case COMP/C-3 /37.990) Commission Decision of 13 May 2009. The Commission describes the test in para 1003 as evaluating 'whether [the dominant firm] itself, in view of its own costs and the effect of the rebate, would be able to enter the market at a more limited scale without incurring losses. It thereby establishes what price a competitor which is "as efficient" as [the dominant firm] would have to offer [the relevant product] in order to compensate [a customer] for the loss of any […] rebate'.

[24] Mario Monti, 'EU Competition Policy' (Fordham Annual Conference on International Antitrust Law and Policy, New York, 31 October 2002).

[25] Lars-Hendrik Röller and Pierre A Buigues, 'The Office of the Chief Competition Economist at the European Commission' (May 2005).

[26] EAGCP, 'An economic approach to Article 82' (n 9).

[27] Ahlborn and Padilla (n 1).

The expression 'Brussels consensus' was used – just like its Washington counterpart – as an umbrella term capturing a set of ideas which had come to be seen as the desirable features of the EU competition law system. It seems useful to go over them in some detail, if only as a point of comparison with the new understanding of competition policy that appears to be emerging in the continent. The philosophy underpinning the 'Brussels consensus' is presented hereinafter around the following three key themes. First, the factors behind the legitimacy of enforcement (that is, what makes competition policy acceptable). Second, the principles around which policy-making would revolve (that is, the overall philosophy). Third, and finally, the tools that are relied upon to implement the said principles.

2.2. The Legitimacy of Enforcement under the 'Brussels Consensus'

Underpinning the 'Brussels consensus' there was a particular understanding of what makes competition policy legitimate; that is, what makes intervention (or its absence) acceptable from the perspective of stakeholders.[28] There are three points that come to mind immediately. The first one is that, under the 'more economics-based approach', what matters is the process though which a decision is reached, not the outcome of an investigation. This is known as 'throughput legitimacy' in the political science literature.[29] What counts, in other words, is not whether administrative action leads to a finding of infringement but whether the authority has asked itself the right questions, followed a sound methodology and considered all the relevant factors. If the appropriate process is followed, then the outcome – whether it is a fine, a structural remedy or, conversely, a decision to close a probe with no further action – will be seen as legitimate. In a sense, the 'more economics-based approach' demands the authority to exercise restraint and acknowledge that there may be instances in which the available evidence does not justify intervention.

Second, competition policy is seen as legitimate under the 'more economics-based approach' where it relies on the best available theoretical and empirical expertise (that is, input legitimacy). Doing so involves, first and foremost, ensuring that administrative action reflects mainstream positions, particularly in relation to economic analysis. The analytical framework, and the methodological tools on which enforcement relies, must be widely understood to reflect the state of the art in the field. An authority that ignores consensus positions in economics and develops its own theoretical framework gives itself, in effect, the ability to

---

[28] Vivien A Schmidt, 'Democracy and Legitimacy in the European Union Revisited: Input, Output and "Throughput"' (2013) 61 Political Studies 2.

[29] Ibid. The concept of throughput legitimacy, as construed by the author, 'focuses on the quality of the governance processes of the EU as contributing to a different kind of normative legitimacy from both the performance-oriented legitimacy of output and the participation-oriented legitimacy of input'.

behave in an arbitrary manner. It would be able to avoid any effective constraints. In the same vein, it would make it impossible for firms to challenge its decisions: as soon as an authority is allowed to choose the expertise on which it relies, it would be able to avoid meaningful scrutiny of administrative action (including judicial scrutiny).

Third, the legitimacy of administrative action depends on it advancing the public interest in a clear, well-defined way. There are two aspects to this idea. In the first place, the 'more economics-based approach' is in part a reaction against a school of thought that sees competition policy as a means to attain a multiplicity of objectives – from workers' rights to environmental protection and the interests of small businesses. The Brussels consensus sees this expansive understanding of law and policy-making as unpredictable and, ultimately, as a source of arbitrary decision-making.[30] Proponents of this consensus questioned, moreover, whether an authority – any authority – can realistically claim to have been entrusted to make and fine-tune policy across the board. Instead, they argued, legitimate enforcement is more modest and more focused.

In the second place, proponents of the Brussels consensus argued that intervention can only be said to advance the public interest where it benefits society as a whole (as opposed to individual firms). This is the point that helps understand why advocates of the 'more economics-based approach' tend to focus on efficiency and consumer welfare as guiding principles. The protection of inefficient firms, they argue, comes at the expense of society: such companies would be, in effect, subsidised through the competition law system. Doing so makes end-users worse off, in the sense that they would not be able to benefit from the cost-savings and quality improvements that are associated with efficiency gains. Firms, moreover, would be disincentivised to improve their methods: efforts to enhance one's efficiency would not only not be rewarded, but would attract public intervention to protect one's rivals.

2.3. Principles of Intervention under the 'Brussels Consensus'

The principles around which the 'more economics-based approach' revolves have been abundantly discussed and identified. Arguably, the overarching idea is that the majority of practices examined by authorities can be plausibly explained on pro-competitive grounds and are not invariably a source of anticompetitive effects. Accordingly, the decision of whether to take action in a particular case should ascertain the likely impact of the practice in the specific economic and legal context of which it is a part. In this regard, the 'more economics-based approach'

---

[30] Okeoghene Odudu, 'The Wider Concerns of Competition Law' (2010) 30 Oxford Journal of Legal Studies 599.

is inimical to blanket prohibitions that are not contingent on an analysis of effects (what is sometimes known as per se infringements, by reference to the US system). This is also true, crucially, when conduct implemented by dominant firms is at stake. The small fraction of practices that would be subject to a blanket prohibition includes, first and foremost, cartels, which are known to lack a credible pro-competitive rationale and necessarily lead, when implemented, to allocative inefficiency.

It follows from the above that, intervention under the 'more economics-based approach' demands a case-by-case assessment of a dual nature. On the one hand, it would be necessary to establish, in light of the relevant economic and legal context, whether a practice is a plausible source of pro-competitive gains. If – as is true of cartel conduct – the available evidence suggests that it is not, the behaviour will be prohibited prima facie without considering its impact. On the other hand, where a practice is known to be capable of improving the conditions of competition, a case-by-case analysis of its negative effects will follow to ascertain whether action is warranted. The reluctance to introduce blanket prohibitions has been explained at length by proponents of the approach. This particular understanding of competition law and policy is sensitive to so-called Type I errors (or false positives).[31] It emphasises that the losses for society of a blanket ban on potentially pro-competitive conduct would far outweigh the gains.

According to the second principle underpinning the 'more economics-based approach', the line between pro- and anticompetitive conduct is to be drawn, whether directly or indirectly, by reference to efficiency considerations. Thus, when it is stated that a practice is pro-competitive it is meant that it is a potential source of (allocative or productive) efficiency gains, which may in turn benefit consumers. Potentially exclusionary conduct such as tying is said to be capable of improving the conditions of competition in the sense that the integration of two complements can, inter alia, improve user experience (and even lead to the emergence of a new product).[32] As far as rebates are concerned, it has already been mentioned that they may allow suppliers to plan their production more effectively and distributors to benefit from lower prices and, generally, better conditions.[33]

Similarly, when it is claimed that a practice is anticompetitive, it is meant that any actual or potential pro-competitive gains that it might generate are not

---

[31] The origins of this understanding are typically traced back to Frank H Easterbrook, 'Limits of Antitrust' (1984) 63 Texas Law Review 1. For a contemporary analysis of the question, see Herbert Hovenkamp, 'Antitrust Error Costs' (2022) 24 University of Pennsylvania Journal of Business Law 293.

[32] Christian Ahlborn, David S Evans and Jorge Padilla, 'The antitrust economics of tying: a farewell to per se illegality' (2004) 49 Antitrust Bulletin 287. On the pro-competitive aspects of tying and bundling, see also EAGCP, 'An economic approach to Article 82' (n 9), 40.

[33] See, from the vast literature, B Douglas Bernheim and Michael D Whinston, 'Exclusive Dealing' (1998) 106 Journal of Political Economy 64; and (for an analysis that is specific to the EU context and the EU case law) Hans Zenger, 'Loyalty Rebates and the Competitive Process' (2012) 8 Journal of Competition Law & Economics 717.

sufficient to outweigh the allocative efficiency losses that result from it. It means, in other words, that the increase in market power resulting from the behaviour is not compensated by other considerations. For instance, the gains generated by the integration of two complements by means of tying may be found to weigh less than the exclusionary effects (with the resulting increase in market power) to which the practice leads. Similarly, a merger between two competitors will be declared to be incompatible with the internal market if the predicted productive efficiency gains will not be passed on to consumers in the form of, for instance, lower prices.

The third principle follows logically from the preceding one and has already been discussed at some length. Under the 'more economics-based approach', the foreclosure of inefficient firms does not justify intervention. Such an outcome would not only be deemed unproblematic, but an expected and desirable consequence of a system based on undistorted competition on the merits. In fact, the exclusion of less efficient rivals would not be attributable to a practice, but to their inability to attract consumers by means of, inter alia, prices, quality or innovation. It would therefore be difficult to justify imputing an outcome to a practice where the requisite causal link is missing. The protection of less efficient rivals would not be a task for competition policy, but for other policies aimed, explicitly or implicitly, at the redistribution and the re-allocation of rents.[34] For instance, the telecommunications regime may seek to assist relatively inefficient firms to inject competition in the early days of the liberalisation of the industry.[35]

According, finally, to the fourth principle, the assessment of the effects of a practice must not be purely hypothetical or based on its abstract potential to cause anticompetitive harm. It must instead be structured around what is known as a theory of harm. This concept can be defined as the mechanism through which behaviour can have a negative impact on competition. To take the expression used by Zenger and Walker, the theory of harm is the map that guides the assessment and against which the facts of the case can be checked.[36] For instance, it demands that an authority be explicit about the strategy through which the vertically-integrated firm resulting from a merger would exclude its upstream or downstream rivals, as well as about why it would be in its interest to do so. The requirement to articulate a theory of harm fulfils two essential roles. In the

---

[34] Ahlborn and Padilla (n 1). One of the points underpinning the 'Brussels consensus', as explained by the authors, is that '[c]ompetition policy should not be concerned with distributional issues. First, those issues can be addressed by other means. Second, as recently argued by Professors Alesina and Tabellini, income distribution is not the sort of policy that should be left to bureaucracies and/or independent agencies'.

[35] Alison Oldale and Jorge Padilla, 'From state monopoly to the "investment ladder": competition policy and the NRF', in Swedish Competition Authority, *The Pros and Cons of Antitrust in Deregulated Markets* (2004).

[36] Hans Zenger and Mike Walker, 'Theories of Harm in European Competition Law: A Progress Report', in Jacques Bourgeois and Denis Waelbroeck (eds), *Ten years of effects-based approach in EU competition law: State of play and perspectives* (Bruylant 2012).

first place, it guarantees that intervention is based on an intellectually robust, internally consistent story (as opposed to an impressionistic intuition about hypothetical harms). In the second place, it ensures that the available evidence supports intervention (and is not relied upon in a piecemeal manner).

2.4. Implementation of the Principles

It has been mentioned above that the 'more economics-based approach' is ultimately concerned with allocative efficiency (or, if one prefers, consumer welfare). Contrary to what is sometimes assumed, the implementation of the approach rarely takes the form of an explicit balancing between the pro- and anticompetitive aspects of potentially anticompetitive behaviour. In the same vein, an authority is not necessarily required to show that consumer welfare will be harmed as a result of the practice. As the various instruments issued by the Commission over the years show, intervention revolves primarily around the impact of conduct on equally efficient rivals' ability and incentive to compete. If these are unaffected, then intervention would not be justified, and this insofar as the behaviour would be unlikely to have anticompetitive effects.

The tools used to establish the effects on rivals' ability and incentive to compete vary depending on the nature of the practice. The 'as efficient competitor test', which has come to epitomise the 'more economics-based approach' itself, is a filter that is typically relied upon when price-based conduct is at stake. The underlying logic is simple: a rival that is as efficient as a dominant firm is unlikely to be excluded when the effective prices charged by the latter remain above cost. In such circumstances, the competitor cannot be expected to incur losses. This basic insight has been used, inter alia, in the context of conditional rebates. Thus, where, given the discounts offered by the dominant firm, an equally efficient rival would not have been forced to offer its products at a loss, the system of rebates is not deemed likely to have exclusionary effects.[37] Where, similarly, the spread between the wholesale and the retail prices charged by a vertically-integrated firm would not force an equally efficient firm to make losses in the downstream market, the practice cannot be expected to amount to an abusive 'margin squeeze'.[38]

More generally, the case-by-case analysis of the actual or potential impact of a practice on competition is undertaken against the relevant counterfactual (that is, the conditions of competition that would have prevailed in its absence).[39] It must take into consideration a number of factors pertaining to the economic and legal context. Thus, the mere fact that one or several firms are affected by the practice is insufficient to justify intervention. When potentially abusive conduct is

---

[37] See Guidance (n 22), paras 37–45; and the Commission Decision in *Intel* (n 23), para 1003, and the discussion at the beginning of this Chapter.
[38] Case C-52/09 *Konkurrensverket v TeliaSonera Sverige AB*, EU:C:2011:83, para 112.
[39] Guidance (n 22), para 21.

at stake, for instance, the factors to consider include the degree of market power enjoyed by the firm(s) involved; the nature of the conduct under examination and its anticompetitive potential; the features of the relevant market (including the position of rivals and that of suppliers and customers) and the coverage of the practice (that is, the extent of the relevant market to which it applies).[40]

Figure 2.1 The 'Brussels consensus'

The 'Brussels consensus'	Features	Explanation
Sources of legitimacy	Input, throughput	Reliance on the mainstream consensus and the best available expertise
Approach	Case-by-case	Most practices can be pro- and anticompetitive, depending on the context
Goals	Efficiency, consumer welfare	Preference for clear, well-defined goals; exclusion of distributional issues
Tools	'As efficient competitor' test	Proxies to ensure the administrability of the system

3. The Consolidation of the 'More Economics-based Approach' in the Case Law

3.1. Introduction

Authors like Sibony have noted that the 'more economics-based approach' represented a major shift for the Commission, not the Court of Justice (hereinafter, the 'Court').[41] The latter's traditional interpretation of competition law provisions has always been more compatible with the mainstream consensus than the administrative practice.[42] In spite of this fact, the question of whether, and to what extent, the Court would accept the Commission's approach, and that of whether the case law would change wherever it was in conflict with it, were widely debated.[43] This was so, in particular, in relation to Article 102 TFEU,

---

[40] Ibid, para 20.
[41] Anne-Lise Sibony, *Le juge et le raisonnement économique en droit de la concurrence* (LGDJ 2008), 245–277.
[42] For an in-depth illustration of this idea, see Pablo Ibáñez Colomo, *The Shaping of EU Competition Law* (Cambridge University Press 2018).
[43] See inter alia Ariel Ezrachi, 'The European Commission Guidance on Article 82 EC – The Way in which Institutional Realities Limit the Potential for Reform' (2009) Oxford Legal Studies Research

where the tension between the emerging paradigm and cases like *Michelin II* and *British Airways* was more apparent.[44] In any event, in the decade that followed the *Post Danmark I* judgment of 2012, the Court's case law moved in a direction that was consistent with the vision underpinning the 'more economics-based approach'. To the extent that this is the case, it is difficult to challenge this approach on grounds that it is at odds with the law as it stands.

One can identify two main trends in the case law in the past decade. First, the Court increasingly relies on formal concepts; second, it makes explicit some of the principles that were already implicit in the relevant precedents. One can think, for instance, of the divide between restrictions by object and effect. In this regard, the Court has consistently favoured a contextual and case-specific interpretation of the issue, which is very much in line with the tenets of the 'more economics-based approach'. In other respects, it has refined its doctrines to reduce or eliminate the frictions with this enforcement paradigm. This is true, in particular, of cases dealing with the interpretation of Article 102 TFEU (and, more specifically, the notion of abuse). In this regard, the Court has introduced adjustments both of a substantive and procedural nature to accommodate economic considerations in the case law.

3.2. The Divide between Restrictions by Object and by Effect

Article 101(1) TFEU distinguishes between restrictions by object and by effect. However, it is only following the adoption of Regulation 1/2003 and the rise of the 'more economics-based approach' that the divide between both acquired theoretical and practical relevance. For as long as the Commission enjoyed a monopoly over the application of Article 101(3) TFEU, the legal question had no actual implications. Understandably, firms were more interested in securing an exemption or a negative clearance decision from the authority, and less in the legal route through which the desired outcome was reached. In that institutional setup, the Commission interpreted Article 101(1) TFEU in a way that blurred the line between restrictions by object and effect. In particular, it displayed a marked tendency to equate a limitation of a firm's freedom of action with an anticompetitive effect.[45]

Paper 27/2009, available at http://ssrn.com/abstract=1463854; Giorgio Monti, 'Article 82 EC: What Future for the Effects-Based Approach?' (2010) 1 Journal of European Competition Law & Practice 2.

[44] John Kallaugher and Brian Sher, 'Rebates revisited: anti-competitive effects and exclusionary abuse under Article 82' (2004) 25 European Competition Law Review 263; and Denis Waelbroeck, 'Michelin II: A Per Se Rule Against Rebates by Dominant Companies?' (2005) 1 Journal of Competition Law & Economics 149.

[45] Giuliano Marenco, 'La notion de restriction de concurrence dans le cadre de l'interdiction des ententes', in Marianne Dony and Aline De Walsche (eds), *Mélanges en hommage à Michel Waelbroeck* (Bruylant 1999).

58 *The Rise and Decline of the 'More Economics-based Approach'*

With the introduction of the 'more economics-based approach' the divide between both categories became a meaningful one. Once the restrictive effects of agreements are assessed by reference to the relevant market (and this on the basis of an internally consistent theory of harm), it becomes significantly more difficult for the authority to discharge its burden of proof. For the same reason, qualifying an agreement as a 'by object' infringement is a more attractive option from an agency's perspective: once it appears that a practice is anticompetitive by its very nature, it is not necessary to evaluate its impact on competition.[46] All things being equal, it is natural for authorities (both the Commission and its national counterparts) to express a preference for a relatively expansive understanding of the 'by object' category and to favour it when interpreting Article 101(1) TFEU.

Unsurprisingly, this preference was expressed as soon as the 'more economics-based approach' was embraced. It was manifested both in the context of direct actions against Commission decisions and in preliminary references from national courts (the origin of which can often be traced back to a domestic challenge against administrative action). The first of the cases revealing the authorities' tendency to favour the 'by object' category reached the Court in the late 2000s. At the time, the legal doctrine on the matter was clear and well-established. From the very early cases, the Court had emphasised the need to consider the nature of agreements in the economic and legal context of which they are a part.[47] It ruled out, from the outset, the idea that formal categories can, alone, determine the legal status of a practice. The case law suggested that establishing the restrictive object of a practice demands, above all, an evaluation of the objective aims pursued by the parties.

The judgments that followed added clarity to the divide between object and effect. They did so by relying upon formal economic concepts to spell out the logic underpinning the preceding case law. The cleanest formula can be found in *Generics*, where the Court held that the 'by object' category applies to practices that cannot be plausibly explained on grounds other than the restriction of competition.[48] These are agreements, in other words, that cannot be rationalised as a means to improve the competitive landscape. By the same token, a practice that is capable of achieving gains that would not have unfolded in its absence does not amount to a 'by object' infringement. As *Cartes Bancaires* shows, this would be the case, for instance, where a set of restraints is a plausible means to

---

[46] Joined Cases 56 and 58/64, *Établissements Consten S.à.R.L. and Grundig-Verkaufs-GmbH v Commission*, EU:C:1966:41, para 342 ('for the purpose of applying Article [101(1)], there is no need to take account of the concrete effects of an agreement once it appears that it has as its object the prevention, restriction or distortion of competition').

[47] Case 56/65, *Société Technique Minière v Maschinenbau Ulm GmbH*, EU:C:1966:38, para 250 ('The competition in question must be understood within the actual context in which it would occur in the absence of the agreement in dispute').

[48] Case C-307/18 *Generics (UK) Ltd and Others v Competition and Markets Authority*, EU:C:2020:52, para 89.

address free-riding concerns.[49] In such circumstances, a restriction can only be established following a case-by-case assessment of its restrictive effects.[50]

A second point to note is the importance attached by the Court to expertise. In *Budapest Bank*, it held that, where there is insufficient experience about the nature of a practice, its categorisation as a 'by object' infringement would not be warranted. It may take time for economists to figure out the rationale behind a new type of agreement.[51] For as long as there is uncertainty about its capacity to yield pro-competitive gains (that is, for as long as there is no consensus about its purpose and impact), only the 'by effect' route would be available to authorities. Experience may show that some practices have no plausible explanation other than the restriction of competition and can thus be safely presumed to lead to allocative inefficiency. Such is the case of price-fixing in the context of a cartel arrangement.[52] Experience may also provide insights about the operation of the relevant market. In *Cartes Bancaires*, for instance, the Court drew insights from the two-sided nature of the ecosystem of which the contentious clauses were a part.[53]

3.3. The Analysis of Anticompetitive Effects

The need to consider, on a case-by-case basis, the actual or potential effects of a potentially anticompetitive practice is, as suggested above, the single most defining principle underpinning the 'more economics-based approach'. The case law has evolved in a manner that is consistent with this prescription, in particular in the context of Article 102 TFEU. In fact, the policy priorities outlined by the Commission in its Guidance Paper have found their way into the case law.[54] One can distinguish three aspects in the rise of effects analysis. The first has to do with the nature and purpose of the assessment (that is, what it means, in concrete terms, to evaluate the actual or potential impact of a practice and the overall principles to follow). The second, with its scope of application (that is, the range of practices that are subject to it). The third, with the tools on which the analysis rests. These are examined in turn.

---

[49] Case C-67/13 P, *Groupement des cartes bancaires v Commission*, EU:C:2014:2204, paras 74–75.
[50] Case C-228/18 *Gazdasági Versenyhivatal v Budapest Bank Nyrt. and others*, EU:C:2020:265, paras 82–83.
[51] *Budapest Bank* (n 50), para 76.
[52] *Cartes Bancaires* (n 49), para 51.
[53] Ibid, para 73.
[54] For an analysis, see Mel Marquis and Ekaterina Rousseva, 'Hell Freezes Over: A Climate Change for Assessing Exclusionary Conduct Under Article 102 TFEU' (2013) 4 Journal of European Competition Law & Practice 32; Pablo Ibáñez Colomo, 'Post Danmark II: The Emergence of a Distinct "Effects-Based" Approach to Article 102 TFEU' (2016) 7 Journal of European Competition Law & Practice 113; and Nicolas Petit, 'The Judgment of the EU Court of Justice in Intel and the Rule of Reason in Abuse of Dominance Cases' (2018) 43 European Law Review 728.

In *Post Danmark I*, the Court made it explicit that not every exclusionary effect is necessarily detrimental to competition.[55] Accordingly, the departure from the market of firms that are less efficient (and thus less attractive in terms of price, quality or innovation) is not problematic.[56] In fact, it would be the very expression of the operation of a system based on undistorted competition. This principle – which can be labelled the 'as efficient competitor principle' – has been consistently relied upon by the Court, including several subsequent landmark judgments. Crucially, the principle is different from – and broader in scope than – the abovementioned 'as efficient competitor' test, which, as already explained, is a tool that assists in the filtering of rebate cases. Because it is broader than the latter, it is relevant both in relation to price-based and non-price-based conduct. This is a point that would be made explicit in *Servizio Elettrico Nazionale*.[57]

The Court expressly held, in *Post Danmark II*, that the assessment of anti-competitive effects must not be 'purely hypothetical'.[58] In other words, it is not sufficient for an authority or claimant to argue that the practice could, in the abstract, have a negative impact on competition, or that it has the theoretical potential to cause harm. Any claims about restrictive effects must be substantiated by evidence drawn from the economic and legal context of which the practice is a part. In other words, an authority or claimant must show why, given the features of the relevant market, the behaviour is capable of affecting competition. In the same judgment, the Court added, in a similar vein, that it is necessary to show a causal link between the practice and any actual or potential effects. More precisely, it held that any impact must be 'attributable' to the conduct.[59]

A second trend in the case law has been the expansion of the range of practices that are subject to an effects analysis (and are thus not subject to a blanket or 'by object' prohibition). Until the mid- to late 2000s, it was not clear whether the lawfulness of potentially abusive practices necessitated an evaluation of their restrictive impact.[60] Cases like *British Airways* gave the impression that an infringement of Article 102 TFEU could be inferred from the mere fact that the behaviour had been implemented by a dominant firm.[61] Subsequent case law, however, made it clear that, at least as far as some practices are concerned, an effects analysis is a precondition for a finding of abuse. Examples include margin squeeze conduct, where the Court held that evidence that rivals are being

---

[55] Case C-209/10 *Post Danmark A/S v Konkurrencerådet*, EU:C:2012:172, para 22.
[56] Ibid.
[57] Case C-377/20 *Servizio Elettrico Nazionale SpA and Others v Autorità Garante della Concorrenza e del Mercato and Others*, EU:C:2022:379.
[58] Case C-23/14, *Post Danmark A/S v Konkurrencerådet*, EU:C:2015:651, para 65.
[59] Ibid, para 47.
[60] For a discussion, see Waelbroeck (n 44).
[61] Case C-95/04 P, *British Airways plc v Commission*, EU:C:2007:166, paras 96–100.

forced to sell at a loss is as such insufficient to trigger Article 102 TFEU;[62] and standardised rebate schemes (such as those at stake in *Michelin II*).[63]

Concerning, finally, the analysis of effects itself, there should be little doubt that the assessment required by the case law is meaningful, as opposed to a mere formality. It is, moreover, an evaluation that is in line with the policy enunciated by the Commission in its Guidance Paper. As the law stands, authorities and claimants must engage with the realities of the market and consider, inter alia, its features, structure and actual or potential evolution. In *Intel*, for instance, the Court introduced a set of five criteria against which the restrictive impact of a practice has to be assessed, namely the extent of the dominant position; the coverage of the practice; the conditions and arrangements for the award of the rebates; the length and amount of the latter; and, finally, the existence of an exclusionary strategy.[64]

3.4. The Use of Procedural Devices

The Court has made use of procedural devices to accommodate economic arguments raised by firms. Where the parties to an agreement, or a dominant firm, provide evidence casting doubts on the facts – presumed or established by the authority – the latter is under a duty to consider them (and, in some cases, to engage in a fully-fledged case-by-case analysis). These procedural devices are a corrective mechanism in those instances where the case law is not fully aligned with the 'more economics-based approach'. By allowing firms to challenge the premises on which the interpretation of the relevant provisions is based, it is possible for them to advance arguments that they would otherwise not have been able to put forward. It represents, in addition, a commitment to the principle of good administration: it is reasonable (and a fundamental tenet of the 'Brussels consensus') to expect that authority's intervention is based on the best available evidence.

The example *par excellence* of this trend in the case law is the *Intel* judgment. The case concerned the area where the tension between the case law and the mainstream consensus was more apparent. At the time of the ruling, exclusive dealing agreements and rebates conditional upon exclusivity were deemed prima facie abusive irrespective of their effects. The Court, while it confirmed that such practices are in breach of Article 102 TFEU by their very nature, it introduced a procedural device allowing dominant firms to provide evidence showing that they are incapable of restricting competition in the relevant economic and legal context.[65] When such evidence is provided to the requisite legal standard,

---

[62] Case C-280/08 P *Deutsche Telekom AG v Commission*, EU:C:2010:603, paras 250–251.
[63] *Post Danmark II* (n 58), paras 28–46.
[64] Case C-413/14 P *Intel Corp. v Commission*, EU:C:2017:632, para 139. See also Case T-286/09 RENV *Intel Corporation Inc. v Commission*, EU:T:2022:19, para 125.
[65] Ibid, para 138.

it triggers a duty on the Commission to engage in a contextual evaluation of the actual or potential impact of the scheme under consideration.[66]

A second, less prominent, example can be found in the *Generics* case. As already explained, the judgment is notable in that the Court held that an agreement should only be categorised as 'by object' infringement where it can solely be plausibly explained as a means to restrict competition. The corollary, made explicit in *Budapest Bank*, is that an agreement that is capable of improving the competitive process would escape such categorisation. These principles have a major procedural implication: it should be possible for the parties to provide evidence showing that the practice is capable of generating pro-competitive effects and therefore that it is not caught by Article 101(1) TFEU by its very nature.[67] The Court accepted that the evaluation of such claims is part of the assessment of the relevant economic and legal context.[68]

4. Why the Tide Turned: The Latent, the Old and the New Debates

4.1. The Latent: The Consensus that Never was?

It is no longer easy to claim that the ideas underpinning the 'Brussels consensus' represent the views of a clear majority of officials and practitioners in Europe. As these pages are written, the 'more economics-based approach' is more likely to spark indifference than debates – let alone unanimity – within the community. A look back at the topics discussed at conferences and workshops suggests that the tide turned, quickly and decisively, at some point in the mid-2010s.[69] There are

---

[66] Ibid, paras 139–143.
[67] *Budapest Bank* (n 50), paras 82–83.
[68] *Generics* (n 48), para 103.
[69] An indicator in this regard is the annual conference organised by CRA, a leading economic consultancy. This conference is one of the largest events organised in Brussels and invariably features leading officials, academics and practitioners. In the 2016 edition, some of the topics that would define the new EU competition law made an appearance, albeit in a tentative manner. For instance, the issue of big data was presented as a potential problem (the 'Search for a competition law problem'). In relation to mergers, in turn, the question was raised about whether markets had become too concentrated. Other topics remain firmly around those raised by the 'more economics-based' approach (including the evaluation of anticompetitive effects by judges and vertical restraints, with a particular focus on exclusivity agreements). The tone and range of issues addressed changed in subsequent editions. In 2017, the conference revisited the issue of market concentration, and introduced views departing from the consensus underpinning the 'more economics-based approach'. One panel was entitled 'Is Big the New Bad (Again)? "Hipster" and "Progressive Antitrust" vs Consumer Welfare'. Other panels marked the shift away from exclusionary matters and towards distribution issues (and more precisely the relationship between the press and Big Tech). The progressive change in the conversation was confirmed in the 2018 edition, with a panel on 'Do We Need a "Radical Antitrust" Answer to "Populist Antitrust"?' and, for the first time, one discussing overtly the need to regulate Big Tech. By 2019, the shift seemed complete, with a panel entitled '"Drums Beating from the Hills": The Global Rise Against

few traces of the questions that kept commentators busy in the preceding decade. Several explanations – not mutually exclusive – can be advanced to explain this rapid shift. The most obvious contributing factor is that the consensus may never have existed and, if it did, it was perhaps overstated or contingent on a very specific set of circumstances. In fact, doubts about the 'more economics-approach' were always raised by certain officials – at the EU and national levels – and in certain academic circles (in particular in some Member States, such as Germany, with a long and illustrious tradition of enforcement).[70]

The 'more economics-based approach' was always criticised from a variety of perspectives. One argument against it focuses on the fact that it leads to suboptimal enforcement. The case-by-case assessment of the actual or potential effects of practices would be problematic in at least two ways, according to this view. First, it would not be conducive to legal certainty. When the lawfulness of a practice depends on a contextual evaluation, it is difficult for stakeholders to anticipate the outcome of administrative action. Accordingly, the 'more economics-based approach' would fail even on its own terms. By the same token, the blanket prohibition of certain practices, which appeared to fall out of favour during the early 2000s, would be preferable as a matter not only of law but of economics. These ideas were expressed particularly eloquently by Wils, a renowned Commission official who has made major scholarly contributions.[71]

A second argument relates to the alleged negative impact of the 'more economics-based approach' on the effectiveness of competition policy. The case-by-case evaluation of the actual or potential effects of a practice is resource-consuming for an authority – more resource-consuming, in any event, than the administration of a blanket prohibition. In addition, gathering the necessary evidence and checking it against the relevant theory of harm necessarily delays intervention. As a result of these factors, it is argued, the 'more economics-based approach' might lead to underenforcement – or, if enforcement eventually takes place, to intervention when the competitive process has been damaged beyond repair. From this perspective, the 'more economics-based approach' would have been too narrowly focused on accuracy in individual cases, and would have missed the administrability of the regime.[72]

"Big Tech"' and one entitled 'Winners and Losers, Concentration, Industrial Policy, Champions, Trade: Competition Tools Under Political Pressure'.

[70] See for instance Drexl, Kerber and Podszun (n 1) and Witt (n 1). See also Paul Nihoul, 'The Ruling of the General Court in *Intel*: Towards the End of an Effect-based Approach in European Competition Law?' (2014) 5 Journal of European Competition Law & Practice 521.

[71] Wouter Wils, 'The judgment of the EU General Court in *Intel* and the so-called 'more economic approach' to abuse of dominance' (2014) 37 World Competition 405.

[72] In addition to Wils (n 71), see for instance Wardaugh (n 1); and Anne C Witt, 'The enforcement of Article 101 TFEU: What has happened to the effects analysis?' (2018) 55 Common Market Law Review 417. The latter author conjectures that the 'more economics-based approach' has led to a decline in cases demanding a case-by-case evaluation of anticompetitive effects.

Finally, a number of commentators – in particular in academic circles – openly questioned the idea that competition policy should revolve around the mainstream consensus. These criticisms were often directed against economics as a discipline and are familiar to social scientists. They have to do not only with the assumptions on which economic analysis is based and with its epistemological limits,[73] but also with the fact that, under the guise of expertise and neutrality, it is said to be politically loaded (and associated with an agenda that was hostile to competition law enforcement and, more generally, State intervention in the economy).[74] Criticism, however, also extends to reliance upon efficiency and/or consumer welfare as guides to law and/or policy making. It has been argued, in this regard, that a consequentialist approach is alien to the European tradition, which seeks to protect competition as a value in itself, not as a means to an end.[75]

The way the Commission has engaged with the 'more economics-based approach' is itself a reliable indicator that the 'Brussels consensus', if it existed, was never as strong as some may have assumed. One aspect that has been widely discussed by commentators relates to the divide that the authority sought to draw between its policy statements and the law. When enforcing Articles 101 and 102 TFEU, the Commission crafted its decisions so that any constraints on administrative discretion would not find their way into the law. This behaviour is particularly apparent in the context of the *Intel* litigation. While the Commission applied the 'as efficient competitor test', it argued in its decision that it was not required to do so as a matter of law.[76] What is more, it challenged attempts by the General Court to enshrine in law the analytical framework laid down in the Guidance Paper.[77]

4.2. The Old: Importing Paradigms from the Past

The decline of the 'more economics-based approach' can also be explained, at least in part, by the revival and influence of some long-forgotten paradigms of analysis. This trend is more marked on the other side of the Atlantic but, just like most debates in the field, it has had an impact in Europe. The search for alternative analytical frameworks in the US is, by and large, the consequence

---

[73] For instance, Wils (n 71), cites Friedrich A Hayek, 'Competition as a Discovery Procedure', in *New Studies in Philosophy, Politics, Economics and the History of Ideas* (University of Chicago Press 1978); and Friedrich A Hayek, 'The Use of Knowledge in Society' (1945) 35 American Economic Review 519.

[74] Ibid. Wils cites heterodox economists like Ha-Joon Chang – referring expressly to Ha-Joon Chang, *Economics: The User's Guide* (Pelican 2014) – and Roger E Backhouse – referring to Roger E Backhouse, *The Puzzle of Modern Economics: Science or Ideology?* (Cambridge University Press 2010).

[75] For an extensive discussion of the divide between the consequentialist and the deontological understandings of competition law, see Ioannis Lianos, 'Some Reflections on the Question of the Goals of EU Competition Law' (2013) CLES Working Paper Series 3/2013, available at https://ssrn.com/abstract=2235875.

[76] Commission Decision in *Intel* (n 23), para 925.

[77] In particular, the Commission appealed the General Court judgment in Case T-286/09 RENV *Intel* (n 64).

of the perceived failure of the so-called consumer welfare standard.[78] It seems difficult to dispute the relative ineffectiveness of antitrust enforcement in North America since the 1980s.[79] Whether or not the said ineffectiveness can be attributed to the prevailing paradigm is a different question.[80] Relatively cautious (or, according to some, lenient) enforcement provided fertile ground for debates around the purpose and operation of the regime. So did the emergence of Big Tech and, more generally, of academic debates around market concentration and rising market power in the economy.[81]

It is in this context that some scholars started to advocate for an approach to enforcement that would be stripped of the sophistication and nuances associated with economic analysis. This school of thought traces its intellectual origins back to the work and thinking of Justice Brandeis.[82] There are two key ideas underpinning this movement that resonate with critics of the 'more economics-based approach'. First, neo-Brandeisians see competition policy (or antimonopoly law[83]) as an essential component of a democracy.[84] In this sense, the goal of antitrust would be, first and foremost to ensure that large corporations (and, more generally, the concentration of power in a few hands) are not an obstacle to meaningful participation in society. An approach grounded on democracy is, almost inevitably, at odds with the technocratic venture that competition policy had progressively become on both sides of the Atlantic.

Second, neo-Brandeisians have openly criticised the consequentialist understanding of competition policy, and, in particular, reliance on consumer welfare as the appropriate benchmark to decide whether intervention is warranted. Instead of turning competition into a means to enhance welfare, this school of thought sees competition as worthy of protection in itself, as a process.[85] For instance, the

---

[78] Some of the most notable criticisms of the consumer welfare standard include Marshall Steinbaum and Maurice E Stucke, 'The Effective Competition Standard' (2020) 87 University of Chicago Law Review 595; and Tim Wu, *The Curse of Bigness: Antitrust in the New Gilded Age* (Columbia Global Reports 2018).

[79] For an overall discussion, see Jonathan B Baker, *The Antitrust Paradigm: Restoring a Competitive Economy* (Harvard University Press); Herbert Hovenkamp, 'Whatever Did Happen to the Antitrust Movement?' (2019) 94 Notre Dame Law Review 58; and Carl Shapiro, 'Antitrust: What Went Wrong and How to Fix It' (2021) 35 Antitrust 33.

[80] For a defence of the consumer welfare standard, see A Douglas Melamed and Nicolas Petit, 'The Misguided Assault on the Consumer Welfare Standard in the Age of Platform Markets' (2019) 54 Review of Industrial 741.

[81] This question has attracted the attention of economists over the past decade. See in particular David Autor, David Dorn, Lawrence F Katz, Christina Patterson and John Van Reenen, 'The Fall of the Labor Share and the Rise of Superstar Firms' (2020) 135 Quarterly Journal of Economics 645; and Gustavo Grullon, Yelena Larkin and Roni Michaely, 'Are US Industries Becoming More Concentrated?' (2019) 23 Review of Finance 697.

[82] Lina Khan, 'The New Brandeis Movement: America's Antimonopoly Debate' (2018) 9 Journal of European Competition Law & Practice 131.

[83] Ibid.

[84] Ibid: 'Brandeis was a strong proponent of America's Madisonian traditions – which aim at a democratic distribution of power and opportunity in the political economy'.

[85] Ibid: 'Antimonopoly must focus on structures and processes of competition, not outcomes'.

66 *The Rise and Decline of the 'More Economics-based Approach'*

fact that a practice leads to the exclusion of a rival (such as tying or an aggressive price campaign) would be deemed problematic irrespective of whether it is, on the whole, pro-competitive. The loss of competition itself would justify intervention. In fact, this school of thought sees value in protecting smaller businesses and in ensuring that economic power remains decentralised.[86]

The neo-Brandeisian School has influenced debates in Europe in a number of ways (in addition to the dissemination of their ideas in European journals[87] and at conferences[88]). First of all, the rejection of the technocratic understanding of competition policy appeals to critics of the 'more economics-based approach' and provides an intellectual foundation for alternative views of the discipline. More generally, the rise of the new Brandeis School signals to the community that a fundamental overhaul is necessary to achieve more vigorous and effective enforcement. Second, neo-Brandeisian scholars have been selected to lead federal enforcement agencies in the US and have been appointed to other influential advisory roles. Lina Khan, for instance, became Chair of the FTC in 2021. In this capacity, she concluded a cooperation agreement with Commissioner Vestager.[89]

4.3. The New: Fairness and Redistribution in Digital Markets and Beyond

It has been suggested above that the coalition around the 'Brussels consensus' may have been contingent on the specific set of circumstances that arose in the late 1990s to mid-2000s. It was a time when a clear majority of stakeholders valued predictability and restraint in administrative action. The preferences lied with modest but sound enforcement, focused on the most obviously harmful behaviour and wary of Type I errors. The circumstances changed during the early 2010s, and a significant fraction of stakeholders started to see the value of expansive, ambitious policy-making, more concerned with addressing perceived market failures than with avoiding enforcement errors. Redistribution – that is, the allocation of rents across the value chain – became, again, a goal worthy of being pursued through competition law.

The climate change that led to different attitudes to enforcement can be attributed, by and large, to the rise of Big Tech. As explained in Chapter 1, the economic dynamics of digital markets tend to favour the emergence of very large players (even dominant, if not quasi-monopolistic) at least in some circumstances

---

[86] Tim Wu, *The Curse of Bigness: Antitrust in the New Gilded Age* (Columbia Global Reports 2018).
[87] See for instance Khan (n 82).
[88] See above, n 69.
[89] European Commission, 'Competition: Second EU-US Joint Technology Competition Policy Dialogue consolidates international cooperation on competition policy and enforcement in technology sector' IP/22/6167 (Brussels, 13 October 2022).

and in some segments of the value chain.[90] In other words, tipping is a relatively frequent occurrence in these markets.[91] The observed dynamics are the consequence of the combination of several economic features, in particular extreme returns to scale (given the high fixed costs and the low to non-existent marginal costs), economies of scope (which result from the importance of data) and network effects (which originate from users' interaction and interdependence).[92]

Given the pervasiveness of digital markets in daily life, the rise of a handful of Big Tech players has had a transformative effect on virtually countless sectors of the economy. In some instances, industries have grown dependent on online platforms; in others, their very existence has come under threat. For instance, featuring on Google may be vital for press publishers or for travel platforms; similarly, selling via an online marketplace, and in particular Amazon, may be crucial for at least some categories of retailers. It is unsurprising that, in these circumstances, competition law has emerged as one of the primary vehicles through which stakeholders express their concerns. Some of these concerns have to do with online platforms' ability to leverage their market power from their core segments to adjacent ones. To come back to the examples already mentioned, the status of Amazon as a marketplace would give it the means to exclude competing online retailers. Similarly, Google's position as the preeminent search engine would allow it to extend its market power to activities that rely on its services, such as online travel platforms.

Other concerns have to do less with exclusion and more with online platforms' ability to capture value in the digital economy. Insofar as they enjoy substantial market power in their core segments, Big Tech players may have the ability to extract supracompetitive rents from their suppliers and customers (that is, exploit their market power vis-à-vis firms in adjacent markets and end-users). To mention some examples drawn from actual disputes, a firm like Apple may, through the operation of its app store, charge excessive commissions to application developers. A social network like Facebook, in turn, may be able to extract excessive amounts of data from individual users. In these cases, competition authorities are not invited to prevent exclusionary conduct, but to reallocate rents to achieve a fairer redistribution of the value generated by online platforms.

It is not difficult to see how, once vast sectors of the economy are affected by the rise of Big Tech and the sense of urgency rises, the compact enshrined in the 'Brussels consensus' becomes less attractive to many stakeholders. The concern with the avoidance of Type I errors (and the importance attached to the careful case-by-case assessment of the actual or potential impact of practices)

---

[90] Jacques Crémer, Yves-Alexandre de Montjoye and Heike Schweitzer, *Competition Policy for the Digital Era* (2019), available at https://ec.europa.eu/competition/publications/reports/kd0419345enn.pdf.

[91] Fiona Scott Morton and others, 'Market Structure and Antitrust Subcommittee Report', in Stigler Committee on Digital Platforms: Final Report (2019), available at https://www.chicagobooth.edu/-/media/research/stigler/pdfs/digital-platforms---committee-report---stigler-center.pdf.

[92] Crémer, de Montjoye and Schweitzer (n 90), 19–20.

may come across, in the new scenario, as a luxury that an effective competition law system can ill-afford. In the same vein, some of the criticisms directed at the 'more economics-based approach' (such as the fact that contextual evaluation of anticompetitive effects is time and resource-consuming and places too high a burden on authorities) are cited as arguments in support of more decisive policy-making.[93]

It is also easy to understand how new paradigms and analytical frameworks are developed in these circumstances. Reliance on efficiency and consumer welfare as guides of enforcement may be seen as overly reductionist. These concepts appear to reflect a lack of concern with exploitative behaviour and, more generally, distributional issues. In addition, they do not seem to be adapted to the very particular scenarios and underlying issues at stake in digital markets. Disputes arising in digital markets are peculiar in a number of ways. They are, first, a mixture of exclusionary and exploitative concerns: they are both about access to the platform and about the price of access. As explained in Chapter 8, moreover, they would not justify action under the 'more economics-based approach' (or as the notion of exclusionary effect has been traditionally construed). Among the responses to the perceived inadequacy of efficiency and consumer welfare, the most prominent one is the rise in popularity of the idea of fairness as a structuring principle.[94]

5. Towards a New Consensus?

5.1. The Changing Legitimacy of EU Competition Policy: From Process to Outcomes

The accelerated changes in the EU competition community, together with the sense of urgency that the rise of Big Tech has created in a majority of stakeholders, seems to be crystallising in the progressive emergence of a new consensus. A highly symbolic milestone occurred as these pages were being finalised. In March 2023, the Commission announced an amendment to the Guidance Paper and the launch of a consultation regarding the adoption of a set of Guidelines on exclusionary abuses.[95] The reform package was accompanied by a Policy Brief[96] signalling the move away from the 'more economics-based approach'. First, the

---

[93] For an overview of these criticisms, see Jason Furman and others, 'Unlocking digital competition: Report of the Digital Competition Expert Panel' (2019), available at http://www.gov.uk/government/publications.

[94] For an in-depth overview of these arguments, see Niamh Dunne, 'Fairness and the Challenge of Making Markets Work Better' (2021) 84 Modern Law Review 230.

[95] European Commission, 'Antitrust: Commission announces Guidelines on exclusionary abuses and amends Guidance on enforcement priorities' IP/23/1911 (Brussels, 27 March 2023).

[96] Linsey McCallum and others, 'A dynamic and workable effects-based approach to abuse of dominance' Competition Policy Brief (March 2023), available at https://ec.europa.eu/competition-policy/publications_en.

document embraces a multiplicity of objectives, not just consumer welfare.[97] Second, it qualifies the Commission's commitment to the 'as efficient competitor' principle.[98] More precisely, the document clarifies that the principle will not guide the authority's enforcement priorities.[99]

The community of officials, practitioners and enforcers may be moving towards a new understanding of the principles driving EU competition policy and about what makes enforcement legitimate in the first place. In short, the community seems now more tolerant of increased administrative discretion and places more value on effective enforcement (and, similarly, less value on predictability and consistency). Perceptions about what makes policy-making legitimate appear to be changing, too. The 'more economics-based approach' is agnostic about the outcome of an investigation and values, above all, the process through which decisions are reached. A decision not to take action is as appropriate as one finding an infringement. Under the emerging consensus, by contrast, it would seem that enforcement is legitimate if it is capable of leading to the outcomes that are perceived to be desirable ex ante (or those that support the authority's policy objectives).

In a sense, the relationship between process and outcomes appears to have been reversed: the latter determines and drives the former, and not vice versa. Accordingly, if the process does not deliver the outcomes that are in line with the policy objectives, it is the process that changes. Output legitimacy, in other words, seems to be replacing throughput legitimacy.[100] Because legitimacy depends on the outcomes reached, the relationship between the emerging consensus and expertise is also in flux. Under the 'more economics-based approach' expertise is relied upon to ensure that the decision-making process is robust and sound. To the extent that this is the case, its role – whether explicitly or implicitly – is to constrain administrative action and limit its reach to the confines allowed by the mainstream consensus. In the new environment, the role of expertise changes: its function is to support the case for intervention or, in the same vein, to enable the administrative authority to attain its policy goals. For the same reasons, the expertise upon which agencies rely need not be the manifestation of the mainstream consensus.

This emerging trend – and, crucially, its impact on policy-making – is nowhere as apparent as in the context of digital markets. The rise of Big Tech and the anxieties that come with its transformative impact have led to a shift in policy-making. The emphasis is now placed on reaching certain goals defined in advance. In fact, agencies have been rethinking enforcement – including from a

---

[97] Ibid, 1: 'The enforcement of competition rules also contributes to achieving objectives that go beyond consumer welfare, at least when the latter is defined strictly in economic terms'.
[98] Ibid, 5: 'The Commission's enforcement experience shows that, while using the notion of foreclosure of as-efficient competitors may be conceptually justified as a general proxy for intervention in pricing abuses, it is important to avoid an unduly strict and dogmatic application of such a standard'.
[99] Ibid, 5.
[100] Schmidt (n 28), 4: 'Output legitimacy is instead concerned with the problem-solving quality of the laws and rules, and has a range of institutional mechanisms to ensure it'.

substantive standpoint – to allow for rapid and decisive action against large online platforms. The Special Advisers' Report on competition policy in the digital era produced for the Commission (hereinafter, the Special Advisers' Report), to take the most prominent example, explores the possibility of moving away from the case-by-case assessment of the actual or potential effects of at least certain practices to make them presumptively unlawful.[101] There is evidence of similar efforts in other systems, including in Germany[102] and the UK.[103]

From an economic perspective, crucially, the Special Advisers' Report does not advocate (at least not unequivocally) a wholesale shift away from the case-by-case evaluation of practices. The experts' overview of the state of the art in the field is prudent in its conclusions and candid about the 'very delicate' balance that authorities must strike when crafting rules and standards in digital markets.[104] In this sense, the report explains that concentration might in fact be desirable, at least from a static efficiency perspective.[105] In addition, it openly concedes that the efficiencies to which online platforms' activities give rise are not yet fully understood.[106] Similarly, it acknowledges nuances in expert debates. In particular, it explains why dominant or quasi-monopolistic positions in digital markets are not necessarily as unassailable or entrenched as some proponents of vigorous intervention assume.[107]

5.2. Principles of Intervention under the New Consensus

If the 'more economics-based approach' sought to address the costs of overenforcement, the avoidance of underenforcement is the central concern in recent policy discussions and in the emerging consensus.[108] The risk of Type I errors, it is frequently argued, should not lead to paralysis or delays in enforcement.[109] This perspective appears to assume – whether explicitly or implicitly – that underenforcement is at least as costly for society and consumers as overenforcement, if not costlier. To a significant extent, the rising concern with Type II errors looks like a reasonable response to the features of digital markets and their tendency towards concentration: where industry dynamics favour the emergence of dominant or quasi-monopolistic positions, enforcement may only attain its aims if it is

---

[101] Crémer, de Montjoye and Schweitzer (n 90), 50–51.
[102] Jens-Uwe Franck and Martin Peitz Digital Platforms and the New 19a Tool in the German Competition Act (2021) 12 Journal of European Competition Law & Practice 513.
[103] CMA, 'A new pro-competition regime for digital markets Advice of the Digital Markets Taskforce'.
[104] Crémer, de Montjoye and Schweitzer (n 90), 37.
[105] Ibid, 22–23.
[106] Ibid, 70.
[107] Ibid, 35–38.
[108] See for instance Johannes Laitenberger, 'Accuracy and administrability go hand in hand' (CRA Conference, Brussels, 12 December 2017).
[109] Jonathan Baker, 'Taking the Error Out of "Error Cost" Analysis: What's Wrong with Antitrust's Right' (2015) 80 Antitrust Law Journal 1.

swift and decisive. The emerging consensus also mistrusts markets' ability to discipline firms and inject competition over the long run, in particular where dominant positions are entrenched.[110]

By definition, this understanding of competition policy demands greater leeway to enforce the law. Agencies' policy space, its advocates argue, should be broader. The constraints to which an authority is subject can be reduced or eliminated in a number of ways. Changing substantive standards is one of them. As proposed in the Special Advisers' Report, the burden of proof can be shifted so that it is for the firms subject to an investigation to prove the absence of effects (or that the practice under investigation is on the whole pro-competitive). It is also possible to relax the threshold for intervention in other ways, for instance by requiring that the probability of anticompetitive effects be plausible, as opposed to likely. Relaxing the procedural requirements (and, similarly, the intensity and scope of judicial review) is another mechanism that can ease the burden on authorities.[111] Cases like *Intel* and *Generics* show how procedural devices can have the effect of adding to the authority's constraints.

In the same vein, efficiency and consumer welfare considerations come across, under this understanding of competition policy, as a straitjacket that can unduly restrain the reach of administrative action. What is more, some of the features of digital markets would plead in favour of abandoning them as benchmarks. It has been frequently argued, for instance, that the consumer welfare standard is not easily administrable in industries where services are provided at a nominal price of zero, and in those where firms compete on innovation and quality (as opposed to price).[112] Similarly, it would be inappropriate to rely on efficiency as a benchmark, it is claimed, because rivals of online platforms may not have the means to reach the minimum efficient scale.[113] It is not surprising, in these circumstances, to see the emergence of alternative benchmarks and analytical frameworks that are looser and less clearly defined, such as fairness.

5.3. Implementation of the Principles

Once enforcement is primarily driven by the outcomes sought in advance, the relationship between policy and the tools through which it is implemented changes.

---

[110] Laitenberger (n 108); and Crémer, de Montjoye and Schweitzer (n 92), 50–51.
[111] See in this sense the ideas advanced in the Furman Report (n 93), 106, which goes as far as to advise judicial deference ('the competition authority should have an appropriate margin of appreciation to reach decisions on digital cases that are likely to be particularly complex and may require elements of expert judgement. A robust appeals process will be vital but its role should be focused on ensuring decisions are founded on procedural regularity, avoid material errors of fact or law, and are reasonable in their exercise of judgement').
[112] This point is noted in Crémer, de Montjoye and Schweitzer (n 92), 40.
[113] McCallum and others (n 96), 5 ('in markets where barriers to entry and expansion are significant, such as in the presence of economies of scale or network effects that lead to the emergence of dominant

72 *The Rise and Decline of the 'More Economics-based Approach'*

Traditionally (including under the 'more economics-based approach'), the purpose of an authority's toolkit was to draw the line between pro- and anticompetitive conduct. Its point was to assist the authority, inter alia, when deciding whether or not a practice amounts to an abuse of a dominant position, or a restriction of competition. The developments of the past few years are indicative that a new relationship between tools and policy-making is under way. Where the available toolkit is incapable of delivering the outcomes that are deemed desirable (or where it is incapable of delivering the outcomes at the appropriate pace), it is replaced by a new one that allows for more streamlined intervention.

From the outset, policy discussions concerning digital markets revolved around the need to develop ad hoc instruments dispensing from the need to establish, case-by-case, the object or effect of practices (or, indeed, the need to identify that a practice has been implemented in the first place) and would maximise the authority's scope for intervention. As already mentioned, the Special Advisers' Report proposed turning some behaviours into presumptive infringements. Other proposals, inspired by the UK competition law regime, advanced the idea of introducing the so-called market investigations, which would allow the Commission to take action without it being necessary to establish an infringement. Under the so-called 'new competition tool', the mere fact that the features of the relevant market are not conducive to competition would suffice to justify intervention.[114] The Digital Markets Act, which was the toolkit eventually adopted, captures this trend effectively. It is discussed in detail in Chapter 5.

Figure 2.2 The emerging consensus

The emerging consensus	Features	Explanation
Sources of legitimacy	Output	Enforcement is legitimate where the policy objectives are attained
Approach	Presumptive prohibitions	Greater tolerance of over-enforcement
Goals	Multiple goals	Growing concern with distributional issues (fairness)
Tools	Development of new and ad hoc tools	Tools (and processes) adjust to meet policy objectives

firms, market challengers may not be expected to be able to achieve the same or even a similar cost structure as the incumbent').

[114] Commission, 'Antitrust: Commission consults stakeholders on a possible new competition tool' IP/20/977 (Brussels, 2 June 2020). See Chapter 5 for a more detailed discussion of the 'new competition tool' and its future in the EU competition law system.

3

Competition Law and Economic Regulation

1. The Overlapping Application of Competition Law and Regulation

1.1. The Interaction between Competition Law and Regulation

1.1.1. The Pervasiveness of Regulation and the Inevitable Overlaps with Competition Law

Regulation is pervasive in the modern administrative state.[1] It is therefore the rule, rather than the exception, to see competition law being enforced alongside other regimes. For instance, the activities of pharmaceutical companies are tightly controlled by the State. All steps leading to the release of a new medicine are closely scrutinised and must comply with strict conditions, including clinical trials and marketing authorisations.[2] Similarly, retailers of consumer products are subject to a wide array of – general and sector-specific – legislation concerning, inter alia, the treatment of data[3] and consumer protection.[4] Regulation, broadly understood, is a part of the canvas on which competition law applies and has a decisive impact on industry dynamics. For instance, it influences the number of players that can profitably operate and thus the level of concentration and, more generally, the features of the relevant market.

Regulation also has an impact on the room for competition law enforcement, as well as on the sort of disputes that arise. Consider again the example of medicines. During the 1990s, pharmaceutical companies put in place several contractual and

---

[1] Some of the most prominent examples of the vast literature on the topic include Robert Baldwin, *Rules and Government* (Oxford University Press 1987); Karen Yeung, 'The Regulatory State', in Robert Baldwin, Martin Cave and Martin Lodge (eds), *The Oxford Handbook of Regulation* (Oxford University Press 2010); Edward L Rubin, 'Law and Legislation in the Administrative State' (1989) 89 Columbia Law Review 369; and Philip Hamburger, *Is Administrative Law Unlawful?* (Chicago University Press 2014).
[2] Emily Jackson, *Law and the Regulation of Medicines* (Hart Publishing 2012).
[3] Peter Carey, *Data Protection: A Practical Guide to UK Law* (6th edn, Oxford University Press 2020).
[4] Stephen Weatherill, *EU Consumer Law and Policy* (2nd edn, Edward Elgar 2013).

unilateral devices to limit cross-border trade within the EU, giving rise to a long saga of cases.[5] This saga cannot be understood without considering the role of national regulation and its influence on prices, which incentivised arbitrage by wholesalers.[6] One can also think of hazardous substances. Regulation applying to such substances may have an impact on wholesalers' and retailers' ability to sell products via certain channels (for instance, Internet sales may be banned, or a permit may be required by resellers). As a result of these requirements, competition enforcement will have to accept that some forms of intra-brand competition will be less intense. For instance, cross-border trade may be significantly curtailed (and online sales may be proscribed altogether in some instances).[7]

As these examples show, economic activities are regulated for myriad reasons. These are often wholly unrelated to the sort of questions that Articles 101 and 102 TFEU seek to address. In reality, discussions around the interaction between competition law and regulation concern the relatively narrow instances where there are commonalities between the two disciplines. These commonalities exist where competition law and regulation share similar preoccupations with market power, market structures and with how certain objectives can be attained by means of proactive or reactive intervention. This subset can be termed economic regulation. It deals with questions such as the conditions under which corporate entry (and exit) takes place, or the ways in which economic activities are organised to attain a particular aim (for instance, low prices, adequate levels of investment and increased innovation).

Two examples of economic regulation, understood in this narrow sense, come to mind immediately. They are particularly relevant in EU competition law, and the discussion that follows (just like the European Commission's policy of the past two decades) focuses on them. First, copyright, patent and trade mark law – inter alia – give an economic operator the exclusive right over an invention, a creation, or a sign.[8] Typically, they seek to attain their aims by creating a legal barrier to entry that regulates the conditions of competition in the relevant market. Often – this is true of copyright and patents – the exclusive right is granted for a limited period of time, after which the protected idea enters the public domain. This legal technique seeks to balance the short-term and long-term dimensions of competition, that is, between rivalry at a given point in time and

---

[5] See in particular Joined Cases C-2/01 P and C-3/01 P *Bundesverband der Arzneimittel-Importeure eV and Commission v Bayer AG*, EU:C:2004:2; and Joined Cases C-501/06 P, C-513/06 P, C-515/06 P and C-519/06 P *GlaxoSmithKline Services Unlimited v Commission*, EU:C:2009:610.

[6] For an analysis of the peculiarities of the economic and legal context, see Andrea Coscelli, Geoff Edwards and Alan Overd, 'Parallel trade in pharmaceuticals: more harm than good?' (2008) 29 European Competition Law Review 490; and Patrick Rey and James S Venit, 'Parallel trade and pharmaceuticals: a policy in search of itself' (2004) 29 European Law Review 153.

[7] See for instance Case C-322/01 *Deutscher Apothekerverband eV v 0800 DocMorris NV and Jacques Waterval*, EU:C:2003:664; and Case C-108/09 *Ker-Optika bt v ÀNTSZ Dél-dunántúli Regionális Intézete*, EU:C:2010:725.

[8] Lionel Bently, Brad Sherman, Dev Gangjee and Phillip Johnson, *Intellectual Property Law* (6th edn, Oxford University Press 2022). See also Chapter 4.

The Overlapping Application of Competition Law and Regulation   75

firms' incentives to create and innovate. The difficult relationship between competition law and intellectual property – and, more generally, intangible property, is explored in detail in Chapters 4 and 7.

A second example is that of network industries regulation – including telecommunications, energy, postal services and transport. The regimes to which these industries are subject determine the conditions of competition in a variety of ways. First, they establish whether market entry is free or whether, instead, one or several activities are protected by exclusive or special rights.[9] Second, they often impose obligations intended to promote and/or to preserve competition at least in some segments of the industry. In particular, these regimes focus on the conditions of access to bottleneck segments within which it may be particularly difficult (if not outright inefficient) to inject rivalry.[10] Regulatory obligations in this sense may include a duty to share the bottleneck segment, to keep different accounts and even to separate (functionally or structurally) the bottleneck segment from adjacent activities.[11] The interaction between competition law and sector-specific regulation is addressed at length in Chapter 6.

1.1.2. Substantive and Temporal Overlaps

Figure 3.1 Substantive and temporal overlaps

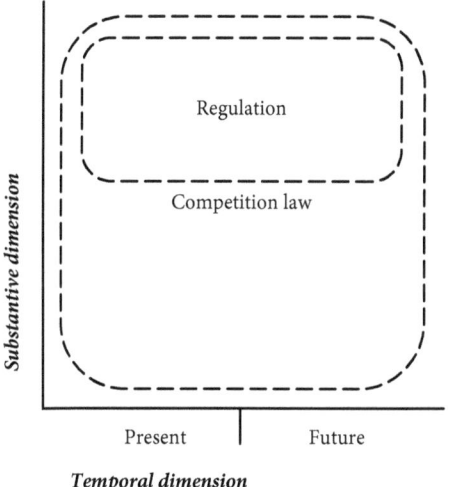

---

[9] Robert Baldwin, Martin Cave, Martin Lodge, *Understanding Regulation: Theory, Strategy, and Practice* (2nd edn, Oxford University Press 2011).

[10] Christopher Decker, *Modern Economic Regulation* (Cambridge University Press 2018). See also the analysis in Chapter 1 in this volume.

[11] See for instance Articles 68–82 in Directive (EU) 2018/1972 of the European Parliament and the Council of 11 December 2018 establishing the European Electronic Communications Code [2018] OJ L321/36, which provide for a wide range of available remedies in the telecommunications sector.

Because overlaps between competition law and regulation are frequent, if not inevitable, it makes sense to think systematically about them. Figure 3.1 breaks down this interaction into two dimensions: substantive and temporal. There are situations where both competition law and regulation apply to a common set of activities, and at the same time. It is sufficient to think, in this regard, of behaviour in the telecommunications sector, which is subject to a dedicated regime and, in addition, may be scrutinised under competition law. As a result, the very same issues (such as access to bottleneck segments) can be addressed by both systems. In fact, the European Commission (hereinafter, the 'Commission') has even evaluated in some instances whether a breach of sector-specific regulation amounts, in addition, to an abuse of a dominant position within the meaning of Article 102 TFEU.[12]

Figure 3.2 'Expectation of regulation'

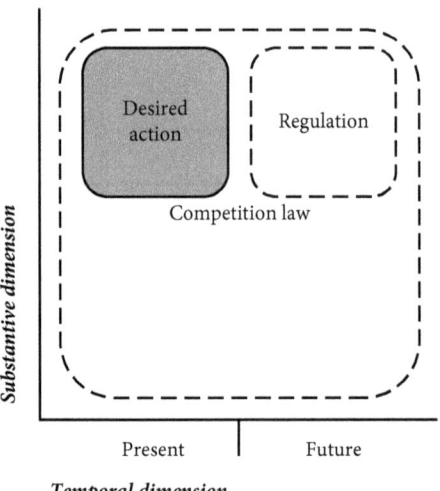

Temporal dimension

In other cases (see Figure 3.2), there is no temporal overlap between the two disciplines. Sometimes, the application of competition law takes place in relation to markets or activities where the adoption of a sector-specific regime is contemplated but has not materialised. These are instances in which there is simply an 'expectation of regulation' while competition law is applied to the issues that, it is anticipated, will also be regulated in the future. Until the adoption of the Digital Markets Act,[13] discussed in Chapter 5, this has been the true of digital platforms.

---

[12] Case C-165/19 P *Slovak Telekom, a.s. v Commission*, EU:C:2021:239.
[13] Regulation (EU) 2022/1925 of the European Parliament and of the Council of 14 September 2022 on contestable and fair markets in the digital sector and amending Directives (EU) 2019/1937 and (EU) 2020/1828 (Digital Markets Act) [2022] OJ L265/1.

Prior to the adoption of a formal sectoral regime, Article 102 TFEU applied to the behaviour of some of the leading platform operators. Similarly, the enforcement of Article 101 TFEU to credit card systems preceded the adoption of a formal regime.[14]

Figure 3.3 Partial overlap and complementarity

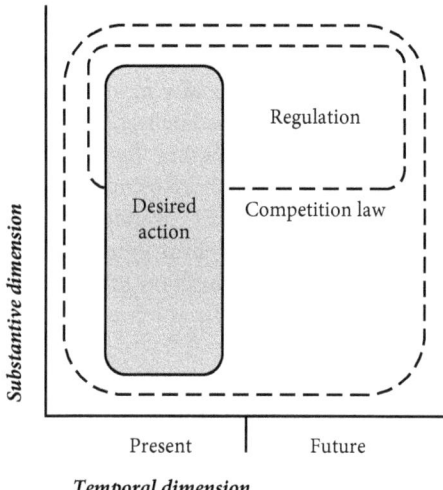

Finally (Figure 3.3), there are instances where there is a temporal overlap between competition law and regulation, but the substantive overlap between disciplines is only partial. Thus, some activities will be subject to regulation, while others fall outside of its scope. Competition law will still apply to the latter. In these circumstances, the two disciplines may play complementary roles. Similarly, Articles 101 and 102 TFEU may effectively address gaps in regulation. Suffice it to think, in this sense, of audio-visual content. Even though they are crucial for the dynamics of rivalry among telecommunications operators (they are a major factor driving subscription to Broadband Internet services[15]), content-related activities are not caught by the EU Regulatory Framework for electronic communications.[16] As a consequence, the impact that such activities have on markets subject to the telecommunications regime will only be addressed by means of competition law enforcement.

---

[14] Regulation (EU) 2015/751 of the European Parliament and of the Council of 29 April 2015 on interchange fees for card-based payment transactions [2015] OJ L 123/1.
[15] For a detailed assessment, see *Liberty Global/Ziggo* (Case M.7000) Commission Decision of 30 May 2018.
[16] See Article 2(4) of Electronic Communications Code (n 11).

1.2. The Applicability of Competition Law to Regulated Activities

Where there is a substantive and temporal overlap between competition law and economic regulation, the question that arises at the outset is whether the former is applicable where the latter already addresses the relevant issue. Suppose that, by virtue of a patent, a firm enjoys a monopoly in the relevant market. It has been explained above that, as a rule, intellectual property regulates competition by granting exclusive rights to the patent holder for a limited period. The point of law, against this background, is whether the intellectual property regime precludes the application of competition law or whether, instead, the latter can apply to address any concerns resulting from the (short-term) monopoly position enjoyed by the patentee. If Articles 101 and 102 TFEU overlap with regulation, conflicting outcomes may result from the concurrent enforcement of both systems. Conduct that is unproblematic under intellectual property law may be deemed restrictive of competition, and vice versa. If, conversely, the two regimes are aligned, there is a risk of double jeopardy.

In principle, it would be reasonable to argue that, where there is a substantive and temporal overlap between competition law and regulation, the former should not come into play. The primacy of dedicated regulation (*lex specialis*) would avoid conflicting outcomes, and, by the same token, it would preserve legal certainty. One should consider, in addition, that competition law applies horizontally across sectors and practices. As a result, regulatory regimes may be superior from a substantive and institutional standpoint. Regulation may be better tailored to the issues falling within its scope of application. For instance, one may expect telecommunications regulation to be well placed to address concerns arising in the industry. From an institutional standpoint, moreover, regulation may be enforced by ad hoc agencies, which may have built the sort of expertise that generalist courts and competition authorities inevitably lack.

This question became a topical and recurrent one in the years that followed the liberalisation of network industries. The position of the Court of Justice (hereinafter, the 'Court') has been consistent. The point of law was definitively settled in *Deutsche Telekom*.[17] In this judgment, the Court ruled that a substantive overlap between competition law and economic regulation does not preclude, in and of itself, intervention under the former. Thus, it is only where a regulatory regime does not leave any scope for manoeuvre to an economic operator – that is, where there is no behaviour attributable to the undertaking – that Articles 101 and 102 TFEU fail to apply.[18] The superior expertise of regulatory authorities, the protection of legitimate expectations or the fact that the application of competition law might lead to inconsistent outcomes were all deemed irrelevant in

---

[17] Case C-280/08 P *Deutsche Telekom AG v Commission*, EU:C:2010:603.
[18] Ibid, para 80.

this regard.[19] In *bpost*, the Court held that competition law and economic regulation can sanction the same conduct independently of one another.[20]

The position expressed by the Court in *Deutsche Telekom* is consistent with the one it adopted in relation to intellectual property in the early days of the discipline. Thus, the fact that a firm's intangible assets are protected by intellectual property rights does not preclude the application of Articles 101 and 102 TFEU. When the question was first raised, the Court distinguished between the existence of intellectual property rights and their exercise. While the former is not as such contrary to EU competition law (and EU law at large), the latter may be subject to scrutiny.[21] In other words, while the market structure resulting from the award of exclusive rights is not questioned, conduct that takes place within the said structure may be, including the licensing or assignment of intellectual property[22] or the refusal to do so.[23]

1.3. Divergences between Competition Law and Regulation: The Formal and the Substantive

1.3.1. Formal Differences between Competition Law and Regulation

Competition law is sufficiently adaptable to allow it to adopt many different forms and guises. One consequence of the adaptability of the discipline is that it can mimic the techniques and operation of other fields of law. Attempts to distinguish between competition law and regulation based on formal considerations often fail to reflect the richness and complexity of enforcement under Articles 101 and 102 TFEU. These attempts are, by and large, artificial. It is always tempting for commentators to argue that regulation intervenes ex ante, whereas competition law comes into play ex post.[24] An overview of the activity of the Commission over the past 15 years exemplifies the various ways in which ex ante action can take place under Articles 101 and 102 TFEU. Ex

---

[19] The first instance ruling (the findings of which were not called into question on appeal) provides more valuable insights in this regard. See Case T-271/03 *Deutsche Telekom AG v Commission*, EU:T:2008:101, paras 263–272.

[20] Case C-117/20 *bpost SA v Autorité belge de la concurrence*, EU:C:2022:202.

[21] Joined Cases 56 and 58/64 *Établissements Consten S.à.R.L. and Grundig-Verkaufs-GmbH v Commission*, EU:C:1966:41, 345.

[22] Case 268/78 *L.C. Nungesser KG and Kurt Eisele v Commission*, EU:C:1982:211; and Case 262/81 *Coditel SA, Compagnie générale pour la diffusion de la télévision, and others v Ciné-Vog Films SA and others*, EU:C:1982:334.

[23] Joined Cases C-241/91 P and C-242/91 P *Radio Telefis Eireann (RTE) and Independent Television Publications Ltd (ITP) v Commission*, EU:C:1995:98 ('*Magill*'); and Case C-418/01 *IMS Health GmbH & Co. OHG v NDC Health GmbH & Co. KG*, EU:C:2004:257.

[24] For a critical overview of these arguments, see Niamh Dunne, *Competition Law and Economic Regulation: Making and Managing Markets* (Cambridge University Press 2015).

ante intervention can occur both through case-by-case enforcement,[25] block exemption regulations and soft law instruments clarifying the Commission's approach to certain issues.[26]

Similarly, it has occasionally been argued that the difference between competition law and regulation has to do with the fact that intervention under the former is proscriptive (it prohibits certain conduct) whereas the latter is typically prescriptive (in the sense that it imposes positive obligations on undertakings).[27] Any attempt to distinguish both disciplines along these lines is not any less artificial. As observed in Chapter 1, not only can competition law lead to intervention of a prescriptive nature; in fact, proactive enforcement is, as explained therein, on the rise. The Court clarified this point of law as far back as *Commercial Solvents*, where it expressly held that remedial action under Article 102 TFEU can result in the imposition of positive obligations.[28] While it is undeniable that proactive intervention poses unique challenges, there is nothing preventing courts and authorities, as a matter of substantive law, from pursuing this course of action where necessary and proportionate.

1.3.2. Substantive Differences between Competition Law and Regulation

Formal attempts to differentiate between competition law and regulation may be artificial. Substantive differences, on the other hand, are frequent and can be expected. These differences may result, first, from the objectives pursued by regulation. The goals of a regime may be – and often are – broadly compatible with those underpinning Articles 101 and 102 TFEU. They are not necessarily identical, however. Following the liberalisation process, the objectives of sector-specific regulation in the telecommunications and energy industries are very much in line with those of competition law. Both see effective competition as the best means to discipline the behaviour of market players and as the default mechanism to attain the desired outcomes (whether it is low prices, innovation or investment). As discussed below, the objectives may be compatible, but they are not the same. More precisely, there is a difference between the protection of competition, which

---

[25] See for instance *Joint selling of the media rights to the FA Premier League* (Case COMP/C-2/38.173) Commission Decision of 22 March 2006. This decision was adopted ahead of the auction for the sale of its media rights by the FA Premier League.

[26] See for instance Guidelines on the applicability of Article 101 of the Treaty on the Functioning of the European Union to horizontal co-operation agreements [2011] OJ C11/1, paras 257–335, where the Commission lays down, ex ante, the criteria for the assessment of the compatibility of standardisation agreements with Article 101 TFEU. See also the Draft Guidelines on the applicability of Article 101 of the Treaty on the Functioning of the European Union to horizontal co-operation agreements C(2022) 1159 final.

[27] For an overview of these arguments, see Pablo Ibáñez Colomo, 'On the application of competition law as regulation: elements for a theory' (2010) 29 Yearbook of European Law 261.

[28] Joined Cases 6 and 7/73 *Istituto Chemioterapico Italiano S.p.A. and Commercial Solvents Corporation v Commission*, EU:C:1974:18, paras 42–50.

is the province of Articles 101 and 102 TFEU, and its promotion, which is the goal of sectoral regulation.

Even when they share the same objectives, competition law and regulation do not necessarily rely on the same techniques. In fact, the techniques pursued by each regime may be in direct contradiction with one another. This is a second source of substantive divergences, which is probably best illustrated by reference to intellectual property systems. As explained at length in Chapter 4, the objectives of competition law and intellectual property are not in conflict. Both seek to create the conditions in which innovation flourishes. The techniques upon which they rely are markedly different, however. It has already been pointed out above that intellectual property seeks to promote investments in creative and inventive activities, first and foremost, by insulating inventors and creators from competition.

1.4. Competition Law as an Instrument of Regulation

The interaction between competition law and regulation can affect the interpretation of Articles 101 and 102 TFEU. Because the two provisions are so malleable, and because the analysis is so context-specific, competition law may be applied to embrace the objectives of the other discipline, as opposed to its own goals. There is, in other words, a risk that competition law becomes, de facto, an instrument of regulation, whether deliberately or in an inadvertent manner. This phenomenon may be manifested in two ways. First, the substantive standards may be altered to accommodate the aims and concerns of regulation. As a result, behaviour that would otherwise not have given rise to an infringement may be found to be in breach of Article 101 and/or 102 TFEU. For instance, a vertically-integrated firm may be required to share access to its infrastructure, even though the existing case law does not support intervention. In other cases, competition law may be applied to challenge market structures as such (as opposed to a behaviour), which is in principle not possible under Articles 101 and 102 TFEU.

The second way in which the phenomenon may be manifested has to do with the proportionality of intervention. There may be scenarios where it is uncontroversial that the practice amounts to an infringement of Article 101 or 102 TFEU. However, action addressing the consequences of the breach may go beyond what would have been necessary to bring it to an end. In particular, structural remedies may be imposed where behavioural intervention alone would have provided an adequate response to the concerns identified during the investigation. Consider the example of a contractual clause prohibiting the export of electricity. There should be little doubt that this practice is presumptively restrictive of competition. It is clear from long-standing administrative practice, moreover, that this infringement can be effectively brought to an end by means of reactive intervention. Where competition law serves the goals of regulation, however, remedial action may be more far-reaching, and may lead to structural changes in the industry.

The use of competition law to attain the objectives of another regime necessarily has an impact on the interpretation of Articles 101 and 102 TFEU. One consequence of the phenomenon is legal inconsistency. If competition law is sometimes relied upon to attain the goals of a regulatory regime, the understanding of the provisions may vary from one industry – or one activity – to another. From a policy perspective, enforcement may be difficult to predict, as several tests and approaches may co-exist alongside one another. From a legal perspective, this reality may lead to fragmentation. In other words, a form of 'sector-specific competition law' (or 'issue-specific competition law'), departing in substance from the default approach, may emerge in practice. For instance, the conditions under which a dominant firm is required to give access to a facility may vary depending on the industry in which the said firm operates.

The risks of legal fragmentation and uncertainty may be manifested in four different scenarios, which are described in detail hereinafter. These scenarios capture the ways in which competition law interacts with regulation. The first is one in which there is a substantive and temporal overlap between the two disciplines, and in which Articles 101 and 102 TFEU act as a safety net that advances, by other means, the objectives of the regulatory regime. The second scenario is one in which competition law fulfils a gap-filling function, in the sense that it addresses the lacunae of a regime already in place. Third, competition law may be instrumentalised with the purpose of rectifying or amending existing regulation. As will be described in detail below, a regulatory regime may be rectified if it is not perceived to be adequately equipped to achieve its objectives, or if it is not deemed to take a set of conflicting objectives sufficiently into consideration. Finally, there are instances in which there is no regulation in place, and in which competition law comes into play to address an 'expectation of regulation' that the legislature, given its intrinsic limitations, may not be able to satisfy.

2. Competition Law as a Safety Net: The Auxiliary Role of Articles 101 and 102 TFEU

2.1. Why Competition Law Acts as a Safety Net

Articles 101 and 102 TFEU frequently overlap in substance and time with regulation. This is true, in particular, of sector-specific regimes designed to promote rivalry in and/or around bottleneck segments in liberalised industries. The Commission has frequently applied competition law to the activities falling within their scope. In particular, Article 102 TFEU has been consistently enforced to address constructive refusals to deal by incumbent operators (such as 'margin squeeze' conduct) and thus preserve emerging rivalry. In some cases, the Commission has found that the very breach of a regulatory obligation amounts to a competition law infringement. In *Slovak Telekom*, for example, it held that the way in which the dominant undertaking had construed the access duties to which it was subject was abusive in and of itself.[29]

What is characteristic about these examples is that the enforcement of Article 102 TFEU had the effect of strengthening the sector-specific regime. From a substantive standpoint, it did so by protecting the market structure that regulation was designed to create (which it achieved, for instance, by taking action against constructive refusals to deal). From an institutional perspective, competition law became an alternative avenue to address breaches of regulation. Where competition law fulfils this role, it can be said to act as a safety net. One can think of several reasons why Articles 101 and 102 TFEU would play this auxiliary role. From the Commission's perspective, the competition law route may be more effective. It may allow for swifter action, open the door to a broader range of remedies and/or may ensure greater deterrence. Crucially, moreover, it has the direct power to enforce Articles 101 and 102 TFEU (which it lacks in telecommunications and energy regulation).

The example of electronic communications, which will be examined at length below and in Chapter 6, eloquently shows the relative advantages of competition law enforcement for an authority like the Commission. Even though it plays a central role in the institutional structure of the telecommunications-specific regime, the Commission is not, strictly speaking, a sectoral authority. Its competences under the latter can in no way be compared to the decision-making powers it enjoys by virtue of Regulation 1/2003. Under the telecommunications framework, it merely has jurisdiction to oversee enforcement by national authorities.[30] It is unsurprising, against this background, that the Commission may seek to attain its preferred outcomes by relying on competition law.

Another factor that may explain the preference for competition law relates to the incentives of sectoral authorities, and to the peculiar institutional setting within which they exercise their powers. The phenomenon of industry capture, whereby agencies may fail to act in the public interest and advance the agenda of private firms instead, is well identified and has been abundantly studied.[31] It is also understood that specialised agencies are more prone to capture than competition authorities with a horizontal remit.[32] In the specific context of the liberalisation of network industries, there is another factor that has the potential to exacerbate the

---

[29] *Slovak Telekom* (Case AT.39523) Commission Decision of 15 October 2014, paras 535–651.

[30] Articles 63–67 of Electronic Communications Code (n 11).

[31] See George J Stigler, 'The theory of economic regulation' (1971) 2 Bell Journal of Economics and Management Science 3; and Jean-Jacques Laffont and Jean Tirole, 'The Politics of Government Decision-Making: A Theory of Regulatory Capture' (1991) 106 Quarterly Journal of Economics 1089. For a discussion of these questions in relation, specifically, to the interaction between competition law and regulation, see Dunne (n 24), 143–146.

[32] OECD, 'Relationship between regulators and competition authorities' DAFFE/CLP(99)8, 28.

phenomenon. The primary goal of sector-specific regulation since the 1990s is to introduce competition on markets that were, as a rule, dominated by a publicly-owned operator enjoying exclusive rights. Accordingly, national regulatory authorities are expected to regulate the incumbent in the country, in which the State may still hold a stake.[33] In these circumstances, the agency may not, or not always, be sufficiently committed to the objectives of the sector-specific regime. Against this background, intervention under competition law may be an effective means to avoid capture, or to remedy its consequences. It is not surprising that commentators have rationalised competition law enforcement in this area as an attempt to address this very concern.[34]

2.2. Compatible, but not Identical, Objectives: Protecting and Promoting Competition

As already pointed out, competition law and regulation sometimes pursue compatible, but not necessarily identical, objectives. A divergence at the level of objectives may be manifested in several ways. It may be reflected, in particular, in the threshold for intervention. For instance, access obligations are more easily imposed under telecommunications or energy regulation than under Article 102 TFEU. It is notorious that, under the latter, mandated shared access to a bottleneck can only be imposed in exceptional circumstances. The *Bronner* case law demands evidence that a refusal to deal would lead to the elimination of 'all competition'.[35] The substantive standards are not as demanding under sectoral regimes. Telecommunications regulation, to mention one example, merely requires authorities to show that lack of access to an infrastructure 'would hinder the emergence of a sustainable competitive market at the retail level, and would not be in the end-user's interest'.[36]

These substantive divergences are a function of the different aims pursued by competition law and sectoral regimes. Telecommunications and energy regulation seek to promote competition. Articles 101 and 102 TFEU, on the other hand, merely aim at protecting it. Sectoral regimes in recently liberalised industries seek to engineer market structures to achieve effective competition. In such scenarios, the purpose of regulation is to reduce the degree of market power enjoyed by the incumbent and, by the same token, increase that of new entrants. Where the promotion of competition is the goal of intervention, what triggers remedial

---

[33] See for instance *Deutsche Telekom AG v Commission* (n 17), para 1.
[34] For a proponent of this explanation, see Giorgio Monti, 'Managing the Intersection of Utilities Regulation and EC Competition Law' (2008) LSE Law, Society and Economy Working Papers 8/2008, available at https://ssrn.com/abstract=1273615.
[35] Case C-7/97 *Oscar Bronner GmbH & Co. KG v Mediaprint Zeitungs- und Zeitschriftenverlag GmbH & Co. KG and others*, EU:C:1998:569, para 41.
[36] Articles 72 and 73 of the Electronic Communications Code (n 11).

action is the very market structure (as opposed to firm behaviour). Under sector-specific regulation, accordingly, dominance will be a concern in and of itself. Since the goal of the regime is to transform the make-up of the industry, it is not necessary to establish, in addition, an abuse (or, indeed, evidence that any practice has been implemented).

Competition law, on the other hand, is concerned with the protection of the competitive process. This is at least clear in the case of the EU system.[37] The point of intervention under Articles 101 and 102 TFEU is not to introduce further market fragmentation, but to preserve market structures and ensure that, imperfectly competitive as they may be, they deliver to their full potential. The concern with the protection of competition is reflected in a variety of ways. In particular, intervention is triggered by a behaviour (such as an agreement or a unilateral practice implemented by a dominant firm), not the market structure as such. For instance, it has already been mentioned that Article 102 TFEU does not prohibit dominant positions, only the abuse thereof. This provision, in other words, seeks to ensure that the conditions of competition are not further deteriorated on a market in which the they are already significantly weakened.[38]

2.3. Consequences for Competition Law

The enforcement of competition law as a safety net has influenced the substantive standards of the discipline. When it fulfilled this auxiliary function, the boundaries of Articles 101 and 102 TFEU were explored, if not stretched, by the Commission. In some instances, competition law was relied upon in the absence of an obvious behavioural trigger (that is, in the absence of an agreement or an abusive practice). In other cases, the scope of existing legal doctrines was expanded; sometimes, new doctrines were introduced. Similarly, remedial action has occasionally aligned with the logic and operation of sector-specific regulation. Several investigations have been closed following commitments fundamentally altering the structure and/or operation of the relevant markets. In a subset of cases, the restructuring has been achieved by means of divestitures; in others, by means of behavioural obligations. These trends in the case law, which suggest that competition law has occasionally embraced the standards of sector-specific regulation, are discussed in detail in Chapter 6.

---

[37] Other systems, like the UK one, go beyond the mere protection of the competitive process, in the sense that they may go as far as to restructure markets by means of a market investigation. See in this sense sections 130–138B of the Enterprise Act 2002. For an overview of the tool, see Massimo Motta, Martin Peitz and Heike Schweitzer, *Market Investigations: A New Competition Tool for Europe?* (Cambridge University Press 2021).

[38] Case C-680/20 *Unilever Italia Mkt. Operations Srl v Autorità Garante della Concorrenza e del Mercato*, EU:C:2023:33, para 36.

3. Competition Law as a Gap-filling Instrument

3.1. Understanding the Gap-filling Role of Competition Law

3.1.1. Why Competition Law Fulfils a Gap-filling Role

It has already been pointed out that competition law has some advantages over most regulatory regimes. Arguably, the biggest of these advantages is the flexibility of Articles 101 and 102 TFEU and their ability to adapt to different scenarios. The formal adoption of regulation typically requires the enactment of legislation. The legislative process is known to be protracted and unpredictable. As a result, regulation may not intervene fast enough to address emerging concerns. Alternatively, it may end up providing a watered-down response to some of the issues. Lobbying efforts, or conflicting interests, may negatively affect the effectiveness of the regime. Even when regulation exists, it is not necessarily nimble enough to address all matters, in particular emerging ones. Legislation is often a snapshot of the concerns arising at a given point in time, and as such one that fails to adjust to changing economic and technological realities.

Competition law, by contrast, does not necessitate the enactment of legislation to address new issues and deal with emerging practices. Because Articles 101 and 102 TFEU are worded in broad and vague terms and have a horizontal scope of application, they can be enforced seamlessly to deal with a wide variety of practices, provided that they can be construed as competition law infringements. The wide range of remedies from which a competition authority can choose, moreover, means that the measures ordered to bring an infringement to an end can adjust to the demands of particular cases. Against, this background, it is not surprising that competition law has often fulfilled a gap-filling role, making up for regulatory regimes' rigidity and inability to anticipte emerging concerns.

3.1.2. How Competition Law Fulfils its Gap-filling Role

Articles 101 and 102 TFEU fulfil their gap-filling role in a variety of ways. It would be wrong to think that these provisions are exclusively enforced by establishing infringements by means of individual decisions. As explained at length in Chapter 1, the Commission relies upon a variety of instruments to formulate policy. For instance, commitments decisions adopted pursuant to Article 9 of Regulation 1/2003 allow for a swift response to an emerging issue without the need to construe Articles 101 and 102 TFEU. In the past two decades, moreover, the Commission has made increasingly frequent use of soft law instruments (including Guidelines). Even though these instruments do not, and cannot, provide for binding obligations vis-à-vis third parties,[39] they can effectively

---

[39] Case C-226/11 *Expedia Inc. v Autorité de la concurrence and Others*, EU:C:2012:795, para 29.

replicate, in substance, regulatory regimes. By the same token, soft law can steer firm behaviour without the need to open formal proceedings.

The treatment of standardisation in the Guidelines on horizontal co-operation agreements[40] provides a concrete example of how soft law can mimic formal regulation. This instrument defines, in the general and abstract way that is characteristic of legislation, the conditions that standard development agreements need to fulfil to comply with Article 101(1) TFEU, as well as the instances in which they can give rise to competition law concerns. The reports issued by the Commission in the context of a sector inquiry provide another example. These documents summarise the potential issues in an industry and signal the authority's enforcement priorities. Because they concern a whole sector, and because they are not subject to the procedural constraints of individual cases, these reports can effectively influence firm conduct. The discussion that follows below will come back to the reports issued by the Commission in the context of its sector inquiry into the energy sector,[41] and those issued in relation to the pharmaceutical industry.[42] These two reports were followed by a steady stream of individual decisions which developed the main ideas found in them.

3.2. The Gap-filling Role of Competition Law in Practice

3.2.1. Intellectual Property

Intellectual property regimes are known to be relatively blunt instruments, in the sense that they are inflexible and revolve around a uniform set of tools that apply irrespective of the nature of the industry and the characteristics of the relevant market.[43] For instance, patent law does not take into consideration the fact that exclusive rights may not always have the same effects on the rate of innovation.[44] Similarly, the factors that justify a case-by-case assessment under competition law are not relevant when protecting inventions or creations under intellectual property. The fact that the exclusive right creates a dominant position, and thus opens the door to exploitative and exclusionary conduct, does not play a role. In the same vein, there are few mechanisms allowing an authority to modulate or correct the degree or range of protection ex post.

---

[40] Guidelines on horizontal co-operation agreements (n 26), paras 257–335.
[41] European Commission, 'Inquiry pursuant to Article 17 of Regulation (EC) No 1/2003 into the European gas and electricity sectors (Final Report)' COM(2006) 851 final.
[42] European Commission, 'Executive Summary of the Pharmaceutical Sector Inquiry Report' COM(2009) 351 final.
[43] For an overview of the differences between competition law and intellectual property, see Chapter 3 of Christina Bohannan and Herbert Hovenkamp, *Creation without Restraint: Promoting Liberty and Rivalry in Innovation* (Oxford University Press 2011). See Chapter 4 for an extensive discussion.
[44] See in this sense Dan L Burk and Mark A Lemley, *The Patent Crisis and How the Courts Can Solve It* (University of Chicago Press 2009).

Commentators and administrative authorities have also noted that intellectual property regimes are based on premises that do not capture – or do so only imperfectly – the contemporary reality of patent and copyright protection. There is a mismatch, in other words, between the assumptions underpinning intellectual property regimes and the reality within which they operate. In particular, commentators have pointed out that, to some extent, legislation appears to be based on the premise that a single patent corresponds to a discrete product that can be readily identified.[45] Reality is considerably more complex (and has become more complex over the years). As a result of this tension between assumptions and reality, claims that intellectual property – especially patent law – no longer works as intended and is in need of fundamental change have become relatively commonplace.[46]

The mismatch between legislation and reality becomes apparent across a number of issues. For instance, many contemporary products are not protected by a single, discrete patent. It is not unusual for modern inventions to be protected by multiple – dozens, if not hundreds or thousands of – patents.[47] As a result, the licensees implementing protected technologies may be required to navigate what is known as a 'patent thicket', which may make market entry complex and less predictable.[48] Second, the boundaries of a patent may not be clearly delineated, or may be difficult to define in practice. In this sense, intellectual property rights are more different from physical property than commonly assumed.[49] One consequence of this reality is that litigation becomes an inevitable feature of patent law: courts, rather than patent authorities will often have the last word about what is covered by the exclusive right and what is not.[50]

The divorce between legislation and reality has led to the emergence of gaps that the intellectual property system is imperfectly equipped to address, if at all. The growing complexity of products – and the need to incorporate multiple patented technologies – is manifested in the rise of standard development organisations, which play a crucial role in many industries.[51] Inter alia,

---

[45] Mark A Lemley and Carl Shapiro, 'Patent Holdup and Royalty Stacking' (2007) 85 Texas Law Review 1991.
[46] See among the vast literature, Adam B. Jaffe and Josh Lerner, *Innovation and Its Discontents: How Our Broken Patent System is Endangering Innovation and Progress, and What to Do About It* (Princeton University Press 2011).
[47] This is the main point underpinning the analysis in Lemley and Shapiro (n 45).
[48] Carl Shapiro, 'Navigating the Patent Thicket: Cross-Licenses, Patent Pools and Standard Setting', in Adam B Jaffe, Josh Lerner and Scott Stern (eds), *Innovation Policy and the Economy*, vol 1 (MIT Press 2006).
[49] Mark A Lemley, 'Ignoring Patents' (2008) Michigan State Law Review 19.
[50] For a US perspective on US patent litigation, see Mark A Lemley, 'The Surprising Resilience of the Patent System' (2016) 95 Texas Law Review 1. The author documents a 350% rise in litigation between 1980 and 2010.
[51] On standardisation and the potential issues to which it might give rise, see Guidelines on horizontal co-operation agreements (n 26), paras 257–335. See also Jorge L Contreras (ed), *The Cambridge Handbook of Technical Standardization Law: Competition, Antitrust, and Patents* (Cambridge University Press 2017).

these bodies are responsible for the selection of the technologies incorporated in complex products and for the definition of the terms under which they are made available to third parties. Standard-setting raises a number of concerns in theory and in practice. In particular, it is often claimed that the holders of patents incorporated in a standard have the ability and incentive to exploit their position vis-à-vis actual or potential licensees (what has come to be known as patent hold-up).[52] In the absence of responses from the intellectual property system, these issues have been addressed via competition law enforcement.

It has also been frequently argued that the intellectual property system is imperfectly equipped to deal with some practices in the pharmaceutical industry. Because patent protection has a major impact on their revenues, drug manufacturers have put in place a range of strategies aimed at delaying entry by generic producers. Some of these strategies exploit the flaws of the patent system; others, the assumptions on which it is based. *AstraZeneca* provides an example of regulatory gaming. In that case, the Commission took action against a drug manufacturer that had provided misleading information to the patent authorities.[53] The phenomenon of patent 'evergreening'[54] is another one. Because a single medicine can be protected by more than one patent, drug manufacturers may attempt (and have in fact attempted) to extend the length of their rights by seeking exclusivity over secondary or adjacent inventions.[55]

The gaps in the intellectual property system have also become apparent in the area of copyright. Technology has eased, and reduced the cost of, reproducing and communicating creative works. Copyright law has consistently tried to adapt to this shifting reality. The past decade has also seen the emergence of platforms which consumers use to access and disseminate protected material. The change in consumer habits has had an impact on the allocation of revenues obtained by some actors in the industry. More precisely, it has been claimed in recent years that the new reality has led to the shift of rents from content creators to platform operators. As a consequence of this phenomenon, it is argued, the revenues generated by online platforms are not (or no longer) commensurate with the remuneration received by authors (and the creative industries). It is claimed, in other words, that a 'value gap' has

---

[52] Patent hold-up refers to an instance where the holder of a patent that is essential to a standard exploits opportunistically its position vis-à-vis firms relying on it to manufacture their products. The phenomenon is described in Lemley and Shapiro (n 45). This is a contentious issue that has generated a sub-literature of its own, focusing on whether the phenomenon exists and, if so, justifies intervention. For an analysis coming to the opposite conclusion, see in particular Alexander Galetovic and Stephen Haber, 'The Fallacies of Patent-Holdup Theory' (2017) 13 Journal of Competition Law & Economics 1.

[53] *AstraZeneca* (Case COMP/A. 37.507/F3) Commission Decision of 15 June 2005.

[54] The phenomenon of evergreening describes an instance where a pharmaceutical company seeks to obtain additional patent protection to prevent or delay the entry of generic manufacturers. C Scott Hemphill and Bhaven N Sampat, 'Evergreening, patent challenges, and effective market life in pharmaceuticals' (2012) 31 Journal of Health Economics 327.

[55] European Commission, 'Executive Summary of the Pharmaceutical Sector Inquiry Report' COM(2009) 351 final (n 42).

emerged.[56] In these circumstances, it is not surprising that the industry has resorted to competition law in an attempt to achieve, through the enforcement of Articles 101 and 102 TFEU, what it also expected to achieve through copyright reform.

For instance, Getty Images brought a complaint before the Commission in which it argued that the operation of Google's search engine (and, more precisely, Google Images) prevents it from generating the revenues it otherwise would.[57] The thrust of the argument is that, as a result of its design, user traffic stays within the search engine, instead of going to other websites. The dispute, which has been framed as a competition law violation, is similar to that between Google and newspaper publishers, which has taken place on many fronts and at many levels.[58] Copyright reform addressing the said 'value gap' has featured prominently in the legislative agenda of the EU since the launch of the Digital Single Market Strategy.[59] Some of the ideas advanced in this context include the expansion of copyright protection to include new activities,[60] and to revise the legal relationship between right holders and online platforms. Other legislative initiatives have sought to exempt certain right holders – in particular newspapers – from competition law rules in an attempt to increase their bargaining power vis-à-vis online platforms.[61]

3.2.2. Network Industries

Gaps have also emerged in the sector-specific regimes applying to network industries. Whether they are made explicit or not, regulation dealing with – inter alia – telecommunications and energy is grounded on a number of assumptions about the economic and technological landscape and, by the same token, about the sort of intervention that is appropriate to achieve the goals of the regime. As is true of intellectual property systems, a mismatch may emerge between the dynamics of the industry and the premises on which legislation is grounded. The reality of the mismatch is manifested in several ways. It may be reflected, for

---

[56] For a discussion of the concept, see Eleonora Rosati, 'Five Considerations for the Transposition and Application of Article 17 of the DSM Directive' (2021) 16 Journal of Intellectual Property Law & Practice 265.

[57] Samuel Gibbs, 'Getty Images files antitrust complaint against Google' *The Guardian* (London, 27 April 2016).

[58] See for instance Décision 20-MC-01 of 9 April 2020 concerning the request for interim measures brought by Syndicat des éditeurs de la presse magazine, l'Alliance de la presse d'information générale e.a. et l'Agence France-Presse. This decision was confirmed once Google desisted in its appeal; see CA Paris, pôle 5, ch. 7, 19 January 2023, *Google LLC and others*.

[59] See in this sense Rosati (n 56).

[60] Ibid. This discussion led, in particular, to the introduction of a new provision creating a right in favour of press publishers. See Article 17 of Directive (EU) 2019/790 of the European Parliament and of the Council of 17 April 2019 on copyright and related rights in the Digital Single Market and amending Directives 96/9/EC and 2001/29/EC [2019] OJ L 130/92.

[61] See, for a discussion, OECD, 'Competition issues concerning news media and digital platforms' (2021) OECD Competition Committee Discussion Paper, available at https://www.oecd.org/daf/competition/competition-issues-in-news-media-and-digital-platforms.htm.

instance, in the scope of the regulatory regime. Some activities that are central to the competitive dynamics of the industry may not be covered by the relevant legislation. In these circumstances, competition law may come into play to fill the gap in the regime.

Gaps may also emerge where sector-specific regulation assumes that there is a finite set of issues that requires intervention. In line with what has already been discussed, post-liberalisation regulation typically focuses on introducing fragmentation in and around the bottleneck segment and, similarly, on easing entry by new players. As a result, a sector-specific regime may find itself powerless where new concerns, unforeseen at the time of the adoption of legislation, emerge. For instance, the fact that regulation is intended to introduce fragmentation does not mean that fragmentation is sustainable in the long run. It may well be the case that, following the initial impetus, certain segments of the value chain develop a tendency towards concentration, and may even be remonopolised. This trend may harm the objectives of the regime – in particular, prices for end-users may go up and the quality of services may go down – but may only be addressed through competition law.

3.3. Consequences for Competition Law

Relying on competition law to remedy gaps in regulatory regimes may have significant consequences for Articles 101 and 102 TFEU. Some of these consequences are substantive in nature and have already been identified above. Where competition law fulfils a gap-filling role, it may embrace the aims of the regime it intends to complete, as opposed to its own. It may also mimic the legislative techniques of economic regulation. For instance, Articles 101 and 102 TFEU may be applied in a way that expands, de facto, the scope of intellectual property. It may, in other words, introduce an exclusive right – or a right to remuneration – by means of case-by-case enforcement. Other consequences of the gap-filling role are procedural and institutional in nature. Where stakeholders perceive that, thanks to their flexibility and adaptability, Articles 101 and 102 TFEU may provide a swifter response to a perceived gap in regulation, competition law institutions may become the arena in which the nature and desirability of intervention are discussed. In other words, the exchanges that typically occur before legislatures and specialised bodies may take place before competition agencies and courts.

4. Competition Law as a Means to Rectify Regulation

4.1. Why Competition Law Rectifies Regulation

Competition law is said to rectify regulation when it overlaps in substance and time with the latter but leads to a different outcome. These are instances, in other words, where the application of Articles 101 or 102 TFEU departs from the solutions provided for in the regime. To begin with, competition law enforcement may introduce additional obligations on regulated firms. For instance, it may require a firm to give access to its (tangible or intangible) property in circumstances where regulation does not. In addition, it may lead to more far-reaching or more stringent intervention. For instance, regulation may simply require a vertically-integrated firm to give access to its property on non-discriminatory terms and conditions. Competition law, by contrast, may take these obligations a step further and order a divestiture.

Rectifying regulation through competition law enforcement means striking a different balance between conflicting objectives within a regime. Patent law, for instance, addresses the trade-off between short-term and long-term competition. As explained above, it deals with it by awarding exclusive rights for a limited period of time. The enforcement of Articles 101 and 102 TFEU will alter the balance enshrined in intellectual property legislation if, for instance, it transforms the exclusive right enjoyed by the patentee into a mere right to receive appropriate remuneration. Consider now telecommunications regulation. This regime needs to navigate the trade-off between promoting competition and preserving firms' incentives to invest in infrastructure. Competition law enforcement may upset the balance struck in the regime if, for instance, it demands the structural divestiture of the bottleneck.

The rectification of regulation may be justified, at least in theory. The balance struck in the intellectual property system or in a sector-specific regime may be suboptimal for a number of reasons. To begin with, it may be grounded on a flawed or obsolete understanding of the reality it intends to regulate. If the economic and technological realities have appreciably changed, and the regime is unable to adjust to them, the solutions for which it provides may have unintended consequences or may underestimate certain factors. Second, the balance struck in regulation is not necessarily the result of an attempt to attain optimal outcomes. As mentioned above, the legislative process is often unpredictable. As a result, the manner in which a regime deals with trade-offs may well be the outcome of a compromise and thus an imperfect solution.

Against this background, it may seem reasonable for competition law to intervene and rectify the outcomes achieved by other regimes. Some of the relative advantages of Articles 101 and 102 TFEU over regulation have already been mentioned above. One must bear in mind, in particular, that competition authorities are relatively well insulated from the pressures and processes that may lead to legislation achieving suboptimal outcomes. If legislation strikes solutions based on some stakeholders' ability to influence the process, a technocratic body like the Commission could in theory be in a better position to advance the general interest.[62] One should consider, in addition, that Articles 101 and 102 TFEU may

---

[62] Bohannan and Hovenkamp (n 43).

sometimes be able to provide a swifter response to changing economic and technological realities.

4.2. The Rectification of Regulation in Practice

4.2.1. *Liberalisation and the Rectification of Regulation*

A look at the history of the liberalisation of network industries in the EU shows that the Commission tends to prefer faster and more far-reaching legislative action than Member States. The experience of decades shows that the latter (or at least some of them) tend to be more reluctant in this sense or prefer a relatively more gradual opening to competition.[63] Inevitably, frictions tend to emerge between the body that proposes legislation (the Commission) and the institutions that adopt it (the Parliament and the Council). Some of the measures that the former proposes have been watered down, delayed or may not be eventually enshrined in legislation.[64] As is true of the examples discussed at length in Chapter 6, the Commission may exploit its dual role as an executive and as a competition authority to rectify, by means of competition law enforcement, the choices made by the legislature.

A cursory look at the evolution of the interaction of competition law and sector-specific regulation sheds light on these dynamics. More specifically, it appears that the Commission has resorted to competition law to attain some outcomes that it was not able to achieve via the legislative process. The liberalisation of the electricity and gas sectors provides an eloquent example in this sense. In the lead-up to the so-called Third Energy Package, the Commission favoured the structural separation of the transmission segments. These preferences were expressed, inter alia, in the report issued in the context of a Sector Inquiry, mentioned above.[65] The EU legislature, on the other hand, settled for less intrusive measures, such as the legal separation of the different activities.[66] It is against this background that

---

[63] For an analysis of the different attitudes in the telecommunications sector, see Chapters 1 and 2 in Pierre Larouche, *Competition Law and Regulation in European Telecommunications* (Hart Publishing 2000). The author describes how the Commission initiated the liberalisation process against the initial reluctance of some Member States (and the Council).

[64] This phenomenon is well documented, for instance, in the energy sector. See for instance Angus Johnston and Guy Block, *EU Energy Law* (Oxford University Press 2013).

[65] Final Report of the Energy Sector Inquiry (n 41), which is unequivocal in pleading for the structural separation of bottlenecks from competitive activities (see in particular para 55: 'Economic evidence shows that full ownership unbundling is the most effective means to ensure choice for energy users and encourage investment. This is because separate network companies are not influenced by overlapping supply/generation interests as regards investment decisions. It also avoids overly detailed and complex regulation and disproportionate administrative burdens. The independent system operator approach would improve the status quo but would require more detailed, prescriptive and costly regulation and would be less effective in addressing the disincentives to invest in networks').

[66] The outcomes achieved via the legislative process can be found in Directive (EU) 2019/944 of the European Parliament and of the Council of 5 June 2019 on common rules for the internal market for

the competition law activity that followed must be understood. In a series of decisions, discussed at length in Chapter 6, the investigations were brought to an end following the structural commitments accepted by the incumbents.

4.2.2. Competition Law as a Means to Rectify Intellectual Property Regimes

As already mentioned, intellectual property regimes achieve their objectives primarily through the award of exclusive rights to authorise or prohibit certain acts pertaining to the relevant intangible asset (which can be, inter alia, a creation, an invention or a brand).[67] It has also been pointed out that these regimes are relatively blunt, in that the mechanisms on which they are based do not vary depending on the degree of market power enjoyed by the right holder or the features of the relevant market. As a result, they may go beyond what is necessary to achieve their objectives. In some cases (that is, some sectors or markets), the length of protection may exceed the requisite period to appropriately reward the inventive or creative efforts of the right holder.[68] In other instances, a system of compulsory licensing (as opposed to the award of exclusive rights) could have been enough to adequately reward such efforts.[69]

Against this background, it is not surprising that commentators and stakeholders often turn to competition law as the instrument that can rectify intellectual property regimes and bring them closer to the optimum by means of piecemeal intervention. A frequent concern among intellectual property scholars is that – at least in some industries – patent protection may have a negative impact on follow-on innovation by third parties.[70] In such circumstances, the argument goes, the award of exclusive rights may, in the long run, go against the declared objectives of the system. Article 102 TFEU may be used – and has been used – to identify instances in which a refusal to license an intellectual property right may be abusive insofar as it limits innovation[71] – or prevents the emergence of a new product for which there is potential consumer demand.[72]

---

electricity and amending Directive 2012/27/EU [2019] OJ L158/125. For an analysis of the unbundling obligations, see Christopher Jones and William-James Kettlewell (eds), *EU Energy Law*, vol 1 (5th edn, Claeys & Casteels 2020), 113–164.

[67] As explained in Chapter 4, intellectual property sometimes resorts to other, less stringent, means of protection, such as a right to receive remuneration.

[68] Burk and Lemley (n 44).

[69] Ian Ayres and Paul Klemperer, 'The old Limiting Patentees' Market Power Without Reducing Innovation Incentives: The Perverse Benefits of Uncertainty and Non-Injunctive Remedies' (1999) 97 Michigan Law Review 985.

[70] Burk and Lemley (n 44).

[71] *Microsoft* (Case COMP/C-3/37.792) Commission Decision of 24 May 2004; confirmed in Case T-201/04 *Microsoft Corporation v Commission*, EU:T:2007:289.

[72] *Magill TV Guide/ITP, BBC and RTE* (Case IV/31.851) Commission Decision of 21 December 1988; confirmed on appeal in *Magill* (n 23).

A similar question, which has attracted the attention of authorities and commentators, relates to the use of injunctions by patent holders. Intellectual property systems are based on the assumption that the balance between short-run and long-run competition is appropriately struck by giving the patent holder the right to seek an injunction against alleged infringers. As pointed out above in relation to standard-setting, entire libraries questioning the validity of this assumption have been written in the past two decades.[73] In particular, it has been argued that the ability to seek injunctions may not strike the right balance where the relevant patent is part of a standard and the right holder has pledged to license its intellectual property on fair, reasonable and non-discriminatory ('FRAND') conditions.[74] In such circumstances, it is claimed, the patent holder may be able to hold up would-be licensees.[75] Again, Article 102 TFEU has been called upon to rectify the logic of intellectual property and to intervene in instances where bringing an injunction would amount to an abuse of a dominant position.[76]

In the EU, the need to rectify regulation may also come from the inherent friction that exists between the geographic reach of intellectual property rights, which is typically national in scope,[77] and the ambition driving the creation of the internal market, which is to create a space without borders across the EU. The Commission may propose legislation aimed at integrating national systems and easing cross-border trade. Legislative action in this sense tends to weaken intellectual property rights, as they tend to follow national borders. For instance, the SatCab Directive introduced the so-called country of origin principle, which allows a licensee in one Member to broadcast via satellite in the whole of the EU.[78] This principle manages the trade-off between market integration and intellectual property protection by favouring the former. For the same reasons, the EU legislature may be reluctant to undermine national regimes. As discussed in Chapter 7, when the Commission is unable to fully advance its market integration agenda via the legislative route, it may choose to do so via competition law enforcement.

---

[73] See above n 72.
[74] See above, Lemley and Shapiro (n 45).
[75] Ibid and above n 72.
[76] Case C-170/13 *Huawei Technologies Co. Ltd v ZTE Corp. and ZTE Deutschland GmbH*, EU:C:2015:477.
[77] Even though harmonisation efforts have reduced this friction, and even though some EU-wide titles have been created in the meantime, the geographic mismatch between national titles and the internal market continues to give rise to disputes and litigation. For an overview of the foundational case law and an explanation of this friction, see Inge Govaere, *The Use and Abuse of Intellectual Property Rights in European Community Law* (Sweet & Maxwell 1996).
[78] Council Directive 93/83/EEC of 27 September 1993 on the coordination of certain rules concerning copyright and rights related to copyright applicable to satellite broadcasting and cable retransmission [1993] OJ L 248/15.

4.3. Consequences for Competition Law

The use of competition law as a means to rectify regulation is not uncontroversial. The main question it raises is whether the application of Articles 101 and 102 TFEU can strike a superior balance between competing aims. The balance enshrined in regulation may be imperfect. However, it is not necessarily any more imperfect than the one that results from the enforcement of competition law. One should note, in this regard, that the latter is, in certain respects, at a relative disadvantage vis-à-vis dedicated regimes. In particular, competition agencies do not have the expertise and resources that their sectoral counterparts do. As a result, it is not clear that, when they strike a different balance (for instance, by forcing a structural divestiture or by banning patentees from bringing an injunction against an alleged infringer), these authorities have the means to evaluate whether their preferred course of action leads to better outcomes.

The enforcement of competition law to rectify regulation is controversial for another reason. It has been frequently claimed, over the past decade, that the application of Articles 101 and 102 TFEU in such a way would lack the necessary legitimacy.[79] Rectifying regulation amounts, the argument goes, to using technocratic mechanisms to overturn the choices made by democratically elected bodies. In the same vein, one could claim, from an administrative law perspective, that this practice amounts to a misuse of power.[80] Articles 101 and 102 TFEU would be enforced, according to this view, to achieve aims other than the creation of a system of undistorted competition. In practice, it may be difficult to substantiate these claims – which, in any event, are not fundamentally different from the concerns expressed above. To the extent that the Commission acts within the scope of its powers and in a lawful manner, it seems difficult to argue that the enforcement of Articles 101 and 102 TFEU is illegitimate, or that it amounts to a misuse of powers.[81]

The fact that using competition law to rectify regulation is not necessarily illegitimate (or does not necessarily amount to a misuse of powers) does not mean that it is without consequences for the system. Addressing matters that are subject to a regulatory regime typically involves the administration of proactive remedies, including ordering divestitures and, more generally, imposing positive obligations. It is not necessary to discuss at length that the enforcement of these obligations is more demanding for a competition authority. As explained in Chapter 1, the design, implementation and monitoring of proactive intervention are, by definition, resource-consuming for an authority. In this sense, rectifying regulation

---

[79] For an in-depth discussion of these arguments, see Niamh Dunne, 'Commitment Decisions in EU Competition Law' (2014) 10 Journal of Competition Law & Economics 399.
[80] See Chapter 15 of Paul Craig, *EU Administrative Law* (3rd edn, Oxford University Press 2019).
[81] Such was the conclusion reached by the General Court in Case T-87/05 *EDP – Energias de Portugal, SA v Commission*, EU:T:2005:333.

exposes the competition law system to the limits of what its institutions can realistically achieve on a sustained basis.

5. Competition Law and the 'Expectation of Regulation'

5.1. Competition Law Intervention as an Anticipation of Regulation

There are two ideas that transpire from the above. The first one is that formal regulation may not be adopted in a timely manner, especially where it requires enacting fresh legislation. In addition, the legislative process does not necessarily yield optimal outcomes. The second idea is that competition law, due to its flexibility, can mimic the techniques and aims that are generally attained via legislation. Against this background, it is not surprising that some stakeholders, and the general public, regard competition law as a blank slate that can readily regulate matters in the same way formal regimes do. Articles 101 and 102 TFEU, in other words, are seen as an off-the-shelf mechanism that can satisfy an 'expectation of regulation', if only on a temporary basis. As mentioned in Chapter 1, competition law is sometimes applied not to fill gaps or to rectify an existing regulatory framework, but to set up one such framework from scratch.

An 'expectation of regulation' tends to develop in industries that – just like telecommunications and energy – feature segments that are structurally unsuited for competition. Because of these features, some market players may find themselves in a position that is not fundamentally different from that enjoyed by incumbents in network industries, in the sense that they have the ability and incentive to leverage their position to adjacent segments and exploit their market power vis-à-vis suppliers and customers. The application of competition law to set up a de facto regime responding to these concerns is a challenge for the competition law system. Absent formal regulation, the design, implementation and monitoring of proactive remedies lies exclusively with the competition authority.

Two examples illustrate how competition law can provide a response to the expectation of regulation (at least temporarily). One is abundantly discussed elsewhere in this volume: online platforms. By the late 2010s, the view among most stakeholders and authorities was that the position enjoyed by Big Tech in at least some digital markets required some form of regulation complementing Articles 101 and 102 TFEU. It is in that context that the Digital Markets Act, analysed in Chapter 5, was proposed and eventually adopted. Prior to submitting its legislative proposal, the Commission opened several competition law investigations addressing the sort of concerns that the ad hoc regime would eventually cover. The remedies administered in these investigations had a distinctive proactive flavour that met the growing expectation of regulatory intervention.

In *Google Shopping*, for instance, the decision ordered the dominant firm to abide by the principle of equal treatment when presenting search results.[82] Intervention in the case amounted, in effect, to requiring the operator of the bottleneck segment to place on an equal footing its own services and those of rivals operating on an adjacent market. As explained above, these non-discrimination obligations are frequent in utilities regulation: they typically accompany access duties. *Android* shared a similar concern with the treatment of rivals on a market adjacent to the bottleneck segment. Inter alia, the Commission argued that tying behaviour gave the dominant firm's services a significant competitive advantage over competing ones.[83] Again, remedial action demanded that the undertaking's affiliate and its rivals be placed on an equal footing.[84] These cases are discussed at length in Chapter 8.

A second example in which competition law applied ahead of a regulatory regime is that of payment systems. Card payment systems, which are best analysed as co-operative joint ventures,[85] share some features with telecommunications activities and other bottlenecks – such as operating systems – in that they display network effects.[86] The fundamental concern behind the investigations opened by the Commission had to do with the fact that the operation of the system tends to lead, by its very nature, to high prices. As explained by the authority in its *MasterCard* decision, the joint venture created an incentive to inflate the fees paid by banks.[87] In addition, the Commission showed that competition between payment systems had the perverse effect of inflating prices across the board.[88]

Dealing with the operation of card payment systems, and remedying the infringements identified, involved engaging in the sort of proactive intervention that competition authorities used to avoid. It is not a secret that the Commission is, and has always been, reluctant to dictate the prices at which products are to be sold, particularly so on a continuous basis.[89] Regulatory authorities, on the other hand, are equipped to administer such obligations, which frequently are central to their remit. Following a saga of cases dealing with card payment systems, the matter was eventually addressed by means of regulation.[90] The legislative

---

[82] *Google Search (Shopping)* (Case AT.39740) Commission Decision of 27 June 2017, para 699.
[83] *Google Android* (Case AT.40099) Commission Decision of 18 July 2018.
[84] Ibid, para 1396.
[85] David S Evans and Richard Schmalensee, 'Economic Aspects of Payment Card Systems and Antitrust Policy Toward Joint Ventures' (1995) 63 Antitrust Law Journal 861.
[86] Case C-67/13 P *Groupement des cartes bancaires (CB) v European Commission*, EU:C:2014:2204, para 74.
[87] *MasterCard, EuroCommerce* and *Commercial Cards* (Cases COMP/34.579, COMP/36.518 and COMP/38.580) Commission Decision of 19 December 2007. See also Case T-111/08, *MasterCard, Inc. and MasterCard Europe v Commission*, EU:T:2012:260, which dismissed the challenge against the decision.
[88] Ibid, para 409.
[89] Niamh Dunne, 'Regulating Prices in the European Union' (2018) 37 Yearbook of European Law 344.
[90] Regulation 2015/751 (n 14).

instrument, adopted in 2015, directly caps the percentage that can be charged per transaction.[91] The level was equivalent to that achieved by the Commission in the aftermath of its competition law investigations.[92]

5.2. Consequences for Competition Law

Dealing with the 'expectation of regulation' by means of competition law enforcement is not without consequences for Articles 101 and 102 TFEU. Some of these consequences have already been addressed. In particular, the sort of remedial intervention that is required from authorities has been discussed at some length. In cases like *Google Shopping* and *Android*, the design and implementation of the relevant remedy was protracted and remained controversial months, if not years, following the finding of infringement.[93] These investigations not only exposed the institutional limits of competition law enforcement. They are also notable in that intervention altered the balance between the various interests that the platform operator sought to advance. In *Android*, for instance, the firm had to find a new way to address the trade-off between the openness of the business model and its ability to appropriate its investments.

One can think of another consequence that arises in instances where Articles 101 and 102 TFEU address, imperfectly, an 'expectation of regulation'. In these instances, competition law may be applied with a view to achieving particular outcomes, as opposed to evaluating, case-by-case, whether a given practice amounts to an infringement. In other words, the relationship between process and outcomes may be reversed: the result sought (a particular form of proactive intervention) would determine whether or not the behaviour amounts to an infringement. As a result, it may not be obvious to reconcile the reasoning in these cases and in the relevant precedents. In the same vein, legal certainty and predictability may suffer. As explained in Chapter 2, the reversal in the relationship between process and outcomes is part of a broader phenomenon in contemporary EU competition law.

---

[91] Ibid, Article 3.
[92] *Mastercard II* (Case AT.40049) Commission Decision of 29 April 2019; and *Visa MIF* (Case AT.39398) Commission Decision of 29 April 2019.
[93] This issue will be addressed at length in Chapter 8.

4

Competition Law and Intangible Property

1. The Features of Intangible Property: Public and Private Responses

The relationship between competition law and intangible assets – whether or not these are protected by intellectual property rights – has never been an easy one. It has given rise to countless discussions in the literature.[1] Such an uneasy balance is, by and large, a function of the nature of intangible property and the consequences that follow from this fact. Non-physical assets are peculiar in the sense that they have the features of a public good.[2] Thus, they are, first and foremost, non-rival in use. This means that consumption of the asset by an individual does not affect consumption by another one.[3] For instance, two individuals can listen simultaneously to the same song or can benefit from the same invention – say, a portable device used to play a recording of the song – without interfering with one another. A pure public good is also non-excludable, by which it is meant that consumption of the asset is in principle very difficult, if not impossible, to prevent.[4]

Because of their nature (that is, because firms that produce them may not be able to reap the fruits of their efforts), investment in intangible assets may be below the social optimum. In other words, the unconstrained play of market forces may not lead to efficient outcomes. If third parties cannot be easily prevented from exploiting a good that is non-rival in use, it is not obvious to see what incentives a profit-maximising firm will have to engage in inventive or creative activities. The risk of underinvestment in public goods elicits responses from public

---

[1] The literature on the topic is virtually countless. Among the many contributions, see Christina Bohannan and Herbert Hovenkamp, *Creation without Restraint: Promoting Liberty & Rivalry in Innovation* (Oxford University Press 2011); Mark Lemley, 'A New Balance between IP and Antitrust' (2007) 13 Southwestern Journal of Law and Trade in the Americas 237; and Ioannis Lianos, 'Competition Law and Intellectual Property Rights: Is the Property Rights' Approach Right?' (2006) 8 Cambridge Yearbook of European Law 153.

[2] For a basic overview of the concept of public good, see for instance Gregory N Mankiw and Mark P Taylor, *Economics* (3rd edn, Cengage 2014), 221–225.

[3] Ibid, 222.

[4] Ibid, 224.

authorities and from the private sector. The point of these interventions is to create mechanisms that allow the appropriability, by inventors and creators, of the social benefits resulting from their investments.[5] Public authorities achieve appropriability either by subsidising their investments or by creating legal mechanisms that make appropriability possible.

There is no need to explain at length that the award of intellectual property rights is among such mechanisms, and the one that will be discussed at length in this chapter.[6] The primary technique on which intellectual property systems rely to provide appropriability is the use of legal barriers preventing third parties from replicating a creation or invention. Typically, these systems give right holders exclusivity over certain acts (for instance, the manufacture and first sale of goods embedding the creation or invention), which they may authorise or prohibit for a limited period (20 years in the case of patents[7] and 70 years after the death of the author in the case of copyright[8]) or, in the case of trade marks, for as long as they are exploited.[9] Other mechanisms to incentivise investments in public goods include the subsidisation of certain activities, such as fundamental research.[10]

Private operators rely on various contractual and non-contractual devices to protect the value of intangible property. A number of reasons explain this behaviour. First, the scope of intellectual property rights is limited. The conditions for protection are not met in all circumstances: some creations or inventions do not satisfy the relevant standards (a given creation, for instance, may not reach the originality threshold required by copyright legislation). Even when a creation or invention fulfils the relevant conditions, exclusivity only encompasses certain activities and leaves others outside of its ambit of protection. Intellectual property rights are said to be 'exhausted' once the activities falling within their scope are performed.[11] For instance, once a good embedding a patent is first put on the market with its consent, the patentee can no longer rely on its title to prevent subsequent sales by third parties.[12]

There is a chance, second, that the creator or inventor prefers not to seek intellectual property protection, as the award of rights comes with trade-offs. Patents,

---

[5] Carl Shapiro, 'Competition and Innovation: Did Arrow Hit the Bull's Eye?' in Josh Lerner and Scott Stern (eds), *The Rate and Direction of Inventive Activity Revisited* (University of Chicago Press 2012), 364.

[6] For an overview, see William M Landes and Richard A Posner, *The Economic Structure of Intellectual Property Law* (Belknap 2003).

[7] Article 63 of the European Patent Convention.

[8] Directive 2006/116/EC of the European Parliament and of the Council of 12 December 2006 on the term of protection of copyright and certain related rights [2006] OJ L372/12.

[9] Regulation (EU) 2017/1001 of the European Parliament and of the Council of 14 June 2017 on the European Union trade mark [2017] OJ L154/1.

[10] Communication from the Commission Framework for State aid for research and development and innovation [2022] OJ C414/1.

[11] See Article 4 of Directive 2001/29/EC of the European Parliament and of the Council of 22 May 2001 on the harmonisation of certain aspects of copyright and related rights in the information society [2001] OJ L167/10 (hereinafter, the InfoSoc Directive).

[12] Ibid, Recital 28.

just to mention the most obvious example, come with a duty to disclose the relevant invention. In addition, exclusivity is limited in time: once the 20-year period of exclusivity comes to an end, the innovator will have to accept competition from third parties. Entry by generic producers in the pharmaceutical sector, which will be discussed at length hereinafter, exemplifies this trade-off well. Against this background (and to the extent that it is feasible), an inventor may conclude that it is in its best interest to keep its invention as an unprotected trade secret. In this vein, the inventor may for instance resort to technological solutions instead of legal devices. Experience suggests that the biggest hurdle for would-be rivals is not necessarily the fact that the relevant information is protected by intellectual property rights, but the fact that it can only be accessed with the holder's consent.[13]

More frequently, third, the holder of an intellectual property right relies on contractual arrangements, such as licensing, to monetise its intangible assets. It may do so because it lacks the technical capabilities or the financial means to exploit an invention (or creation); or it may simply be the case that it is more convenient to rely on a third party to make the most of it. A licensing agreement is likely to provide for restraints aimed at protecting the value of the relevant intellectual property right. For instance, the contract may confine the licence to a particular application of the invention (what is known as a field-of-use restriction).[14] Similarly, it may provide for contractual restrictions aimed at ensuring that the exploitation of the right by a third party in a given territory does not affect its own exclusivity in other areas.[15]

Decades of competition law enforcement provide countless examples of how contractual arrangements may be relied upon to preserve the value of intangible assets – irrespective of whether these are protected by intellectual property. A few factual scenarios exemplify the role of agreements in this regard. Consider, first, the dispute in *Remia*.[16] That case concerned a non-compete obligation imposed by the seller of a business to its buyer. As explained by the Court of Justice (hereinafter, the 'Court') in its ruling, the point of such a contractual device is to preserve the value of the intangible property (the goodwill) associated with the physical assets that are transferred to the buyer.[17] *Coty* provides a similar example. This case concerned the lawfulness of a selective distribution system. As part of the agreement, the supplier imposed on its distributors a range of contractual restraints aimed at protecting its luxury image by preventing, inter alia, the sale of its product via third-party online marketplaces with which it was not affiliated.[18]

---

[13] John Temple Lang, 'Mandating Access: The Principles and the Problems in Intellectual Property and Competition Policy' (2004) 15 European Business Law Review 1087.
[14] Guidelines on the application of Article 101 of the Treaty on the Functioning of the European Union to technology transfer agreements [2014] OJ C89/3, paras 208–215.
[15] Ibid, paras 105–114.
[16] Case 42/84 *Remia BV and others v Commission*, EU:C:1985:327.
[17] Ibid, para 19.
[18] Case C-567/18 *Coty Germany GmbH v Amazon Services Europe Sàrl and Others*, EU:C:2020:267.

Consider, in addition, the preliminary reference in *Pronuptia*. In that case, the Court evaluated the compatibility of franchising agreements with Article 101(1) TFEU. The point of franchising as a distribution system is to allow a firm to exploit its formula by relying on independent third parties. Franchising involves the licensing of intellectual property (such as trade marks) and know-how (including trade secrets) to ensure that the look-and-feel of the franchisor's premises can be replicated by third parties. The transfer of intangible property comes with a number of restraints aimed at preserving its value. In particular, the franchisor will seek to ensure that its assets do not benefit economic activities competing with its own and, conversely, that its brand image is not negatively affected by the activities of the franchisee.[19]

Finally, there is a long line of case law and administrative practice dealing with territorial restraints imposed in the context of licensing agreements. Think of the dispute at stake in *Coditel II*.[20] The copyright holder had given territorial exclusivity to its Belgian licensee for a period of seven years. As part of this agreement, the latter had the right to authorise or prohibit, within Belgium, any broadcasting of the film.[21] As noted by the Advocate General in his Opinion, the rationale for the restraint was the protection of the intangible property that was covered by the licence.[22] Since a broadcast is itself non-rival in use, it is reasonable to expect that a would-be recipient will demand protection from broadcasts coming from other territories as a condition for the award of the licence.[23]

2. The Complex Relationship between Competition Law and Intellectual Property

2.1. Objectives: Static and Dynamic Competition

Virtually any text dealing with the relationship between competition law and intellectual property will start by clarifying that, in spite of the appearances and the occasional conflicts between them, both disciplines pursue the same objectives.[24] Even though there is no real controversy around the point, it makes sense to address at some length why such conflict may be said to exist, and why

---

[19] Case 161/84 *Pronuptia de Paris GmbH v Pronuptia de Paris Irmgard Schillgallis*, EU:C:1986:41, paras 16–17.
[20] Case 262/81 *Coditel SA, Compagnie générale pour la diffusion de la télévision, and others v Ciné-Vog Films SA and others*, EU:C:1982:334.
[21] Ibid, para 3.
[22] Opinion of Advocate General Reischl in Case 262/81 *Coditel SA, Compagnie générale pour la diffusion de la télévision, and others v Ciné-Vog Films SA and others*, EU:C:1982:290, 3411–3412.
[23] Ibid.
[24] See for instance the Guidelines on technology transfer agreements (n 14), para 7.

it is more seeming than real. The argument can be summarised as follows: both competition law and intellectual property are concerned with the static and dynamic dimensions of competition and both disciplines agree that the latter dimension is more important for long-term prosperity and the welfare of consumers. By the same token, it would be incorrect to state that competition law is not concerned with innovation and/or dynamic competition, or that intellectual property is only preoccupied with these.

Static competition refers to the intensity of rivalry that exists at a given point in time. It is generally associated with the notion of market power.[25] The task of modern competition law is precisely the prevention of the creation or the strengthening of positions of market power. The protection of the static dimension of the process can be expected to bring benefits in the form of allocative and productive efficiency and, in the same vein, the protection of consumers' interests.[26] Intellectual property, by contrast, works precisely by raising legal barriers to entry (that is, by creating the legal conditions in which right holders can enjoy and exercise market power). From this perspective, the latter discipline can be said to be at odds with the protection of static competition. This view, however, ignores that intellectual property is typically enjoyed for a limited period of time. As mentioned above, the patent system (just to mention an example) is designed to undermine the market power enjoyed by the incumbent after the period of protection.[27]

Dynamic competition, on the other hand, refers to the long-run dimension of the phenomenon. The expression refers, in other words, to a reality in which firms seek to outperform one another by improving existing products and services, and by developing new ones (as opposed to competing at a given point in time with an existing product or technology). It is the process that leads, for instance, to the replacement of cassettes by mp3 and then by streaming,[28] or to the rise of smartphones as a substitute of regular mobile phones. If market power is central to the concept of static competition, dynamic competition revolves essentially around innovation. The consensus among economists is that innovation, rather than short-run allocative and productive efficiency, is more important for prosperity and consumers' well-being.[29]

As explained above, intellectual property is based on the idea that erecting legal barriers to entry (and thus creating the conditions for the creation and exercise of market power positions) provides the necessary incentives for firms

---

[25] For an overview, see J Gregory Sidak and David J Teece, 'Dynamic Competition in Antitrust Law' (2009) 5 Journal of Competition Law & Economics 581.
[26] Guidelines on the application of Article 81(3) of the Treaty [2004] C101/97, para 13.
[27] In particular, Article 83 of the European Patent Convention requires the disclosure of the invention as a quid pro quo for the award of the exclusive rights associated with the patent.
[28] Example used in Mark A Lemley, 'Industry-Specific Antitrust Policy for Innovation' (2011) Columbia Business Law Review 637 ('ask yourself whether you would rather have a monopolistically-priced iPod or a perfectly competitive market for 8-track tapes').
[29] Ibid.

to create and innovate.³⁰ One may be tempted to argue, conversely, that competition law is not concerned with innovation. There would be reasons to claim that Articles 101 and 102 TFEU are at odds with intellectual property. To the extent that they seek to prevent the creation and the strengthening of positions of market power, they would be directly at odds with the spirit and operation of, inter alia, patent and copyright legislation. If intellectual property sees the (temporary) insulation from the static dimension of the process as essential to innovation, competition law is based on the opposite idea.

This understanding of competition law, however popular, does not accurately reflect the reality of the discipline. Articles 101 and 102 TFEU are concerned with the dynamic dimension of the competitive process, as well as with innovation. What is more, competition law does not dispute that innovation drives prosperity in the long run and that protecting intangible assets is necessary to attain long-run inter-firm rivalry. The case law that best exemplifies how the discipline deals with dynamic competition is the *Magill* doctrine.³¹ This line of case law addresses the question of whether a refusal to license an intellectual property right amounts to an abuse of a dominant position. If the discipline were only concerned with the static dimension of competition, any refusal to deal would be a breach of Article 102 TFEU. Once produced, information can be easily reproduced. From a purely static standpoint, mandating shared access to intellectual property would be the efficient outcome.

However, the Court ruled in *Magill* (and then again in *IMS Health*³²) that a refusal to license an intellectual property right is only abusive in exceptional circumstances, to be established on a case-by-case basis. The rationale behind these conditions was lucidly spelled out by Advocate General Jacobs in *Bronner*.³³ In line with the discussion above, the Opinion noted that, in the short term, requiring a right holder to share its intellectual property with third parties may seem pro-competitive, and this insofar as it increases rivalry and is likely to lead to a drop in prices. In the long run, however, allowing holders to make use of their property as they see fit would be more conducive to competition. This is so, as explained by Advocate General Jacobs, because mandating shared access too readily would impact negatively on firms' incentives to invest and innovate.³⁴ This same reasoning was embraced by the Court in *Slovak Telekom*.³⁵

---

[30] The idea underlying intellectual property is not universally accepted. See in particular Michele Boldrin and David Levine, 'The Case against Intellectual Property' (2009) 92 American Economic Review 209.
[31] Joined Cases C-241/91 P and C-242/91 P *Radio Telefis Eireann (RTE) and Independent Television Publications Ltd (ITP) v Commission*, EU:C:1995:98 ('*Magill*').
[32] Case C-418/01 *IMS Health GmbH & Co. OHG v NDC Health GmbH & Co. KG*, EU:C:2004:257.
[33] Opinion of AG Jacobs in Case C-7/97 *Oscar Bronner GmbH & Co. KG v Mediaprint Zeitungs- und Zeitschriftenverlag GmbH & Co. KG and others*, EU:C:1998:264.
[34] Ibid, para 57.
[35] Case C-165/19 P *Slovak Telekom, a.s. v Commission*, EU:C:2021:239, para 47.

Article 101 TFEU case law also provides abundant examples showing that competition law is concerned with the dynamic dimension of rivalry, and that limiting static competition may be justified to preserve firms' incentives to invest and innovate. *Nungesser*,[36] for instance, concerned the lawfulness of an exclusive territorial licence covering a plant variety. As part of the agreement, the licensor committed not to exploiting the intangible property itself in the territory covered by the licence and not to giving a licence to third parties in that same territory.[37] In its assessment of the question, the Court noted that the development of the plant variety was the result of years of 'research and experimentation' and that the exclusivity made it possible to offer a technology in another territory where it was unknown.[38] In those circumstances, the Court ruled that the abovementioned restraints – which inevitably affected static competition – did not violate Article 101(1) TFEU.[39]

2.2. Balance between Appropriability and Contestability

Once it is accepted that both competition law and intellectual property are concerned with static and dynamic competition, and that ultimately the latter is more relevant for long-term prosperity and consumer well-being, the question that follows is how to make sense of the seeming divergence between competition law and intellectual property. As already explained above, the former is primarily concerned with preventing the creation and strengthening of market power, whereas the second favours structures in which market power can both emerge and be exercised. While they may seem contradictory on the surface, both disciplines promote the two necessary ingredients to achieve dynamic competition, namely appropriability and contestability. This framework was relied upon by Carl Shapiro in a celebrated piece.[40]

The concept of appropriability has been discussed at some length above. Creative and inventive activities are unlikely to take place (and if they do take place, they are likely to be below the social optimum) where firms or individuals lack the means to reap the fruits of their efforts (or, as Shapiro puts it, the 'social benefits resulting from [their] innovation'[41]). The intellectual property system incentivises innovation by signalling to firms and individuals that they will be insulated, to some degree, from imitation. Contestability is an equally important ingredient for innovation. As explained by Shapiro, this concept refers to the prospect of gaining market share by offering new or better products and services.

---

[36] Case 268/78 *L.C. Nungesser KG and Kurt Eisele v Commission*, EU:C:1982:211.
[37] Ibid, para 49.
[38] Ibid, para 56.
[39] Ibid, para 58.
[40] Shapiro (n 5).
[41] Ibid, 364.

Innovation is unlikely to happen if the position enjoyed by incumbents cannot be challenged by new entrants. In such circumstances, established players will not fear the threat of entry (and thus would not be pressed to innovate) and potential entrants would not see the interest in engaging in creative or inventive activities, as the effort would not pay off. Once the contestability principle is considered, it is easy to understand why preserving static competition may be conducive to innovation. A merger between the only two firms in a market with very high (or insurmountable) barriers to entry[42] would make it unlikely to see new players, at least in the short term. Following the merger, it is not immediately obvious to see where the impetus for innovation might come from.

Summing up, incentives to innovate can be expected to exist, according to Shapiro, where firms and individuals have the prospect that their creative and innovative efforts will pay off. They will pay off when they can be expected to result in them gaining market share at the expense of actual or potential rivals (contestability) all while allowing them to capture the benefits flowing from them (appropriability). A legal regime that seeks to incentivise innovation will, accordingly, try to promote both contestability and appropriability, and strike the right balance between both. Competition law is one such regime. While the discipline is typically associated with the protection of static competition (and thus contestability), the examples discussed above show that concerns with appropriability are at the heart of many legal doctrines.

In fact, one could characterise competition law as a discipline that revolves around the balance between contestability and appropriability. From this perspective, the essential task of courts and authorities is to identify which restraints limiting static competition are acceptable in the name of appropriability, and which amount to a breach. Rules are crafted and refined accordingly. In some cases, a practice linked to the appropriability of a creation or an invention, such as a refusal to license an intellectual property right, will be deemed lawful absent exceptional circumstances. In other instances, a more in-depth case-by-case assessment is required to establish whether appropriability justifies restraining static competition. If, as in *Nungesser*, it appears that territorial restraints are objectively necessary for a licensee to invest in the development of a new technology, the relevant clauses will escape the prohibition altogether. The opposite may be true where the factual circumstances differ.

Conversely, it is difficult to argue that intellectual property is not concerned with contestability. In line with the points made above, contestability is at the heart of the discipline. For instance, the fact that the award of a patent is subject to a disclosure obligation, and that it is granted for a limited period of time, shows that intellectual property systems have in-built mechanisms to discipline incumbent

---

[42] Shapiro (n 5) mentions the example of the *Genzyme/Novazyme* merger (*Genzyme Corporation/Novazyme Pharmaceuticals, Inc.*, File No. 021 0026), which involved the only two firms engaged in research and development in relation to a particular drug.

players. One should bear in mind, in addition, that many sub-fields (suffice it to think of copyright) provide for exceptions to exclusivity that allow for entry and the use of protected information. Finally, intellectual property is compatible with contestability in a different sense: by promising a reward for inventive and creative efforts, the system offers the prospect of challenging existing players with superior goods and services; and provides the impetus for entry to happen.

2.3. Techniques: Case-by-case vs Across-the-board Intervention

The discussion above shows that competition law and intellectual property do not diverge because of the objectives they pursue, or because they have different priorities. The divergence has to do, instead, with the techniques through which the two disciplines attain their aims. Competition law follows an approach that can be labelled contextual, in the sense that it is tailored to the specific circumstances of each case (and the economic and legal context of which the behaviour is a part). As a result, the balancing between appropriability and contestability is undertaken on a case-by-case basis. Intellectual property, on the other hand, follows an approach that is cruder in nature, and this insofar as it provides the same response across the board and leaves little room, if any, for contextual considerations.

If there is something that characterises contemporary competition law, it is the fact that intervention demands a context-specific assessment of behaviours and transactions. A restriction of competition within the meaning of Article 101(1) TFEU, or an abuse of a dominant position under Article 102 TFEU, cannot be established in the abstract. The question of whether the object and/or the effect of a practice amounts to a prima facie breach necessitates an evaluation of the relevant economic and legal context. For instance, the very same agreement (from a formal standpoint) may be deemed anticompetitive by its very nature in a particular factual scenario, but not in another one. Similarly, the assessment of the impact of conduct on competition is sensitive to factors such as the coverage of the practice, the nature of the product and the degree of market power.

Suffice it to mention some examples to show how contextual considerations impact on the balance between appropriability and contestability. To begin with, the holder of an intellectual property right cannot be compelled to deal with would-be licensees unless the latter (or a competition authority) can show, to the requisite legal standard, that the title in question is indispensable. As explained by the Court in *IMS Health*, establishing indispensability demands assessing whether there are alternative ways, even if less advantageous, to compete on the relevant adjacent market and whether it is economically feasible to duplicate the input.[43]

---

[43] *IMS Health* (n 32), para 28.

By definition, an assessment of this nature is context-specific and can only be undertaken by paying attention to the competitive dynamics of the relevant market. The same is true of the so-called 'new product' condition, which demands evidence that the refusal would prevent the launch of a new product for which there is potential consumer demand.[44]

The *Nungesser* case, discussed above, provides an additional example of how contextual considerations may influence (or even determine) the outcome of a case. As already pointed out, the Court, when concluding that the territorial restraints fell outside the scope of Article 101(1) TFEU, gave particular weight to the fact that the technology was new and that it was the result of considerable research efforts.[45] In addition, it emphasised the importance of allowing the licensee to appropriate the fruit of its efforts in the new territory.[46] The conclusion may have been a different one in another economic and legal context. A similar approach can be found in the Block Exemption Regulation on technology transfer agreements, which makes the legality of licensing arrangements hinge, in particular, on the degree of market power enjoyed by the parties. More precisely, the instrument relies on market share thresholds to identify the instances in which appropriability is unlikely to give rise to concerns.[47]

The operation of intellectual property regimes is markedly different. The protection awarded by virtue of a patent, or copyright, is not the outcome of a contextual evaluation of the adequate length of protection to incentivise investment and innovation. A patent is granted for a period of 20 years irrespective of the features of the relevant economic sector and irrespective of the market power it confers on the title holder.[48] In addition, there are virtually no ex post mechanisms aimed at evaluating whether the degree of protection was excessive, or whether the exercise of the rights conferred by a title hinders follow-on innovation that would be socially beneficial.[49] From this perspective (and in particular when compared with the operation of competition law), intellectual property is a fairly blunt instrument. It has frequently been criticised, in fact, for that very reason. Some authors, for instance, point out that the assumptions underpinning the patent system do not reflect the reality of how intellectual property is exploited.[50]

---

[44] Ibid, para 49.
[45] *Nungesser* (n 36), para 56.
[46] Ibid, para 57.
[47] Commission Regulation (EU) No 316/2014 of 21 March 2014 on the application of Article 101(3) of the Treaty on the Functioning of the European Union to categories of technology transfer agreements [2014] OJ L93/17.
[48] For a critical analysis of the blunt nature of patent protection, see Dan L. Burk and Mark A. Lemley, *The Patent Crisis and How the Courts Can Solve It* (University of Chicago Press 2011).
[49] A compulsory licence may be imposed in a restrictive set of circumstances. For an overview, see Lionel Bently and others, *Intellectual Property Law* (5th edn, Oxford University Press 2018). For an application, see Siva Thambisetty and others, 'Addressing Vaccine Inequity During the COVID-19 Pandemic: The TRIPS Intellectual Property Waiver Proposal and Beyond' (2022) 81 Cambridge Law Journal 384.
[50] See for instance Mark A Lemley and Carl Shapiro, 'Patent Holdup and Royalty Stacking' (2007) 85 Texas Law Review 1991.

2.4. Discussion: Between Deference and Fine Tuning

The analysis above suggests that any tension between competition law and intellectual property, to the extent that it exists, is the result of a difference concerning the techniques on which they rely to attain their aims. Both disciplines agree on the necessary ingredients to preserve firms' ability and incentives to invest and innovate, but they do so in a different way. If competition law favours a case-by-case, context-specific calibration of the balance between appropriability and contestability, intellectual property provides a uniform response that does not adjust the degree or length of protection to the idiosyncrasies of the industry or the market where the title is awarded. As a result of this tension in terms of techniques, authorities and claimants may feel tempted to rely on competition law provisions to reduce the reach of intellectual property, or to limit the range of rights over which it confers control. In other words, Articles 101 and 102 TFEU could be used as a means to correct the perceived excesses of the latter. Competition law may also be relied upon to achieve, case-by-case, the opposite, that is, to extend the reach of intellectual property protection beyond its formal scope of application.

Against this background, and to the extent that Articles 101 and 102 TFEU can intervene on a piecemeal basis to address suboptimal outcomes, competition law could in theory become a 'catch-all' corrective mechanism. Such an (interventionist) approach to the enforcement of Articles 101 and 102 TFEU would allow courts and authorities to interfere with any aspect of the intellectual property regime (such as the length or scope of protection, or the range of acts that the right holder can authorise or prohibit). An alternative approach can be termed deferential. Under this second understanding of the relationship between the two disciplines, competition law would refrain from second-guessing intellectual property systems, at least absent exceptional circumstances. By the same token, case-by-case intervention under Articles 101 and 102 TFEU would only come into play outside the range of acts covered by the relevant title.

Competition law regimes oscillate between the temptation to interfere with intellectual property regimes in the name of static rivalry and the reluctance to do so. The EU system is not an exception in this sense. Fine-tuning intellectual property titles often demands the sort of proactive intervention discussed in Chapter 1 and is therefore typically resource-consuming and challenging. A deferential approach, on the other hand, may leave a wide range of acts outside of the reach of competition authorities and thus err on the side of underenforcement. The European Commission's (hereinafter, the 'Commission') approach to intellectual property (and to intangible property more generally) has followed the same path as the rest of its policy-making activity. Accordingly, it has progressively become less deferential and less reluctant to venture into the very scope of the titles protecting intangible assets.

3. The Deferential Approach to Intangible Property

3.1. The Existence/Exercise Divide in Competition Law

The deferential approach to intangible property (including intellectual property) dominated the enforcement landscape during the formative years of the discipline. It has a number of distinctive features. The first of these, already apparent in *Consten-Grundig*, is the divide between the existence and the exercise of intellectual property rights. While competition law can apply to the latter, it does not question the former.[51] Accordingly, a title existing under national law will be assumed to exist, be valid, and remain in force, when the application of Articles 101 and 102 TFEU is at stake. In the same vein, a finding of infringement cannot be based, inter alia, on the fact that the right is weak, that the title may have been wrongly granted and/or is of dubious validity. For instance, claims to the effect that process patents in the pharmaceutical sector tend to be declared invalid would not be relevant.

There are two central judgments that confirmed the deferential attitude. One of them is *Magill*. A question that dominated the dispute, both implicitly and explicitly, was the controversy around whether the information at stake in the case (programme listings issued by broadcasters) was worthy of protection.[52] While protected by copyright in the relevant Member State – Ireland – it would not have met the threshold of originality in continental systems. Moreover, it was deemed a mere by-product that did not require any inventive or creative efforts.[53] The Court could have chosen to rule that the refusal to share the relevant data was not abusive insofar as the programme listings were not the sort of information that deserves to be insulated from rivalry. However, its ruling did not rely on this fact, and took the existence of copyright as given. Thus, the conditions set out in the judgment apply irrespective of whether intellectual property protection is controversial.

A second judgment is *Generics*, in the pharmaceutical industry.[54] Process patents are a central aspect of the relevant economic and legal context of this and other cases raising similar issues. They were central because intellectual protection could no longer be claimed in relation to the active ingredient itself (as the period of protection had already come to an end). Accordingly, the only plausible means to prevent entry by generic manufacturers was to claim that, even though the active ingredient no longer benefitted from protection, the manufacturing

---

[51] Joined Cases 56 and 58/64 *Établissements Consten S.à.R.L. and Grundig-Verkaufs-GmbH v Commission*, EU:C:1966:41, 345.
[52] See in this sense Opinion of Advocate General Gulmann in Joined Cases C-241/91 P and C-242/91 P *Radio Telefís Eireann (RTE) and Independent Television Publications Ltd (ITP) v Commission*, EU:C:1994:210.
[53] For a discussion, see Eleonora Rosati, *Originality in EU Copyright Full Harmonization through Case Law* (Elgar 2013).
[54] Case C-307/18, *Generics (UK) Ltd and others v Competition and Markets Authority*, EU:C:2020:52.

process did. The peculiarity of process patents is that they are found, relatively frequently, to be invalid when challenged.[55] Accordingly, one could have argued that such titles do not prevent entry insofar as the probability of them being declared invalid is high (or higher than their validity being upheld).[56] As in *Magill*, however, the Court rejected this route. It instructed the national court to perform its analysis as if the process patents were valid and in force.[57] The question to be answered, accordingly, did not have to do with the relative strength of the process patent but with whether it raises 'insurmountable barriers to entry' precluding actual or potential competition from a generic manufacturer.[58]

3.2. The Scope for Intervention under the Deferential Approach

The second feature of the deferential approach relates to the reach of intervention under Articles 101 and 102 TFEU. Under the deferential approach, the acts that are covered by the intellectual property right escape the application of competition law provisions, at least absent exceptional circumstances. If, for instance, an industrial property title gives its holder the exclusive right to manufacture a good incorporating the technology, any practice relating to the exercise of this right would, in principle, fall outside the reach of competition law. On the other hand, Articles 101 and 102 TFEU would come into play where the rights in question are 'exhausted', that is, once the beneficiary can no longer rely on them to prohibit acts by third parties.

This idea can be illustrated by reference to the rights conferred by a patent. As the Court explained in *Centrafarm v Sterling Drug*, industrial property, as a reward for the inventive efforts of the title holder, gives it 'the exclusive right to use an invention with a view to manufacturing industrial products and putting them into circulation for the first time, either directly or by the grant of licences to third parties, as well as the right to oppose infringements'.[59] Under the deferential approach, any practice that remains within the scope of these two activities, pictured in Figure 4.1, would not be subject to scrutiny. Competition law would only come into play once the products are put into circulation by the patentee or with its consent (that is, once the rights conferred by virtue of the patent are exhausted).

---

[55] For a discussion, see *Lundbeck* (Case AT.39226) Commission Decision of 19 June 2013, paras 76–83.
[56] Such, in fact, was the way in which the issue was framed by the Competition Appeal Tribunal in its reference to the Court in *Generics* (n 54), para 21.
[57] Ibid, para 121.
[58] Ibid, para 58.
[59] Case 15/74 *Centrafarm BV and Adriaan de Peijper v Sterling Drug Inc*, EU:C:1974:114, para 9.

Figure 4.1 The deferential approach and the specific subject-matter of a patent

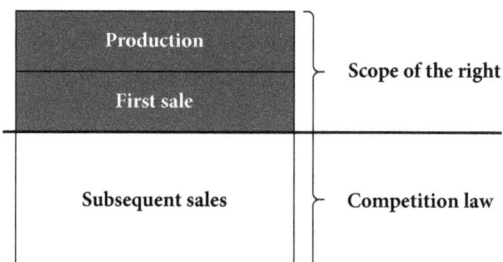

It makes sense to mention some of the activities that escape competition law scrutiny under the deferential approach. For instance, the patentee would be able to bring proceedings against an alleged infringer and, by the same token, reach an out-of-court settlement to avoid litigation. As noted by the Court in *Centrafarm v Sterling Drug*, the exercise of the patent also comprises the exploitation of the title through a licensee (exclusive or non-exclusive), which may manufacture and/or sell the goods incorporating the technology on behalf of the licensor. Where the licence does not exceed the scope of the exclusive rights conferred by virtue of the patent, it would not be in breach of Articles 101 and 102 TFEU. Such an agreement would not give the licensee any more rights than the licensor would have been able to exercise. Similarly, a patentee would also be able to refuse to deal with a third party without being in breach of competition law – at least in principle.

Traditionally, competition law refrained from interfering with the scope of intellectual property rights. *Coditel II*, mentioned above, is an example.[60] As already explained, the exclusive licensee of a film in Belgium sought to prohibit a cable operator from broadcasting it in the territory covered by the agreement. The right invoked in the case was the very right a copyright holder would have been able to invoke to prevent unauthorised broadcasts in the same circumstances. The Court ruled in *Coditel II* that an exclusive territorial licence such as the one at stake in the case is not, in and of itself, contrary to Article 101(1) TFEU. This outcome is not surprising considering that the agreement remained within the scope of the relevant right, which confers on its holder exclusivity over every communication to the public of the protected work (without the right being subject to exhaustion).[61]

Where, conversely, the range of acts covered by the agreement goes beyond the range of acts that the holder can authorise or prohibit by virtue of the intellectual property regime, competition law will apply. According to a long line of case law, agreements giving absolute territorial protection to a distributor, as well as those prohibiting the export of goods to other EU Member States, are prohibited

---

[60] *Coditel II* (n 20).
[61] See in this sense Article 4.2 of the InfoSoc Directive.

as restrictive of competition by object.[62] These cases differ from *Coditel II* in that the rights at stake (the right to distribute the goods embedding the intellectual property on the market for the first time) are subject to the exhaustion doctrine within the EU. Accordingly, the right holder cannot prevent the import and export of products that have been put on the market by it or with its consent. Such activities would fall outside the scope of the intellectual property regime.

One can think of other examples that reflect the deferential approach to intellectual property well. The analysis of the Court in *Windsurfing*, for instance, revolves entirely around whether the restraints imposed by the licensor were within the scope of the patent.[63] The clauses at stake in the case limited the freedom of action of licensees in a number of ways. For instance, they required them to use and sell the invention together with certain products;[64] and to refrain from challenging the validity of the titles.[65] Because they were deemed to fall outside the scope of the patent, these contractual duties were found to be caught by Article 101(1) TFEU. On the other hand, the method of calculating the royalty of the protected invention was not considered to have as its object or effect the restriction of competition, as the remuneration did not exceed what the licensor could obtain from the exploitation of its exclusive right.[66]

Arguably, the *Erauw-Jacquery* judgment,[67] on the exploitation of plant varieties, is even more eloquent about the operation and practical implications of the deferential approach. The case is notable in that it concerned an export prohibition, which is in principle restrictive by object. Because such a restraint is inherently at odds with market integration, it is very unlikely to satisfy the conditions set out in Article 101(3) TFEU.[68] In the specific context of *Erauw-Jacquery*, however, the Court ruled that the export prohibition was not in breach of Article 101(1) TFEU, whether by object or effect.[69] The outcome is explained by the fact that the ban on cross-border sales concerned basic seed, the protection of which is indispensable for the preservation of the plant variety (which has to be distinct, uniform and stable).[70] As noted by the Advocate General in his Opinion, absent these clauses, the intangible property would be lost.[71]

---

[62] *Consten-Grundig* (n 51).
[63] Case 193/83 *Windsurfing International Inc. v Commission*, EU:C:1986:75.
[64] Ibid, para 54.
[65] Ibid, para 89.
[66] Ibid, para 67.
[67] Case 27/87 *SPRL Louis Erauw-Jacquery v La Hesbignonne SC*, EU:C:1988:183.
[68] This principle stems from *Consten-Grundig* (n 51). For an extensive discussion, see Pablo Ibáñez Colomo, 'Article 101 TFEU and Market Integration' (2016) 12 Journal of Competition Law & Economics 749.
[69] *Erauw-Jacquery* (n 67), para 20.
[70] Ibid, para 9. See also Article 6 of Council Regulation (EC) No 2100/94 of 27 July 1994 on Community plant variety rights [1994] OJ L227/1.
[71] Opinion of AG Mischo in Case 27/87 *SPRL Louis Erauw-Jacquery v La Hesbignonne SC*, EU:C:1987:538, para 11 (where the Advocate General explains that '[b]asic seed is to a certain extent comparable to a manufacturing process protected by a patent, since certified seed of the first and second generation intended for sale to farmers for use in cereal production is produced from it').

Finally, *BAT (Toltecs-Dorcet)*,[72] illustrates neatly the room for competition law intervention under the deferential approach. The case concerned a trade mark delimitation agreement, the purpose of which is to deal with a dispute between two title holders. In principle, such arrangements remain within the scope of the exclusive rights, just like licensing. To the extent that they do, a deferential understanding of Article 101(1) TFEU would not see them as restrictive of competition, whether by object or effect. Such, in fact, was the position expressed by the Court in its judgment.[73] In the specific circumstances of the case, however, the agreement could not be said to be a genuine delimitation arrangement and thus fell outside the scope of the intellectual property right. This is so because one of the parties (BAT) sought to obtain, by means of the agreement, the protection that it would no longer be able to attain by means of its trade mark.[74]

In a system that follows the deferential approach, acts that remain within the scope of the title are only anticompetitive in exceptional circumstances, to be established on a case-by-case basis. As already pointed out above, showing that a refusal to license an intellectual property right is abusive is very demanding for authorities and claimants. In accordance with the *Magill* doctrine, it would be necessary for them to show that access to the intellectual property right in question is indispensable for competition on an adjacent market and that, in addition, it prevents the emergence of a new product for which there is potential consumer demand.[75] As clarified by the Court in *IMS Health*, a duty to license cannot be imposed if the third party merely seeks to duplicate the products already offered by the right holder.[76]

3.3. The Balance between Contestability and Appropriability

Because the deferential approach does not question the existence of intellectual property rights and leaves the acts falling within its scope outside of competition law scrutiny, it accepts, as given, the balance between contestability and appropriability that is built into the intellectual property regime (at least so as a matter of principle). Accordingly, it does not enter into the fine-tuning of, inter alia, patent and copyright systems. In particular, the deferential approach does not

---

[72] Case 35/83 BAT *Cigaretten-Fabriken GmbH v Commission*, EU:C:1985:32.
[73] Ibid, para 33 ('[t]he Court acknowledges that, as the applicant and [Germany] submit and the Commission also concedes, agreements known as "delimitation agreements" are lawful and useful if they serve to delimit, in the mutual interest of the parties, the spheres within which their respective trade marks may be used, and are intended to avoid confusion or conflict between them [...]'.
[74] The title at stake was dormant and no longer benefitted from protection, given that the relevant period had expired. In the specific circumstances of the case, given the expiry of the period, the trade mark could be removed upon application by any interested third party. Ibid, para 35.
[75] *Magill* (n 31), paras 52–54.
[76] *IMS Health* (n 32), para 49.

ask whether the incentives to innovate could be preserved – even enhanced – by adjusting the scope, the nature or the length of protection (for instance by turning an exclusive right into a right to receive remuneration, or by ruling that a shorter period of protection is adequate to provide the necessary rewards for inventive and creative efforts). Similarly, it does not enter into an evaluation of whether the innovation that could have been achieved in the absence of protection would be superior, qualitatively or quantitatively, to that which is achieved through intellectual property.

Again, it is only in exceptional circumstances that the competition law regime would, under the deferential approach, overrule the balance between appropriability and contestability achieved under the intellectual property regime. Under the *Magill* case law, a court or authority can strike a new balance if it can show that the refusal to license brings about an immediate and substantial improvement to the conditions of competition that would otherwise have been impossible to achieve. Such an improvement to the conditions of competition would have to be immediate in the sense that it is not based on speculation about future market developments, but on a specific product, the emergence of which is being prevented. It would, in addition, be substantial insofar as it would be new (that is, it would not face competitive pressure from existing products[77]).

3.4. Rationale Behind the Deferential Approach

The choice for a deferential approach can be rationalised in a number of ways. One could argue, first, that the approach is an expression of a well-established doctrine in EU competition law. Since the very early days of *Société Technique Minière*, the Court has insisted that the lawfulness of practices has to be assessed in light of the conditions of competition that would exist in their absence.[78] Accordingly, behaviour that is objectively necessary to attain a pro-competitive objective falls outside the scope of Articles 101 and 102 TFEU. The same is true of conduct that increases, rather than decreases, competition.[79] Simply put, the EU competition law regime does not take for granted the positive aspects of a practice or system, nor does it assume that they would exist irrespective of intervention aimed at injecting static competition. Rather, the Court has always accepted that some short-term obstacles to rivalry are inextricably linked to the pro-competitive benefits of a practice, and that it would be misguided (and incorrect as a matter of law) to evaluate one in isolation from the other.

---

[77] For a systematic discussion of this question, see Robert O'Donoghue and Jorge Padilla, *The Law and Economics of Article 102 TFEU* (3rd edn, Hart Publishing 2020), 656–657.
[78] Case 56/65 *Société Technique Minière*, EU:C:1966:38, 249–250.
[79] Case C-228/18 *Gazdasági Versenyhivatal v Budapest Bank Nyrt. and others*, EU:C:2020:265, paras 82–83.

Arguably, the deferential approach is nothing more than the encapsulation of these principles. Thus, the restrictions to static rivalry that result from the operation of the intellectual property regime would be inextricably linked to the benefits that flow from it. Some of the examples discussed above illustrate this idea. Consider the preliminary reference in *Pronuptia*. The Court understood that franchising agreements would simply not occur in the absence of effective protections against free-riding by actual or potential competitors and against actions damaging the image and uniformity of the formula. Accordingly, any clauses in an agreement aimed at preserving the know-how and the brand image of the franchisor escape the prohibition altogether.[80] Similarly, in *Nungesser*, the Court conceded that, in the specific circumstances of the case, the technology might never have been licensed (and thus may never have reached a new territory) in the absence of some insulation against free-riding.

In the same vein, one cannot assume that the incentives to engage in inventive and creative activities would remain unaffected and would continue to be delivered at the same rate if competition law interfered frequently with intellectual property by limiting the reach or length of protection through case-by-case intervention. The relevant counterfactual, in other words, may not be one in which static competition is enhanced, but one in which the innovation would not have been delivered to begin with. As noted by Advocate General Jacobs in *Bronner*, the fact that forcing a firm to share its intangible assets appears to increase short-term rivalry does not mean that it is pro-competitive. Against this background, it is reasonable for courts and authorities to be deferential vis-à-vis intellectual property regimes: it is an acknowledgement of the nature of intangible property and the need to preserve firms' incentives to develop it.

The second way in which one could rationalise the deferential approach is linked to the first one. Courts and competition authorities are generalist bodies: they are expected to apply the relevant provisions across a number of sectors and practices and typically lack the resources and the necessary expertise to engage in the fine balancing between appropriability and contestability. For instance, they would not be in a position to overrule a patent office when deciding on whether, say, a process patent is worthy of protection. In the same way that review courts typically give discretion to expert authorities in relation to 'complex economic assessments',[81] it would make sense for the competition law regime to err on the side of caution and defer to the intellectual property system. From this perspective, the fact that the latter is imperfect – even prone to errors – would not be sufficient to second-guess its operation. There is no reason to assume that the generalist authority can or would strike a better balance between appropriability and contestability than the expert one.

---

[80] *Pronuptia* (n 19), paras 16–17.
[81] *Consten-Grundig* (n 51), 347; *Remia* (n 16), para 34; and Case T-201/04 *Microsoft Corporation v Commission*, EU:T:2007:289, para 88.

118 *Competition Law and Intangible Property*

Finally, the deferential approach appears to be based on a particular conception of the relationship between competition law and intellectual property. It considers the two disciplines as complementary, each of them with their respective area of application. In a sense, intellectual property would be the exception to the rule. Within its scope of application, competition law would not interfere, and its techniques of protecting appropriability and contestability would prevail. If at all, Articles 101 and 102 TFEU would play a subsidiary role in that context, coming into play in exceptional circumstances. Outside the scope of intellectual property rights, on the other hand, the techniques that are typical of competition law – and in particular the case-by-case, context-specific approach to the balancing of appropriability and contestability – would apply.

4. The Decline of the Deferential Approach

4.1. Explaining the Decline of the Deferential Approach

One of the most identifiable trends in contemporary competition law is the progressive decline of the deferential approach to intellectual property. Over the years, authorities in Europe – including the Commission – have become less reluctant to extend the reach of competition law provisions and to engage in the sort of context-specific fine-tuning that is characteristic of the discipline. Accordingly, the authority seems far less hesitant to conclude that some manifestations of the exercise of intellectual property rights are unlawful or that the latter strike the wrong balance between appropriability and contestability. Interestingly, Articles 101 and 102 TFEU are being invoked not just to reduce the scope and reach of intellectual property regimes but also to expand them. In other words, the provisions have occasionally been relied upon to insulate firms from static competition in relation to activities that would not have benefitted from protection. If these ideas gain traction, competition law would become a fine-tuning tool moving in both directions: depending on the circumstances of each case, the discipline may expand or reduce the reach of exclusive rights.

Several factors explain the decline of the deferential approach to intellectual property. Growing dissatisfaction with intellectual property systems is one of them. Specialist scholars (or at least a subset thereof) have argued at length why the patent system is broken and not fit for purpose.[82] It is mentioned, in this sense, that protection is granted too readily and that it is difficult for the current institutions (such as patent offices and review courts) to deal effectively

---

[82] See for instance Burk and Lemley (n 48). See also Adam B Jaffe and Josh Lerner, *Innovation and its Discontents: How Our Broken Patent System is Endangering Innovation and Progress, and What to Do About It* (Princeton University Press 2004).

with stakeholders' demands.[83] It is also mentioned that the intellectual property system was designed in a different world, and on the basis of a set of assumptions that do not hold true today. Lemley and Shapiro, for instance, explain that contemporary products incorporate hundreds – if not thousands – of technologies, each of which may be protected by one or several patents.[84] This reality is at odds with the idea of a product incorporating a single invention protected by a patent.[85]

As a consequence of these discontents, stakeholders turn to competition law as the mechanism to address the flaws of intellectual property regimes. Articles 101 and 102 TFEU – and equivalent provisions in other jurisdictions – have several advantages. First, competition law does not necessitate a legislative amendment to deal with instances of exclusionary and/or exploitative conduct. Given the malleability of the two provisions, a court or authority can bring an immediate response to alleged anticompetitive behaviour. As pointed out in Chapter 3, it is not a secret that amending legislation – in particular intellectual property legislation – is a lengthy process the outcome of which is difficult to predict.[86] Second, competition law can provide targeted responses with a degree of specificity that is unlikely to be found in intellectual property. As already explained above, the latter is a much cruder instrument and far less prone to incorporating adjustments pertaining to the specifics of a market or an industry.

One can think of another key factor behind the decline of the deferential approach. Intangible property has grown in importance over the past decades.[87] Innovation as a parameter of competition is far more relevant in the world economy than it used to be. It is not difficult to think of economic sectors where rivalry among firms no longer revolves around price or output but around the quality of their products (and the brand image associated with them) and their ability to offer new and improved ones. It is inevitable that, where innovation becomes one of the major drivers of the competitive process, disputes around the existence and/or the exercise of intellectual property rights grow in prominence. The so-called smartphone wars[88] among major manufacturers in the industry, which had a competition law component, is a leading example of the contemporary

---

[83] See for instance Mark A Lemley, 'Can the Patent Office Be Fixed?' (2011) 15 Marquette Intellectual Property Review 295.
[84] Lemley and Shapiro (n 50).
[85] Alain Pottage and Brad Sherman, *Figures of Invention: A History of Modern Patent Law* (Oxford University Press 2010).
[86] For a discussion, see Benjamin Farrand, 'Lobbying and Lawmaking in the European Union: The Development of Copyright Law and the Rejection of the Anti-Counterfeiting Trade Agreement' (2015) 35 Oxford Journal of Legal Studies 487.
[87] Jonathan Haskel and Stian Westlake, *Restarting the Future: How to Fix the Intangible Economy* (Princeton University Press 2022).
[88] For an overview of the topic, see Jorge L Contreras (ed), *The Cambridge Handbook of Technical Standardization Law: Competition, Antitrust, and Patents* (Cambridge University Press 2017).

importance of intangible assets and of how they impact on the nature of disputes. The role of data in several economic sectors is another one.[89]

4.2. Manifestations of the Decline

The decline of the deferential approach has been manifested in the Commission's practice in a number of ways. One of them is the tendency to water down or circumvent the legal doctrines that apply to the exercise of intellectual (and, more generally, intangible) property. Evidence of this tendency was already apparent in the interim measures decision issued by the Commission in the *IMS Health* saga.[90] The authority argued that the conditions laid down in *Magill* were alternative, not cumulative. Accordingly, a firm could be ordered to license its intellectual property without it being necessary to show, to the requisite legal standard, that the refusal prevents the emergence of a new product for which there is potential consumer demand.[91] Evidence of indispensability, alone, would be sufficient to establish an abuse. The President of the General Court concluded that this interpretation of the case law was sufficiently dubious to suspend the interim measures.[92]

Microsoft I is, in any event, the saga that marks the decline of the deferential approach. The case is notable for several reasons. Suffice it to focus on one of them. In its analysis, the Commission never sought to claim that Microsoft's refusal to provide interoperability information to a rival on an adjacent market prevented the emergence of a new product for which there was potential consumer demand. Instead of identifying a specific new product, the decision pointed to the fact that the dominant firm's conduct limited follow-on innovation. By denying access to interoperability information, the argument went, the refusal would affect the rate of innovation on the relevant market, insofar as it would deny rivals the ability to introduce incremental improvements and would lock consumers into a homogeneous ecosystem.[93]

The Commission's reasoning is notable, first and foremost, because it amounts to second-guessing the balance between appropriability and contestability. The authority (and then the General Court) did not question that the contentious information was protected by intellectual property.[94] However, it implied that the exercise of the rights as foreseen in the intellectual property regime would not provide the optimal incentives to invest and innovate. By the same token, the Commission concluded that the optimal balance would be achieved by turning

---

[89] See Jacques Crémer, Yves-Alexandre de Montjoye and Heike Schweitzer, *Competition Policy for the Digital Era*, available at http://ec.europa.eu/competition/publications, 24–29.
[90] *NDC Health/IMS Health: Interim measures* (Case COMP D3/38.044) Commission Decision of 3 July 2001.
[91] Ibid, paras 68–70.
[92] Case T-184/01 R *IMS Health Inc. v Commission*, EU:T:2001:259.
[93] *Microsoft* (Case COMP/C-3/37.792) Commission Decision of 24 May 2004, para 647.
[94] Microsoft (n 73), paras 283–290.

an exclusive right into a right to receive a fair and reasonable remuneration.[95] The General Court endorsed this analysis. More precisely, it ruled that any negative effects on innovation coming from Microsoft would be more than compensated by rivals' increased incentives to invest in inventive activities.[96]

None of the hallmarks of the deferential approach seem to be present in *Microsoft I*. In spite of it being a generalist authority – and not one with the specific expertise to promote innovation – the Commission expressed its confidence in its ability to strike the right balance between appropriability and contestability. The consequences of this approach cannot be overestimated. The reasoning behind the duty to license in *Microsoft I* – that is, the fact that promoting static competition at the expense of appropriability increases the overall incentives to invest and innovate – can plausibly apply to virtually every instance in which the exclusive exercise of intangible property is at stake.[97] In fact, it is difficult to see how the reasoning advanced by the Commission could ever fail. From this perspective, the approach heralded in *Microsoft I* paves the way for the rise of competition law as a tool for the fine-tuning of intellectual property regimes.

A second way in which the deferential approach is being abandoned is through the application, to intangible property, of legal doctrines that were conceived for instances in which physical assets are at stake. It has been explained above how the competition law system adjusts its substantive tests when intangible property is involved. Some practices that would otherwise be restrictive by their very nature may escape the prohibition altogether. *Coditel II* is one example. The exclusive territorial agreement in the case gave absolute protection to the licensee, in the sense that it gave it the right to prohibit any broadcast originating from other licensees or assignees based in other Member States.[98] If the agreement had concerned the distribution of goods (and thus exhausted rights), it would have been deemed restrictive by its very nature. It was found not to be restrictive, in and of itself, precisely because it involved the exploitation of a copyright-protected work in an intangible manner (that is, a broadcast).[99]

Subsequent Commission practice, however, sought to expand the scope of the doctrines originally designed for the distribution of goods (and, more generally, instances in which intellectual property rights could not be invoked to authorise or prohibit the relevant acts[100]). Accordingly, enforcement has interfered with the very exclusive rights granted by virtue of legislation and this, without

---

[95] Ibid, paras 637–665.
[96] Ibid, paras 688–712.
[97] For a discussion, see Pablo Ibáñez Colomo, 'Restrictions on innovation in EU competition law' (2016) 41 European Law Review 201.
[98] Case 62/79 *SA Compagnie générale pour la diffusion de la télévision, Coditel, and others v Ciné Vog Films and others*, EU:C:1980:84, para 5.
[99] *Coditel II* (n 20), para 11.
[100] Practices aimed at restricting cross-border trade are also restrictive by object when the 'country-of-origin' principle applies. In such instances, the licensee in one territory cannot invoke its rights to limit cross-border transmissions (which are deemed to take place only on the country of origin). See Joined Cases C-403/08 and C-429/08 *Football Association Premier League Ltd and Others v QC Leisure and Others and Karen Murphy v Media Protection Services Ltd*, EU:C:2011:631.

invoking any exceptional circumstances. The *Cross-border access to pay-TV* case[101] exemplifies this transition better than any other. In 2014, the Commission opened proceedings against a broadcaster and the Hollywood major studios. The authority argued, in the context of its preliminary assessment, that the clauses in the agreement that required the Sky UK to limit online broadcasting to the territories covered by the licence were restrictive of competition within the meaning of Article 101(1) TFEU.[102]

The claim is notable in that the transmission of content, online, outside the territories covered by the licence would have amounted to a copyright breach by the broadcaster. The Commission's analysis was therefore based on the idea that unlawful competition (that is, market access contingent on an intellectual property infringement) is worthy of protection under Article 101(1) TFEU, and that the exercise of intellectual property is restrictive of competition. This understanding of EU competition law would result, de facto, in the transformation (if not the elimination) of the right to communication to the public. The licensees would have to accept competition from other licensees in the territory where – in theory – it enjoys exclusivity. Accordingly, it would empty the right of its substance.[103]

4.3. Moving Forward: Fully-fledged Fine-tuning under Competition Law?

So far, the decline of the deferential approach has described instances in which static competition is injected at the expense of appropriability. There are, however, hints at moves in the opposite direction – that is, where Articles 101 and 102 TFEU are relied upon to increase appropriability at the expense of static competition. In effect, such moves lead to the extension of the logic and operation of intellectual property regimes beyond their formal scope of application. Occasionally, intellectual property systems are criticised for being insufficiently protective of inventive and creative activities.[104] There are instances, the argument goes, where intellectual property fails to fulfil its function. In such cases, competition law is called upon to play its gap-filling role by mimicking intellectual property regimes (that is, by making intangible assets appropriable).

---

[101] *Cross-border access to pay-TV* (Case AT.40023). There are several decisions associated with this case.

[102] See for instance *Cross-border access to pay-TV* (Case AT.40023) Commission Decision of 26 July 2016, paras 45–49.

[103] The Commission Decision was eventually annulled by the Court of Justice. This factor seemingly played a central role in the outcome of the case. Canal+, the rights of which would have been emptied of their substance, was not involved in the proceedings. See Case C-132/19 P *Groupe Canal + v Commission*, EU:C:2020:1007.

[104] For a discussion on various issues, see Thomas Höppner, 'EU Copyright Reform: The Case for a Publisher's Right' (2018) Intellectual Property Quarterly 1; and Andrei Hagiu, Tat-How Teh and Julian Wright, 'Should platforms be allowed to sell on their own marketplaces?' (2022) 53 RAND Journal of Economics 297.

One of the Commission investigations concerning Amazon – eventually closed with commitments[105] – exemplifies this trend. The authority expressed concerns, inter alia, about the fact that the said firm was using the non-public data generated by its marketplace to benefit its own activities at the expense of competitors.[106] The case is of particular interest in that intervention did not rely on the fact that Amazon was in breach of third parties' intellectual property. Instead, it was grounded on the idea that privileged access to some data gave the online platform an undue competitive advantage. This behaviour would, the argument goes, negatively impact rival retailers' incentives to innovate. The case was closed once Amazon accepted to refrain from using this data – that is, once it accepted to increase third parties' ability to appropriate their inventive and creative efforts.[107]

One can think of other examples. The display by Google of third-party information in its search engine is a recurrent one. Content providers regularly argue that embedding content in the search engine amounts to a competition law infringement. As explained in Chapter 3, Getty brought a competition law complaint against Google in which it claimed that the way its images are displayed in the results lists is abusive within the meaning of Article 102 TFEU.[108] Similarly, Genius accused Google of scraping song lyrics from its website and reposting them directly on the search results page.[109] Establishing a competition law infringement in either of these two cases would involve the administration of remedies aimed at increasing the appropriability of the relevant information (and thus aimed at mimicking the operation of copyright regimes).

If the idea that competition law can apply to increase – and not just to reduce – appropriability is accepted, then Articles 101 and 102 TFEU would become a tool for the fine-tuning, case-by-case, of intellectual property regimes. In some cases (as in the *Amazon* investigation mentioned above), intervention may expand, in effect, the reach of exclusive rights. In other cases, including *Microsoft I* and *IMS Health*, competition law enforcement would lead to the adjustment of intellectual property; for instance, by turning the exclusive right into a right to receive appropriate remuneration, or by limiting the range of remedies available to the right holder. In practice, competition law would become a generalist intellectual property regime sitting above legislation and addressing individual areas.

---

[105] *Amazon* (Case COMP/AT.40462 and Case COMP/AT.40703) Commission Decision of 20 December 2022.

[106] European Commission, 'Antitrust: Commission sends Statement of Objections to Amazon for the use of non-public independent seller data and opens second investigation into its e-commerce business practices' IP/20/2077 (Brussels, 10 November 2020).

[107] European Commission, 'Antitrust: Commission accepts commitments by Amazon barring it from using marketplace seller data, and ensuring equal access to Buy Box and Prime' IP/22/7777 (Brussels, 20 December 2022).

[108] Samuel Gibbs, 'Getty Images files antitrust complaint against Google' *The Guardian* (London, 27 April 2016).

[109] Paresh Dave, 'Genius Media, The Nation sue Google in advertising antitrust lawsuit' *Reuters* (Oakland, 17 December 2020).

5

The DMA as the Expression (and Endgame) of the New Competition Law

1. The DMA as the Endgame of the New EU Competition Law

1.1. A Blend of Competition Law and Sector-specific Regulation

In October 2022, Digital Markets Act (hereinafter, the 'DMA' or the 'Regulation') was published in the Official Journal.[1] The enactment of this Regulation is the culmination of a two-year process during which the European Commission (hereinafter, the 'Commission') considered the various responses that the EU could give to the rise and consolidation of Big Tech – the so-called digital 'gatekeepers' in regulatory parlance.[2] One of the legal paths contemplated – as proposed in the Special Advisers' Report and discussed in Chapter 2 – was the tweaking of substantive competition law provisions to make it easier to establish infringements in digital markets.[3] This route would have led to the emergence of a form of sector-specific competition law, premised on the idea that the power enjoyed by Big Tech, together with the features of the industries in which they operate, justify the re-calibration of legal tests to minimise enforcement errors in certain markets.

A second route (also mentioned in Chapter 2, and explored by the Commission in a consultation) was the adoption of a 'new competition tool' that would have

---

[1] Regulation (EU) 2022/1925 of the European Parliament and of the Council of 14 September 2022 on contestable and fair markets in the digital sector and amending Directives (EU) 2019/1937 and (EU) 2020/1828 (Digital Markets Act) [2022] OJ L265/1.

[2] Commission, 'Commission launches consultation to seek views on Digital Services Act package' IP/20/962 (Brussels, 2 June 2020) and Commission, 'Antitrust: Commission consults stakeholders on a possible new competition tool' IP/20/977 (Brussels, 2 June 2020).

[3] Jacques Crémer, Yves-Alexandre de Montjoye and Heike Schweitzer, *Competition Policy for the Digital Era* (2019), available at https://ec.europa.eu/competition/publications/reports/kd0419345enn.pdf.

empowered the Commission to take action in relation to some market features without it being necessary to establish that there is a behaviour that amounts to an infringement.[4] This second approach, inspired by the market investigations that exist in the UK competition law regime, is best understood as a reverse merger control regime. Like the latter, it is a tool that is structural – not behavioural – in nature. Instead of preventing the creation and the strengthening of market power, however, it seeks to undo structural obstacles to competition and inject rivalry where such obstacles exist. Unlike the first one, this second route would not necessarily have been confined to digital markets.[5]

The path eventually chosen by the Commission and the EU legislature is the enactment of sector-specific legislation, comparable in several respects to the one that applies to telecommunications[6] and energy (electricity[7] and gas[8]) activities. At least formally speaking, the DMA is not a competition law regime. In fact, the Preamble itself is explicit about the role of the regulatory apparatus as a complement to Articles 101 and 102 TFEU. Accordingly, enforcement under the DMA is not constrained by the substantive or institutional limits that would be relevant when EU competition law is enforced.[9] In particular, firms subject to the regime would not be able to escape intervention on grounds that their conduct is incapable of causing actual or potential effects,[10] or on grounds that the efficiency gains to which they give rise outweigh any such effects.[11]

The Preamble clarifies that the objectives of the DMA, while they may be compatible with – and similar to – those underpinning Articles 101 and 102 TFEU, they are not the same. If the latter seek to ensure that competition within the internal market is not distorted, the aim of the DMA is to promote fairness and contestability in digital markets.[12] The Regulation is based on the premise that these two objectives are autonomous (and thus not defined by reference to

---

[4] Commission, 'Antitrust: Commission consults stakeholders on a possible new competition tool' IP/20/977 (Brussels, 2 June 2020).

[5] Ibid, where the Commission referred to 'a possible new competition tool to deal with structural competition problems across markets which cannot be tackled or addressed in the most effective manner on the basis of the current competition rules (e.g. preventing markets from tipping)'.

[6] See in particular Directive (EU) 2018/1972 of the European Parliament and the Council of 11 December 2018 establishing the European Electronic Communications Code [2018] OJ L321/36 (Electronic Communications Code).

[7] See in particular Directive (EU) 2019/944 of the European Parliament and of the Council of 5 June 2019 on common rules for the internal market for electricity and amending Directive 2012/27/EU (recast) [2019] OJ L158/125.

[8] Directive (EU) 2019/692 of the European Parliament and of the Council of 17 April 2019 amending Directive 2009/73/EC concerning common rules for the internal market in natural gas [2019] OJ L117/1.

[9] Digital Markets Act (n 1), Recitals 10 and 11.

[10] Ibid.

[11] Ibid, Recital 23 ('Any justification on economic grounds seeking to enter into market definition or to demonstrate efficiencies deriving from a specific type of behaviour by the undertaking providing core platform services should be discarded, as it is not relevant to the designation as a gatekeeper').

[12] Ibid, Recital 7.

competition law concepts).¹³ Contestability appears to refer to the ability of new entrants to challenge the position of gatekeepers. Intervention in the name of this objective is deemed necessary on account of the features of digital markets (namely extreme returns to scale and network effects).¹⁴ Fairness, in turn, appears to refer to distributional issues (that is, the allocation of rents and power across digital value chains).¹⁵

Even though the DMA is designed to be formally distinct from competition law, a cursory reading of the Regulation reveals that it draws inspiration from it, both from a procedural and a substantive standpoint. The provisions that are the heart of the regime – and that impose a number of duties on firms designated as gatekeepers – are, by and large, a codification of past, ongoing and contemplated Article 101 and 102 TFEU investigations. Just to mention two examples, one of the provisions generalises the ban on the sort of self-preferencing conduct that is at central to the *Google Shopping* case.¹⁶ Another one introduces a prohibition on the use by gatekeepers of data that is not publicly available and that would give vertically-integrated players such as Amazon an edge over rivals on one of the markets within which they operate.¹⁷

The procedural and institutional apparatus of the DMA, in turn, is arguably best described as a *pastiche* bringing together various elements of EU competition law. The procedure for the designation of firms as gatekeepers, to begin with, is similar in its logic and operation to the EU merger control regime, at least in the sense that it relies on proxies such as company turnover and user numbers to identify the entities that are subject to the substantive obligations laid down in Articles 5 to 7.¹⁸ The mechanisms to ensure compliance and to gather information, in turn, are not fundamentally different from those enshrined in Regulation 1/2003. This is true, just to mention some examples, of the investigative, enforcement and monitoring powers with which the Commission is vested.¹⁹

All in all, the DMA comes across as a genuine hybrid that is half way between traditional forms of both competition law and regulation. To the extent that it does, it shows how increasingly artificial it may be to try and draw a precise line between one and the other, whether from a formal or a substantive standpoint. It has already been explained in Chapter 3 that there are not any marked differences between competition law and regulation. The example of the DMA further illustrates why any attempts to distinguish between the former and the latter may be futile. In the same way competition law mimics regulation, the latter may also

---

[13] Ibid, Recital 11.
[14] Ibid, Recital 32.
[15] Ibid, Recital 33.
[16] See Article 6(5) DMA.
[17] Article 6(2) DMA.
[18] See in particular Article 3(2) DMA.
[19] See in particular Articles 16–34 DMA.

replicate the former. The Regulatory Framework for electronic communications[20] adopted in 2002 is an earlier example of a regime that can be seen as both a form of competition law (it revolves, in fact, around competition law concepts) and of sector-specific regulation.[21]

1.2. A Compendium of Emerging Trends in EU Competition Law

The interest of the DMA goes beyond it being a hybrid. As a regime, it encapsulates the trends in competition law discussed in the preceding chapters. First, it marks, perhaps better than any other development, the shift towards proactive enforcement. The duties enshrined in Articles 5 to 7 DMA aim at restructuring value chains in digital markets in fundamental ways. Suffice it to mention some examples of the scale and ambition of intervention. Pursuant to Article 7, firms that are designated as gatekeepers have a duty to provide interoperability of their 'number-independent interpersonal communications services'.[22] More precisely, a firm like Meta would be under a duty to redesign its WhatsApp application to ensure it gives other services such as Telegram the chance to compete with it. Article 6(11), in turn, requires that a gatekeeper operating a search engine, such as Google, share with third parties the 'ranking, query, click and view data' that its service generates.[23]

Second, the DMA can be seen as the culmination of the trend towards 'policy-driven' enforcement identified in Chapter 1. It is a regime narrowly targeted at a small subset of companies with the clear objective of achieving fairness and contestability. Unlike intervention under EU competition law, it is designed in a way that dispenses with the need for the Commission to show that a particular provision has been infringed. The substantive aspects of the regime deal exclusively with the obligations imposed on firms and do not demand an evaluation of the actual or potential (pro- and anticompetitive) effects of the

---

[20] Electronic Communications Code (n 6).
[21] For an extensive discussion, see Pablo Ibáñez Colomo, 'Future-Proof Regulation against the Test of Time: The Evolution of European Telecommunications Regulation' (2022) 42 Oxford Journal of Legal Studies 1170.
[22] Pursuant to Article 7(1) DMA: 'Where a gatekeeper provides number-independent interpersonal communications services that are listed in the designation decision pursuant to Article 3(9), it shall make the basic functionalities of its number-independent interpersonal communications services interoperable with the number-independent interpersonal communications services of another provider offering or intending to offer such services in the Union, by providing the necessary technical interfaces or similar solutions that facilitate interoperability, upon request, and free of charge'.
[23] In accordance with Article 6(11) DMA: 'The gatekeeper shall provide to any third-party undertaking providing online search engines, at its request, with access on fair, reasonable and non-discriminatory terms to ranking, query, click and view data in relation to free and paid search

relevant practices. This feature of the Regulation is also indicative of a parallel trend identified in Chapter 2, which is the shift from process to outcomes – with the latter determining (and, if necessary, altering) the former. It can be seen, in fact, as the epitome of the phenomenon. The processes around which the DMA revolves make it possible to attain the outcomes sought in advance more swiftly and effectively.

Third, the DMA signals a shift from a different perspective. As explained in the preceding chapters, the legitimacy of intervention under Articles 101 and 102 TFEU traditionally hinged on due process and on relying upon the best available expertise. This is due to the fact that competition law enforcement has long been seen as a technocratic venture enforced by an administrative authority. By contrast, the legitimacy of the DMA primarily hinges on the fact that, as a legislative instrument, it has been agreed upon by democratically elected bodies. These bodies have decided to exercise their powers to restructure digital markets in the pursuit of a particular vision and are less bound (or, if one prefers, not bound in the same way or to the same extent) by expertise and the best available evidence. For the same reason, some of the questions that are central to Articles 101 and 102 TFEU enforcement are arguably not relevant (and, insofar as they are, less so) under the DMA.

This legitimacy shift – and its impact on theoretical and practical discussions – can be illustrated by reference to some examples. For instance, some commentators have wondered whether the balance struck in the DMA, which does not allow for efficiency-related arguments to be advanced, is the right one.[24] Similarly, other authors have raised the issue of whether, and to what extent, the regime faithfully reflects, and is supported by, the expert consensus.[25] These questions are central to enforcement by an administrative agency in charge of construing, case by case, broad and vague provisions such as Articles 101 and 102 TFEU. They would also have been at the heart of discussions if the EU legislature had chosen to address the challenge of digital markets by means of the reform of the Commission's competition law powers. Because the Parliament and Council ultimately agreed to set up a sector-specific regime, the said questions are, at best, of marginal importance. If at all, they could be considered if the compatibility of the legislation itself with the TFEU – as opposed to individual instances of intervention – were to be challenged.[26]

---

generated by end users on its online search engines. Any such query, click and view data that constitutes personal data shall be anonymised'.

[24] Monopolkommission, 'Recommendations for an effective and efficient Digital Markets Act' Special Report 82 (2021).

[25] Pablo Ibáñez Colomo, 'The Draft Digital Markets Act: A Legal and Institutional Analysis' (2021) 12 Journal of European Competition Law & Practice 561.

[26] See in this sense Alfonso Lamadrid de Pablo and Nieves Bayón Fernández 'Why the Proposed DMA Might Be Illegal under Article 114 TFEU, and How to Fix It' (2021) 12 Journal of European Competition Law & Practice 576.

2. From a Law-driven Process to Policy-driven Outcomes

2.1. The Shift of the Burden of Intervention

One of the most distinctive aspects of the DMA is that it relieves competition authorities from the need to show that certain conditions are met before intervening. As already pointed out, the Commission does not need to establish that a gatekeeper holds a dominant position or that its behaviour has, as its object or effect, the restriction of competition. The change introduced in the DMA, in any event, is more fundamental than simply shifting the burden of proof or simplifying the procedures to reach the stage at which duties are made binding upon firms. The shift is fundamental in that the initiative no longer lies with the authority, but with the gatekeeper. The latter bears what can be termed the burden of intervention. Enforcement under Articles 101 and 102 TFEU depends on the opening of proceedings and the adoption of a decision by the Commission (or its national counterpart). The same is true of the Regulatory Framework for electronic communications.[27] Under the DMA, on the other hand, the obligations, from the outset, lie with firms identified as gatekeepers.

Article 3 DMA lays down the procedure for the designation of undertakings as gatekeepers (that is, a provider of core platform services[28] within the meaning of Article 2 that 'has a significant impact on the market' and that enjoys – or it is foreseeable that will enjoy – an 'entrenched and durable position' therein[29]). The default mechanism to identify gatekeepers is provided for in Article 3(2) and relies, as mentioned above, on a number of proxies based on the firm's turnover, capitalisation and user numbers. As soon as these turnover thresholds are met, the undertaking in question is under a duty to notify its status to the Commission and is deemed subject to the substantive obligations laid down in Articles 5, 6 and 7. Accordingly, the role of the authority is confined to designating the firm as gatekeeper.[30]

In the same vein, a firm that is presumptively subject to the regime bears the burden of providing evidence to the effect that, even though it meets the thresholds laid down in Article 3(2), it does not meet the qualitative conditions set out in Article 3(1). Pursuant to Article 3(6), an undertaking may provide 'sufficiently substantiated arguments' showing that, 'exceptionally' it should not be designated

---

[27] See Article 67 of the Electronic Communications Code (n 6).
[28] Core platform services are defined as follows pursuant to Article 2(2): '"core platform service" means any of the following: (a) online intermediation services; (b) online search engines; (c) online social networking services; (d) video-sharing platform services; (e) number-independent interpersonal communications services; (f) operating systems; (g) web browsers; (h) virtual assistants; (i) cloud computing services; (j) online advertising services, including any advertising networks, advertising exchanges and any other advertising intermediation services, provided by an undertaking that provides any of the core platform services listed in points (a) to (i)'.
[29] Article 3 DMA.
[30] Article 3(4) DMA.

as gatekeeper. The Commission may then evaluate whether the arguments advanced by the firm are sufficient to 'manifestly call into question' its designation as gatekeeper. If it comes to the conclusion that they do, it will open a market investigation in accordance with the procedure laid down in Article 17(3); if it takes the view that they do not, it will designate the firm as a gatekeeper pursuant to Article 3(4).[31]

The same shift in the burden of intervention can be observed in relation to the substantive obligations set out in Articles 5 to 7 of the Regulation. Article 8 provides that undertakings designated as gatekeepers 'shall ensure and demonstrate compliance' with the said substantive obligations, without it being necessary for the Commission to adopt a decision to this effect. In fact, the DMA goes as far as to demand from firms subject to the regime the setting up of a 'compliance function'. Thus, in accordance with Article 28, the gatekeeper is to create an office that is independent from the undertaking's 'operational functions'[32] and that has the necessary resources and human capital to carry out its activities.[33] The role of the compliance function comprises the internal monitoring of its duties and cooperation with the Commission.[34]

Even though the burden of compliance is firmly placed with gatekeepers, the DMA itself acknowledges, in its Preamble, that some of the obligations laid down in Articles 6 and 7 are sufficiently far-reaching and complex that they are not self-executing and may need to be further specified. Notably, however, Article 8 does not require the Commission to clarify its understanding of these obligations, nor is compliance contingent on such clarification being provided. Instead, the provision simply indicates that the authority may decide, on its own motion or at the request of a designated undertaking, to open proceedings with a view to the adoption of an 'implementing act' specifying the meaning and scope of the abovementioned obligations. Similarly, it is for the gatekeeper to request from the Commission guidance about whether the measures it implements achieve the objectives set out in the regime.[35]

2.2. The Expansion of the Commission's Leeway

A second factor that paves the way for outcome-driven policy-making is the expansion of the leeway enjoyed by the Commission. The DMA reduces the constraints faced by the authority in three ways. It does so, first, by dispensing it from the need to establish an infringement, which is a factor that limits the scope

---

[31] Article 3(5) DMA.
[32] Pursuant to Article 28(1) DMA: 'Gatekeepers shall introduce a compliance function, which is independent from the operational functions of the gatekeeper and composed of one or more compliance officers, including the head of the compliance function'.
[33] Article 28(2) DMA.
[34] Article 28(5) DMA.
[35] Article 8(3) DMA.

for intervention under Articles 101 and 102 TFEU. Second, the DMA adopts a new set of goals and benchmarks against which administrative action is assessed. In this regard, it expressly deviates from concepts such as dominance and overarching ideas such as the 'as efficient competitor' principle. For the same reason, the Commission is not subject to the boundaries defined over the years in the case law. Third, it expands the leeway through very choice of goals and benchmarks, which are inherently broad and vague.

The discretion enjoyed by the Commission can be observed at the two crucial stages of the analysis. The designation of a firm as a gatekeeper within the meaning of Article 3 is one of them. The applicability of the regime to a particular undertaking relies on three qualitative criteria. These are broad enough to encompass the activities of any major provider of core platform services. What is more, the Commission is entrusted with the power to expand or reduce the number of firms subject to the regime on the basis of a combination of quantitative and qualitative factors. Thus, it may designate as gatekeeper an undertaking that does not satisfy the applicable thresholds and, conversely, it may conclude that a firm that meets the quantitative criteria set out in Article 3(2) should nevertheless not be subject to the regime.

To begin with, Article 3(8) gives the Commission the power to designate as gatekeepers undertakings that do not satisfy the quantitative thresholds described above. What is more, this provision does not lay down a structured legal test, or a set of conditions that the authority would need to satisfy. Instead, the Regulation identifies a number of factors that the Commission is entitled to consider in its analysis, such as the size of the undertaking, the features of the activity (for instance, whether there are network effects or data-driven advantages and whether there is customer lock-in).[36] However, nowhere does Article 3(8) provide that all factors be present, or that they be weighed against one another. It is explicit about the fact that it may take into account 'some or all' of them. Similarly, there is no threshold of significance or appreciability. As already mentioned, the authority may also come to the opposite conclusion (that is, that the undertaking is not a gatekeeper even though the quantitative thresholds are met) pursuant to Article 3(5) DMA.[37]

---

[36] The factors included in Article 3(8) DMA are the following: '(a) the size, including turnover and market capitalisation, operations and position of that undertaking; (b) the number of business users using the core platform service to reach end users and the number of end users; (c) network effects and data driven advantages, in particular in relation to that undertaking's access to, and collection of, personal data and non-personal data or analytics capabilities; (d) any scale and scope effects from which the undertaking benefits, including with regard to data, and, where relevant, to its activities outside the Union; (e) business user or end user lock-in, including switching costs and behavioural bias reducing the ability of business users and end users to switch or multi-home; (f) a conglomerate corporate structure or vertical integration of that undertaking, for instance enabling that undertaking to cross subsidise, to combine data from different sources or to leverage its position; or (g) other structural business or service characteristics'.

[37] In such circumstances, Article 3(5) DMA requires the Commission to open a market investigation pursuant to Article 17(3) DMA.

The Commission also enjoys significant leeway when assessing compliance with the substantive obligations laid down in Articles 5 to 7. This is so for substantive and procedural reasons. From a substantive standpoint, compliance is to be assessed by reference to the two objectives underpinning the regime, namely fairness and contestability. Again, there are no obvious boundaries to these concepts. Intervention in the name of fairness, for instance, allows the Commission to redistribute power across digital value chains without it being checked against a legal test like the one that applies, under Article 102 TFEU, to exploitative pricing.[38] The same is true of contestability. Because economic power and barriers to entry are pervasive in the (digital) economy, there are no obvious ex ante limits to market restructuring to inject or preserve rivalry in a given area of activity.

Procedural factors are central to the discretion given to the Commission. Nowhere does Article 8 require the Commission to adopt a decision declaring that the measures put in place by the gatekeeper adequately meet the objectives of the regime (and of the specific obligation which they intend to implement). Instead, the provision gives the Commission the discretion to follow several procedural avenues to engage with the undertaking. Thus, it may adopt an 'implementing act' setting out in detail the sort of steps that the gatekeeper is to take to fulfil its duties; however, it is under no obligation to do so.[39] Alternatively, the Commission may decide to engage in a process to determine, by means of regulatory dialogue, whether the measures put in place by the firm 'ensure effective' compliance.[40]

In principle, judicial review could constrain administrative action. The designation of an undertaking as gatekeeper and an 'implementing act' can both be challenged by virtue of Article 263 TFEU. The Court of Justice, in turn, could come to interpretations that are different from those favoured by the Commission. Such interpretations, in turn, could reduce the leeway enjoyed by the authority. By design, however, judicial review is relatively unlikely to come into the picture. As far as the designation of firms as gatekeepers is concerned, the legislature has deliberately chosen to widen the scope for administrative action. Article 3(5) DMA sets a high bar for entities, in the sense that their arguments must 'manifestly' call into question the presumptions drawn from the administration of the quantitative thresholds. Concerning the substantive obligations, the regime appears to be designed to ensure compliance by the firm. Contrary to what is true under Articles 101 and 102 TFEU, the annulment of a Commission decision would not preclude the application of the duties enshrined in Articles 5 to 7 DMA. What is more, delayed compliance is disincentivised.[41]

---

[38] Recital 33.
[39] Article 8(2) DMA.
[40] Article 8(3) DMA.
[41] The DMA provides for a sliding scale of sanctions, whereby the penalty for failing to comply is progressively increased. In this sense, the Regulation distinguishes between 'non-compliance' and 'systematic non-compliance'. Accordingly, the Commission may adopt a non-compliance decision

There is another factor that may make judicial review less likely. The DMA allows the Commission to exercise its discretion in a way that avoids the adoption of formal decisions – thereby minimising the chances of a direct action. The experience of two decades under Regulation 1/2003 suggests, in fact, that this behaviour can be expected. In the same way that the Commission has expressed a preference for commitments decisions over proceedings formally leading to a finding of infringement, it may follow similar routes under the DMA. The preference for informal or negotiated outcomes may be even stronger than in the context of the enforcement of Articles 101 and 102 TFEU, if one considers that the DMA limits the scope for business users to challenge administrative action where they consider that the implementation of the obligations remains ineffective.

3. From Exclusion to Restructuring and Redistribution

3.1. The Limits of Exclusion as the Basis of Intervention

As explained in Chapter 2, the focus on exclusionary behaviour is one of the most distinctive features of the 'Brussels consensus'. It is an indicator of a relatively modest approach to competition law enforcement. By taking action against certain practices only insofar as they are a potential source of foreclosure (or exclusion), it is a policy choice that refrains from intervening against the exploitation of market power and, more generally, one that is not concerned with the allocation of rents and/or power across the supply chain. To the extent that the distribution of wealth warrants intervention, the task is best left to other regulatory regimes. Under the 'more economics-based approach', moreover, the evaluation of exclusionary effects is not a mere formality. Ascertaining the actual or potential impact of a practice on rivals demands a meaningful analysis of the relevant economic and legal context.

It is not necessary to explain at any length how these constraints reduce the scope for intervention in digital markets. They have already been identified elsewhere in this volume. In particular, the need to articulate a coherent theory of harm and assess whether the available evidence is compatible with it necessarily has a significant impact on the frequency and reach of administrative action. These constraints became apparent in some of the cases investigated by the Commission. Consider the Statement of Objections sent to Apple in April 2021.[42]

---

pursuant to Article 29 where, inter alia, the gatekeeper fails to honour 'any of the obligations laid down in Article 5, 6 or 7' or any of the 'measures specified by the Commission in a decision adopted pursuant to Article 8(2)'. Under Article 18, moreover, the authority is entitled to open a market investigation into 'systematic non-compliance' by the gatekeeper. The remedies under Article 18 may be behavioural and structural in nature (and thus may include a divestiture). What is more, Article 18(2) provides that, with a view to restoring the conditions of competition, the gatekeeper may be prohibited from taking part in a concentration within the meaning of Regulation 139/2004.

[42] European Commission, 'Antitrust: Commission sends Statement of Objections to Apple on App Store rules for music streaming providers' IP/21/2061 (Brussels, 30 April 2021).

The investigation focused on Apple's design choices, which involved, among others, charging a 30 per cent commission to third-party application developers.[43] The publicly available information suggests that building a case of exclusion would not have been an easy task for the authority.

The complainant in this case, to begin with, is the leader in the segment allegedly affected by the practice (music streaming services).[44] What is more, Apple's practices only cover a fraction of the said segment. In fact, the Commission's publicly available analysis refrains from referring to exclusion or foreclosure, and simply mentions the distortion of competition resulting from the contentious practice, and the fact that it raises rivals' costs.[45] To the extent that the investigation was genuinely driven by concerns with exclusion, the Commission seemingly embraced a threshold of effects that is markedly lower than that deriving from the case law and, indeed, its past administrative practice. The available information suggests that this sui generis threshold would be met merely by virtue of the fact that the practice gives a competitive advantage to an affiliate over rivals, irrespective of its impact on the latter's ability and incentive to compete. For the same reason, the analysis would not have been obvious to uphold if challenged. It is not surprising, against this background, that the exclusionary aspects of the case were eventually dropped by the Commission in a second Statement of Objections issued in February 2023.[46]

This case is just an example of a peculiar set of investigations in digital markets (for other similar cases, it is sufficient to think of the disputes involving Amazon). Insofar as they do not meet the prevailing threshold of effects, these investigations cannot be said to be purely or firmly about exclusion. In fact, they typically reflect a concern, more or less explicit, with exploitation (arguably, disputes around the 30 per cent commission charged by Apple are, above all, about the latter's alleged ability to extract supracompetitive rents in its dealings with application developers; similarly, Amazon's ability to use the data generated by its marketplace is deemed unfair in itself, irrespective of whether it leads to foreclosure). This new generation of hybrid cases – partially about exclusion, partially about exploitation – is not easy to accommodate with the traditional approach to Article 101 and 102 TFEU enforcement, and even less so with the logic underpinning the 'more economics-based approach'.

---

[43] Ibid: 'The mandatory use of Apple's proprietary in-app purchase system ("IAP") for the distribution of paid digital content. Apple charges app developers a 30% commission fee on all subscriptions bought through the mandatory IAP. The Commission's investigation showed that most streaming providers passed this fee on to end users by raising prices'.

[44] Ibid, where the Commission indicates that the investigation 'follows-up on a complaint by Spotify'.

[45] Ibid, 'Apple's rules distort competition in the market for music streaming services by raising the costs of competing music streaming app developers'.

[46] European Commission, 'Antitrust: Commission sends Statement of Objections to Apple clarifying concerns over App Store rules for music streaming providers' IP/23/1217 (Brussels, 23 February 2023). This second investigation focused on the so-called anti-steering provisions preventing application developers from informing users of alternative purchasing possibilities.

It is only natural, against this background, that the DMA is seen both by the Commission and the legislature as the natural avenue to deal with these hybrid cases and, similarly, as the obvious instrument to address the limits of exclusion-based theories of harm. Unlike traditional competition law enforcement, there is no stark divide (or hierarchy) between exclusion and exploitation under the Regulation. The explicit goals of the DMA, namely fairness and contestability, seek to promote competition both by improving firms' ability and incentive to rival gatekeepers and by allowing them to extract a larger share of the value generated by their activities. However, Articles 5 to 7 do not distinguish neatly between the obligations that are driven by potential exclusionary considerations and those that seek to reallocate rents.

In fact, the DMA blurs the line between exclusion and exploitation.[47] Fairness is seen to contribute to contestability, and vice versa. For instance, the strict ban on self-preferencing is both a mechanism to prevent the raising of rivals' costs and to redistribute rents. Prohibiting the gatekeeper from favouring its affiliates on adjacent segments, is expected to preserve competitors' ability and incentive to remain in the relevant segment, and to lead a more even allocation of resources. The creation of a level playing field between a gatekeeper's affiliate and its rivals creates the conditions in which the latter can capture a larger share of, say, the advertising revenue generated on the adjacent segment. Similarly, a duty to share data with any willing third party will necessarily have distributional effects, in addition to creating chances for rivals to compete and expand their activities at the expense of gatekeepers.

3.2. Contestability as Market Restructuring

An overview of the obligations laid down in Articles 5 to 7 DMA reveals the market restructuring ambitions of the regime. Just like the EU Electronic Communications Code, the purpose of the DMA is not simply to preserve competition, but to promote competition by reshaping digital ecosystems and value chains. Articles 5 to 7 seek to make markets more contestable by pursuing three main regulatory strategies. First, by changing the operation of an activity to nullify or reduce an advantage enjoyed by the gatekeeper in its core segment. For instance, a firm subject to the regime may be required to give up its ability to exploit the synergies it derives from the aggregation of data.[48] Second, the DMA opens up layers within an ecosystem that were not accessible to rivals. Just to mention an example, a gatekeeper may be required to allow third parties to run an app store alongside its own.[49] Third, there are obligations that regulate the

---

[47] See in particular Recital 34, where the Regulation points out that '[c]ontestability and fairness are intertwined'.
[48] Article 5(2) DMA.
[49] Article 6(4) DMA.

terms and conditions under which the gatekeeper deals with rivals and/or end-users. For instance, the gatekeeper may have to refrain from using, to its own advantage, the non-public data generated by its marketplace.[50]

3.2.1. Changing the Operation of Gatekeepers' Core Segments

It makes sense to discuss, at greater length, each one of these three regulatory strategies. The first (changing the operation of a core segment to nullify a gatekeeper's competitive advantage) is arguably the most intrusive, in the sense that it goes as far as to alter the underlying dynamics of the relevant market in the name of contestability. The strategy is an attempt to tame some of the features that favour the emergence of monopolies and quasi-monopolies in some layers within digital value chains. The DMA focuses on two of these features: network effects and returns to scale (and scope). As far as the former are concerned, the regime seeks to alter the prevailing dynamics so that all players – and not just the gatekeeper – benefit from them. The threat to competition coming from returns to scale and scope, in turn, is addressed by constraining the extent to which the gatekeeper can exploit some of its advantages.

Article 7 DMA provides the prime example of an instance in which the regime addresses the risk of monopolisation resulting from the operation of network effects. Pursuant to this provision, gatekeepers providing number-independent interpersonal communications services (such as WhatsApp) are required to make the basic functionalities of the said services interoperable with competing ones.[51] Put differently, the DMA demands that, at least in relation to some of the features (including, inter alia, text messaging, sharing of voice messages and calls), their communications services be redesigned so they communicate with rival ones. In this regard, the regime replicates, in essence, the interconnection obligations that define the conditions of competition in the telecommunications sector, and which prevent the 'tipping' of the industry in favour of the preeminent player.[52]

Other provisions in the DMA come across, at least in part, as a response to gatekeepers' ability to exploit some of their conglomerate advantages. More precisely, Article 5(2) DMA limits firms' ability to use personal data when providing their services. To the extent that data is central to some gatekeepers'

---

[50] Article 6(2) DMA.
[51] Pursuant to Article 7(1) DMA: '1. Where a gatekeeper provides number-independent interpersonal communications services that are listed in the designation decision pursuant to Article 3(9), it shall make the basic functionalities of its number-independent interpersonal communications services interoperable with the number-independent interpersonal communications services of another provider offering or intending to offer such services in the Union, by providing the necessary technical interfaces or similar solutions that facilitate interoperability, upon request, and free of charge'.
[52] See in particular Articles 60 and 61 of Electronic Communications Code (n 6). The Code did not extend to providers of number-independent interpersonal communications services the interconnection duties that apply to other operations. See in this sense Article 61(2)(c) DMA.

monetisation strategies, this provision may attenuate the economies of scale and scope that give them an edge in some of their core segments. By the same token, the constraints enshrined in the provision may contribute to levelling the playing field. Specifically, Article 5(2) DMA prohibits, inter alia, the combination of personal data from different services and the use of personal data across services unless the end-user has been presented with a choice and unless consent has been given in accordance with the data protection regime.[53]

Figure 5.1 Changing the operation of the gatekeeper's core segment via interoperability

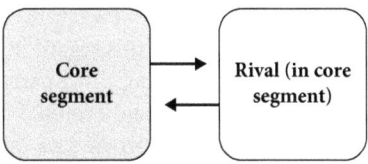

3.2.2. Opening up Layers within Ecosystems

Gatekeepers rarely follow a uniform strategy across all levels of the value chain. They may be active at some levels, but not others. Similarly, some layers may be open to third-party business users, whereas others may not. For instance, an integrated firm operating an ecosystem may choose to open it to applications developed by third parties; on the other hand, it may choose to keep the app store layer exclusively to itself. Another gatekeeper, in turn, may allow third parties to sell products via its online marketplace whereas other activities (such as the fulfilment of orders) may be closed to rivals. Several reasons explain why digital ecosystems are, more often than not, partially open and partially closed. It may be the case, for instance, that the exclusive control of one layer of the value chain is central to a firm's monetisation strategy. More precisely, precluding rivals from accessing a layer is what allows the firm to capture the value generated by the ecosystem. Alternatively, it may be the case that the exclusive control of one layer is driven by quality considerations. For example, the gatekeeper may not trust third parties to be able to fulfil its quality requirements.

Several provisions in the DMA are designed to open up layers of the value chain so that third parties can access them. The regime achieves this goal by relying on different techniques. It does so, first, by requiring gatekeepers to allow the installation and 'effective use' of third-party applications (and app stores). Among others, this obligation, enshrined in Article 6(4) DMA, seeks to ensure that mobile applications are accessible other than via the app store run by the gatekeeper (what

---

[53] Article 5(2) DMA refers to 'consent within the meaning of Article 4, point (11), and Article 7 of Regulation (EU) 2016/679'.

is known as sideloading).[54] Second, the DMA imposes vertical interoperability obligations, whereby software and hardware products developed by third-party providers are entitled to communicate effectively with the hardware and software features that are accessed or controlled by the gatekeepers' operating system or virtual assistant.[55]

Third, there are instances where the DMA opens up a layer of the value chain not by mandating access by rivals to a given segment, but by requiring firms to share an input with third parties. These are scenarios in which intervention does not simply lead to entry by third parties to a segment monopolised by the gatekeeper, but results, in effect, in the creation of new layers of activity. Article 6(11) DMA provides the most eloquent example in this regard. By mandating operators of online search engines to provide any willing third party with 'ranking, query, click and view data in relation to free and paid search',[56] the regime sets up, ex novo, both an upstream segment for the supply of data inputs by the gatekeeper and a downstream segment where the latter competes, on an equal footing, with rivals offering search engine services to end-users.

Figures 5.2.1 and 5.2.2 Opening up layers within the ecosystem

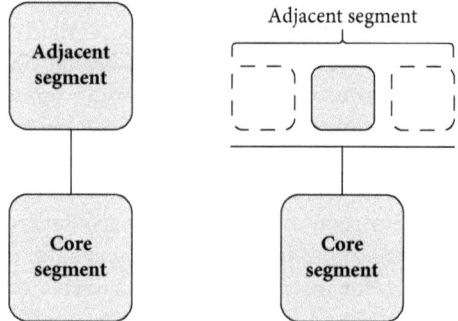

3.2.3. Regulating the Terms and Conditions of Access

There are other instances where the DMA does not seek to alter the operation of a segment or to force gatekeepers to deal with rivals. The purpose, instead, is to regulate existing arrangements and contractual relationships. More precisely, the point is to define the terms and conditions under which gatekeepers deal with business and end users. These measures seek to promote contestability by levelling the playing field in vertical settings (both by minimising the competitive advantages

---

[54] Article 6(4) DMA prohibits, among others, 'allow and technically enable the installation and effective use of third-party software applications or software application stores using, or interoperating with, its operating system and allow those software applications or software application stores to be accessed by means other than the relevant core platform services of that gatekeeper'.
[55] Article 6(7) DMA.
[56] Article 6(11) DMA.

enjoyed by integrated gatekeepers and reducing the obstacles that third parties face when rivalling them). The measure that perhaps best reflects this ambition is the blanket ban on self-preferencing enshrined in Article 6(5) DMA. In accordance with this provision, it is prohibited for gatekeepers to treat more favourably their own activities in adjacent segments when ranking and indexing products and services. In this sense, firms subject to the regime are required to apply transparent, fair and non-discriminatory criteria when listing products and services.

Article 6 DMA provides additional duties, some of which have featured in past competition law investigations. As mentioned above, for instance, Article 6(2) DMA prohibits gatekeepers from using the non-public data generated by their own core platform services to exploit a competitive advantage over business users in an adjacent segment.[57] Similarly, Article 6(3) DMA reflects a concern with gatekeepers' ability to benefit from the 'status quo bias' that might result from some services or products being presented as the default choice in an operating system, web browser or virtual assistant. In this regard, the provision seeks to level the playing field in two ways. First, by enabling the uninstallation of the gatekeeper's applications;[58] and, second, by imposing a positive duty on them to prompt end users to choose from a list of services when setting up their devices.[59]

3.3. Fairness as Redistribution

It has already been mentioned above that market restructuring in the name of contestability necessarily leads to the redistribution of rents: minimising or nullifying a gatekeeper's competitive advantage allows rivals to improve their relative position and capture a larger share of the rents. To the extent that this is the case, the measures discussed in the preceding sub-sections contribute to fairness in digital markets. There are, in addition, obligations in the DMA where the relationship between fairness and contestability is the reverse. These measures, in other words, focus on achieving a fair distribution of value, and contestability is expected to follow as a side effect. It is possible to identify two categories of these (primarily fairness-driven) obligations. In some instances, the relevant obligations benefit business users the activities of which do not overlap with

---

[57] More precisely, Article 6(2) DMA prohibits gatekeepers from using, 'in competition with business users, any data that is not publicly available that is generated or provided by those business users in the context of their use of the relevant core platform services or of the services provided together with, or in support of, the relevant core platform services, including data generated or provided by the customers of those business users'.

[58] The first paragraph of the provision requires the gatekeeper to 'allow and technically enable end users to easily un-install any software applications on the operating system of the gatekeeper'.

[59] The second paragraph, in turn, mandates gatekeepers to 'allow and technically enable end users to easily change default settings on the operating system, virtual assistant and web browser of the gatekeeper that direct or steer end users to products or services provided by the gatekeeper. That includes prompting end users, at the moment of the end users' first use of an online search engine, virtual assistant or web browser of the gatekeeper listed in the designation decision pursuant to Article 3(9), to choose, from a list of the main available service providers […]'.

the gatekeeper's own activities. Alternatively, they may benefit end users. In other instances, redistribution comes across as the primary concern behind the substantive obligation.

The most obvious example of the first category of fairness-driven duties can be found in the provisions regulating the relationship between gatekeepers, on the one hand, and advertisers and publishers, on the other. These duties are to be found in Articles 5(9), 5(10) and 6(8) DMA. These three provisions seek to address the power that some firms enjoy in the online advertising space.[60] The purpose of Articles 5(9) and 5(10) DMA is to improve the transparency of these activities by requiring gatekeepers to provide daily information, free of charge, about prices and remunerations, in addition to the metrics on the basis of which both are calculated. Article 6(8) DMA, in turn, introduces an obligation to give access to the 'performance measuring tools' and data so that advertisers and publishers can carry out their own independent verification of the 'advertisements inventory'.[61]

The redistribution of power transpires very clearly as the key concern underpinning some of the obligations. This is true, in particular, of Article 6(12) DMA, which imposes a duty on gatekeepers to apply 'fair, reasonable, and non-discriminatory' conditions of access by business users to 'software application stores, online search engines and online social networking services'. The obligation of fairness extends not just to the conditions of access as such, which are to be published and apply across the board, but to the settlement of disputes. In this sense, the general conditions of access are to include an 'alternative dispute settlement mechanism'. The concerns underpinning these obligations can be traced back to disagreements between Apple and application developers. As discussed above, it was not obvious to discern an exclusionary dimension in these cases, the core of which related to the allocation of the value between the platform and business users.

4. The Shift in the Centre of Gravity of Enforcement

4.1. Proactive Intervention as the Centre of Gravity of Enforcement

Chapter 1 described the rise of proactive enforcement as one of the most distinctive features of contemporary competition law. Because of the nature and demands

---

[60] See in this sense Recitals 45 and 58. This is a topic that has been followed closely by competition authorities. See in particular Competition and Markets Authority, *Online platforms and digital advertising: market study final report* (1 July 2020).

[61] In accordance with the provision, the gatekeeper is under a duty to 'provide advertisers and publishers, as well as third parties authorised by advertisers and publishers, upon their request and free of charge, with access to the performance measuring tools of the gatekeeper and the data necessary for advertisers and publishers to carry out their own independent verification of the advertisements inventory, including aggregated and non-aggregated data'.

of positive obligations (whether behavioural, such as a duty to deal; or structural, such as a divestiture), this trend in policy-making has the effect of moving the centre of gravity of the system towards implementation, and away from establishing the facts to the requisite legal standard and/or evaluating whether a practice amounts to an infringement. As the culmination of the new competition law, the DMA reflects this shift. One could argue, in fact, that it both epitomises and exacerbates the trend. This is so for three main reasons. First, the DMA dispenses from the need to engage in any sort of case-by-case assessment. Second, because it generalises interventions that were exceptional under competition law. Third, because it pushes intervention beyond what would have been achieved by means of the enforcement of Articles 101 and 102 TFEU.

The first point has been abundantly discussed above and in the preceding chapters. The hallmark of the 'more economics-based approach', which is the case-by-case evaluation of the effects of practices, has been questioned as the pendulum of opinion swung in favour of presumptively prohibiting conduct irrespective of its impact. In this regard, the DMA pushes the trend to its outer limits by shifting the burden of intervention altogether and focusing exclusively on compliance. The second point demands further elaboration. Several of the obligations enshrined in Article 6 DMA can only be attained via competition law enforcement, if at all, in exceptional circumstances (at least so in principle). In fact, they have only been imposed relatively sparingly (even after the rise of proactive enforcement), as they are known to be distinctly difficult to design, implement and monitor.

The above is true, in particular, of most provisions aimed at opening layers to rivals. This is so to the extent that they amount to an obligation to deal. Access duties requiring gatekeepers to provide access to search data to would-be downstream rivals, for instance, would fall squarely within the scope of the *Bronner* and *Magill/IMS Health* lines of case law if examined under Article 102 TFEU. As a result, intervention would have to satisfy the strict conditions laid down in the three rulings. The same can be said of vertical interoperability obligations that have the object or effect of allowing business users to enter layers that the gatekeeper had chosen to keep for itself. As explained in *Slovak Telekom*, action under Article 102 TFEU requires evidence of indispensability whenever the remedy amounts, in effect, to forcing a dominant firm to deal with third parties with which it has chosen not to deal.[62]

In some instances, third, the DMA pushes the boundaries of what would have been possible to achieve by means of Article 102 TFEU enforcement (at least as the law stands). Unconstrained by the potential boundaries to intervention under competition law, the legislature could venture into questions for which there were no precedents. Consider the example of the refusal to deal case law. Not only is a duty to share an input or infrastructure confined to exceptional circumstances

---

[62] Case C-165/19 P *Slovak Telekom, a.s. v Commission*, EU:C:2021:239.

under Article 102 TFEU, but the relevant judgments concern a very specific factual scenario. More precisely, the *Bronner* and *Magill/IMS Health* lines of case law apply in instances where a vertically-integrated dominant firm that operates on two adjacent markets faces actual or potential competition on the upstream or the downstream levels. The relevant question in these cases is whether the integrated undertaking can be required to share an input or infrastructure to prevent the elimination of competition on a related market.

Access under the DMA, by contrast, is not confined to these factual circumstances. Suffice it to mention, in this sense, Article 7. An interoperability obligation (such as the one enshrined in the provision) amounts, in practice, to a duty to deal with third parties. The peculiarity of this duty (and the reason why it stands apart from the existing case law and, indeed, other interoperability obligations under the regime) is that the vertical integration element is missing. Put differently, the point of Article 7 is not to preserve competition on an adjacent market, but to change the dynamics of the core market to accommodate rivalry and ensure that network effects do not lead to its monopolisation by a gatekeeper. It is debatable whether a refusal to provide interoperability can amount to an abuse of dominance.[63] What seems difficult to dispute, in any event, is that, by introducing this additional scenario, the DMA has expanded the reach of, and scope for, proactive enforcement.

4.2. Institutional Implications of the Shift

Moving the centre of gravity towards the implementation stage has important consequences from an institutional perspective. Given the nature of proactive intervention and the difficulties associated with it, the shift demands the reorientation of resources towards the design, implementation and monitoring of the obligations. This is an area of enforcement where the limits of competition law systems have regularly been exposed. As explained at length in Chapter 8, the aftermath of the *Google Shopping* and *Android* cases reveals the extent to which competition authorities are unequipped to deal with the administration of proactive remedies; and, similarly, the extent to which the regime had not been designed with proactive intervention in mind. Even though the two abovementioned decisions were adopted, respectively, in 2017 and 2018, it was still being discussed, at the time of writing, whether the dominant firm had brought the remedy effectively to an end.[64] What is more, the Commission does not have the power to declare, by

---

[63] See in particular Kevin Coates, *Competition Law and Regulation of Technology Markets* (Oxford University Press 2011).

[64] See in particular the contributions by lawyers acting for complainants, including Thomas Höppner, 'Google's (Non-) Compliance with the EU Shopping Decision' (2020), available at https://ssrn.com/abstract=3700748; and Philip Marsden, 'Google Shopping for the Empress's New Clothes –When a Remedy Isn't a Remedy (and How to Fix it)' (2020) 11 Journal of European Competition Law & Practice 553.

means of a formal decision, that the changes introduced by Google to its activities bring the latter in line with Article 102 TFEU.

In addition, the shift in the centre of gravity of enforcement demands the development of a new kind of expertise. Under the influence of the 'more economics-based approach', the sort of expertise that competition authorities developed focused on the evaluation, case-by-case, of the impact of behaviour on competition. The DMA (and, indeed, any system that relies on the administration of complex positive duties) demands technical knowledge of a different kind. The restructuring of digital markets necessitates a detailed, in-depth understanding of the industry. The role of the authority, in this new scenario, is not dissimilar from that of regulatory agencies in the telecommunications and energy sectors. This new role replaces economists with engineers and computer scientists to enact the requisite changes to markets, products and business models. It is not surprising that, at the time of writing, the Commission had announced the creation of the office of the Chief Technology Officer.[65]

The structure of the DMA and the substantive choices made may exacerbate one of the major trends since the adoption of Regulation 1/2003, which is the rise of negotiated procedures (in particular by means of commitments decisions). Given that the shift in the burden of intervention and given the consequences that non-compliance for firms (which may go as far as to mandate the structural separation of the gatekeeper),[66] the regime is designed to achieve the swift implementation of the obligations and, by the same token, to disincentivise litigation. In fact, Article 8(3) DMA provides for an explicit avenue to ensure a negotiated outcome. Pursuant to this provision, the gatekeeper may trigger a process to determine, in the context of a dialogue with the Commission, whether the measures it has introduced ensure compliance with the substantive obligations enshrined in Articles 6 and 7.[67]

5. A 'Third Way' to Promote Dynamic Competition

5.1. Dynamic Competition under the DMA: The Explicit and the Implicit

5.1.1. *The Explicit: Increasing Appropriability and Contestability*

Innovation is at the heart of the DMA. The efforts aimed at making activities more contestable are deemed beneficial for competition both from a static and

---

[65] Janith Aranze, 'Guersent: EU considering new chief tech officer role to assist antitrust cases' *Global Competition Review* (London, 15 June 2022).
[66] Article 18(1) and above n 41.
[67] See above n 40.

a dynamic standpoint. Put differently, the market restructuring ambition underpinning regulation is expected to increase the rate of innovation by favouring business users' ability to capture the fruits of their efforts and by lowering barriers to entry and expansion. In this sense, the assumptions on which the DMA is based are in line with the analytical framework around which Chapter 4 revolves.[68] By improving the prospect of successful entry (that is, by achieving contestability) and by redistributing rents to enable firms to capture a larger share of the value they generate (that is, by promoting appropriability), the legislature hopes to promote long-run competition.

The Preamble is particularly explicit about these assumptions. The expected impact of increased appropriability on the rate of innovation is addressed in Recital 33. According to the legislature, gatekeepers receive a 'disproportionate advantage' from their relationship with business users due to the imbalance between the rights and obligations of the latter. As a result, the Preamble continues, market participants are not in a position to capture the benefits from, inter alia, their innovative efforts.[69] This is the background without which the fairness-driven duties enshrined in the DMA cannot be fully rationalised. The point of intervention, according to Recital 33, is to ensure that business users are adequately rewarded for their contributions to the platform or ecosystem and that gatekeepers do not impose unbalanced conditions for the use of their services.[70]

Some of the fairness-driven measures discussed above are designed to allow business users to appropriate a larger share of the value they generate within platforms and ecosystems. This is true, for instance, of Article 6(12) DMA, which, as already pointed out, seeks to ensure that gatekeepers deal with third parties on 'fair, reasonable, and non-discriminatory' terms and conditions. Other provisions are conceived to enable business users to effectively capture and exploit the intangible assets that their activities generate when interacting with platform operators. More precisely, Article 6(10) DMA requires gatekeepers to give third parties effective access, free of charge, to the (aggregated and non-aggregated) data provided for or generated in the context of the use of the relevant core platform services.

Recital 32 of the Preamble, in turn, addresses the relationship between contestability and dynamic competition and, similarly, how intervention in the name of the former contributes to the latter. In this regard, the EU legislature notes that barriers to entry and expansion by firms in digital markets have a negative impact on their incentives to invest and innovate.[71] This is so both in the core

---

[68] Carl Shapiro, 'Competition and Innovation: Did Arrow Hit the Bull's Eye?' in Josh Lerner and Scott Stern (eds), *The Rate and Direction of Inventive Activity Revisited* (University of Chicago Press 2012).

[69] See Recital 33, where the EU legislature notes that '[…] Market participants, including business users of core platform services and alternative providers of services provided together with, or in support of, such core platform services, should have the ability to adequately capture the benefits resulting from their innovative or other efforts […]'.

[70] Ibid.

[71] See Recital 32: '[…] The features of core platform services in the digital sector, such as network effects, strong economies of scale, and benefits from data have limited the contestability of those

markets in which gatekeepers operate and in adjacent ones. In the same vein, the Preamble notes that intervention in the name of contestability should seek to promote competition not just at the inter-platform level (and thus rivalry within the gatekeeper's core segment, such as the interoperability obligations enshrined in Article 7), but also at the intra-platform one too (and thus in the activities around the core segment, such as the prohibition against self-preferencing or allowing of the sideloading of applications).

5.1.2. The Implicit: Reducing Gatekeepers' Appropriability and Contestability

The DMA is less explicit in relation to the mechanisms that limit gatekeepers' ability to appropriate the fruits of their efforts and, by the same token, to reduce their chances of challenging the position of other firms on adjacent segments. Simply put, there are instances in which the DMA intervenes to hinder appropriability (and not just to promote it). These mechanisms are no less central to the operation of the regime. In fact, one of the key assumptions underpinning the legislation is that there may be circumstances where gatekeepers' ability to capture the value generated by their platform or ecosystem can make digital markets less contestable and, by the same token, less conducive to innovation. Accordingly, the DMA fine-tunes innovation incentives based on the degree of economic power that firms enjoy. More precisely, the regime promotes appropriability and contestability where it favours business uses over gatekeepers. It does the opposite where it would strengthen the position of the latter.

These ideas are best illustrated by reference to some concrete examples. Article 6(2) DMA is one of them. As explained above, this provision seeks, in essence, to prevent gatekeepers' ability to exploit a competitive advantage they may derive from a set of intangible assets (non-public data). In other words, the regime prohibits the platform operator from capturing part of the value generated by its activity. Some of the provisions imposing positive access obligations illustrate equally eloquently how the DMA fine-tunes appropriability and contestability (and this in a way that sometimes favours the former at the expense of the latter). The substance of Article 6(11) DMA, for instance, has already been addressed. This provision, in essence, requires that search engine operators share their click and query data with any third party. In other words, it turns an exclusive right to exploit its search data into a right to receive fair remuneration for it.

services and the related ecosystems. Such a weak contestability reduces the incentives to innovate and improve products and services for the gatekeeper, its business users, its challengers and customers and thus negatively affects the innovation potential of the wider online platform economy'.

5.2. A New Relationship between Appropriability and Contestability

The mechanisms to promote dynamic competition underpinning the DMA set it apart from both intellectual property and competition law. It is in this sense that the regime can be said to be a third way between both disciplines. To begin with, the DMA differs from intellectual property insofar as the ability to capture the value generated by innovative activity appears to be contingent on the degree of power and/or control enjoyed by a firm. In other words, the regime does not protect against appropriation based on whether the intangible asset is worthy of protection, but based on the position of the firm which generated the asset in question. Accordingly, a gatekeeper operating a search engine will be required to share the data generated by its activity irrespective of whether it involves an innovative and creative effort. The crucial consideration, under the DMA, is that the control of the intangible asset raises barriers to entry and expansion within a segment where there are structural obstacles to competition.

From this perspective, the DMA introduces a degree of flexibility that is not found in intellectual property regimes. As discussed at length in Chapter 4, patent and copyright systems provide for relatively crude instruments that do not pay due regard to the economic and technological context within which exclusive rights are awarded. By contrast, the DMA is based on the idea that appropriability is not necessarily conducive to innovation – or to socially desirable innovation – where the asset holder enjoys a substantial degree of control over an activity or around an ecosystem. This premise does not lack foundations. It is an acknowledgement that, absent contestability, appropriability alone may not deliver the expected benefits in terms of dynamic competition. This, in fact, is a point that has been explored in the economic literature.[72]

The DMA is also at odds, in several important respects, with competition law. The divergence between disciplines is obvious if one considers that Articles 101 and 102 TFEU, which address behavioural issues (as opposed to structural), are considerably more modest in their nature and potential reach. As pointed out above, Articles 5 to 7 DMA go beyond what would be possible to attain under competition law in several important respects. For instance, fairness-driven obligations, such as that enshrined in Article 6(10), do not depend on evidence that the terms and conditions applied by the gatekeeper are exploitative within the meaning of Article 102 TFEU. Similarly, the duty to share the data generated as a result of their interaction with platforms is not contingent on evidence of indispensability.

The DMA differs from Articles 101 and 102 TFEU enforcement in another fundamental respect. Unlike competition law, the regime dispenses from the need to engage in a context-specific evaluation of the impact of a practice (and, indeed, a

---

[72] Maarten de Ridder, 'Market Power and Innovation in the Intangible Economy' (2022), available at http://www.maartenderidder.com/research.html.

given market structure) on firms' incentives to invest and innovate. The *Magill* and *IMS Health* case law, even after the General Court's reinterpretation in *Microsoft I*, demands a case-by-case evaluation of whether, in the relevant circumstances, the refusal to license would have a negative impact on dynamic competition.[73] The same is true, for instance, in relation to non-compete obligations (and, more precisely, the extent to which they are necessary to preserve the intangible assets that come with the sale of a business).[74] The DMA, by contrast, is based on a number of structural assumptions about market structures and the rate of innovation that inform the various ex ante obligations.

Figure 5.3 The DMA as a tool to promote innovation

Regime	Ex ante vs ex post	Relevance of market power
Intellectual property	Ex ante	No
Competition Law	Case-by-case	Yes
Digital Markets Act	Ex ante	Yes

6. The End of Competition Law or a New Relationship with Regulation?

The DMA both encapsulates the contemporary transformation of competition law and transcends it. The trends that have reshaped policy-making since Regulation 1/2003 appear to be so potent that they ultimately result in the adoption of a sector-specific regime replacing Articles 101 and 102 TFEU. This evolution should not come as a surprise. The competition law system is unlikely to be able to provide a fully satisfactory answer where enforcement is driven by outcomes (as opposed to process) and the law is less relevant in the overall equation. When policy-making mutates and takes a turn in this direction, any legal and non-legal constraints – such as the need to establish dominance or the anticompetitive object or effect of a practice – ultimately become difficult to sustain and to justify. For the same reason, a regulatory regime that does away with such constraints and

---

[73] Case C-418/01 *IMS Health GmbH & Co. OHG v NDC Health GmbH & Co. KG*, EU:C:2004:257 and Case T-201/04 *Microsoft Corporation v Commission*, EU:T:2007:289.
[74] Case 42/84 *Remia BV and others v Commission*, EU:C:1985:327.

shifts the centre of gravity to the implementation of a particular policy vision may become inevitable.

Against this background, the example of the DMA raises the question of whether the new competition law will, ultimately, lead to the demise of the discipline, at least in relation to some industries and practices. The emerging ethos may result in the progressive replacement of competition law with a patchwork of formal and informal, outcome-driven regulatory schemes (such as the DMA itself). In the new environment, the enforcement of Articles 101 and 102 TFEU may come to be seen – at best – as a transitory and imperfect second-best. There is a chance, however, that the competition law system proves able to adapt to this new reality, if Articles 101 and 102 TFEU are replaced from within the system. The 'new competition tool' – the adoption of which was, as discussed above, contemplated by the Commission – may become the privileged instrument to attain the outcomes sought by authorities and, in the same vein, do away with the existing legal and institutional constraints.

Alternatively, the potential demise of Articles 101 and 102 TFEU may not necessarily be seen as the end of competition law, but rather as the beginning of a different relationship of the discipline with economic regulation. It has been explained at length in Chapter 3 that there are not necessarily formal and substantive differences between one domain and the other. Articles 101 and 102 TFEU have the necessary flexibility to functionally mimic economic regulation. In addition, it has been suggested that competition law and economic regulation may become blended to such an extent that it may become difficult to try and distinguish between one and the other in any meaningful way. Competition law would not just act as a safety net or a mechanism to rectify other regimes. It would become ingrained in legislation. Articles 101 and 102 TFEU would give way to other instruments, such as the 'new competition tool', which would free competition authorities from the legal and institutional constraints that are inherent to the two provisions.

The hybridisation – to borrow the expression used by Dunne[75] – of competition law and regulation is not a new phenomenon. The example of the EU Regulatory Framework for electronic communications – which can be seen, in substance, as a branch of competition law – has been mentioned in Section 1. Similarly, market investigations have long been a central feature of the UK competition law regime. This said, the new environment may lead to the acceleration of the trend in the EU, whether by means of legal transplants (such as the 'new competition tool', which essentially borrows from the UK system), by means of ad hoc regulatory instruments or through a combination of both. The novelty of the emerging landscape may be not so much hybridisation as the resulting fragmentation of the legal and institutional system. A multiplicity of – partially or totally – overlapping regimes may coexist alongside one another, each seeking to promote and/or preserve competition in their particular, idiosyncratic ways.

---

[75] Niamh Dunne, 'Between competition law and regulation: hybridized approaches to market control' (2014) 2 Journal of Antitrust Enforcement 225.

The End of Competition Law or a New Relationship with Regulation?   149

Table 5.1 A taxonomy of regulatory obligations under the DMA

Nature of the obligation	Purpose of the obligation	Technique	Provision
Contestability-driven (fairness follows)	Change the operation of the gatekeeper's core segment	Limit exploitation of economies of scale and scope	Article 5(2) DMA
		Horizontal interoperability	Article 7 DMA
	Open up layers within the ecosystem to business users	Unbundled access to business users' services	Article 5(7) DMA
		Sideloading allowed and technically enabled	Article 6(4) DMA
		Vertical interoperability	Article 6(7) DMA
		Access to search data by other search engines	Article 6(11) DMA
	Regulate the terms and conditions of access to a layer	Ban on the use of non-public data	Article 6(2) DMA
		Allow and enable uninstallation and default setting	Article 6(3) DMA
		Ban on self-preferencing	Article 6(5) DMA

(continued)

Table 5.1 (Continued)

Nature of the obligation	Purpose of the obligation	Technique	Provision
Fairness-driven (contestability follows)	Facilitate and ensure cross-platform access by business and end users	Ban on most-favoured-nation clauses	Article 5(3) DMA
		Right to promote offers accessible by other means	Article 5(4) DMA
		Access to services acquired outside the platform	Article 5(5) DMA
		Data portability	Article 6(9) DMA
	Regulate the conditions for access and use of the platform	No additional registration	Article 5(8) DMA
		Ability to switch services within the platform	Article 6(6) DMA
		FRAND access to the platform	Article 6(12) DMA
	Regulate access to tools and data by business users	Information to advertisers on price and fees	Article 5(9) DMA
		Information to publishers on price and fees	Article 5(10) DMA
		Access to performance measuring tools	Article 6(8) DMA
		Access to the data generated by the business	Article 6(10) DMA
	Contractual termination and dispute settlement	Guaranteed access to courts and authorities	Article 5(6) DMA
		Proportionate termination	Article 6(13) DMA

PART II
Case Studies

6

Energy and Telecommunications

1. Competition Law in the Telecommunications and Energy Sectors

1.1. How and Why Competition Law Contributes to Liberalisation Efforts

Competition law played a fundamental role in the liberalisation of telecommunications and energy. Articles 101 and 102 TFEU accompanied the opening of both sectors to competition and contributed to the success and consolidation of the process. The Table provided at the end of this chapter gives an idea of the scale of enforcement in absolute and relative terms, if only from a quantitative standpoint. At various points in time over the past two decades, telecommunications and energy have been the focus policy-making. It is sufficient to think, in this sense, of the decisions issued prior to, and in the immediate aftermath of, the adoption of the so-called Third Energy Package by the EU legislature[1] and of the string of Article 102 TFEU decisions taken against telecommunications incumbents.[2] Similar efforts were subsequently extended to conduct in other network industries.

EU competition law contributes to liberalisation in three primary ways. These modes of interaction with economic regulation have been identified and discussed in Chapter 3. First, competition law has repeatedly acted as a safety net,

---

[1] See in particular Directive 2009/72/EC of the European Parliament and of the Council of 13 July 2009 concerning common rules for the internal market in electricity and repealing Directive 2003/54/EC [2009] OJ L211/55 (no longer in force); Regulation (EC) No 714/2009 of the European Parliament and of the Council of 13 July 2009 on conditions for access to the network for cross-border exchanges in electricity and repealing Regulation (EC) No 1228/2003 [2009] OJ L211/15 (no longer in force); and Regulation (EC) No 713/2009 of the European Parliament and of the Council of 13 July 2009 establishing an Agency for the Cooperation of Energy Regulators [2009] OJ L211/1. The Third Energy Package was subsequently replaced and superseded by the so-called Fourth or Winter Package of 2019. See in particular Directive (EU) 2019/944 of the European Parliament and of the Council of 5 June 2019 on common rules for the internal market for electricity and amending Directive 2012/27/EU [2019] OJ L158/125.

[2] *Deutsche Telekom AG* (Case COMP/C-1/37.451, 37.578, 37.579) Commission Decision of 21 May 2003; *Wanadoo Interactive* (COMP/38.233) Commission Decision of 16 July 2003; *Wanadoo España v Telefónica* (Case COMP/38.784) Commission Decision of 4 July 2007; *Telekomunikacja Polska* (COMP/39.525) Commission Decision of 22 June 2011; and *Slovak Telekom* (Case AT.39523) Commission Decision of 15 October 2014.

in the sense that it has become a parallel avenue through which the objectives of liberalisation regimes have been preserved or attained. This mode of interaction is relevant where the contentious practice falls firmly within the substantive scope of a sectoral regime and where the latter is principle adequately equipped to deal with the issue. Even in these circumstances – or, rather, in particular in these circumstances – Articles 101 and 102 TFEU have been frequently relied upon. The series of decisions concerning incumbent operators in the telecommunications industry provide an eloquent illustration of how and when competition law acts as a safety net.

Second, competition law has played a gap-filling role. Even when they are expressly designed to be future-proof[3] (just like the Regulatory Framework for electronic communications was in the early 2000s), sectoral regimes are not necessarily, or not always, fully equipped to deal with every concern or with every structural change in the industry. They may be based on a particular assumption about the evolution of market dynamics, and thus may not adequately respond to every emerging challenge. Similarly, the sort of intervention that the sector might require may not be easily attained by means of regulatory action. Whenever such gaps emerge, Articles 101 and 102 TFEU may be able to address them, even if partially or imperfectly. Competition law enforcement is, in fact, often an intermediate step that takes place prior to subsequent regulatory reform. In the energy sector, for instance, the European Commission's (hereinafter, the 'Commission') activity enabled some structural changes that prepared the ground for effective competition.

Finally, Articles 101 and 102 TFEU have occasionally been applied in a way that amounts, in effect, to the rectification of regulation. In the telecommunications and energy industries, competition law enforcement has sometimes led to more far-reaching intervention than that achieved under sectoral regimes. To the extent that secondary legislation is by necessity the product of a compromise, regulation may not always be as ambitious as it could be. It may also fall short of the vision offered in the original legislative proposal. It is not surprising, against this background, that the Commission, in the exercise of its powers to enforce Articles 101 and 102 TFEU, has explored the extent to which these provisions can be relied upon to attain some policy outcomes where it deems formal regimes insufficiently bold.

The decision-making practice in the telecommunications and energy industries illustrates the relative advantages of Articles 101 and 102 TFEU in a multi-level system of enforcement. That sector-specific regulation is more effective

---

[3] The idea of future-proof regulation refers to the design of legislation so that it can seamlessly adapt to changes in the economic and technological landscape. For a discussion of the concept, see Pablo Ibáñez Colomo, 'Future-Proof Regulation against the Test of Time: The Evolution of European Telecommunications Regulation' (2022) 42 Oxford Journal of Legal Studies 1170.

than competition law is typically considered to be self-evident – and for good reasons. The substantive threshold for intervention is generally lower under a dedicated regime; in addition, the latter is implemented by a specialised agency with the necessary resources and expertise. The picture changes however, where enforcement is structured around two or more levels. In such an institutional setup, competition law may present advantages in a number of respects, at least from the perspective of some players. For instance, action under Articles 101 and 102 TFEU gives the Commission the ability to intervene directly and bypass national agencies. It lacks similar powers under either telecommunications and energy regulation (the enforcement of which is entrusted to the said national agencies) or through the legislative process (where its role is confined to presenting legislative proposals).

In the same vein, the administrative practice of the past decades also shows that competition law enforcement may be an effective mechanism to address the imperfect operation of sector-specific regulation. For instance, a dedicated regime does not necessarily provide the Commission with a swift and adequate route to address enforcement failures at the national level. Such regulatory failures may arise, for instance, where a national authority is insufficiently committed to the liberalisation process. In such instances, the Commission, instead of opening infringement proceedings against the Member State in question, may decide to enforce Articles 101 and 102 TFEU. EU competition law, in other words, may provide for a more direct route for the Commission to signal its concerns about the perceived failures of sector-specific regulation.

1.2. How Enforcement in Regulated Markets has Shaped Competition Law

Just like the liberalisation process cannot be understood without the enforcement of Articles 101 and 102 TFEU, the application of both provisions in the telecommunications and energy sectors has had a major impact on the substantive evolution of EU competition law. To begin with, the Commission's practice – and the case law that followed – has settled the terms of the interaction of competition law and sectoral regimes. It has defined, in other words, the space where Articles 101 and 102 TFEU apply. In addition, enforcement in the two sectors has clarified some fundamental principles of EU competition law. In many respects, the relevant decisional practice paved the way for the rise of the 'more economics-based approach' during the late 1990s to early 2000s. Administrative action has also led to the introduction of new legal doctrines and the expansion of existing ones. What is more, network industries provided the ideal factual scenarios within which to experiment with the sort of proactive remedies that had been rarely imposed until then.

1.2.1. The Terms of the Interaction between Competition Law and Regulation

The first contribution concerns the terms of the interaction between competition law and economic regulation. In order to conceptualise the interplay between both disciplines, one must bear in mind that sector-specific regimes (including in the telecommunications and energy industries) frequently craft artificial market structures to attain their goals. These structures are artificial in the sense that they originate thanks to, and are sustained by, the regulatory duties imposed upon some operators. As discussed in Chapter 3, such duties include access and non-discrimination obligations, which allow new players to enter the sector under favourable terms and conditions (by, inter alia, setting access prices and by allowing them to compete in the market without building their own infrastructure) and which address, pre-emptively, the risk of leveraging conduct.

The question, from a competition law standpoint, is how Articles 101 and 102 TFEU interact with the structures created by regulation. Under one understanding of this interaction, artificially engineered markets cannot be the background against which competition law infringements are assessed. To the extent that they are a creature of regulation, such markets cannot determine the applicability of Articles 101 and 102 TFEU. They cannot be taken as given, according to this approach. Instead, the argument goes, intervention under competition law should consider the conditions that would have prevailed in the absence of regulatory intervention. Thus, if the relevant markets exist only because of the regime, Articles 101 and 102 TFEU would not be applicable to them. Suppose that an incumbent gives access to its infrastructure to its downstream rivals only because there is a sectoral mandate in place. Because the wholesale access market that results from this obligation would disappear if regulation were to be withdrawn, competition law should not be enforced in it.

Under a second understanding of the interaction, the market structure crafted by the regime would be the relevant background against which the lawfulness of practices is assessed. From this perspective, the fact that, absent regulation, the market would not have existed is not a relevant consideration. Whether or not the ecosystem is an artificial creature of the sectoral regime would be equally immaterial. Artificial or not, the prevailing conditions of competition would be taken as given for the purposes of the application of Articles 101 and 102 TFEU. In *Deutsche Telekom*[4] and the cases that followed (in particular *TeliaSonera*[5] and *Slovak Telekom*[6]) the Court of Justice (hereinafter, the 'Court' or the 'ECJ') opted decisively for this second understanding. The implications for competition law enforcement are significant. By taking the markets crafted by regulation as given (as opposed to speculating about the conditions that would have prevailed in the

---

[4] Case C-280/08 P *Deutsche Telekom AG v Commission*, EU:C:2010:603.
[5] Case C-52/09 *Konkurrensverket v TeliaSonera Sverige AB*, EU:C:2011:83.
[6] Case C-165/19 P *Slovak Telekom, a.s. v Commission*, EU:C:2021:239.

absence of the sectoral regime), Articles 101 and 102 TFEU have a much greater scope for application in the energy and telecommunications industries. In this sense, the Court opted for a model that maximises the potential contribution of competition law in liberalised industries.

1.2.2. Liberalised Industries and the 'More Economics-based' Approach

The liberalisation of the telecommunications and energy industries took place at the same time as the Commission's policy was firmly shifting towards a 'more economics-based' approach. It is therefore not surprising that the administrative practice of the time is infused with the analytical spirit of the latter. In particular, seminal cases like *Deutsche Telekom* were premised on the idea that a practice is only unlawful where it has the potential to exclude rivals that are as efficient as the dominant firm.[7] Accordingly, the foreclosure of firms that are less efficient, in the sense that they have a higher cost structure or their products are otherwise less attractive, would be unproblematic from a competition law standpoint. This position reflects a characteristic concern of the time, namely the need to distinguish between the 'protection of competition' and the 'protection of competitors'.[8]

The 'as efficient competitor' principle found its way, in particular, in 'margin squeeze' cases. The concern underpinning this category is that a vertically-integrated firm, which provides a wholesale input to its downstream rivals, may exclude the latter by leaving them an insufficient margin to operate profitably.[9] The Commission and the EU courts agreed that this practice can only be a concern under Article 102 TFEU where it would drive equally efficient third parties out of the market, which can only occur where the dominant firm's downstream division would not have been able to operate at a profit given the wholesale prices charged by its own upstream arm.[10] This would be the case, for instance, where the wholesale prices charged by the vertically-integrated undertaking are higher than the retail prices paid by its end-users (that is, a negative 'margin squeeze').[11]

---

[7] *Deutsche Telekom* (n 4), para 143.

[8] Eleanor M Fox, 'We Protect Competition, You Protect Competitors' (2003) 26 World Competition 149.

[9] *TeliaSonera* (n 5), para 32 ('In the present case, there would be such a margin squeeze if, inter alia, the spread between the wholesale prices for ADSL input services and the retail prices for broadband connection services to end users were either negative or insufficient to cover the specific costs of the ADSL input services which TeliaSonera has to incur in order to supply its own retail services to end users, so that that spread does not allow a competitor which is as efficient as that undertaking to compete for the supply of those services to end users'.

[10] Ibid, para 33: 'In such circumstances, although the competitors may be as efficient as the dominant undertaking, they may be able to operate on the retail market only at a loss or at artificially reduced levels of profitability'.

[11] Ibid, para 73.

158 *Energy and Telecommunications*

The case law and administrative practice on 'margin squeeze' conduct have clarified the case law in another sense. In its *Deutsche Telekom* judgment, the Court did not hold that the anticompetitive effects of this practice can be simply assumed merely by virtue of the fact that equally efficient rivals would be forced to sell at a loss.[12] The exclusionary impact of a 'margin squeeze' would have to be established, case-by-case, in light of the economic and legal context.[13] Thus, the assessment of the anticompetitive effects of practices is sometimes part of the evaluation of their lawfulness under Article 102 TFEU. This position, which is in line with the core tenets of the 'more economics-based' approach, would be confirmed in subsequent case law. There is little doubt now, over a decade later, that the context-specific evaluation of potentially abusive practices is the rule, not the exception, under Article 102 TFEU. From this perspective, 'margin squeeze' cases changed the case law for good.

1.2.3. *The Expansion of Existing Doctrines and the Creation of New Ones*

The enforcement of Articles 101 and 102 TFEU in regulated markets provided fertile ground for the expansion of existing legal doctrines and the introduction of new ones. One of the main reasons telecommunications and energy are subject to a sector-specific regime is that they are structured around a bottleneck segment where it is difficult – if not inefficient from an economic standpoint – to inject competition. Thus, promoting and/or preserving effective rivalry in adjacent markets typically involves mandating shared access to the bottleneck. It is notoriously difficult for a competition authority to impose such access obligations under Article 102 TFEU. Under the *Bronner* doctrine, it would be necessary for the authority to show not only that the infrastructure is indispensable for competition on an adjacent market, but also that a refusal to deal would lead to the 'elimination of all competition' therein.[14]

As already pointed out in Chapter 1, it is not surprising, against this background, that authorities explore new interpretations of the law allowing them to circumvent, in effect, the substantive hurdles imposed by the *Bronner* doctrine. In the energy sector, for instance, the Commission has taken action against incumbents controlling bottlenecks on grounds of discrimination, rather than

---

[12] *Deutsche Telekom* (n 4), para 250: 'With regard to the third part of the second ground of appeal, it must be held at the outset that, in paragraphs 234 to 244 of the judgment under appeal, the General Court correctly rejected the Commission's arguments to the effect that the very existence of a pricing practice of a dominant undertaking which leads to the margin squeeze of its equally efficient competitors constitutes an abuse within the meaning of Article 82 EC, and that it is not necessary for an anti-competitive effect to be demonstrated'.

[13] Ibid, para 255, where the Court undertakes an evaluation of the effects of the practice in the specific circumstances of the case.

[14] Case C-7/97 *Oscar Bronner GmbH & Co. KG v Mediaprint Zeitungs- und Zeitschriftenverlag GmbH & Co. KG and others*, EU:C:1998:569, para 41.

the indispensability of the infrastructure at stake. In *German Electricity Balancing Market*, for instance, the authority argued that the incumbent's vertical integration created a conflict of interest that led it to favour its own electricity generation activities over competing ones.[15] In *ENI*, it claimed that the said conflict of interest led to 'strategic underinvestment' in capacity, allowing the firm to preserve its position in the relevant downstream market.[16] In other words, rather than claiming that the dominant firm had refused to give access to its infrastructure, it argued that it had failed to accommodate rivals.

1.2.4. Remedies in Liberalised Industries

The structural make-up that explains why intervention in regulated industries often involves access obligations also explains why the Commission's action has led to innovations when addressing concerns and bringing infringements to an end. As explained in Chapter 1, intervention in markets structured around a bottleneck is often proactive in nature. In this regard, the administrative practice has resulted in the imposition of a variety of relatively intrusive obligations. In some cases, the Commission has gone as far as to mandate a structural breakup (more precisely, the divestiture of the bottleneck segment).[17] Behavioural remedies, in turn, have led to, inter alia, the restructuring of the electricity transmission market in Sweden,[18] the creation of a power exchange,[19] and a wholesale review of Gazprom activities in Central and Eastern Europe in order to facilitate the integration of the various regional markets and ensure the cross-border flow of gas.[20]

1.3. The Institutional Dimension of the Interaction between Disciplines

Two main themes emerge from a substantive overview of EU competition law enforcement in the telecommunications and energy sectors. The first is the expansion of legal doctrines and the development of new ones. This phenomenon appears to be – at least in part – a predictable response to the relatively strict substantive standards enshrined in the relevant case law, which limit the scope for intervention. The phenomenon may also be the consequence of the influence of sector-specific regulation and the objectives underpinning it. A second

---

[15] *German Electricity Wholesale Market* (Case COMP/39388) and *German Electricity Balancing Market* (Case COMP/39389), Commission Decision of 26 November 2008, paras 50–55.
[16] *ENI* (Case COMP/39.315) Commission Decision of 29 September 2010.
[17] *German Electricity Balancing Market* (n 15).
[18] *Swedish Interconnectors* (Case 39351) Commission Decision of 14 April 2010.
[19] *BEH Electricity* (Case AT.39767) Commission Decision of 10 December 2015.
[20] *Upstream Gas Supplies in Central and Eastern Europe* (Case AT.39816) Commission Decision of 24 May 2018.

theme relates to the nature of intervention under Articles 101 and 102 TFEU. As the examples mentioned above show, the enforcement of competition law in the telecommunications and energy industries not only mimics the sort of measures adopted in sectoral regimes but is also particularly far-reaching (and might go as far as to lead to structural divestitures).

These substantive trends must be placed in the institutional framework that allowed for their emergence and evolution. The expansion of legal doctrines and the development of new ones was facilitated by two of the instruments that the EU legislature introduced in Regulation 1/2003, namely commitments decisions and sector inquiries. It is by means of these instruments that the Commission was able to signal its policy priorities while minimising the constraints defined by law. Commitments decisions have effectively complemented more traditional forms of intervention – and, in particular, decisions establishing an infringement and imposing fines. The Energy Sector Inquiry, in turn, allowed the Commission to lay out a plan of action without identifying individual breaches of Articles 101 and 102 TFEU.

1.3.1. Quasi-legislation in EU Competition Law: Soft Law and Sector Inquiries

It has already been mentioned that the powers that the Commission enjoys as a competition agency are not comparable to the position it has in the context of the adoption of primary legislation. Its role is confined, under the latter, to proposing texts to the EU legislature. The practical consequence is that the Parliament and the Council may not always follow the vision laid out by the Commission (and, even if they do, they may disagree in some respects). In relation, specifically, to network industries regulation, experience suggests that Member States tend to be less ambitious in their plans to promote competition and/or may focus on the need to balance competition against other considerations. Given the importance of the energy sector for economic and non-economic reasons and given the status of incumbent operators at the national level, the EU legislature may have a more prudent vision than the Commission's about the pace, scope and reach of legal reform. Where such differences of views emerge, competition law may be relied upon to outline the authority's preferences and signal how Articles 101 and 102 TFEU might complement – and in some respects rectify – legislation.

The Commission's ability to issue competition-related secondary legislation akin to that of formal regulatory regimes is significantly constrained under the Treaty. By and large, it remains confined to block exemptions applying to certain categories of agreements and specifying the conditions under which the said agreements fall outside the scope of Article 101(1) TFEU.[21] As a result of these

---

[21] As discussed in Chapter 1, the instrument that enables the Commission to adopt block exemption regulations is defined and constrained by the scope of application enshrined in Regulation No 19/65/EEC of 2 March of the Council on application of Article 85 (3) of the Treaty to certain categories

constraints, the Commission is not able to rely on its competition law powers to regulate sectors on the basis of legally binding general and abstract duties and prohibitions. However, this fact has not prevented it from making a creative use of its powers to outline its vision about how Articles 101 and 102 TFEU are to be enforced in certain industries. As discussed in Chapter 1, soft law instruments have played a major role in this sense. For instance, a set of Guidelines[22] and a Notice on access agreements[23] accompanied the opening of telecommunications activities to competition during the 1990s.

In the process that would lead to the adoption of the so-called Third Energy Package, the Commission launched a Sector Inquiry pursuant to Article 17 of Regulation 1/2003. Formally speaking, the role of this instrument is to gather information about whether, and to what extent, competition is restricted or distorted within the internal market. The focus, in this sense, is on the 'agreements, decisions and concerted practices'.[24] The Energy Sector Inquiry fulfilled this role, and identified a series of markets and activities where there were persistent obstacles to competition. In particular, the Commission placed an emphasis on exclusivity contracts leading to vertical foreclosure[25] and on practices aimed at restricting cross-border trade between Member States.[26] The principles laid down in the Final Report provided a template that would then be implemented in the series of decisions that followed.

However, the Report issued by the Commission at the end of the inquiry was not confined to breaches of competition law, and directly addressed some of the obstacles to competition in gas and electricity resulting from legacy market structures. In other words, the document did not just identify conduct potentially infringing Articles 101 and 102 TFEU. It also discussed how competition could be promoted by tweaking the prevailing market structures. The latter is the natural province of sector-specific regulation, not of competition law. In spite of this fact, the Commission went as far as to advocate changes aimed at injecting competition, such as a duty to share virtual electricity generation capacity to third parties[27] and,

---

of agreements and concerted practices [1965] OJ 36/533. One should consider, in addition, that the Commission may issue Directives in accordance with Article 106(3) TFEU.

[22] Guidelines on the application of EEC competition rules in the telecommunications sector [1991] OJ C233/2.

[23] Notice on the application of the competition rules to access agreements in the telecommunications sector [1998] OJ C265/2.

[24] See Article 17(1) of Council Regulation (EC) No 1/2003 of 16 December 2002 on the implementation of the rules on competition laid down in Articles 81 and 82 of the Treaty [2003] OJ L1/1, which in the second sub-paragraph provides that '[t]he Commission may in particular request the undertakings or associations of undertakings concerned to communicate to it all agreements, decisions and concerted practices'.

[25] European Commission, 'Inquiry pursuant to Article 17 of Regulation (EC) No 1/2003 into the European gas and electricity sectors (Final Report)' COM(2006) 851 final, paras 18–20 and 35–37.

[26] Ibid, paras 21–23.

[27] Ibid, para 43: 'Energy release programmes (i.e. electricity Virtual Power Plant auctions and gas release programmes) are a means to develop market liquidity and increase entry opportunities. They constitute suitable remedies to competition concerns not only in the merger area but also under antitrust rules. In order to be fully effective they must be well-designed and large scale [...]'.

in particular, the so-called ownership unbundling of bottleneck segments (that is, the structural separation of these segments).[28] Ownership unbundling was, in fact, at the heart of the legislative proposals issued by the Commission.[29]

1.3.2. The Role of Commitments Decisions

The Commission's enforcement activity in the telecommunications and energy sectors has relied on infringement decisions adopted in accordance with Article 7 of Regulation 1/2003 and, in particular, on commitments decisions pursuant to Article 9. The choice between one instrument or the other was seemingly based on the nature of intervention. Reactive measures that can be effectively implemented via a one-off, cease-and-desist order were introduced by means of an infringement decision. Proactive intervention, on the other hand, has been the privileged realm of Article 9 of Regulation 1/2003. The use of the latter is, from an institutional standpoint, the single most salient aspect of the Commission's enforcement activity in the energy and telecommunications markets. In many respects, commitments as an instrument came of age when relied upon in these two industries. For a period of time – and, more precisely, from the mid-2000s to the early to mid-2010s – Article 9 decisions were a central feature of the enforcement landscape at the EU level. It is precisely during this period that the Commission's focus on recently liberalised markets was particularly intense. As a result, these two industries account, even to this day, for a substantial fraction of the total number of commitments decisions adopted since 2005.[30]

Article 9 enforcement has been so central to the application of Articles 101 and 102 TFEU in energy and telecommunications markets (in particular the former) that some of the trends and developments discussed above cannot be fully grasped without taking into account the role they played; and how their nature and operation influenced policy choices. As observed in Chapter 1, these instruments facilitate innovative enforcement in three interrelated ways. To begin with, they do not require that the Commission establish an infringement of Articles 101 and 102 TFEU. What is more, the substantive analysis can remain speculative, in the sense that it is confined to outlining, in the context of a preliminary assessment, the concerns raised by the contentious practice. Finally, it is unlikely to see commitments decisions challenged before the EU courts (whether by the addressees of these decisions or third parties). These distinctive features, taken together,

---

[28] Ibid, para 55: 'Economic evidence shows that full ownership unbundling is the most effective means to ensure choice for energy users and encourage investment. This is because separate network companies are not influenced by overlapping supply/generation interests as regards investment decisions'.

[29] European Commission, 'Prospects for the internal gas and electricity market' COM(2006) 841 final.

[30] See the Table provided at the end of this Chapter.

allow the Commission to venture into new doctrines or to test the boundaries of existing ones.

It is not surprising, against this background, that a significant fraction of commitments decisions in the energy sector concern the conditions of access to essential facilities. Showing, in the context of a prohibition decision, that the conditions laid down in *Bronner* are met is notoriously difficult for any authority. Reaching certain outcomes – such as mandating shared access to an infrastructure or a divestiture – is markedly easier in the context of a negotiated procedure with the undertakings. Avoiding the need to establish an infringement to the requisite legal standard, moreover, facilitates the tentative expansion of existing doctrines in a number of ways. It allows, for instance, to introduce the idea that a refusal to invest in capacity is anticompetitive, or the idea that discrimination by a vertically-integrated firm against its upstream or downstream rivals amounts, in and of itself, to a breach of Article 102 TFEU.

Commitments decisions also facilitate innovative policy-making at the remedy stage. Where the Commission adopts a decision establishing an infringement within the meaning of Article 7 of Regulation 1/2003, remedies must keep proportion with the breach.[31] What is more, the bar to impose structural measures (such as a divestiture) is distinctly high.[32] Administrative action under Article 9, on the other hand, is not subject to such constraints, both in effect and as a matter of law. To the extent that commitments are submitted by the firms subject to an investigation, they may go beyond what is strictly necessary to address the consequences of a potential infringement. In *Alrosa*, the Court confirmed that, from a legal standpoint, the proportionality assessment that needs to be undertaken in the context of commitment proceedings cannot be compared to that required under Article 7 of the Regulation.[33]

2. Autonomous Forms of Abuse in Regulated Markets: 'Margin Squeeze' and Beyond

Action against 'margin squeeze' and similar conduct marks the symbolic start of enforcement in the post-liberalisation context. In many ways, it exemplifies how fragile and unusual competition is in the early stages of the process. 'Margin squeeze' concerns arise in instances where one or several firms operating on a retail market depend on access to a wholesale input provided by a vertically-integrated

---

[31] Article 7 of Regulation 1/2003 (n 24), which requires that remedies be 'proportionate to the infringement committed and necessary to bring the infringement effectively to an end'.
[32] Ibid. The Regulation confines the administration of structural remedies to instances 'where there is no equally effective behavioural remedy or where any equally effective behavioural remedy would be more burdensome for the undertaking concerned than the structural remedy'.
[33] Case C-441/07 P *Commission v Alrosa Company Ltd*, EU:C:2010:377.

undertaking (which is therefore both a supplier and a rival). This form of retail competition is fragile in the sense that it depends on a regulatory apparatus imposing and maintaining a combination of obligations designed to allow new entrants to thrive downstream. The market setting is unusual insofar as a firm's ability to compete at the retail level rarely depends on access to a wholesale input supplied by a rival. If dominance is a relatively rare occurrence in the economy, a position of superdominance allowing a rival to control downstream competition is rarer (even after the rise of the digital economy).

2.1. 'Margin Squeeze' as a Constructive Refusal to Deal: Legal and Policy Considerations

The legal treatment of 'margin squeeze' conduct under Article 102 TFEU became a subject of interest during the early to mid-2000s. The approach to this issue, about which entire libraries were written,[34] has major implications for the role of competition law in regulated industries. The terms of the debate are relatively simple. Should a 'margin squeeze' be treated as a refusal to deal, or should it be treated as an autonomous form of abuse? Opting for the former would mean that the practice would only be abusive where the conditions laid down in *Bronner* (or *Magill* and *IMS Health*) are met. An inevitable consequence of that approach is that the scope for intervention under Article 102 TFEU would be limited. Conversely, treating 'margin squeeze' conduct as an autonomous form of abuse would allow for competition law to play a frequent and meaningful role as a safety net.

The arguments in favour of treating this practice as a refusal to deal subject to the *Bronner* case law have been abundantly discussed in the literature.[35] The fundamental premise underpinning this position is that a 'margin squeeze' and an outright refusal to deal have an identical object and effect. In one scenario, rivals would be driven out of the market as a result of the spread between the wholesale and the retail prices; in the other, exclusion would be more direct. From an economic standpoint, however, there would be no difference between one strategy and the other. Consistency would demand, in the same vein, that they be subject to the same treatment as a matter of law. Thus, if a refusal to deal is only abusive where, inter alia, the relevant input is indispensable for downstream competition, the same should be true of a 'margin squeeze'. It is occasionally pointed out, in

---

[34] See in particular and Damien Geradin and Robert O'Donoghue, 'The Concurrent Application of Competition Law and Regulation: The Case of Margin Squeeze Abuses in the Telecommunications Sector' (2005) GCLC Working Paper No. 04/05; Niamh Dunne, 'Margin squeeze: theory, practice, policy, part I' (2012) 33 European Competition Law Review 29; and Friso Bostoen, 'Margin Squeeze: Where Competition Law and Sector Regulation Compete' (2016–17) 53 Jura Falconis 3.

[35] Damien Geradin, 'Refusal to supply and margin squeeze: A discussion of why the 'Telefonica Exceptions' are wrong' (2011) TILEC Discussion Paper 2011-051; and Pablo Ibáñez Colomo, 'Indispensability and Abuse of Dominance: From Commercial Solvents to Slovak Telekom and Google Shopping' (2019) 10 Journal of European Competition Law & Practice 532.

addition, that it would be paradoxical to treat more leniently the more extreme manifestation of the conduct – the outright refusal – than a milder variation thereof.[36]

These ideas were deemed persuasive enough to find their way into the Guidance Paper. In this policy document, the Commission presented a 'margin squeeze' as a potential manifestation of a refusal to deal, which would as such be scrutinised in light of the same conditions as the latter.[37] Accordingly, the Guidance Paper defines a set of prioritisation criteria that applies in principle to both outright and constructive refusals, and which is directly inspired from *Bronner*.[38] On the other hand, the document clarifies that intervention could be justified even when a wholesale input is not indispensable within the meaning of the case law. However, the exceptions to the principle apply indistinctly to all refusals to deal, and not just to 'margin squeeze' conduct.[39] In other words, the facts surrounding the case, as opposed to the formal manifestation of the practice, determine the applicable criteria.

The approach enshrined in the Guidance Paper is, in essence, the same as that endorsed by the US Supreme Court in *linkLine*,[40] and – with some caveats – by Advocate General Mazák in *TeliaSonera*.[41] In the former, Justice Roberts held that a 'margin squeeze' (or 'price squeeze', as it is termed on the other side of the Atlantic) does not give rise to an autonomous claim under Section 2 of the Sherman Act. Accordingly, a claimant would need to show either that the vertically-integrated firm has an antitrust duty to deal (and, in the same vein, that the 'price squeeze' would be in breach of the said duty) or that the prices charged by its downstream affiliate are predatory.[42] Under this approach, whether or not

---

[36] See, for instance, Geradin (n 35).

[37] Guidance on the Commission's enforcement priorities in applying Article 82 of the EC Treaty to abusive exclusionary conduct by dominant undertakings [2009] OJ C45/7, para 80.

[38] Ibid, para 81, which propose to prioritise the assessment of refusal to deal and margin squeeze conduct in accordance with the same criteria, set out in para 81 and inspired from *Bronner* (n 14) namely:

> 'The Commission will consider these practices as an enforcement priority if all the following circumstances are present:
> - the refusal relates to a product or service that is objectively necessary to be able to compete effectively on a downstream market,
> - the refusal is likely to lead to the elimination of effective competition on the downstream market, and
> - the refusal is likely to lead to consumer harm'.

[39] Ibid, para 82.

[40] *Pacific Bell Telephone Co. v. linkLine Communications, Inc.*, 555 U.S. 438 (2009).

[41] Opinion of Advocate General Mazák in Case C-52/09 *Konkurrensverket v TeliaSonera Sverige AB*, EU:C:2010:483.

[42] *linkLine* (n 40): 'Plaintiffs' price-squeeze claim, looking to the relation between retail and wholesale prices, is thus nothing more than an amalgamation of a meritless claim at the retail level and a meritless claim at the wholesale level. If there is no duty to deal at the wholesale level and no predatory pricing at the retail level, then a firm is certainly not required to price both of these services in a manner that preserves its rivals' profit margins'.

there is a sector-specific regime mandating shared access to the relevant inputs would not be a material consideration in the analysis. Advocate General Mazák, by contrast, argued that the *Bronner* conditions would be applicable where there is no regulatory obligation imposing an access duty.[43]

Several arguments have been advanced to claim that a 'margin squeeze' can justify intervention even when the – strict – conditions set out in *Bronner* are not met. One of these arguments has to do with the fact that the practice, unlike an outright refusal, is manifested where the vertically-integrated firm already supplies its inputs to its downstream rivals (whether because the firm does so voluntarily or because there is a sector-specific regime in place). A finding of infringement in a 'margin squeeze' case, accordingly, does not lead a *de novo* duty to supply (or at least not in principle). In such circumstances, the argument goes, the justifications that explain the reluctance to take action in refusal to deal cases would not be relevant. In particular, remedial intervention would not compel the competition authority to deal with third parties. Similarly, the authority would not be required to craft a complex proactive remedy.

A second, related, argument is that intervention in a 'margin squeeze' case does not impact negatively on firms' incentives to invest and innovate.[44] Where the dominant firm is already dealing with third parties (whether voluntarily or because it is required by regulation to do so), this concern would not be at stake. Remedial action in a 'margin squeeze' does not require the firm to change its monetisation strategy. Rather than asking the firm to alter the mechanism by which it recoups its investments, intervention would simply prohibit it from dealing with third parties on unfair terms and conditions. In other words, the infringement can be effectively brought to an end by means of a reactive measure. By the same token, the practice could be abusive irrespective of whether the relevant input is indispensable for competition on an adjacent market.

Other arguments against treating a 'margin squeeze' as a refusal to deal reflect a concern with policy-making, as opposed to strictly legal considerations. As already pointed out, requiring evidence that the input is indispensable reduces the scope for competition law enforcement. This is so, in particular, considering that bottlenecks in the telecommunications and energy industries are not necessarily indispensable within the meaning of the *Bronner* doctrine. Where there is an alternative infrastructure (such as a cable television network), a refusal to deal would not lead to the 'elimination of all competition', as the relevant case law would require. In such circumstances, an expansive interpretation of the scope of Article 102 TFEU would ensure that the provision can act as a safety net in regulated markets. From a policy-making perspective, in other words, a lower threshold for intervention in 'margin squeeze' cases could be justified to maximise the frequency and effectiveness of competition law enforcement.

---

[43] Opinion of AG Mazák in *TeliaSonera* (n 41), para 11.
[44] See in particular *Telefónica* (n 2), para 303 and Guidance (n 37), para 82.

2.2. The Court's Position: From *Deutsche Telekom* and *TeliaSonera* to *Slovak Telekom*

2.2.1. *Deutsche* Telekom, TeliaSonera *and its Immediate Aftermath*

The Court considered the legal status of 'margin squeeze' practices in *Deutsche Telekom*. However, it did not directly address the question of whether this behaviour is abusive only where the input is indispensable within the meaning of *Bronner*. As explained above, the point of law addressed in this case was whether evidence of a 'margin squeeze' is sufficient, in and of itself, to establish a breach of Article 102 TFEU. The Court ruled that this behaviour does not amount to an abuse by its very nature. A finding of infringement therefore necessitates an analysis of its anticompetitive effects.[45] In the specific circumstances of the case, the infrastructure was indispensable for downstream competition. This aspect was, in fact, the crucial consideration in the Court's assessment of the restrictive potential of the 'margin squeeze'.[46]

Deutsche Telekom could be interpreted as meaning that indispensability is a sufficient, but not necessary, condition to establish a breach of Article 102 TFEU. Alternatively, one could have argued that the practice is only abusive where the *Bronner* conditions are met (as they were in the case). It did not take long for the Court to be directly confronted with the question. Its preliminary ruling in *TeliaSonera* contradicted the position expressed by Advocate General Mazák (and, indeed, that outlined by the Commission in its Guidance Paper). It held that a 'margin squeeze' can be abusive irrespective of whether the input is indispensable (and, similarly, regardless of whether there is a regulatory obligation in place).[47] The Court advanced several reasons in support of its conclusions. First, it interpreted *Bronner* as addressing a narrow legal question, namely whether it is abusive for a dominant firm to refuse to deal with a rival.[48] It pointed out, in this regard, that the legal question at stake in *TeliaSonera* (and, indeed, any 'margin squeeze' case) is a different one, and relates to whether the spread between the wholesale and the retail prices is unfair under Article 102(a) TFEU (and this, to the extent that it is capable of excluding equally efficient rivals).[49]

Second, the Court held that the position advocated by the dominant firm in the case would impact negatively the effectiveness of Article 102 TFEU enforcement.

---

[45] *Deutsche Telekom* (n 4), para 250.
[46] Ibid, para 255: 'In the present case, since [...] the wholesale local loop access services provided by the appellant are indispensable to its competitors' effective penetration of the retail markets for the provision of services to end-users, the General Court was entitled to hold [...] that a margin squeeze [...] hinders the growth of competition in the retail markets in services to end-users, since a competitor who is as efficient as the appellant cannot carry on his business in the retail market for end-user access services without incurring losses'.
[47] *TeliaSonera* (n 5), para 55.
[48] Ibid, para 57.
[49] Ibid, para 34.

It would require an authority to provide evidence of indispensability prior to taking action in a 'margin squeeze' dispute.[50] Instead, *TeliaSonera* interpreted *Deutsche Telekom* as meaning that the indispensable nature of an input is a particularly relevant consideration when evaluating the likelihood of anticompetitive effects, but not a necessary condition to establish an abuse.[51] In fact, evidence of indispensability was deemed to be sufficient, alone, to establish the potential anticompetitive effects of the practice.[52] On the other hand, the ECJ does not rule out the possibility that, in a particular economic and legal context, a 'margin squeeze' leads to the actual or potential exclusion of equally efficient rivals even absent indispensability.[53]

2.2.2. Slovak Telekom, *or 'Margin Squeeze' by Other Means*

As far as 'margin squeeze' conduct is concerned, the applicability of the indispensability condition seemed settled since *TeliaSonera*. In spite of this fact, questions about the scope of the *Bronner* doctrine arose again in subsequent cases. Several of the grounds of appeal in *Telefónica*, for instance, insisted on the need for the Commission to establish the essentiality of the relevant infrastructure.[54] Because the Court had already held that a 'margin squeeze' is an autonomous form of abuse, these arguments were summarily dismissed. *Slovak Telekom*, on the other hand, raised novel points of law. The latter case is distinctive in that, unlike *Deutsche Telekom* and *TeliaSonera*, it deals both with price and non-price conduct. More precisely, the Commission decision[55] took issue not only with a 'margin squeeze' but also with other non-price strategies having the same object and effect. Such strategies include conduct such as withholding information that rivals needed to compete[56] or reducing the scope of the dominant firm's regulatory obligations.[57]

The said non-price practices can be aptly described as a 'margin squeeze' by other means, as they seek to limit downstream rivals' ability to compete, just like leaving an insufficient spread between wholesale and retail prices does. On the other hand, they could also be categorised as a refusal to deal, which is precisely what the Commission decision did.[58] Against this background, the point of law that required clarification was whether the abusive nature of every refusal must

---

[50] Ibid, para 58: 'Moreover, if *Bronner* were to be interpreted otherwise, in the way advocated by TeliaSonera, that would, as submitted by the European Commission, amount to a requirement that before any conduct of a dominant undertaking in relation to its terms of trade could be regarded as abusive the conditions to be met to establish that there was a refusal to supply would in every case have to be satisfied, and that would unduly reduce the effectiveness of Article 102 TFEU'.
[51] Ibid, para 70.
[52] Ibid, para 77.
[53] Ibid, para 72.
[54] Case C-295/12 P *Telefónica SA and Telefónica de España SAU v Commission*, EU:C:2014:2062.
[55] Commission Decision in *Slovak Telekom* (n 2).
[56] Ibid, paras 431–534.
[57] Ibid, paras 535–651.
[58] Ibid, paras 355–371.

be examined against the *Bronner* conditions or whether there are circumstances where a lower substantive threshold applies. In its decision, the Commission interpreted *TeliaSonera* as meaning that evidence of indispensability is not required whenever a dominant firm imposes unfair trade terms on its downstream rivals, irrespective of whether these result from price or non-price behaviour (and, by the same token, irrespective of whether the practice can be categorised as a refusal to deal).[59]

In line with the Opinion expressed by Advocate General Saugmandsgaard Øe,[60] the Court held that, in the specific circumstances of the case, *Bronner* was not the relevant benchmark against which the lawfulness of the contentious practices had to be assessed.[61] The reasoning appears to depart from *TeliaSonera* in some respects. The factor that determines the applicability of the *Bronner* criteria, in *Slovak Telekom*, is whether remedial action would result in the imposition of a duty to deal. Thus, where intervention would lead to proactive intervention, indispensability would be an element of the legal test.[62] By the same token, where there is a regulatory regime in place imposing access obligations, or where the dominant undertaking voluntarily shares its infrastructure, it would not be necessary to show that the *Bronner* criteria are met.[63] In the latter two scenarios, an abuse can be established by providing evidence of the actual or potential anticompetitive effects of the practice.

The Court's position regarding the scope of the *Bronner* criteria is justified on two grounds. First, requiring a firm to deal with third parties interferes with its freedom of contract and with its right to property.[64] Second, an overly liberal attitude vis-à-vis access obligations can be expected to have a negative impact on firms' incentives to invest and innovate.[65] To the extent that it does, it would be at odds with the objectives of Article 102 TFEU. This second point echoes Advocate

---

[59] Ibid, para 366: 'The Commission considers first that the Court of Justice is not referring at paragraph 55 of its TeliaSonera judgment only to margin squeeze, but generally, to "conduct such as supplying services or selling goods on conditions which are disadvantageous or on which there might be no purchaser"'.

[60] Opinion of Advocate General Saugmandsgaard Øe in Cases C-152/19 P and C-165/19 P *Deutsche Telekom AG and Slovak Telekom a.s.* EU:C:2020:678.

[61] *Slovak Telekom* (n 6), para 53.

[62] Ibid, para 49: 'The application, to a particular case, of the conditions laid down by the Court of Justice in the judgment in *Bronner*, set out in paragraph 44 of the present judgment, and in particular the condition relating to the indispensability of the access to the dominant undertaking's infrastructure, allows the competent authority or national court to determine whether that undertaking has a genuinely tight grip on the market by virtue of that infrastructure. Thus, that undertaking may be forced to give a competitor access to an infrastructure that it has developed for the needs of its own business only where such access is indispensable to the business of such a competitor, namely where there is no actual or potential substitute for that infrastructure'.

[63] Ibid, para 50: 'By contrast, where a dominant undertaking gives access to its infrastructure but makes that access, provision of services or sale of products subject to unfair conditions, the conditions laid down by the Court of Justice in paragraph 41 of the judgment in Bronner do not apply'.

[64] Ibid, para 45.

[65] Ibid, para 47.

General Jacobs' Opinion in *Bronner*[66] (also reiterated by Advocate General Saugmandsgaard Øe), where he noted that, even though a duty to deal seemingly promotes competition in the short term (in the sense that it leads to new entry and an increase in rivalry), it is detrimental to it in the long run insofar as it discourages the development of new efficient facilities.[67] These two considerations, however, would not be relevant in a factual scenario such as the one at stake in *Slovak Telekom*.

2.3. Analysis and Implications of the Court's Position

TeliaSonera and *Slovak Telekom* address the central aspect of the interaction between competition law and regulation. By holding that the *Bronner* doctrine is not relevant where there is a sector-specific regime in place, the Court ruled, in effect, that the (artificial) market structure created by means of regulatory intervention is the playing field where anticompetitive effects are assessed. Put differently, the ECJ accepts the reality of the sector as a regulated one and takes it as given. It does not require the Commission to consider what the conditions of competition would have been in the absence of sector-specific intervention. *TeliaSonera* is explicit about the rationale behind this choice. The Court emphasises that requiring evidence of the indispensability of the infrastructure would have a negative impact on the effectiveness of Article 102 TFEU enforcement in regulated industries.

In a multi-level institutional landscape such as the EU one, it is not surprising that the Court chose to prioritise effective enforcement over other considerations. In line with what has been discussed above, it is reasonable to ensure that competition law preserves a meaningful role in recently liberalised markets. The factual background of some of the cases discussed above provides concrete illustrations of the value of Articles 101 and 102 TFEU as a safety net. For instance, it has not escaped commentators that *Deutsche Telekom* cannot be fully understood without taking into account the broader institutional context, and in particular the fact that there were legitimate doubts about the commitment by the national regulatory authority to the liberalisation process. Some aspects of the case reveal that some decisions adopted by the German sectoral agency at least facilitated, if not contributed to, the 'margin squeeze'.[68]

Favouring effective enforcement over other considerations is not without implications for the legal order. One consequence is that the discipline may be applied

---

[66] Opinion of Advocate General Jacobs in Case C-7/97 *Oscar Bronner GmbH & Co. KG v Mediaprint Zeitungs- und Zeitschriftenverlag GmbH & Co. KG and others*, EU:C:1998:264.

[67] Ibid, para 57.

[68] See Chapter 3, which refers to Giorgio Monti, 'Managing the Intersection of Utilities Regulation and EC Competition Law' (2008) LSE Law, Society and Economy Working Papers 8/2008, available at https://ssrn.com/abstract=1273615.

in a way that advances the objectives of sector-specific regulation, as opposed to its own. In the telecommunications context, this may mean enforcing Articles 101 and 102 TFEU as a means to promote competition (and not just to protect it). *Deutsche Telekom* illustrates this mutation in the competition law regime. In its decision, the Commission argued that the dominant firm could have avoided a finding of abuse by raising its retail prices so as to allow downstream rivals to operate at a profit at the retail level.[69] Under this understanding of competition law (very much aligned with the logic of post-liberalisation regulation), the discipline would be enforced to create the conditions in which new entrants can thrive, even if it comes under the expense of consumers. As observed by Larouche, the analysis in *Deutsche Telekom* seems to be predicated on the idea that rivals should be in a position not just to compete effectively, but to profitably offer each of the dominant firm's products (or bundles thereof).[70]

A second major consequence of prioritising effectiveness is the emergence of frictions and potential substantive inconsistencies within and across provisions. Outright and constructive refusals are not always treated in the same way under Article 102 TFEU, even when they have the same object and effect. As observed by countless commentators, the differential treatment of both expressions of refusal to deal conduct may have unintended consequences. In *TeliaSonera*, for instance, the incumbent operator would have avoided liability if it had chosen not to deal voluntarily with its downstream rivals. Lack of access to the infrastructure at the bitstream level (the relevant level in the case) would not have led to the elimination of 'all competition' within the meaning of *Bronner*.[71] Applying a lower substantive threshold to instances of voluntary dealing, authors have observed, incentivises outright refusals (and thus may lead to less, not more, competition than there would otherwise have been).[72]

The rationale behind this difference in treatment was spelled out in *Slovak Telekom*. As already pointed out, the Court chose to confine the higher substantive threshold – laid down in *Bronner* – to instances where competition law would require, in effect, a firm to deal with third parties with which it has chosen not to deal. The dividing line is thus not whether the practices have an equivalent object and/or effect, but whether intervention would lead to proactive remedial action. In this sense, the Court confined the scope of the *Bronner* doctrine to scenarios where the competition law system would be required to assume the role of a sector-specific regime. Where, conversely, there is regulation already in place, the system would not be subject to the pressures that come with the definition of

---

[69] Commission Decision in *Deutsche Telekom* (n 2), paras 163–175.
[70] Pierre Larouche, 'Contrasting Legal Solutions and the Comparability of EU and U.S. Experiences' (2006) TILEC Discussion Paper No. 2006-028, available at https://ssrn.com/abstract=943615.
[71] This is so because there was a regulatory obligation to provide unbundled access to the local loop, which would have allowed downstream rivals to compete. See *TeliaSonera* (n 5), para 5.
[72] For an overview of these arguments, see Ibáñez Colomo (n 35).

proactive remedies, namely setting the terms and conditions of access to the infrastructure. For the same reason, indispensability is not an element of the legal test.

Making the nature of remedial intervention the line defining the confines of the *Bronner* doctrine creates a symbiotic relationship between competition law and regulation. The symbiosis between disciplines goes well beyond the former acting as a safety net to advance the objectives of the latter. The fact that there is a sector-specific regime in place means that competition law can delegate, in effect, the design, implementation and monitoring of proactive remedies to the specialised authority. In *Deutsche Telekom* and the cases that followed, for instance, the Commission was able to bring the remedy effectively to an end by simply ordering the dominant undertaking to cease its conduct (that is, a negative obligation administered on a one-off basis).[73] The sector-specific regime was in a position to take over the burden that comes with the day-to-day administration of the proactive duties; competition law, in turn, could retain its role as a discipline that comes into play on a case-by-case basis.

The symbiosis manifests itself in other ways. *Slovak Telekom* shows not only that competition law can come into play when there is regulation in place, but that a breach of the sector-specific regime can also amount to a competition law violation. In other words, the mere fact that the firm has failed to comply with its regulatory duties can also trigger the application of Articles 101 and 102 TFEU.[74] It would not be necessary to show that action under competition law complements the sector-specific regime. In the specific circumstances of *Slovak Telekom*, the Commission took issue, in particular, with the fact that the firm had chosen to interpret its obligations under the sector-specific regime in a narrow manner.[75] In *bpost*, in turn, the Court confirmed that competition law and regulation can indeed apply to the same conduct.[76]

3. The Expansion of Existing Doctrines and the Creation of New Ones

3.1. Strategic Underinvestment and Capacity Hoarding

The traditional refusal to supply doctrines, from *Magill* to *Bronner*, addressed the question of whether it is abusive for a dominant undertaking to deny access to an input or infrastructure. These doctrines do not deal with capacity constraints pertaining to the relevant input or infrastructure. If capacity is at all relevant in the leading cases, it is to allow dominant undertakings escape liability. The Court

---

[73] Article 2 of Commission Decision in *Deutsche Telekom* (n 2).
[74] See the Commission Decision in *Slovak Telekom* (n 2), paras 535–651; and the discussion above.
[75] Ibid.
[76] Case C-117/20 *bpost SA v Autorité belge de la concurrence*, EU:C:2022:202.

has consistently held that potentially abusive conduct falls outside the scope of Article 102 TFEU where it is objectively justified or where the pro-competitive gains that result from it outweigh any negative effects.[77] In the specific context of *Bronner*, it has always been assumed as given by commentators that, where the dominant undertaking lacks the necessary capacity to meet rivals' requests, a refusal to deal does not amount to an abuse of a dominant position.[78] The *Bronner* doctrine, in other words, cannot be interpreted as imposing a mandate to invest in the necessary capacity for effective competition to emerge or, similarly, a duty to share existing capacity with third parties.

This is the background against which the analysis in *GDF foreclosure*[79] and *ENI*[80] must be understood. In these two cases, the Commission advanced the idea that dominant undertakings must not only grant access to an essential facility but are under a duty to ensure that such indispensable infrastructure can accommodate the demands of would-be rivals, both by expanding capacity and by re-allocating existing capacity. From this perspective, the very failure to invest (as opposed to a mere refusal to give access) would amount to an abuse of a dominant position. The same would be true of a decision to retain the capacity a firm enjoys (as a result, for instance, of a legacy advantage). The effect of these two cases would be to turn an objective justification into an autonomous form of abuse, thereby expanding the scope of Article 102 TFEU. This legal interpretation was never tested before the EU courts (or, indeed, an infringement decision). However, it allowed the Commission to obtain commitments from the two dominant firms.

3.1.1. Strategic Underinvestment: A Duty to Invest in Capacity?

It is worth explaining the Commission's reasoning in *ENI* and *GDF foreclosure* at greater length. The former concerned the cross-border infrastructure necessary to import gas into Italy, which was solely or jointly controlled by ENI.[81] As a result, the firm was found to enjoy a dominant position on the markets for the transport of gas and for the downstream supply of the product in the said Member State.[82] What is more, the infrastructures controlled by ENI were deemed to be indispensable for competition on the relevant downstream market.[83] The Commission identified a number of refusal to supply strategies implemented by the State-owned

---

[77] See for instance Case C-413/14 P *Intel Corp. v Commission*, EU:C:2017:700, para 140.
[78] Robert O'Donoghue and Jorge Padilla, *The Law and Economics of Article 102 TFEU* (3rd edn, Hart Publishing 2020) 657–664.
[79] *Gaz de France* (Case COMP/39.316) Commission Decision of 3 December 2009.
[80] *ENI* (Case COMP/39.315) Commission Decision of 29 September 2010.
[81] Ibid, para 18.
[82] Ibid, para 29.
[83] Ibid, para 41.

174 *Energy and Telecommunications*

undertaking. First, the decision argued that ENI had hoarded capacity, thereby limiting access by third parties.[84] Second, it took the view that the undertaking, when providing capacity, did so on disadvantageous terms and conditions.[85]

Third, and more importantly, the Commission's preliminary assessment concluded that the investment decisions adopted by ENI amounted, in and of themselves, to an abuse of a dominant position.[86] This conduct has been labelled 'strategic underinvestment'. More precisely, the authority claimed in the decision that the dominant firm decided not to invest sufficiently in the expansion of its infrastructure,[87] even though it was aware that there was growing long-term demand of capacity from third parties.[88] According to the decision, the firm's approach to these strategic decisions was driven by a conflict of interest. Thus, even though it would have been profitable for ENI to expand capacity, it chose not to, since doing so would have led to increased downstream competition and, by the same token, would have undermined the profitability of its affiliate in that market.[89]

Strategic underinvestment was also present in *GDF foreclosure*, where the Commission's preliminary assessment concluded that GDF Suez enjoyed a dominant position in the relevant markets for the import and supply of gas into and in France.[90] In addition to other practices identified below, the decision took issue with the firm's refusal to expand the capacity of an LNG terminal.[91] This strategic choice made it even more difficult for third parties to import gas into France. The single most significant aspect of the Commission's analysis is the claim that investing in capacity would have been 'sufficiently profitable' for GDF Suez.[92]

---

[84] Ibid, para 45: '[...] there is evidence that ENI may have implemented a strategy to systematically reduce access to capacity for third parties on its gas transport infrastructure to Italy'.

[85] Ibid, para 51: '[...] even when capacity on the pipelines was offered by ENI, its purchase was made more difficult and less valuable to third parties by various means'.

[86] Ibid, para 55.

[87] Ibid, para 57: 'ENI's decisions to enhance transport capacity were mainly based on ENI's own needs resulting from new long-term contract commitments and the goal of keeping gas supply tight, while refusing to consider and eventually carry out expansions of capacity that would have allowed responding to third-party requests'.

[88] Ibid, para 56: '[...] there was significant and credible long term capacity demand by third party shippers on ENI's international pipelines. Furthermore ENI was aware that additional capacity was necessary to satisfy these capacity requests as possible expansion projects were studied [...]'.

[89] Ibid, para 58: 'the strategic limitation of investment in transport pipelines was driven by ENI's objective to keep a tight control over transport capacity. In particular, ENI was aware that if directly allocated to third parties additional capacity would boost competition on the downstream markets. Hence, limitation of investments was not driven by the lack of profitability of an increased transportation activity for ENI as a TSO. Rather, the Commission's concern is that such a strategy has been the result of ENI's conflict of interest'.

[90] *GDF foreclosure* (n 79), para 18.

[91] Ibid, para 37: '[...] the Commission identified competition problems relating to a possible refusal by GDF Suez to supply import capacity at the Montoir de Bretagne LNG terminal as a result of the company's strategic limitation of investment in additional capacity there [...]'.

[92] Ibid, para 39: '[...] given the firm capacity requests received in the open season procedure, extension of the capacity at the Montoir de Bretagne terminal would have been sufficiently profitable [...]'.

The Expansion of Existing Doctrines and the Creation of New Ones   175

This passage in the decision appears to suggest that a dominant firm would be under a duty to expand their infrastructure provided that doing so would not be loss-making.

3.1.2. Capacity Management: A Duty to Share Capacity?

In addition to strategic underinvestment, *GDF foreclosure* addressed two other practices. The analysis in the decision suggests that dominant firms are under a duty to allocate existing capacity in a non-discriminatory manner. The Commission's preliminary assessment explains that GDF Suez had potentially abused its dominant position by reserving long-term capacity in France, first;[93] and by refusing to share its assets in two separate LNG terminals, second.[94] In relation to the first of these practices, the decision argues that the dominant firm's infrastructure was indispensable within the meaning of *Bronner*, and that, by reserving capacity it enjoyed for historical reasons, GDF Suez was preventing effective competition on the relevant downstream markets. The decision implies that the firm had a duty to allocate existing capacity at regular intervals and in accordance with a transparent and non-discriminatory procedure.[95]

As far as the second practice is concerned, the Commission expands the prevailing refusal to supply doctrines in several directions. In line with what has already been pointed out, the authority took issue with the fact that the firm had not organised an open procedure to allocate capacity; what is more, it suggested that the terms and conditions of access were in themselves anticompetitive. More precisely, it claimed that third parties were asked for strategic non-monetary assets as consideration.[96] The relevant passage suggests that it is abusive for a dominant firm not to accept requests from third parties to co-finance the infrastructure (thereby allowing it to accommodate rivals' requests for access). Finally, it is argued in the decision that GDF Suez had reserved more capacity than it actually needed.[97]

3.2. Market Integration

As explained in Chapter 1, market integration has always been a central goal of EU competition law. From the very early days, the Court has held that practices aimed at restricting cross-border trade are deemed anticompetitive by their very nature,

---

[93] Ibid, para 26.
[94] Ibid, paras 31 and 37.
[95] Ibid, paras 42–50.
[96] Ibid, para 32: '[…] [t]he preliminary assessment showed that GDF Suez made third-party access to the Fos Cavaou terminal conditional on receiving nonmonetary strategic assets in return and that, as a result, no third party (other than Total) obtained long-term capacity at the Fos Cavaou terminal […]'.
[97] Ibid, para 35.

without it being necessary to evaluate their effects on competition.[98] These behaviours include both agreements between undertakings and unilateral behaviour implemented by dominant firms.[99] Some of the earliest Article 102 TFEU cases, such as *United Brands*, dealt with conduct aimed at drawing artificial boundaries between Member States.[100] The focus on market integration is particularly pronounced in electricity and gas markets. As explained by the Commission in its Energy Sector Inquiry, the relevant markets in the industry are typically national or sub-national in scope.[101] What is more, electricity and gas activities were historically organised around legal monopolies by Member States. As a result, cross-border trade offers some of the best prospects of injecting effective competition within the EU.

An overview of the Commission practice since the adoption of Regulation 1/2003 reveals the extent to which market integration has been central to its enforcement efforts in the energy sector. It is sufficient to mention some examples. In *DE-DK Interconnector*, the investigation concerned practices having the object and/or effect of curtailing the cross-border sale of electricity.[102] In *BEH Electricity*, the preliminary assessment focused on the destination clauses included by the Bulgarian incumbent in the contracts concluded with its wholesale customers on the market for freely negotiated prices.[103] Such clauses worked, according to the decision, as cross-border restraints.[104] *Gazprom*, in turn, dealt with a market segmentation strategy aimed at limiting the free flow of gas across Central and Eastern Europe.[105]

In many respects, these cases reflect the consistent case law and administrative practice of decades. Price discrimination and market segmentation strategies are presumptively anticompetitive; what is more, they are unlikely to be justified. In particular, claims that restrictions to cross-border trade are efficiency-enhancing are, as the law stands, unlikely to be sufficient to escape the prohibition.[106] In other respects, however, some of these cases venture into the limits of intervention under Articles 101 and 102 TFEU. There are indeed restrictions to cross-border trade in the sector that are not necessarily the consequence of an agreement or a unilateral

---

[98] Joined Cases 56 and 58/64 *Établissements Consten S.à.R.L. and Grundig-Verkaufs-GmbH v Commission*, EU:C:1966:41, 339.

[99] Case 26/75 *General Motors Continental NV v Commission*, EU:C:1975:150; and Joined Cases C-468/06 to C-478/06 *Sot. Lélos kai Sia EE and Others v GlaxoSmithKline AEVE Farmakeftikon Proïonton, formerly Glaxowellcome AEVE*, EU:C:2008:504.

[100] Case 27/76 *United Brands Company and United Brands Continentaal BV v Commission*, EU:C:1978:22.

[101] Final Report of the Energy Sector Inquiry (n 25), para 14.

[102] *DE/DK Interconnector* (Case AT.40461) Commission Decision of 7 December 2018.

[103] *BEH Electricity* (n 19), para 49.

[104] Ibid, para 50: '[…] these destination clauses amount to territorial restrictions on the resale of electricity insofar as they limit the buyers' freedom to choose whether to sell the purchased electricity in the territory of Bulgaria or to export the electricity'.

[105] *Gazprom* (n 20).

[106] *Sot. Lélos* (n 99), para 49.

The Expansion of Existing Doctrines and the Creation of New Ones 177

practice, but a function of the underlying market structure. For instance, capacity constraints may limit the extent to which gas and electricity can be moved across borders.[107] Other restraints may be a necessary response to the specific features of gas and electricity markets.

These ideas were expressed by the Commission in the context of its Sector Inquiry. The Final Report acknowledges that the main obstacles to cross-border trade are not attributable to firm behaviour but to other structural factors. First, the Commission noted that vertical integration may prevent competition originating in other Member States. Entities operating at several levels of the value chain may have an incentive to discriminate in favour of their own affiliates, thereby limiting imports.[108] Similarly, the report identifies the main capacity constraints preventing market integration. In electricity markets, for instance, the extent of cross-border trade depends on the interconnection capacity available (which incumbents are not necessarily incentivised to increase) and on legacy rights.[109]

Some of the commitments decisions addressing market integration concerns appear to take issue not so much with an agreement or a unilateral practice but with the very structural factors identified by the Commission in its Sector Inquiry. One example in this regard is *German Electricity Balancing Market* case.[110] The concerns raised in this investigation related, by and large, to the fact that the dominant firm, E.On, was vertically-integrated. In the specific context of the case, the relevant markets were the upstream market for the supply of balancing power and the downstream market where this power is purchased.[111] Because E.On operated at the two levels of the value chain, the Commission argued, it had an incentive to favour its own activities[112] and, by the same token, to discriminate against suppliers of balancing power originating in other Member States.[113]

The Commission's analysis in *German Electricity Balancing Market* is remarkable in that it appears to suggest that the logical and inevitable consequence of vertical integration – which is to rely on in-house production – is problematic under EU competition law. To the extent that it does, the decision appears to express a concern with the market structure, not with a practice – as Article 102 TFEU requires by definition. The implication of this analysis is that dominant firms are under a duty to place their affiliates and third parties on an equal footing. The decision is notable in that it takes issue, moreover, with the way in which vertically-integrated entities adopt decisions pertaining to the allocation of costs among the various divisions. More precisely, the Commission argued that

---

[107] Final Report of the Energy Sector Inquiry (n 25), paras 21–23.
[108] Ibid, para 22.
[109] Ibid, para 23.
[110] *German Electricity Balancing* (n 15).
[111] Ibid, para 46.
[112] Ibid, para 50.
[113] Ibid.

178 *Energy and Telecommunications*

the choice to favour the in-house supply of electricity had the effect of inflating the costs of E.On's downstream division (which would then be passed on to end-users).[114]

The Commission's interpretation of the notion of abuse in *German Electricity Balancing Market* seems difficult to square not only with Article 102 TFEU, but with EU merger control. The central question, under Article 2 of Regulation 139/2004, is not whether the transaction is likely to lead to discrimination. In and of itself, it is unproblematic, as a matter of law, that a firm would favour its own activities in the post-merger scenario. After all, some of the expected pro-competitive benefits of vertical integration are inextricably linked to discriminatory conduct.[115] Accordingly, it is not sufficient to show that the new entity would have the ability and incentive to favour its own affiliates. In EU merger control, the assessment revolves around whether such strategy, if feasible and profitable, can be expected to lead to anticompetitive foreclosure.[116]

A second case that is worth discussing at some length is *Swedish Interconnectors*.[117] Like some of the decisions analysed above, the investigation concerned export restrictions imposed by the operator of the transmission network in Sweden.[118] The context and rationale of these restrictions, however, was somewhat unusual, and markedly different from the run-of-the-mill market integration scenarios. In the circumstances of the case (as the decision itself recognises), the curtailment of cross-border flows of electricity was a necessity given the features and operation of the relevant market.[119] Because of the capacity constraints within the network and the distance between generation-heavy and consumption-heavy areas, the transmission operator addressed the risk of internal congestion by reducing the amount of electricity sent to other Member States (which in turn reduced the amount of electricity that had to be transported to consumption-heavy areas).[120]

The question that arises, against this background, is whether the measures put in place by the firm to address congestion would not be objectively justified given that the Commission not only acknowledged the risk of congestion but accepted that it is one of the three possible (and necessary) responses that a transmission

---

[114] Ibid, para 53.
[115] For a discussion, see Pablo Ibáñez Colomo, 'Self-Preferencing: Yet Another Epithet in Need of Limiting Principles' (2020) 43 World Competition 417.
[116] Guidelines on the assessment of non-horizontal mergers under the Council Regulation on the control of concentrations between undertakings [2008] OJ C265/6.
[117] *Swedish Interconnectors* (n 18).
[118] Ibid, para 27.
[119] Ibid, para 37: 'Whereas in the long term investments to expand or reinforce capacity in the network can primarily remedy this congestion, SvK can adopt essentially three types of measures to relieve internal network congestion in the shorter term. [...] Lastly, SvK can limit (curtail) available transmission capacity for trade with another zone, to relieve the foreseen congestion on the bottleneck within its network'.
[120] Ibid, para 38: '[...] SvK limited electricity exports, due to internal bottlenecks, on several interconnectors during a significant number of hours in the period January 2002- April 2008 [...]'.

operator can adopt to deal with the issue.[121] This point of law, however, is never really considered. The decision notes that, by curtailing cross-border trade, the transmission operator engaged in discriminatory conduct based on residence[122] so as to reserve electricity for domestic consumption.[123] In addition, the Commission expresses the view that the behaviour amounts to treating equivalent transactions in a dissimilar way. Finally, it points out that the transmission operator had not provided an objective justification.[124]

3.3. Analysis and Implications of the Commission's Approach

The new doctrines discussed in this section were never tested before the Court, as the cases were closed with commitments. In spite of their novelty, the undertakings were willing to offer far-reaching obligations as part of the negotiated procedure. In cases like *ENI* and *German Electricity Balancing Market*, the dominant undertakings agreed to a structural divestiture. As already pointed out, these remedies are most unusual in the Commission's practice and can only be imposed in exceptional circumstances when contemplated under Article 7 of Regulation 1/2003. Other behavioural commitments were no less far-reaching. In *Swedish Interconnectors*, as mentioned above, the negotiated outcome resulted in the restructuring of the national market and in the dominant undertaking changing its operations.[125]

The legal interpretation underpinning these far-reaching obligations is premised on an expansive understanding of the scope of Articles 101 and 102 TFEU. It is an interpretation that appears to create new duties on vertically-integrated undertakings. The combined reading of *GDF foreclosure*, *ENI* and *German Electricity Balancing Market* suggests that, at least where they control an indispensable infrastructure, dominant firms are required to ensure that they have enough capacity to accommodate access requests by third parties, even if it means expanding it. In addition, they are under an unqualified obligation to place third parties and their own affiliate on an equal footing. This duty may mean, in circumstances like those at stake in *ENI*, allocating capacity in an open procedure; it may also mean, as *German Electricity Balancing Market* shows, purchasing electricity without discriminating against non-affiliated producers.

Taken together, these decisions mean that a firm controlling an essential facility has a duty not just to share access to its infrastructure with would-be

---

[121] Ibid, para 37.
[122] Ibid, para 42: '[...] Discrimination between customers based on residence constitutes, in view of the Court's case law, an abuse of dominant position in violation of Article 102 TFEU'.
[123] Ibid, para 44. See also the analysis below.
[124] Ibid, para 45.
[125] Ibid, paras 47–49.

competitors (which is what the traditional understanding of the *Bronner* doctrine would support), but also to ensure that the market conditions allow rivals to thrive in the marketplace. In other words, the obligation to deal, as re-interpreted by the Commission in the abovementioned decisions, involves not just a behavioural obligation to share an input or infrastructure but one to alter, if necessary, the market structure itself, whether by structural or behavioural means. The change relative to the preceding case law is significant. Where *Bronner* took the market structure as given, the three decisions suggest that the infringement may comprise a failure to have modified the market structure to make way for effective competition.

Swedish Interconnectors is also indicative of this expansive understanding of the scope of Article 102 TFEU. The Commission's analysis suggests that a dominant firm would not be able to escape liability by arguing that restrictions to cross-border trade are a necessary and proportionate response to congestion. According to the reasoning in the decision, if congestion can be managed in a different way, curtailing exports will be prohibited as abusive. This is so, most notably, even if it involves a change in the way that the dominant firm organises its internal operations. In other words, the duty to ensure that cross-border activities are not restricted implicitly includes a mandate to restructure an undertaking's activities. In the specific circumstances of the case, such mandate resulted in the transmission operator managing congestion differently.

This interpretation of Articles 101 and 102 TFEU is not wholly uncontroversial. The first reason, which is implicit in the above discussion, is that the Commission's interpretation of the two provisions appears to express a concern with the market structures as such, as opposed to an agreement or a unilateral practice. *ENI* and *German Electricity Balancing Market* exemplify one aspect of this idea. A reading of the decisions suggests that the real obstacle to competition that the Commission sought to tackle was vertical integration, as opposed to a particular line of conduct. This, in fact, is the conclusion one can draw from the Final Report the authority issued in the context of its Energy Sector Inquiry. *Swedish Interconnectors* provide another example. It is apparent from the decision that the problem at stake in the case could only be effectively addressed, at least in the long run, by adding capacity to the transmission network – in fact, the restrictions to cross-border trade were an imperfect and short-term response to this structural issue.

The legal interpretation of Articles 101 and 102 TFEU is controversial for a second reason. One of the most remarkable aspects of the analysis in cases like *ENI* and *GDF foreclosure* is that the Commission does not hesitate to engage in the evaluation of the profitability of the expansion of the dominant firm's capacity. Both decisions suggest that competition law can interfere with business decisions adopted and require structural changes. In *ENI*, for instance, the Commission notes that capacity expansion would have been profitable. This fact, alone, would seemingly justify questioning the firm's investment decisions. The decision implies that ENI should have approached capacity expansion in the way a non-vertically-integrated entity would (that is, by not prioritising its overall profitability, but rather the profitability of some segments of the value chain considered in isolation). The Commission hints at a similar understanding of its powers in *German Electricity Balancing Market*. In more specific terms, the decision suggests that there is something inherently anticompetitive about the fact that the firm had chosen to raise the costs of its transmission division by acquiring balancing electricity from its own generation affiliate (as opposed to third parties) and them allegedly passing them on to end-users.

It is not easy to find precedents in the relevant Article 102 TFEU case law. It seems difficult to claim that dominant undertakings have a special responsibility to engage in profitable investments or to allocate costs as if they were not vertically-integrated. The Court held, in *AKZO*, that pricing or investment decisions that are prima facie irrational (in the sense that they would not be adopted by a profit-maximising entity) are not compatible with competition on the merits. This principle applies, in particular, to pricing below average variable costs, which cannot be plausibly explained (at least not in principle) if it is not as a means to exclude rivals. The reasoning in the abovementioned commitments decisions is markedly different from *AKZO*. Unlike the latter, the lack of investment or the allocation of costs were not deemed irrational; they were, in fact, the expected conduct of a vertically-integrated, profit-maximising firm.

This difference in approach between the case law and the Commission's practice in the energy sector marks a major shift in the substantive understanding of the discipline. Cases like *AKZO* are an expression of an interpretation of competition law that interferes with business choices at the margins – that is, where such decisions are manifestly at odds with competition on the merits. The commitments decisions discussed above are indicative of a manifestation of Articles 101 and 102 TFEU that supports more intrusive intervention. Arguably, the observed shift is an inevitable side-effect of the proactive turn in EU competition policy, discussed in Chapter 1. Such an approach to policy-making inevitably leads to the authority exploring the outer boundaries of what is permitted by law and, similarly, advances an interpretation that amounts, in some cases, to second-guessing core business choices.

4. Exploring the Limits of Market Restructuring

4.1. The Limits to Market Restructuring under Competition Law

The extent to which the Commission can engage in market restructuring when adopting an infringement decision is constrained by the logic of remedial action in EU competition law (and, more generally, by the rationale and operation of the discipline). This logic is encapsulated in Article 7 of Regulation 1/2003. First, the point of a remedy in the system is to bring the infringement effectively to an end.[126] The purpose of intervention, in other words, is to cease the implementation of the practice, not to rebuild the relevant markets in accordance with a particular vision or to create the structures that might otherwise have existed. As explained at length in Chapter 3, EU competition law seeks to protect competition, not to promote it. Second, intervention must be proportionate to the breach of Articles 101 and 102 TFEU. In this sense, a finding of infringement cannot be seen as a pretext to inject more rivalry at the remedy stage than existed prior to the implementation of the practice or, similarly, demand from the undertaking more than what is strictly necessary to address any concerns underlying the decision.

The limits to remedial action are particularly apparent in relation to the imposition of divestitures and similar duties. Even though these measures have been a feature of Article 102 TFEU enforcement since the very first abuse case brought by the Commission (*Continental Can*[127]) the authority's powers to order them were only made explicit in Article 7 of Regulation 1/2003. In this provision, the EU legislature expressly provides that infringements may be assorted with obligations of a structural nature. However, these powers are qualified, in the sense that they are subject to stricter standards than measures simply aimed at changing the conduct of an undertaking. More precisely, the Commission would have to show either that behavioural remedies would not be equally effective or that they would be more burdensome for the undertaking subject to the measure.[128]

These constraints to intervention are particularly relevant in the energy and telecommunications markets. One major consequence that flows from them is that the Commission cannot enforce Articles 101 and 102 TFEU to promote competition. To the extent that the purpose of intervention is to bring the infringement to an end, the abovementioned provisions cannot be relied upon to undermine dominant positions within the bottleneck segment or in adjacent markets. In the context of a refusal to deal, for instance, the infringement is effectively addressed by mandating shared access to an infrastructure. Whether or not the remedy would successfully inject competition on a lasting basis on the adjacent market is not a relevant consideration. In the same vein, where a duty to deal would be effective, a structural separation of the bottleneck segment would no longer be an available remedy. The Court has consistently held that the Commission cannot impose a

---

[126] Pursuant to Article 7(1) of Regulation 1/2003 (n 24), the Commission may 'may by decision require the undertakings and associations of undertakings concerned to bring such infringement to an end'.

[127] *Europemballage Corporation* (Case IV/26811) Commission Decision of 9 December 1971; and Case 6/72 *Europemballage Corporation and Continental Can Company Inc. v Commission*, ECLI:EU:C:1973:22. In accordance with Article 2 of the decision, the dominant firm was order to bring the infringement (consisting of the acquisition of 80% of the shares of a rival) to an end.

[128] See above n 32. For a discussion of the issue, see Frank P Maier-Rigaud, 'Behavioural versus Structural Remedies in EU Competition Law', in Philip Lowe, Mel Marquis and Giorgio Monti (eds), *European Competition Law Annual 2013 – Effective and Legitimate Enforcement of Competition Law* (Hart Publishing 2016).

particular obligation if there is a less onerous means to bring the infringement to an end.[129]

Intervention in the telecommunications and energy industries has ventured into the limits of remedial action under Articles 101 and 102 TFEU by means of both behavioural and structural measures. The limits have been explored in two ways, which are examined in turn. In some cases, there is not an obvious link between the practice and the obligations imposed upon the undertakings, in the sense that remedy appears to respond to the structural features of the relevant market (as opposed to a specific line of conduct). In other instances, the remedy does not necessarily keep proportion with the (alleged or established) infringement. As explained above, commitments decisions, given their nature (and in particular the fact that they are not subject to strict proportionality requirements) make it easier for the Commission to explore the outer boundaries of intervention.

4.2. Structural Intervention and Proportionality

As already pointed out, the Commission decisions in *German Electricity Balancing Market* and *ENI* are remarkable not only because of the interpretation of Article 102 TFEU advanced in them but due to the far-reaching nature of the obligations accepted by the firms. In both cases, the undertakings committed to selling their stakes in the bottleneck segment. The table provided at the end of this chapter shows that these measures are not the only instances of structural intervention in the telecommunications and energy industries. It is sufficient to mention some examples at this stage to highlight how frequent divestitures became (in absolute and relative terms) during the period. In *German Electricity Wholesale Market* and *CEZ*, the undertakings accepted to sell part of their production capacity to third parties.[130] In *BEH Electricity*, the dominant firm accepted, inter alia, to set up a viable and independent power exchange and divest it from the rest of its interests.[131]

4.2.1. The Link between the Behaviour and the Commitments

The second set of cases cited above provides, in fact, valuable illustrations of instances where the link between the potential infringement and the

---

[129] Joined Cases 6/73 and 7/73 *Istituto Chemioterapico Italiano S.p.A. and Commercial Solvents Corporation v Commission*, ECLI:EU:C:1974:18, para 45. For a discussion, see Cyril Ritter, 'How Far Can the Commission Go When Imposing Remedies for Antitrust Infringements?' (2016) 7 Journal of European Competition Law & Practice 587.

[130] *German Electricity Wholesale Market* (n 15), paras 59–68 (under the heading 'Divestiture of the power plants'); and *CEZ* (Case AT.39727) Commission Decision of 10 April 2013, para 39.

[131] *BEH Electricity* (n 19), para 111 ('[…] the Commission considers that BEH's commitment to establish a viable day-ahead market on the power exchange and to enter into a service agreement with an independent service provider with expertise in the operation of a power exchange […] under which the market functions of the day-ahead market will be operated by that service provider, is appropriate'.

commitments offered by the undertaking is less obvious to establish. Consider *German Electricity Wholesale Market*. This case was based on the premise that two or three of the main electricity generators were collectively dominant on the German wholesale market for electricity[132] (which, in itself, is an unusual occurrence in the context of Article 102 TFEU[133]). According to the preliminary assessment, the practices raising concerns were the (tacitly) coordinated withdrawal of capacity with a view to raising electricity prices[134] and the determent of entry by means of long-term supply agreements and by offering a share in its plants to potential competitors.[135]

The commitments offered by E.On – that is, the sale of generation capacity to third parties – are an effective means to tackle the position of collective dominance enjoyed by the incumbent producers. By injecting competition and altering the features of the relevant market, these firms' ability to coordinate their conduct in a sustained manner would be undermined. The Commission, in its decision, explains that the goal of intervention is to ensure that E.On would no longer have the means to profitably withdraw capacity at the wholesale level. The immediate question that emerges, against this background, is whether the obligations sought to bring the infringement to an end, or whether, instead, the goal was to alter the market structure by injecting competition. The Sector Inquiry suggested that the concern underpinning the case was structural more than behavioural. More precisely, the Final Report drew a link between the level of concentration at the generation level and undertakings' ability to withdraw capacity to raise prices.[136]

BEH Electricity is more explicit about the market restructuring goal underpinning intervention. In its preliminary assessment, the Commission raised concerns about the territorial sale restrictions imposed by the Bulgarian incumbent operator at the wholesale level.[137] The decision takes issue with the fact that the wholesale commercialisation of electricity was carried out bilaterally between the suppliers and their customers. This is the market feature that allowed wholesalers to limit cross-border trade. Contractual restrictions on the resale of goods, which are deemed anticompetitive by their very nature, can be effectively brought to an end by means of reactive measures, that is, a one-off cease-and-desist order. It would be sufficient, in other words, to remove the contentious clauses from the bilateral deals. In *BEH Electricity*, however, the commitments offered by the undertaking resulted in the alteration of the structure and operation of the market.

---

[132] *German Electricity Wholesale Market* (n 15), paras 13–24.
[133] For a discussion, see Nicolas Petit, 'The Oligopoly Problem in EU Competition Law', in Ioannis Lianos and Damien Geradin (eds), *Handbook on European Competition Law: Substantive Aspects* (Edward Elgar 2013).
[134] *German Electricity Wholesale Market* (n 15), paras 28–40.
[135] Ibid, paras 41–44.
[136] Final Report of the Energy Sector Inquiry (n 25), para 16.
[137] *BEH Electricity* (n 19), para 49.

Exploring the Limits of Market Restructuring 185

It makes sense to be more specific about the obligations. The proceedings were brought to an end once the undertaking accepted to set up a functionally independent power exchange and to take steps to divest itself from it. When assessing the proportionality of the remedies offered, the Commission noted that a cease-and-desist order mandating the firm to refrain from introducing territorial sales restrictions would not be sufficient to address the concerns. This aim would only be attained, according to the decision, by introducing a 'more transparent market structure' with an 'anonymised sales channel'.[138] In this regard, the Commission suggests that it would not be enough to prohibit a practice. Altering the conditions of competition so that the possibility of engaging in the practice was deemed necessary. This position is indicative of an approach to intervention that is not easy to square with the nature of remedial action under Articles 101 and 102 TFEU. It is more in line with the goals of intervention under EU merger control, which is structural by definition.

4.2.2. *The Proportionality of the Commitments*

Because *German Electricity Balancing Market* and *ENI* provide for structural obligations, they raise the question of whether the commitments accepted by the undertakings were proportionate to the concerns identified in the preliminary assessment. This question is particularly relevant considering that the regulatory responses eventually enshrined in the Third Energy Package were not as far-reaching as those achieved by means of competition law enforcement. The EU legislature did not consider that the effective separation of bottleneck segments and competitive activities required ownership unbundling, as advocated by the Commission in its sector inquiry. As mentioned in Chapter 3, the options finally enshrined in the regime fell short of mandating a divestiture, even if the latter remained the default option.[139] A look at other regulatory regimes, and in particular the EU Electronic Communications Code suggests that there might have been less restrictive alternatives to address the conflicts of interests of vertically-integrated incumbents.[140]

The commitments decisions, however, are succinct about the proportionality of the obligations accepted by the firms. Before the Court clarified that the Commission has a margin of discretion when choosing whether to bring an

---

[138] Ibid, para 110.
[139] See Directive 2019/944. For an analysis of the unbundling obligations, see Christopher Jones and William-James Kettlewell (eds), *EU Energy Law*, vol 1 (5th edn, Claeys & Casteels 2020), 113–164, mentioned in Chapter 3.
[140] See Directive (EU) 2018/1972 of the European Parliament and the Council of 11 December 2018 establishing the European Electronic Communications Code [2018] OJ L321/36, which provide for a broad range of remedial alternatives to a structural divestiture. For an analysis, see Martin Cave, 'Six Degrees of Separation Operational Separation as a Remedy in European Telecommunications Regulation' (2006) 64 Communications & Strategies 89.

investigation to an end following the commitments offered by the parties, the authority was required to undertake a proportionality assessment. This, at least, was the condition introduced by the General Court in its first instance ruling in *Alrosa*.[141] In spite of this fact, the Commission's assessment in cases like *German Electricity Balancing Market* – delivered prior to the appeal judgment – was not a particularly detailed one. For instance, the proportionality of the divestiture of the transmission network is addressed in not more than three paragraphs,[142] and the question of whether there might have been other means to remedy the authority's concerns, a single one.[143]

The brief analysis of proportionality of the measures stands in stark contrast with the requirements that exist under sector-specific regulation. Under the EU Electronic Communications Code, for instance, national regulatory authorities must respect strict proportionality requirements when choosing the obligations to impose on undertakings with Significant Market Power. More precisely, they are under a duty to choose the 'least intrusive way' of addressing any concerns.[144] What is more, the burden is substantially higher where an agency contemplates the functional separation of an operator's wholesale access activities from the rest of its divisions.[145] Such measures can only be imposed 'on an exceptional basis', where there are 'important and persisting' problems and once it is established that the rest of the obligations (such as access and non-discrimination duties) have failed to achieve effective competition on the relevant markets.[146]

4.3. Market Restructuring Through Behavioural Obligations

The discussion above shows that the Commission has frequently engaged in significant market restructuring by means of behavioural measures. In *GDF foreclosure*, for instance, the commitments did not lead to a structural divestiture. However, the changes accepted by the firm greatly altered the conditions of competition in the industry. In essence, the incumbent operator accepted to share existing capacity so that third parties would be in a position to compete. The commitments specified the exact amounts to be released by the firm over the short term,[147] and

---

[141] Case C-170/06 *Alrosa Company Ltd v Commission*, EU:T:2007:220.
[142] *German Electricity Balancing Market* (n 15), paras 86–88.
[143] Ibid, para 86.
[144] Article 68(2) of the Electronic Communications Code (n 140).
[145] Ibid, Article 77(1).
[146] Ibid. Pursuant to Article 77(1), the functional separation of the different activities may only be imposed 'on an exceptional basis'. The regulatory authority would need to show that other remedies 'have failed to achieve effective competition and that there are important and persisting competition problems or market failures identified in relation to the wholesale provision of certain access product markets'.
[147] *GDF foreclosure* (n 79), paras 43–45.

placed limits over the market share that the incumbent could reserve, long-term, for its own activities.[148] More precisely, the decision sought to ensure that GDF would not be able to control over 50 per cent of the available capacity. Proactive intervention stretched into 2029.[149] A similar form of restructuring took place in *Romanian Gas Interconnectors*, decided in 2020.[150]

Swedish Interconnectors provides another example of significant market restructuring. Leaving aside the question of whether the export restrictions amounted to an infringement and/or were objectively justified, already discussed above, the nature and scale of the structural change in response to the Commission's concerns is extraordinary. In particular, the Swedish operator agreed to change the operation of the country's transmission system so that it would be organised around two or more bidding zones.[151] The point of the measure was to ensure that congestion would be managed by the price system by adjusting supply and demand on each bidding zone (and not by curtailing interconnection capacity).[152] In addition, the operator agreed to build a new transmission line where there was no less restrictive alternative.[153]

5. Analysis: Expansion, Fragmentation, Symbiosis

5.1. Summary

The application of Articles 101 and 102 TFEU in the telecommunications and energy sectors, discussed in the preceding sections, is remarkable in several ways. It is remarkable, first, because of the volume of decisions involved. As observed in Chapter 1, a substantial fraction of 'law-intensive' enforcement under Regulation 1/2003 is made up of decisions in these two industries. This is so even after the significant decline of activity – at the EU level – since the late 2010s.[154] Second, administrative action has been characterised by its boldness. The *Bronner* line of case law, which typically comes into play in exceptional circumstances, is at the heart of several decisions discussed above. What is more, some cases explore the outer boundaries defined in that ruling and, by extension, of Article 102 TFEU. Enforcement can be said to be bold in a second sense. The changes introduced by

---

[148] Ibid, paras 47–48.
[149] Ibid, para 48.
[150] *Romanian gas interconnectors* (Case AT.40335) Commission Decision of 6 March 2020.
[151] *Swedish Interconnectors* (n 18), para 47.
[152] Ibid, para 80.
[153] Ibid, para 82.
[154] Enforcement at the national level has not declined, however. For an example, see Case C-377/20 *Servizio Elettrico Nazionale SpA and Others v Autorità Garante della Concorrenza e del Mercato and Others*, EU:C:2022:379.

188 *Energy and Telecommunications*

the Commission had a transformational impact, leading in some cases to a fundamental restructuring of the relevant activities.

It is worth discussing three trends that emerge from the issues analysed in the preceding sections. The first one is the growing focus of enforcement on market structures as opposed to anticompetitive conduct (or, if one prefers, a behavioural trigger). Even though the enforcement of Articles 101 and 102 TFEU is by definition constrained by the need to identify a practice, several of the cases discussed challenged, above all, the nature and operation of the relevant market. Energy and telecommunications are not the only industries in which the shift has been observed, but they are the ones where the phenomenon was more widespread and was manifested earlier. A second trend is the move towards the sectoral fragmentation of competition law. To a significant extent, the cases discussed in this section come across as a self-contained world within the competition law universe that contrasts in a number of respects with other areas of enforcement. Finally, it is worth discussing the symbiotic relationship between competition law and regulation.

5.2. Expansion: From the Behavioural to the Structural

It has already been pointed out that the Commission's administrative practice in the energy and telecommunications sectors has been characterised by a relative tendency to expand the scope of existing doctrines. For instance, the idea that the strategic underinvestment in capacity amounts to an abuse of a dominant position takes the scope of Article 102 TFEU a step beyond *Bronner*, insofar as it imposes a duty not just to share an infrastructure, but to ensure that the infrastructure can accommodate rivals' needs. What is more, there are commitments decisions where the Commission came close to suggesting that vertically-integrated dominant firms have a strict duty of non-discrimination vis-à-vis suppliers and/or customers. The expansive approach is also observed in relation to the administration of remedies, which in a number of instances appear to go beyond what was necessary to bring the potential infringement to an end.

More remarkable than the expansion of the existing doctrines itself (and more interesting than the administration of far-reaching proactive remedies itself) is the fact that some cases challenge the very market structure in which dominant firms compete, as opposed to a specific practice. A decision like *ENI*, for instance, takes issue, first and foremost, with the fact that the combined effects of vertical integration and lack of capacity (that is, structural issues) prevent rivals from competing. By the same token, several of the remedies that the Commission administered sought to alter the operation of the relevant market (as opposed to, or in addition to, bringing the alleged infringement to an end) *BEH Electricity*, which resulted in the introduction of a power exchange (within which the contentious bilateral operations at stake in the case would no longer take place), is the example that comes to mind immediately.

The trend observed in these two sectors is suggestive of the substantive transformation of Articles 101 and 102 TFEU and their mutation into provisions enabling courts and authorities to rectify market structures and inject competition in segments suited for rivalry. Reliance on EU competition law to enact structural change in the energy and telecommunications industries should not come across as surprising if one considers that enforcement was aimed at rectifying economic regulation and/or providing an alternative avenue to attain the aims enshrined in it. To the extent that the point of the sectoral regime was to promote competition by reshaping markets, it seems inevitable that its objectives find their way into competition law enforcement and lead to changes in the interpretation of Articles 101 and 102 TFEU. The substantive consequences of relying on competition law as an instrument of regulation were identified in Chapter 3.

There are reasons to wonder, however, whether the shift in enforcement, from the behavioural to the structural, may progressively expand to other sectors. The rest of the network industries are obvious candidates in this regard. In *Baltic Rail*,[155] for instance, the Commission took issue with the Lithuanian incumbent's decision to dismantle 19 kilometres of its own railway tracks. The case is remarkable not so much because of the finding of infringement – sacrificing profits and destroying one's property can be safely presumed to have an anticompetitive object – but because of the remedy. The Commission did not require the dominant firm to bring the infringement to an end, but to restore the conditions of competition – which ultimately led to intervention aimed at rebuilding the infrastructure.[156] Digital markets are another obvious candidate for the shift towards market restructuring. As discussed in Chapters 3 and 5, the ambition to reconfigure industries is particularly pronounced in the digital arena.

More generally, there are reasons to wonder whether the shift towards structural intervention is a necessary and expected side-effect of the sort of 'market-shaping' intervention that has characterised the application of Articles 101 and 102 TFEU to 'law-intensive' matters. As soon as the competition authority adopts a role akin to that of a utilities regulator (whether or not competition law is enforced alongside a sectoral regime), the line between the structural and the behavioural may become blurred. As pointed out in Chapter 5, the pressure to reshape markets may eventually lead to the adoption of a 'new competition tool'. One should note, in this regard, that the purpose of this new instrument is to allow the Commission

---

[155] *Baltic Rail* (Case AT.39813) Commission Decision of 2 October 2017. The challenge against the decision was dismissed on appeal (with a rectification in the amount of the fine) in Case T-814/17 *Lietuvos geležinkeliai AB v Commission*, EU:T:2020:545.

[156] 'Lithuanian Railways can sign Renge rebuilding contract – commission' (*Baltic Times*, 15 March 2019).

190 *Energy and Telecommunications*

to effectively achieve the outcomes at which it can only hint in the context of a sector inquiry conducted in accordance with Article 17. In this sense, the 'new competition tool' would be the logical and inevitable evolution of an approach to enforcement that started in the energy sector.

5.3. The Sectoral Fragmentation of Competition Law

One may argue, in reaction to the above, that the shifts that one might infer from the application of Articles 101 and 102 TFEU to the energy and telecommunications sectors may not occur in other industries. They may be confined to the specific circumstances in which the decisions discussed in this chapter were adopted. Such circumstances include not only the influence of sector-specific regulation but also the broader context within which intervention takes place. One cannot ignore that most of the cases analysed above were closed following a negotiation between the firm and the Commission. As discussed in Chapter 1, the commitments route allows competition authorities to attain certain policy outcomes that they may have struggled to achieve by means of an infringement decision. From this perspective, the observed substantive expansion of Articles 101 and 102 TFEU would be contingent on firms' willingness to cooperate with the authority and introduce the necessary changes to address any concerns.

There may be a number of reasons why, in some sectors or areas of activity, firms are more inclined to seek a negotiated outcome, even if intervention relies on a controversial, unorthodox or untested interpretation of competition law provisions. Incumbents in the energy and telecommunications sectors, which are traditionally subject to strict regimes and have benefitted from exclusive rights, may be particularly likely to offer commitments. The same may be true where there is a sectoral regime overlapping in substance with Articles 101 and 102 TFEU. Following the adoption of the Digital Markets Act, which – as mentioned in Chapter 5 – codifies several past, ongoing and contemplated competition law investigations, gatekeepers falling within the scope of the legislation have a strong incentive to reach a negotiated outcome.

In other sectors, however, the opposite may be true. As a result, the observed expansion of the substantive scope of Articles 101 and 102 TFEU may be confined to some sectors. In other words, and as anticipated in Chapter 3, competition law may become fragmented. Instead of a set of provisions with a uniform interpretation across all sectors and activities, the scope and meaning of Articles 101 and 102 TFEU would vary based on the context in which it applies. For instance, failure to invest in the requisite capacity may only amount to an abuse in the energy sector (and, more generally, in the network industries). In other industries, by contrast, *Bronner* might remain the only set of circumstances in which a dominant firm is required to share its infrastructure with would-be rivals. Such substantive fragmentation may occur in a formal (if acknowledged by the Court) or an informal way (where it results from the administrative practice).

It is inevitable that fragmentation negatively affects legal certainty and makes enforcement less predictable. Whenever several substantive interpretations of Articles 101 and 102 TFEU coexist, it may not be easy to anticipate which of the two applies to a novel factual scenario or industry. What is more, experience suggests that, even when there is an attempt to circumscribe a particular interpretation to a very specific set of circumstances, it may over time extend its reach to other areas. It is sufficient to think, in this sense, of Article 106 TFEU case law, which applies, in principle, to measures adopted by Member States in relation to the activities of firms that benefit from exclusive or special rights. In spite of this fact, some principles originally introduced in that context have been transposed to cases dealing with the application of Articles 101 and 102 TFEU.[157]

5.4. Towards a Symbiotic Relationship with Regulation

The analysis of the Commission's administrative practice in the energy and telecommunications sectors shows the extent to which competition law and economic regulation can become embedded. Referring to the complementarity between the two regimes does not appear to fully reflect the nature and depth of the interaction. Their relationship is much more profound than typically assumed. Whole swathes of competition law enforcement can only be explained by the presence of an institutional framework that makes intervention possible and workable. Conversely, the success of the liberalisation process is, as the beginning of this chapter pointed out, in part contingent on the frequent and robust application of Articles 101 and 102 TFEU. It is in this sense that competition law and economic regulation can be said to be in a symbiotic relationship.

As *Slovak Telekom* shows, some Article 101 and 102 TFEU cases can be brought precisely because (and only because) there is a sectoral apparatus in place. In such instances, the relationship is symbiotic in that competition law enforcement relies on the ability of economic regulation to handle the consequences of intervention. The Commission was able to sanction the breach of the firm's sectoral duties under Article 102 TFEU without the need to administer complex proactive remedies. The symbiotic relationship with the telecommunications regime allowed for a one-off, reactive intervention. *Deutsche Telekom*, in turn, exemplifies how competition law can correct the – institutional and substantive – flaws of economic regulation. Where sectoral agencies are insufficiently (or imperfectly) committed to the objectives of the regime, Articles 101 and 102 TFEU can act as a safety net.

---

[157] Pablo Ibáñez Colomo, 'Will Article 106 TFEU Case Law Transform EU Competition Law?' (2022) 13 Journal of European Competition Law & Practice 385.

Table 6.1 Energy and telecommunications decisions adopted under Regulation (EC) 1/2003

Case	Name	Sector	Provision	Nature of the case
39839	Telefónica and Portugal Telecom	Telecommunications	101	Fact-intensive Reactive
40305	Network sharing – Czech Republic	Telecommunications	101	Law-intensive Proactive
40335	Romanian Gas Interconnectors (Transgaz)	Gas	102	Law-intensive Proactive
39849	BEH Gas	Gas	102	Law-intensive Proactive
40461	DK/DE Interconnector (TenneT)	Electricity	102	Fact-intensive Proactive
39816	Upstream gas supplies in Central and Eastern Europe	Gas	102	Fact-intensive Proactive
39767	BEH Electricity	Electricity	102	Law-intensive Proactive
39523	Slovak Telekom	Telecommunications	102	Law-intensive Reactive
39952	Power exchanges cartel	Electricity	Cartels	Fact-intensive Reactive
39984	OPCOM / Romanian Power Exchange	Electricity	102	Fact-intensive Reactive
39727	CEZ	Electricity	102	Law-intensive Proactive
39525	Telekomunikacja Polska	Telecommunications	102	Law-intensive Reactive
39315	ENI	Gas	102	Law-intensive Proactive
39317	E.On gas foreclosure	Gas	102	Law-intensive Proactive
39351	Swedish Interconnectors	Electricity	102	Law-intensive Proactive

(continued)

Table 6.1 *(Continued)*

Case	Name	Sector	Provision	Nature of the case
39386	Long-term electricity contracts in France	Electricity	102	Law-intensive Proactive
39316	GDF foreclosure	Gas	102	Law-intensive Proactive
39401	E.On-GdF collusion	Gas	Cartels	Fact-intensive Reactive
39402	RWE gas foreclosure	Gas	102	Law-intensive Proactive
39388	German electricity wholesale market	Electricity	102	Law-intensive Proactive
39389	German electricity balancing market			
37966	Distrigaz	Gas	102	Law-intensive Proactive
38784	Wanadoo España/Telefónica	Telecommunications	102	Law-intensive Reactive
38662	GDF	Gas	101	Fact-intensive Reactive

7

Patents and Copyright

1. Intellectual Property and its Discontents

1.1. The Malaise with and within Intellectual Property Systems

The application of Articles 101 and 102 TFEU to the exercise of copyright and patent rights can only be fully understood if one considers the persistent malaise with and within intellectual property regimes. As discussed in Chapters 3 and 4, these regimes are characterised by their relative inflexibility. Unlike competition law, their design and operation make it difficult for them to adjust to the features of the industries in which they display their effects. In principle, the same degree of protection is granted irrespective of its impact on innovation, and irrespective of whether less protection (or different type thereof) would have provided adequate incentives to engage in inventive and creative activities. The relative inflexibility gives rise to tensions, both among stakeholders and between stakeholders and authorities. Occasionally, these tensions are channelled through competition law enforcement. This Chapter examines two areas where the malaise was manifested: standard development (and the exploitation of the so-called standard-essential patents, hereinafter 'SEPs') and the pharmaceutical industry.

The Chapter also addresses a third, quintessentially European, type of malaise with patents and copyright: the mismatch between the cross-border nature of the EU internal market and the national scope of most intellectual property rights. In spite of the creation of EU-wide regimes (namely the EU trade mark[1] and design[2]) national systems of protection have not disappeared. In some cases, in particular copyright, they are unlikely to ever disappear. As a result, frictions persist, and may never completely be eliminated. To the extent that bringing down barriers to trade may come at the expense of appropriability, Member States may be reluctant (and have proved to be reluctant) to harmonise domestic regimes.[3] This is the context

---

[1] Regulation (EU) 2017/1001 of the European Parliament and of the Council of 14 June 2017 on the European Union trade mark [2017] OJ L154/1.
[2] Council Regulation (EC) No 6/2002 of 12 December 2001 on Community designs [2002] OJ L3/1.
[3] Richard Arnold, 'An Overview of European Harmonization Measures in Intellectual Property Law', in Justine Pila and Ansgar Ohly (eds), *The Europeanization of Intellectual Property Law: Towards a European Legal Methodology* (Oxford University Press 2013).

that explains the enforcement of Article 101 and 102 TFEU in the name of market integration.

As explained in Chapter 3, competition law enforcement in these three areas has fulfilled two roles. In some instances, the application of Articles 101 and 102 TFEU has filled gaps in intellectual property regimes. It has become apparent that the latter may not be fully equipped to deal with the strategies pursued by some stakeholders (as is true of some practices in the pharmaceutical industry) and/or with the growing complexity of business realities (for instance, some aspects of standard development processes and, more generally, the multiplication of patents in certain industries). In other instances, the application of competition law was aimed at rectifying intellectual property systems. The fundamental legal issue at stake in relation to the exploitation of SEPs, for example, is whether Article 102 TFEU can be relied upon to limit the extent to which a patent holder can seek an injunction before a court; that is, whether it is abusive for a patentee to exercise its core rights against an alleged infringer.

The cases discussed in the preceding chapter show that, when Articles 101 and 102 TFEU are enforced as a means to rectify and/or fill gaps in regulatory regimes, formal legislation often follows, or is at least contemplated. In such instances, competition law sometimes fulfils a brewing 'expectation of regulation'. The three case studies are not any different in this regard. The string of decisions dealing with the friction between copyright and the free movement of services must be read against the background of attempts to favour market integration and the cross-border provision of content. In a similar vein, the complex issues around the development of standards and the exploitation of SEPs have been eventually addressed by means of ad hoc regulation, which had been proposed but not yet adopted at the time of writing.[4]

1.2. The Potential and Limits of Competition Law to Address the Malaise

The enforcement of competition law provisions to fill gaps and/or to rectify intellectual property regimes exposes courts and authorities to the outer boundaries of Articles 101 and 102 TFEU. Across a number of dimensions, the cases that will be discussed hereinafter explore the limits of what can be achieved through the competition law system, both from a substantive and an institutional standpoint. This trailblazing feature is to be expected, considering the deferential approach to intellectual property that traditionally dominated policy-making and considering that intervention aimed at rectifying and/or filling gaps in regulatory regimes often

---

[4] Proposal for a Regulation of the European Parliament and the Council on standard essential patents and amending Regulation (EU)2017/1001 COM(2023) 232 final.

involves the administration of proactive remedies that test the sort of 'market-shaping' restructuring that can be realistically attained via Articles 101 and 102 TFEU.

Two of the substantive limits have been identified in Chapter 4. To begin with, competition law (and EU law at large) does not question the existence of intellectual property rights. It can only interfere, if at all, with their exercise.[5] As a result, a competition authority cannot challenge the validity of, say, a title. Similarly, the analysis cannot be grounded on the assumption that the said title is weak, that it is unlikely to survive scrutiny or that the probability of it being declared invalid is above 50 per cent. The assessment under competition law must take intellectual property rights as given and assume that they are in force. Some of the cases that follow this introduction question, if not challenge, this principle, both implicitly and explicitly. Enforcement in the pharmaceutical industry, in particular, cannot be disentangled from the suspicion surrounding the validity of the contentious patents. This, in fact, is a central aspect in the cases discussed in Section 3.

A second substantive boundary that these cases explored relates to the 'exceptional circumstances' doctrine, whereby the unilateral exercise of market power by dominant firms is only abusive if the strict conditions laid down in *Magill* and *IMS Health* are met.[6] A breach of Article 102 TFEU is contingent, in particular, on evidence that the conduct prevents the emergence of a new product for which there is potential consumer demand.[7] The applicability of competition law to the unilateral exercise of their rights by SEP holders gives rise to legal issues that are not fundamentally different from those at stake in *Magill* and *IMS Health*. One may argue that, from an economic perspective, seeking an injunction against an alleged infringer is essentially identical to a refusal to license an exclusive right.[8] For the same reason, these cases raise the question of whether the 'new product' criterion is a precondition for competition authorities to rectify the operation of intellectual property systems in SEP-related contexts or whether, instead, there are 'exceptional circumstances' other than those originally defined in *Magill*.

The existence-exercise dichotomy and the 'exceptional circumstances' doctrine have already been discussed in the preceding chapters. It is worth addressing two additional ways in which the cases that follow test the limits of what can be achieved under competition law. As already pointed out, the theory

---

[5] Joined Cases 56 and 58/64 *Établissements Consten S.à.R.L. and Grundig-Verkaufs-GmbH v Commission*, EU:C:1966:41, 345.

[6] Joined Cases C-241/91 P and C-242/91 P *Radio Telefis Eireann (RTE) and Independent Television Publications Ltd (ITP) v Commission*, EU:C:1995:98 ('*Magill*'); and Case C-418/01 *IMS Health GmbH & Co. OHG v NDC Health GmbH & Co. KG*, EU:C:2004:257.

[7] *Magill* (n 6), para 54.

[8] For a discussion of this argument, see Robert O'Donoghue and Jorge Padilla, *The Law and Economics of Article 102 TFEU* (3rd edn, Hart Publishing 2020) 854–856.

of intervention in SEP-related disputes revolves around the idea that starting litigation amounts, or can amount, to an abuse of a dominant position. Claiming that the very exercise of a fundamental right, recognised in the EU Charter[9] and the ECHR,[10] may be in breach of competition law is controversial. One could convincingly argue that seeking an effective remedy before a court is not abusive – at least not where the right holder has a legitimate claim (that is, where the claim is genuine and not merely a pretext to restrict competition). The interest of this question is compounded by the fact that, when SEP-related disputes reached the Court of Justice (hereinafter, the 'Court', or the 'ECJ') there were precious few precedents addressing the matter.[11]

Finally (and as far as substantive boundaries are concerned), these cases raise the issue of whether unlawful market activity (that is, market entry that contravenes the relevant legislation) can be considered as 'competition' for the purposes of the application of Articles 101 and 102 TFEU. In intellectual property-related contexts, the issue, more precisely, is whether a firm that must breach another's rights in order to provide its goods or services counts as a 'competitor' within the meaning of the case law. Suppose, for instance, that the relevant copyright regime precludes a licensee in one territory from providing its content, across borders, in the territory of another licensee. One could reasonably argue, against this background, that the relevant copyright legislation (as opposed to terms and conditions laid down by the licensor) prevents competition between the two licensees, irrespective of any conduct. However, the European Commission (hereinafter, the 'Commission'), in some of its decisions, has suggested that an agreement can be in breach of Article 101(1) TFEU even when it seeks to prevent market entry that would have been unlawful in any event.

From an institutional standpoint, the analysis that follows shows that it may not be possible to attain some policy outcomes by means of proactive enforcement. This may be the case, first, because of the technical nature and sheer complexity of some areas. It appears, for instance, that Articles 101 and 102 TFEU can only meaningfully intervene, at best, at the margins of SEP-related matters. The cautious, procedural approach taken by the Court confirms, as will be shown below, this conclusion. Second, the case studies suggest that changing the operation of a system of intellectual property may be beyond the reach of a competition authority. The sort of case-by-case intervention that is characteristic of competition law regimes does not appear to be a practical means to alter the relationship between content producers and licensees across a whole industry. Finally, the discussion below also exposes the limits of what can be attained by means of commitments decisions.

---

[9] Article 47 of the Charter of Fundamental Rights of the European Union [2012] OJ C326/391.
[10] Articles 6 and 13 of the European Convention of Human Rights.
[11] Case T-111/96 *ITT Promedia NV v Commission*, EU:T:1998:183; and Case T-119/09 *Protégé International Ltd v Commission*, EU:T:2012:421.

2. Standards and Standard Development

2.1. Standard Development: A Necessity and a Source of Tensions

Standards are pervasive in the economy and have a decisive influence over the dynamics of competition in some industries, from high-technology markets to agricultural products. They vary widely in their nature and purpose. This Section focuses on a particular sub-set of standards, namely those that define the technical specifications with which a product must comply.[12] Examples of this sub-set include the DVD system for video and data storage;[13] the Universal Serial Bus (USB),[14] which applies to cables and connectors; or 5G, for mobile telecommunications.[15] Standards emerge in different ways. In some cases, they are the result of State involvement.[16] In others, they arise spontaneously, as a result of market dynamics. The rise of Windows as the de facto standard operating system has been frequently cited as an example.[17] This Section deals with instances in which the specifications are defined by industry stakeholders, typically in the context of a standard-setting (and/or standard-development) organisation.[18]

It is not necessary to explain at length how inter-firm cooperation to define and develop a standard can be beneficial for the competitive process (including both its static and dynamic dimensions) and society at large. Where a standard emerges spontaneously (as was true of Windows), a single firm may enjoy a monopolistic position. This firm may refuse to allow third parties to produce in accordance with the specifications it has defined unilaterally. In such circumstances, moreover, the de facto standard may not incorporate the best technologies (or may not always do so). Inter-firm cooperation, by contrast, expands the pool of potentially available technologies and gives participants the chance to choose the ones that suit their needs best. From the perspective of end-users, cooperation (as opposed to unilateral action) may be beneficial for several reasons, including the fact that

---

[12] Guidelines on the applicability of Article 101 of the Treaty on the Functioning of the European Union to horizontal co-operation agreements [2011] OJ C11/1, para 257. As these pages were being completed, the adoption of a new set of Guidelines seemed imminent. See Draft Guidelines on the applicability of Article 101 of the Treaty on the Functioning of the European Union to horizontal co-operation agreements C(2022) 1159 final.
[13] 'DVD Read-Only Disk File System Specifications' ECMA Technical Report TR/71 (February 1998).
[14] USB 2.0 Specification, available at https://www.usb.org/document-library/usb-20-specification.
[15] 'Technical Specifications and Technical Reports for a 5G based 3GPP system', available at https://portal.3gpp.org/.
[16] Guidelines on horizontal co-operation agreements (n 12), para 258.
[17] Michael L Katz and Carl Shapiro, 'Systems Competition and Network Effects' (1994) 8 Journal of Economic Perspectives 93.
[18] Mark A Lemley, 'Intellectual Property Rights and Standard-Setting Organizations' (2002) 90 California Law Review 1889.

rivalry typically results in greater choice of products and lower prices. The formal definition and development of standards may also reduce consumer uncertainty, in the sense that they signal that the relevant products are less likely to become obsolete (or the 'losing' ones) and may ensure compatibility and interoperability with complementary goods and services.

Given the importance of standards in some sectors of the economy, it is inevitable that tensions arise within organisations in charge of defining them. Such tensions are in part a consequence of the divergent interests and incentives of the stakeholders taking part in the process. Firms creating the technologies that are incorporated into a standard will be interested in maximising the revenues generated by means of licensing. Firms incorporating those technologies into finished products, by contrast, have incentives to contain the costs involved in acquiring them. Frictions may also result from the design and operation of the standardisation process. In particular, the criteria for the participation in the organisation and in the selection of a technology may prove controversial. Concerns may be raised where involvement in the process is restricted,[19] or where the criteria to select technologies are opaque.[20]

The remainder of this Section addresses a different source of tensions, namely relating to the implications of standardisation for firms and, more generally, the dynamics of competition. The incorporation of a technology into a standard has important consequences for the firm having developed it. Once selected, its value increases substantially.[21] For the same reason, it opens the door to opportunistic behaviour. Because of its improved bargaining position, the firm may seek to extract excessive royalties from would-be licensees (or 'implementers', as they will be referred to generically hereinafter). If it is vertically-integrated (in the sense that it acts both as a licensor and as an implementer), the firm may be tempted to exploit its position to exclude actual or potential rivals on the relevant downstream market.

Technologies incorporated into a standard may be protected by intellectual property rights, in particular patents. However, intellectual property regimes do not deal with standardisation as such and/or with opportunistic conduct as such. In the absence of ad hoc legislation addressing the matter, standard development organisations have sought to define rules of conduct by its members. One mechanism addressing the risk of opportunism is the requirement that technologies incorporated in a standard be licensed to third-party implementers on fair, reasonable and non-discriminatory conditions (hereinafter, 'FRAND').[22] Another mechanism is to mandate the disclosure of any intellectual property interests.

---

[19] Guidelines on horizontal co-operation agreements (n 12), para 295.
[20] Ibid, para 282.
[21] O'Donoghue and Padilla (n 8) 807.
[22] Guidelines on horizontal co-operation agreements (n 12), para 287.

This tool, which is intended to address the phenomenon of 'patent ambush'[23] will typically be assorted with penalties for failure to comply (namely licensing on royalty-free terms).

In spite of the (private) ex ante regulation of standard development, it is frequently claimed that the ability of patent holders to behave opportunistically is not fully addressed merely by requiring FRAND licensing or the disclosure of their intellectual property interests. As explained in Chapter 3, it has been argued over the past decades that the mere threat that the patent holder could seek an injunction against an implementer could be problematic in and of itself.[24] This is so, in particular, in relation to the SEPs, mentioned above. Implementers, once committed to a standard, are not able to circumvent patents that are deemed essential to comply with the technical specifications. As a result of the threat posed by the potential injunction, the argument goes, patent holders would not be negotiating on a level playing field. This reality would lead to royalties that exceed the incremental contribution of the technology to the standard[25] and in the slowing down of innovation. According to this view, further intervention, including limiting SEP holders' ability to exercise their rights,[26] would be needed.

The purpose of this Section is not to examine whether these claims (generally referred to as the 'patent holdup' theory) are an accurate description of the contemporary reality of standard development activities and/or whether regulatory intervention in some form is warranted. As briefly mentioned in Chapter 3, they are and have been contested and there is no consensus around them.[27] The point of the analysis that follows is instead to note that claims of 'patent holdup' have reached competition authorities, including the Commission. It has been argued that the level of royalties demanded by SEP holders amounts to excessive pricing within the meaning of Article 102 TFEU.[28] As early as 2007, for instance, the Commission opened proceedings looking into licensing practices by Qualcomm.[29] It has also been claimed that it is abusive for an SEP holder to seek an injunction. The remainder of the Section focuses on the latter question.

---

[23] Ibid, para 286. Ruben Schellingerhout and Piero Cavicchi, 'Patent ambush in standard-setting: the Commission accepts commitments from Rambus to lower memory chip royalty rates' (2010) 1 Competition Policy Newsletter 32.

[24] See in particular Mark A Lemley and Carl Shapiro, 'Patent Holdup and Royalty Stacking' (2007) 85 Texas Law Review 1991, and the discussion in Chapter 3.

[25] Ibid, 1993 ('[…] the threat of an injunction can enable a patent holder to negotiate royalties far in excess of the patent holder's true economic contribution […]'.

[26] Ibid, 2035–2039.

[27] For an example of a piece challenging this idea, see Alexander Galetovic and Stephen Haber, 'The Fallacies of Patent-Holdup Theory' (2017) 13 Journal of Competition Law & Economics 1, cited in Chapter 3.

[28] For an overview of these arguments, see Marco Botta, 'Unfair Pricing and Standard Essential Patents' (2020) EUI Working Paper RSCAS 2020/60, available at https://cadmus.eui.eu/.

[29] European Commission, 'Antitrust: Commission initiates formal proceedings against Qualcomm' MEMO/07/389 (Brussels, 1 October 2007). These proceedings were subsequently closed without a finding of infringement.

2.2. Injunctions as an Abuse of Dominance: Issues and Frictions

As noted above, the idea that Article 102 TFEU can be relied upon to limit dominant firms' ability to seek an injunction before a court or tribunal is controversial, to begin with, from a fundamental rights perspective. It is therefore easy to understand why the General Court was cautious when first confronted with the question. In *ITT Promedia*,[30] it ruled that starting litigation can only be deemed abusive in 'wholly exceptional circumstances'.[31] In line with the Commission's position in the case, the General Court concluded that seeking relief before a court can only amount to an abuse of a dominant position where doing so can only be plausibly rationalised as a means to exclude competition. This idea was turned into a legal test revolving around two cumulative conditions that an authority or claimant would need to satisfy. First, it would be necessary to show that the action 'cannot reasonably be considered as an attempt to establish the rights of the undertaking concerned and can therefore only serve to harass the opposite party' and that 'it is conceived in the framework of a plan whose goal is to eliminate competition'.[32] These two conditions were confirmed and further fleshed out in *Protégé International*, delivered in 2012.[33]

The test laid down in *ITT Promedia* sets a very high bar of intervention, in the sense that Article 102 TFEU would only be applicable where the legal action sought by the dominant right holder has an exclusionary object. Accordingly, the behaviour would not be abusive even when the injunction would have actual or potential exclusionary effects. Against this background, the question is whether there is something specific about SEP-related disputes that might justify departing from the *ITT Promedia* doctrine. An immediate differential factor that comes to mind is the fact that the behaviour occurs in a standard development context. One could therefore argue that the injunction sought cannot be examined in isolation from the FRAND commitment given by the SEP holder and from the expectations that the said commitment creates in the industry. It would not be unreasonable to claim, in the same vein, that, in this particular economic and legal context, seeking an injunction is at odds with the logic underlying the standardisation process (at the very least where the injunction is sought against a willing licensee).

The application of Article 102 TFEU to the exercise of patent rights could be seen as controversial insofar as it clashes with the deference that EU competition law has traditionally shown vis-à-vis intellectual property. In line with this

---

[30] *ITT Promedia* (n 11).
[31] Ibid, para 60.
[32] Ibid, para 55.
[33] *Protégé International* (n 11).

deferential attitude, the Court has confined to 'exceptional circumstances' the instances in which Article 102 TFEU interferes with the unilateral exercise of substantial market power. It is not necessary to discuss again the conditions set out by the Court in *Magill* and *IMS Health*, addressed in Section 1 and in previous chapters. It is sufficient to point out that, in the context of an SEP-related dispute, it may be difficult to show that all these conditions are satisfied. In particular, it may not be obvious to establish that the injunction would prevent the emergence of a new product for which there is potential consumer demand. An overview of the relevant cases suggests that they do not necessarily relate to the launch of a new product. Because disputes are, almost by definition, bilateral, an authority or claimant may also struggle to argue, convincingly, that the injunction leads to the elimination of 'all competition', which is the threshold set in the case law.

As is true of the *ITT Promedia* doctrine, the open question is whether there are reasons to depart from the conditions laid down in *Magill* in a standard development context. One should point out, generally speaking, that the Court, in *IMS Health*, clarified that the said conditions are 'sufficient' to establish an abuse.[34] It did not hold that they are necessary for the unilateral exercise of intellectual property rights to fall within the scope of Article 102 TFEU. It is thus conceivable that there is a diverse range of exceptional circumstances that justify the application of that provision. A second key difference has to do with the fact that, in a standard development context, the SEP holder will typically have made a FRAND commitment. By virtue of that commitment, the firm will have voluntarily decided to limit its own contractual freedom. For that very reason, the factual scenario in the typical SEP-related case would not be comparable to the one at stake in *Magill* (or *IMS Health*).

Arguably, the factual differences between the two scenarios could justify the adoption of a different, less stringent test, for three interrelated reasons. By making a FRAND commitment, implementers would have the legitimate expectation that they would be able to receive a licence on such terms. No such legitimate expectations exist in the context of a traditional refusal to license case. Second, one could argue (as it has been argued) that seeking an injunction before a court or tribunal would be inconsistent with the firm's own FRAND commitments. Some authors have coined the term 'estoppel abuse' to refer to these instances.[35] The argument, in essence, is that dominant firms would be abusing their dominant position when they go back on their own word. The third argument can be drawn from the line of case law discussed in the preceding Chapter. As cases like *TeliaSonera* and *Slovak Telekom* show, the Court has held that the *Bronner* doctrine does not apply where the dominant firm is dealing with rivals on a voluntary basis or where there is a regulatory obligation. In such circumstances,

---

[34] IMS Health (n 6), para 38.
[35] Kevin Coates, 'The Estoppel Abuse' (*21st Century Competition*, 28 October 2013).

Article 102 TFEU would not interfere with the right to property and/or with the dominant firm's freedom of contract.[36]

2.3. From Motorola and Samsung to Huawei

2.3.1. *The Commission Decisions in* Motorola *and* Samsung

Uncertainty around the applicability of EU competition law to injunctions sought by SEP holders, and the risk of legal fragmentation within the internal market, help explain why the Commission adopted two decisions addressing the status of these practices in the mid-2010s.[37] In *Motorola*,[38] delivered in April 2014, the authority concluded that, by seeking, obtaining and enforcing an injunction against Apple, the firm had abused its dominant position. In *Samsung*, it accepted commitments from the undertaking.[39] The Commission's approach introduced an ad hoc legal test that departed in several respects from the case law discussed above. On the one hand, it concluded that *ITT Promedia* is not applicable, and that it cannot be interpreted as overruling the precedents specifically dealing with the unilateral exercise of intellectual property rights.[40] On the other hand, and while its decision expressly builds on *Magill* and *IMS Health*, it is not constrained by them. More precisely, the Commission introduced a new set of 'exceptional circumstances' justifying the application of Article 102 TFEU.

The legal test devised in *Motorola* is relatively strict vis-à-vis dominant SEP holders. Seeking an injunction, in a standard development context, was treated as presumptively abusive conduct.[41] Thus, where the SEP holder has made a FRAND commitment, the behaviour will be in breach of Article 102 TFEU unless the SEP holder can show that the implementer is not a willing licensee, is in financial distress or its assets are in locations that do not provide adequate means of enforcement.[42] What is more, the decision is clear in stating that these three exceptions are considered at the objective justification stage, that is, once a prima facie abuse is established.[43] Thus, under the test proposed by the Commission, it would be for the SEP holder to prove that the implementer is not a willing licensee.

---

[36] Case C-165/19 P *Slovak Telekom, a.s. v European Commission*, EU:C:2021:239, para 46. See Chapter 6 for an extensive discussion.

[37] For a background discussion, see Nicolas Petit, 'EU Competition Law Analysis of FRAND Disputes', in Jorge L Contreras (ed), *The Cambridge Handbook of Technical Standardization Law: Competition, Antitrust, and Patents* (Cambridge University Press 2017).

[38] *Motorola – Enforcement of Standard Essential Patents* (Case AT.39985) Commission Decision of 29 April 2014.

[39] *Samsung – Enforcement of (UMTS) Standard Essential Patents* (Case AT.39939) Commission Decision of 29 April 2014.

[40] *Motorola* (n 38), paras 531-534.

[41] For a discussion, see Igor Nikolic, *Licensing Standard Essential Patents: FRAND and the Internet of Things* (Hart Publishing 2021) 203–204.

[42] *Motorola* (n 38), para 427.

[43] *Motorola* (n 38), para 434.

2.3.2. The Court Judgment in Huawei

Given the economic salience of the issue and the uncertainty surrounding the lawfulness of injunctions, it seemed inevitable that the matter would eventually reach the Court. The *Huawei* judgment was delivered in July 2015.[44] On the point of principle, the ECJ accepts the idea that Article 102 TFEU can be enforced to limit the exercise by dominant SEP holders of their rights. Compared to the Commission decisions in *Motorola* and *Samsung*, however, the judgment is more nuanced. Crucially, it is not presumptively abusive for an SEP holder to seek an injunction. Generally speaking, such behaviour is only caught by Article 102 TFEU when it would be inconsistent with the spirit of its FRAND commitments. In the same vein, the evaluation of whether the implementer is a willing licensee is not undertaken at the objective justification stage.

The Court justifies its decision on two main grounds. First, it relies on the relevant case law, and more precisely on the 'exceptional circumstances' doctrine described above. Second, it takes into account the relevant context, which is deemed to justify a finding of abuse in circumstances differing from the ones at stake in *Magill* and *IMS Health*. More precisely, the fact that the dispute arises in a standard development context and that the patent holder has committed to licensing on FRAND terms would warrant interfering with the enforcement of intellectual property rights before courts.[45] The Court notes, in this regard, that the ex ante commitment made by the firm influences market dynamics by creating legitimate expectations.[46] As a consequence of the commitment, the SEP holder has the ability to exclude actual or potential rivals and to 'reserve to itself the manufacture of the products in question'.[47]

In such 'exceptional circumstances', constraining the exercise of a patent right is not at odds with fundamental rights and with the EU's commitment to a 'high level' of protection of intellectual property.[48] The judgment introduces a set of requirements with which the SEP holder must comply to ensure it acts within the boundaries of what is allowed under Article 102 TFEU. These requirements are, in essence, a structured procedural framework that seeks to ensure, by proxy, that the patentee acts in accordance with the legitimate expectations it has created and, by the same token, that the implementer behaves as a willing licensee would. Accordingly, the SEP holder is expected to alert the implementer that its rights are being infringed and present a licensing offer on FRAND terms.[49] Conversely, the implementer will not only have to express its willingness to conclude a licensing agreement, but diligently must present a counter-offer in the

---

[44] Case C-170/13 *Huawei Technologies Co. Ltd v ZTE Corp. and ZTE Deutschland GmbH*, EU:C:2015:477.
[45] Ibid, para 59.
[46] Ibid, para 52.
[47] Ibid, para 53.
[48] Ibid, paras 57–58.
[49] Ibid, para 60.

event of a disagreement⁵⁰ and must, in addition, show its good faith by providing 'appropriate security' (by means, for instance, of a bank guarantee) and by refraining from engaging in any delaying tactics.⁵¹

The Court ruling in *Huawei* was criticised by some leading commentators. These practitioners and scholars pointed out, for instance, that the framework created by the judgment ignores the reality of licensing negotiations in a standard development context and that it leaves many crucial questions unanswered.⁵² It became apparent, in subsequent litigation at the national level, that the approach taken by the Court may come across as overly formalistic. In *Unwired Planet*, for instance, Birss J (High Court of Justice) noted that *Huawei* could lead too readily to a finding of abuse if the framework it sets out is taken literally, rather than as the expression of the overall attitude that SEP holders must adopt in the event of a patent dispute.⁵³ According to this view, only the general duty of 'notice and prior consultation', laid down in para 60 of the Huawei judgment would be really binding.⁵⁴ The UK Supreme Court would subsequently agree with this interpretation.⁵⁵

This Chapter is not the place to engage with these criticisms and interpretations. The legal test crafted in the judgment is interesting from a different perspective. The single most notable feature of the approach taken by the Court is that it chose to address a substantive matter (that is, the interpretation of the notion of abuse in the relevant context) by means of a procedural device. Instead of getting into the technical details around licensing negotiations (including the meaning of FRAND), it stayed at the margins of such negotiations. This approach is not difficult to rationalise if one takes into account the institutional constraints of the competition law system and the demands that proactive intervention would place upon authorities and courts. Following the judgment, the role of Article 102 TFEU in SEP-related disputes is likely to be a relatively minor one. The Court appeared to see competition law as a safety net, rather than as the forum regulating the details of the said disputes.

2.4. Towards the Formal Regulation of Standardisation and SEP Licensing

The litigation that ultimately led to the Court judgment in *Huawei* arose in a very specific industry context: the development of smartphones (in fact, the said

---

⁵⁰ Ibid, para 65.
⁵¹ Ibid, para 67.
⁵² Miguel Rato and Mark English, 'An Assessment of Injunctions, Patents, and Standards Following the Court of Justice's Huawei/ZTE Ruling' (2016) 7 Journal of European Competition Law & Practice 103.
⁵³ *Unwired Planet International Ltd v Huawei Technologies Co. Ltd & Anor* [2017] EWHC 711 (Pat).
⁵⁴ Ibid, para 740.
⁵⁵ *Unwired Planet International Ltd & Anor v Huawei Technologies (UK) Co Ltd & Anor* [2020] UKSC 37, para 149.

disputes have often been dubbed the 'smartphone wars') and the various mobile communications standards used with them. The economic and technological landscape is changing, inter alia, with the rise of the Internet of Things.[56] The fundamental implication of this phenomenon is that a considerable number of everyday appliances and devices (such as cars and fridges) will be connected to the Internet and will work, at least to some degree, as a smartphone. SEP-related disputes are likely to become more complex and multi-layered. The profile of potential litigants is also different, and less homogeneous (the 'smartphone wars' involved a small subset of relatively sophisticated firms). In this new landscape, it seems almost inevitable that a number of stakeholders will attempt to construe some of the disputes as competition law breaches.

An idea of the potential disputes that might arise in the future was provided by a preliminary reference submitted by the *Landgericht Düsseldorf* (and ultimately withdrawn following an agreement between the parties[57]) in the *Nokia v Daimler* case.[58] One of the questions raised by the national court related to the level at which FRAND licensing is to take place, and more precisely whether a FRAND commitment comprises a duty to deal with third-parties at every level of the supply chain or whether, instead, patent holders retain the freedom to decide who is to receive the licence. In a case like *Nokia v Daimler*, the question would be whether a patent holder like Nokia can require the car manufacturer to take the licence or whether, instead, it can be compelled to license its technology upstream in the supply chain, at the component level.

This new generation of questions confirms, just like the *Huawei* judgment, that SEP-related disputes are unlikely to be satisfactorily regulated by Article 102 TFEU enforcement. In line with what has been suggested above, this is a matter that demands formal ad hoc intervention. As this book was being completed, a Proposal for a Regulation on Standard-Essential Patents was announced.[59] In essence, this proposed legislation would give the responsibility of proactively overseeing SEP licensing to the EU Intellectual Property Office (EUIPO) and, more precisely, a 'competence centre' under its purview.[60] The proposal suggests that the EUIPO will be responsible for issues such as keeping a record of SEPs, evaluating whether a patent is essential to a standard and, more importantly and overseeing FRAND determinations when disputes are submitted to the competence centre.[61]

---

[56] European Commission, 'Final report – Sector inquiry into consumer Internet of Things' SWD(2022) 10 final.
[57] Foo Yun Chee, 'Daimler to pay Nokia patent fees, ending German legal spat' *Reuters* (Brussels, 1 June 2021).
[58] Case C-182/21 *Nokia Technologies Oy v Daimler AG*, EU:C:2021:575.
[59] Proposal for an SEP Regulation (n 4).
[60] Ibid, Article 4.
[61] Ibid, Title III.

3. Intellectual Property and the Regulation of Medicines

3.1. Patents and Regulatory Gaming in the Pharmaceutical Sector

Patents and related rights[62] are a central feature of the pharmaceutical sector. It is not seriously disputed that intellectual property protection is indispensable to provide the adequate incentives for the development of new and better treatments.[63] The convenience of awarding exclusive rights may be (and is) controversial in relation to other economic activities (such as the development of software applications[64]), but not pharmaceuticals. Because patent protection is so important from the perspective of firms developing new drugs (hereinafter, the 'originator companies'[65]), these firms have designed, over the years, a number of strategies aimed at preserving or extending in time the exclusive rights that they enjoy. These have been briefly discussed in Chapter 3. The incentive to engage in the said strategies is all the more important if one takes into account the fact that originator companies' revenue typically relies on a limited number of best-selling drugs (the so-called blockbusters[66]).

In some instances, originator companies have sought to exploit the gaps and flaws in the regulatory regime. One such example is provided by the *AstraZeneca* case,[67] also mentioned in Chapter 3. A peculiarity of patented pharmaceuticals is that they may benefit from sui generis protection by virtue of the so-called Supplementary Protection Certificates ('SPCs'). These titles allow right holders in the industry to effectively extend the period of exclusivity.[68] The award of SPCs is intended to make up for the time that lapses between the filing of the patent application and the marketing authorisation. This is the background against which the *AstraZeneca* case must be understood. The firm provided misleading information to national patent offices with a view to (i) extending the length of protection beyond the period to which it was entitled; and (ii) obtaining an SPC to which it was not entitled.[69]

---

[62] Regulation (EC) No 469/2009 of the European Parliament and of the Council of 6 May 2009 concerning the supplementary protection certificate for medicinal products (Codified version) [2009] OJ L152/1.

[63] Dan L Burk and Mark A Lemley, *The Patent Crisis and How the Courts Can Solve It* (University of Chicago Press 2009), 4.

[64] Ibid.

[65] Expression taken from European Commission, 'Pharmaceutical Sector Inquiry: Final Report' (Brussels, 8 July 2009).

[66] Ibid, 6, which defines a blockbuster medicine as 'being one which achieves annual revenues of over US$ 1 billion at global level'.

[67] *AstraZeneca* (Case COMP/A. 37.507/F3) Commission Decision of 15 June 2005.

[68] Article 13 of the SPC Regulation (n 62).

[69] *AstraZeneca* (n 67), para 144.

In other instances, originator companies attempt to preserve or extend their exclusive rights by seeking additional legal protection, above and beyond that granted to the active ingredient. If successful, this strategy can lead to the award of a number of secondary patents adding to – or replacing – the primary (or base) patent.[70] In other words, the originator company may seek to build a 'cluster' (or 'fortress') made up of secondary patents; it may also seek to add layers of protection to the exclusive rights around the core title. Such secondary patents may cover aspects such as the process by which the active ingredient is turned into a medicine, or the development of new formulations. As a result of this strategy, generic manufacturers may not be able to compete with the originator company even when the primary patent is declared invalid, or expires.[71]

As a complementary or additional strategy, originator companies may rely on litigation. As will be discussed at length below, entry 'at risk' by generic manufacturers (that is, entry even when there are doubts as to whether the generic producer is in a position to lawfully operate on the relevant market[72]) is a feature of competition in the pharmaceutical industry. It is not difficult to rationalise this reality: experience shows that secondary patents are frequently declared to be invalid or not infringed when challenged.[73] As a result, entry 'at risk' may have good chances of success in a given case. In spite of this fact (or, rather, precisely because of it), originator companies may respond by vigorously asserting their rights before courts. Given the costs involved in litigation, such an attitude, which signals a strong commitment to enforcement, may deter or delay entry by generic manufacturers.[74]

Another strategy that complements the preceding one, and on which the remainder of this Section focuses, is reliance on out-of-court settlements. Such agreements are ubiquitous and, more often than not, uneventful, if not beneficial for competition and society.[75] Competition authorities have focused their attention on a particular type of settlements. In lieu of litigation, a generic manufacturer

---

[70] Final Report of the Pharmaceutical Sector Inquiry (n 65), para 476: 'To ensure exclusivity at least until the end of the patent protection period of the base patent, originator companies may file for a multitude of patent applications (on process, reformulation, etc.) protecting the product in addition to the base patent with the aim of creating several layers of defence […]'.

[71] Ibid: 'Thus where generic companies might manage to invalidate the base patent before its regular expiry they still cannot enter the market, if the originator company has succeeded in creating what some originator companies call "a multilayered defence" by other patents for such aspects as different dosage forms, the production process or for particular pharmaceutical formulations […]'.

[72] Ibid, para 538.

[73] Ibid, para 628.

[74] Ibid, para 540.

[75] Guidelines on the application of Article 101 of the Treaty on the Functioning of the European Union to technology transfer agreements [2014] OJ C89/3, para 235: 'Settlement agreements in the context of technology disputes are, as in many other areas of commercial disputes, in principle a legitimate way to find a mutually acceptable compromise to a bona fide legal disagreement. The parties may prefer to discontinue the dispute or litigation because it proves to be too costly, time-consuming and/or uncertain as regards its outcome. Settlements can also save courts and/or competent administrative bodies effort in deciding on the matter and can therefore give rise to welfare enhancing benefits […]'.

may agree to delay the launch of its version of the drug and not to challenge the validity of the contentious patents. As consideration, the originator company may agree to compensate the generic manufacturer. It may do so in a number of ways. It may, for instance, agree to a direct monetary transfer. Alternatively, it may reach a distribution arrangement: for instance, the generic manufacturer may be designated as the exclusive reseller in a given territory[76] or may conclude a licensing agreement.[77]

These agreements are known as 'reverse payment' of 'pay-for-delay' settlements. The compensation is said to be 'reverse' in the sense that the transfer flows from the patent holder to the alleged infringer – and not, as one would expect, from the latter (which is said to have breach the presumptively valid exclusive rights). This feature of the settlements is what explains the scrutiny they have attracted, both from an intellectual property and a competition law standpoint. The fact that the right holder is willing to compensate the generic manufacturer can be taken (and has been taken by authorities and some stakeholders) as an indicator that the patents at stake in the settlement are weak (and thus likely to be declared invalid by a court) or that they have not been infringed. From this perspective, the agreement would be giving the patent holder a degree of protection exceeding what it would have been able to obtain in litigation.

Competition authorities on both sides of the Atlantic have followed closely reverse payment settlements over the past decades. In the US, the Federal Trade Commission challenged an agreement of this nature concluded between Solvay Pharmaceuticals and two generic manufacturers.[78] This litigation would ultimately reach the US Supreme Court. Justice Breyer delivered his Opinion in *Actavis* in 2013.[79] On the other side of the Atlantic, patent settlements between originator companies and generic manufacturers featured prominently in the Final Report issued by the Commission in the context of its Sector Inquiry into the pharmaceutical sector.[80] At very much the same time the US Supreme Court issued its *Actavis* ruling, the Commission issued a prohibition decision in *Lundbeck*,[81] the first of a string of cases addressing the legal status of 'pay-for-delay' agreements.[82]

---

[76] For an example, see *Paroxetine* (Case CE-9531/11) Decision of the Competition and Markets Authority of 12 February 2016, para 3.12 ('[...] Under those terms, IVAX became the exclusive distributor in the UK for GSK's unbranded paroxetine and subsequently supplied Tillomed Laboratories Limited ('Tillomed'), GUK and Alpharma with GSK's unbranded paroxetine under the terms of separate supply agreements with each of those companies [...]').

[77] Ibid, para 3.83 ('[...] A settlement may also include a licence from the originator company to the generic supplier authorising the latter to use the invention, with or without royalties').

[78] Federal Trade Commission, 'FTC Sues Drug Companies for Unlawfully Conspiring to Delay the Sale of Generic AndroGel Until 2015' (Washington DC, 2 February 2009).

[79] *FTC v Actavis, Inc.*, 570 U.S. 136 (2013).

[80] Final Report of the Pharmaceutical Sector Inquiry (n 65), paras 702–855.

[81] *Lundbeck* (Case AT.39226) Commission of 19 June 2013.

[82] *Fentanyl* (Case AT.39685) Commission Decision of 10 December 2013; *Perindopril (Servier)* (Case AT.39612) Commission Decision of 9 July 2014; *Cephalon* (Case AT.39686) Commission Decision of 26 November 2020.

3.2. The Economic and Legal Context of Reverse Payment Settlements

At first glance, reverse payment settlements come across as problematic from a competition law standpoint. An agreement whereby a firm agrees, with an incumbent operator, to delay its entry into a market in exchange for a transfer of value is, at the very least, superficially similar to a market-sharing cartel. Instead of competing with one another (bringing down prices in the process), the two firms (incumbent and challenger) would be seemingly sharing monopoly profits at the expense of consumers and society. The very fact that an intellectual property dispute is in the background means, however, that the economic and legal context of reverse payment settlements is typically more complex than the one at stake in an ordinary market-sharing cartel. In fact, it would not be unreasonable to argue, as some (including the minority in *Actavis*) have, that these settlements are not only not akin to cartels, but that they should be presumptively lawful, if not escape competition law scrutiny altogether.

The attitude of the Commission vis-à-vis reverse payment settlements in the very early days illustrates well the complexities surrounding the economic and legal context of which these agreements are a part. When the Danish competition authority initially informed the Commission of the arrangements at stake in *Lundbeck*, the EU agency was not even certain that they were a competition law matter (let alone a restriction of competition by its very nature). In a note, it pointed out to its Danish counterpart that the practice was in a 'gray area' and that, moreover, 'it was unclear' how close the case was to the 'black area'.[83] The Commission announced that it would 'initiate a general analysis of these types of cases, which shall result in the development of a general standard for how they should be handled'.[84]

3.2.1. Settlements as Pro-competitive Arrangements

One reason why it may not be immediately obvious to compare 'pay-for-delay' agreements with cartels is that out-of-court settlements are a normal feature of the competitive process in industries where patents play a central role. One could argue, in the same vein, that they are both normal and the very expression of the exercise of intellectual property rights. From this perspective, a settlement would not be any different from a licensing agreement or from seeking relief before a court. Just like the patent holder is entitled to allow a third party to manufacture

---

[83] Danish Competition Authority, 'Press Release: Investigation of Lundbeck – Council Meeting' (Copenhagen, 28 January 2004), as cited in Michael Clancy, Damien Geradin and Andrew Lazerow, 'Reverse-payment patent settlements in the pharmaceutical industry: An analysis of US antitrust law and EU competition law' (2014) 59 Antitrust Bulletin 153.

[84] Ibid.

its products, it should be entitled to choose a settlement over court proceedings. It is often argued, in this regard, that a settlement remains within the scope of the acts that a patent holder is allowed to authorise or prohibit. Thus, such an agreement would not be restricting competition any more than the intellectual property regime does.

Arguably, in fact, out-of-court settlements are to be preferred over litigation. One need not explain at length that they are an efficient way of solving disputes. In this sense, they would be beneficial not only for the parties (which can avoid the costs associated with litigation) but for society at large (insofar as valuable resources are not diverted to proceedings and that they make an effective use of courts). This point is acknowledged by the Commission in its Guidelines on technology transfer agreements, where it states that settlements are 'in principle a legitimate way to find a mutually acceptable compromise to a bona fide legal disagreement'.[85] Against this background, one could argue that it is open to question, at the very least, whether 'pay-for-delay' agreements have, as their object, the restriction of competition. To the extent that they are a plausible source of efficiency gains, one could credibly claim that they should only be prohibited, if at all, where they have restrictive effects on competition.

The case law provides support for this conclusion. In *BAT (Toltecs-Dorcet)*,[86] mentioned in Chapter 4, the Court addressed the legal status of trade mark delimitation agreements. These can be likened to reverse payment settlements in that they deal with a similar reality in a comparable way: in lieu of litigation, the parties define the areas within which their respective trade marks may be used. The Court held in *BAT (Toltecs-Dorcet)* that a genuine trade mark delimitation agreement is not restrictive of competition, whether by object or effect.[87] Where, on the other hand, the settlement is not a genuine one, it may be caught by Article 101(1) TFEU (and may also amount to an abuse within the meaning of Article 102 TFEU). This may be the case, for instance, where the agreement conceals a market-sharing cartel[88] or where it exceeds the scope of the trade mark rights – as was the case in *BAT (Toltecs-Dorcet)*.[89]

3.2.2. *The Uncertain Status of Generic Manufacturers as Potential Competitors*

There is a second reason why it may not always be obvious to compare reverse payment settlements with cartels. As far as the latter are concerned, there is no

---

[85] Guidelines on technology transfer agreements (n 75), para 235.
[86] Case 35/83 *BAT Cigaretten-Fabriken GmbH v Commission*, EU:C:1985:32.
[87] Ibid, para 33.
[88] See by analogy, Case C-9/93 *IHT Internationale Heiztechnik GmbH and Uwe Danzinger v Ideal-Standard GmbH and Wabco Standard GmbH*, EU:C:1994:261.
[89] *BAT (Toltecs-Dorcet)* (n 86).

doubt that the parties are actual, or at least potential, competitors.[90] It is a precondition to categorise an arrangement as a cartel. Where intellectual property rights are at stake, by contrast, it is not always possible to tell whether there is a competitive relationship between the originator company and the generic manufacturers. Where there is a genuine intellectual property dispute between the parties, it may not be possible to tell, ex ante, whether or not the generic manufacturer would have been in a position to enter the market in the absence of the agreement. As already pointed out above, only lawful entry counts as actual or potential competition for the purposes of the application of Articles 101 and 102 TFEU.[91] Accordingly, whether or not a generic manufacturer qualifies as a competitor may well hinge on the outcome of litigation. If the patent is declared valid and infringed, it would not have been able to enter the market, even if the settlement would never have been concluded.

The difficulty of determining the competitive relationship between originator companies and generic manufacturers is compounded by the fact that, in the context of a reverse payment settlement, competition law is enforced before the outcome of litigation is known. The validity of the patent may or may not be upheld; the patent may or may not be found to have been infringed. There is a probability that the generic manufacturer is a potential competitor and a probability that it is not. Put differently (and to use a graphic analogy), there is a state of 'quantum superposition' whereby the generic manufacturer is and is not a potential competitor at the same time. It is not surprising that courts and authorities have struggled with this particular point. As explained above, competition law cannot, and does not, question the existence of intellectual property rights and therefore cannot challenge the validity of the patent. On the other hand, it may be difficult to decide whether there is a restriction of competition without going into the matter (or at least, without speculating about the probability of the patent being declared valid and infringed).

3.3. The Legal Categorisation of Reverse Payment Settlements: Issues and Choices

3.3.1. A Context-Dependent Exercise

One of the main conclusions to draw from the analysis above is that the legality of reverse payment settlements is very much context-dependent. The complexity

---

[90] C-373/14 P *Toshiba Corporation v Commission*, EU:C:2016:26.
[91] See in this sense Case T-360/09 *E.ON Ruhrgas AG and E.ON AG v Commission*, EU:T:2012:332. In relation to intellectual property agreements in particular, see Guidelines on technology transfer agreements (n 75), para 32 ('In the specific context of intellectual property rights, an additional factor for assessing whether the parties are potential competitors on a particular market is the possibility that their intellectual property rights are in a blocking position, that is to say that the licensee cannot enter the respective market without infringing the intellectual property rights of the other party').

of the legal and economic circumstances in which they arise reveals, first and foremost, that their status under Article 101 and 102 TFEU cannot be established in the abstract, or in categorical terms. In spite of the formal similarities, reverse payment settlements vary widely from one another. In some instances, 'pay-for-delay' agreements may be indistinguishable from a cartel. This is the case, in particular, where the settlement gives the originator company more protection than it would have been able to obtain by enforcing its patent rights before a court. There are other instances, however, where such settlements pursue a legitimate purpose and, as such, are a natural expression of competition on the merits. Whether the agreement at stake in a given case resembles a cartel or a genuine means to bring an intellectual property dispute to an end depends on the circumstances of each case.

Suppose for instance that the declared purpose of the reverse payment is to settle a dispute around a secondary patent that is not necessary to enter the market. Suppose, in addition, that the primary title – covering the active ingredient – has already expired. If it can be shown that generic manufacturers were willing and able to rely on non-infringing methods, they would qualify as potential competitors. For the same reason, it would be difficult to dispute that the agreement has, as its very object, the restriction of competition. It would not be possible to rationalise the settlement as a genuine attempt to bring an end to an intellectual property dispute. In all likelihood, the objective purpose of the agreement is to share supra-competitive profits with a potential entrant (which is tantamount to saying that it is a cartel arrangement). Other factors, such as the size of the payment, could reinforce this conclusion.

As shown in Figure 7.1, this conclusion may be a different one if one or several of the factors identified in the preceding example change. Suppose, for instance, that the settlement concerns not a secondary patent but the base patent, without which generic manufacturers cannot enter the market. Suppose, in addition, that the reverse payment is intended to cover the costs of litigation. In such circumstances, it is possible (at least in principle) to rationalise the agreement as a means to settle a genuine intellectual property dispute. First, there may be genuine doubts about generic manufactures' ability to enter the market without infringing the base patent. Second, the transfer of value could be explained on grounds other than the restriction of competition. Rather than a mechanism to share profits with a potential entrant, the compensation may well reflect a relatively risk-averse attitude vis-à-vis litigation by the originator company.[92]

---

[92] Avantika Chowdhury and Helen Jenkins, 'Inference or Evidence? The Uncertain Fate of Patent Settlement Agreements' (2018) 9 Journal of European Competition Law & Practice 449.

214 *Patents and Copyright*

Figure 7.1 Reverse payment settlements as a context-dependent exercise

Factors	Less likely to restrict competition	More likely to restrict competition
Status of the base (primary) patent	Presumptively valid and in force	Expired
Object of the dispute	Around the base patent	Around the secondary patent(s)
Nature and size of the payment	Covers cost of litigation	Covers new entrant's expected profits

3.3.2. Approaches to the Assessment of Potential Competition

A second conclusion from the analysis above is that the legal treatment of reverse payment settlement under Articles 101 and 102 TFEU is sensitive to the approach that courts and authorities take vis-à-vis the relationship between intellectual property and competition law, in particular when evaluating the issue of potential competition. The scope for, and frequency of, intervention, varies depending on how issues surrounding the validity and/or the infringement of patents are tackled. The room for competition law enforcement will be relatively limited where courts and authorities defer to the intellectual property system and its operation. Where, conversely, the scope of patent rights is not deemed to be a relevant consideration in the analysis (in the sense that it does not define the boundaries of intervention), the potential for the application of Articles 101 and 102 TFEU would be greater.

As shown in Figure 7.2, one can distinguish between three potential approaches that competition authorities and courts can take in the above regard. They range from the least to the more deferential to the intellectual property system. At one end of the spectrum, the question of whether the generic manufacturer is a potential competitor and that of whether the settlement has a restrictive object and/or effect would be assessed as an autonomous competition law matter that is independent from any consideration pertaining to patent law. A second approach would engage in a probabilistic assessment of the likelihood of the patent being declared valid an infringed. The most deferential approach would be one that would treat settlements as presumptively valid where they remain within the scope of the patent.

Figure 7.2 Approaches to the assessment of potential competition

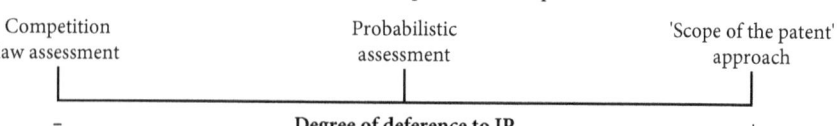

3.4. The Legal Status of Reverse Payment Settlements in the Case Law

3.4.1. *The Choices Made by the Commission in* Lundbeck

In *Lundbeck*, the Commission eventually found that the agreements at stake in the case were not only restrictive of competition by their very nature, but akin to a market-sharing cartel.[93] Accordingly, it imposed a fine in excess of €93 million on Lundbeck (the originator company) and fines on four generic manufacturers amounting to a total of over €52 million.[94] The agreements at stake in the case follow the basic pattern described above. In addition to the base patent (expired, for instance, in 2002 in the UK),[95] Lundbeck had obtained a number of secondary patents covering several manufacturing processes. These secondary patents were obtained by the originator company in the UK at roughly the same time the base patent expired.[96] In parallel with this strategy, Lundbeck concluded the contentious settlements with the generic manufacturers.[97] In spite of slight variations, they all shared the same basic features.

The Commission concluded that these agreements had, as their object, the restriction of competition.[98] First, the authority regarded the parties as competitors. Second, it pointed out that all these settlements involved a transfer of value and that, as consideration, the generic manufacturers delayed market entry (more precisely, they accepted not to sell a generic version of the drug during the period agreed between the parties). Third, the Commission estimated that the transfer of value corresponded roughly to the profit that the generic manufacturers would have made if they had decided to enter the market. Fourth, it argued that the settlements went beyond the scope of Lundbeck's patents, in the sense that the originator company was trying to achieve a degree of protection that intellectual property would not have afforded.

The facts of the case, as established by the Commission, suggest that a restriction of competition could have been established under the most deferential of the approaches described above. As confirmed by Lundbeck itself,[99] the decision shows that the originator would not have been able to prevent entry by virtue of the secondary patents at stake in the case. There were, as explained by the Commission, several alternative routes available to generic manufacturers.[100] What is more,

---

[93] *Lundbeck* (n 81).
[94] European Commission, 'Antitrust: Commission fines Lundbeck and other pharma companies for delaying market entry of generic medicines' IP/13/563 (Brussels, 19 June 2013).
[95] *Lundbeck* (n 81), para 111.
[96] Ibid, para 113–115.
[97] Ibid, paras 172–217.
[98] Ibid, paras 1169–1174.
[99] Ibid, para 364.
[100] Ibid, para 635.

some of these manufacturers had already taken active steps to produce the drug relying on non-infringing processes. In such circumstances, it would be difficult to argue that the originator company did not face (at least) potential competition. For the same reason, it would be inevitable to conclude that the very object of the settlements is anticompetitive.

However, the Commission argued in its decision that the agreements would have been restrictive of competition even under the least deferential of the approaches described above. In this vein, the authority took the view that, had there been genuine uncertainty about the generic manufacturers' ability to enter the markets (and, by the same token, a genuine patent dispute), the latter would still have qualified as potential competitors. It claimed, in this regard, that challenging patents and 'entry at risk' are natural manifestations of competition on the merits in the pharmaceutical industry.[101] According to the Commission, this conclusion would be reinforced by the fact that the originator company's own assessment suggested that the secondary patent that was central to its litigation strategy had a 60 per cent chance of being declared invalid.[102]

The inevitable implication of the Commission's expansive (or non-deferential) approach to the notion of potential competition is that reverse payment settlements amount, by definition, to a restriction of competition by object. Under the authority's interpretation of the notion, whether or not the agreement relates to a genuine dispute is an irrelevant consideration. For the same reason, any settlement is in principle comparable to a market-sharing cartel, in the sense that any such settlement can be easily construed as an attempt to share monopoly profits with a would-be rival. Even though the Commission explains in its decision that not all patent settlements are restrictive of competition by their very nature[103] including those that involve 'payments of some kind'.[104] However, the examples provided differ significantly from the basic factual scenario described in this section.[105]

---

[101] Ibid, para 624.
[102] Ibid, para 627.
[103] Ibid, para 638.
[104] Ibid, para 639.
[105] Ibid: '[…] Payments may, in specific legal and commercial circumstances, be instrumental to the finding of an acceptable and legitimate solution for both parties. This is the case in particular but not exclusively in cases where, for example, the generic undertaking had already entered the market and if each party in the course of litigation comes to consider that the likelihood of patent validity and infringement is high, a patent settlement may legitimately include […] a payment from the generic undertaking to the originator undertaking to settle the damage suffered by the latter. Likewise, a patent settlement could include a [reverse] payment […] if originally, through legal threats or court action of the originator undertaking, the generic undertaking had refrained from entering the market and both parties come to consider later on […] that there is in fact a high likelihood either that the patent is invalid or that it is not infringed. If in that case a patent settlement is concluded that allows for immediate market entry by a generic undertaking, such a settlement could legitimately include a payment by the originator company compensating the damage suffered by the generic company […]'.

3.4.2. The Court in Generics: A Nuanced Approach

In March 2021, the Court dismissed in its entirety the appeal against the Commission decision in *Lundbeck*. A year earlier, it had delivered its preliminary ruling in *Generics*,[106] which defined the legal status of reverse payment settlements under Articles 101 and 102 TFEU. Even though the Court's approach left largely intact the scope of intervention in relation to these practices, it is more nuanced than that adopted by the Commission. Unlike the latter, the ECJ took a more deferential stance vis-à-vis intellectual property. This is reflected both in the way it evaluated potential competition and in the way it went about determining whether reverse payment settlements have the object or effect of restricting competition. The Court rejected both the Commission's non-deferential approach, but also emphatically dismissed the idea that it is necessary to engage in an assessment of the strength of the patents. In the spectrum depicted in Figure 7.2, *Generics* is, if anything, closer to the left end.

On the issue of potential competition, the *Generics* judgment explains that the evaluation must consider a number of circumstances pertaining to the structure of the relevant market and the economic and legal context of which the settlement is a part.[107] This analysis provides a number of direct and indirect indicators regarding generic manufacturers' ability and incentive to enter the market. It is necessary to consider, first, the regulatory framework, including the intellectual property system. The relevant question, in this regard, is whether there are 'insurmountable barriers' precluding entry.[108] Where, as in *Lundbeck* and *Generics*, the base patent is in the public domain and the settlement concerns a secondary patent, no such barriers exist, according to the judgment.[109] As noted above, the Court avoids engaging in a probabilistic assessment about the validity of the patent. Unlike the Commission, on the other hand, the analysis in the judgment is limited to the specific circumstances of the case and fails to make any general statement about 'entry at risk' in the pharmaceutical industry.

One must consider, second, the objective behaviour of the parties to the agreement, which is deemed to provide indirect evidence of the competitive relationship between them. The fact that generic manufacturers take active steps towards offering their versions of the medicine (such as seeking the relevant administrative permits and keeping adequate stocks) should be taken as an indicator that they have the 'firm intention and inherent ability' to enter the market.[110] Another

---

[106] Case C-307/18 *Generics (UK) Ltd and Others v Competition and Markets Authority*, EU:C:2020:52.
[107] Ibid, para 39.
[108] Ibid, para 45.
[109] Ibid, para 46.
[110] Ibid, paras 44, 46 and 54.

indicator, according to the judgment, would come from the very fact that an agreement is concluded[111] and that, moreover, it provides for a transfer of value. The Court points out, in the latter regard that, the size of the transfer is also a factor in the assessment: the higher the transfer of value, the more reliable as indirect evidence of a competitive relationship between the parties.[112]

On the question of whether reverse payment settlements restrict competition the Court emphasised, in line with the relevant case law, that the inquiry is a context-specific one. Accordingly, the anticompetitive nature of these agreements cannot be established in the abstract. When figuring out the object of the settlement, the assessment revolves around whether it can be rationalised on grounds other than the restriction of competition; whether, in other words, it can be plausibly explained other than as a means to share monopoly profits with a potential entrant.[113] The transfer of value from the originator company to the generic manufacturer is the central consideration in this regard. A settlement will be deemed to restrict competition by object where the 'net gain is sufficiently large actually to act as an incentive to the manufacturer concerned of generic medicines to refrain from entering the market concerned'.[114] Where, conversely, there is a legitimate justification for the payment, as would be the case where the originator company compensates for the costs of litigation, the agreement will not be caught by Article 101(1) TFEU by its very nature. Accordingly, even a reverse payment settlement can escape the prohibition. On this point, the Court comes across as more nuanced than the Commission decision in *Lundbeck*.

Where the agreement is not found to have, as its object, the restriction of competition, it is necessary to engage in an evaluation of its actual or potential impact on competition. On the analysis of effects, the Court clarifies that it does not require a probabilistic inquiry about the validity of the patent or about the likelihood of it being declared invalid.[115] The evaluation, including the analysis of the counterfactual, can be conducted, according to the judgment, without speculating about the chances of the generic manufacturer prevailing in litigation. The Court, again, showed deference to the intellectual property regime and refrained from interpreting Articles 101 and 102 TFEU in a way that would amount to questioning the existence of the patent, or in a way that would account for its relative weakness.

---

[111] Ibid, para 55 ('the conclusion of an agreement between a number of undertakings, operating at the same level in the production chain, some of which had no presence in the market concerned, constitutes a strong indication that a competitive relationship existed between those undertakings').
[112] Ibid, para 56.
[113] Ibid, para 89.
[114] Ibid, para 93.
[115] Ibid, para 119 ('It follows that, in a situation such as that at issue in the main proceedings, the establishment of the counter-factual does not involve, on the part of the referring court, any definitive finding in relation to the chances of success of the manufacturer of generic medicines in the patent proceedings or to the probability of the conclusion of a less restrictive agreement').

4. Copyright Harmonisation via Competition Law Enforcement? The *Pay-TV* Saga

4.1. The Digital Single Market Strategy and Copyright

The creation of the Digital Single Market was one of the flagship policies of the Juncker Commission, which took office in 2014.[116] The initiative sought to ensure that the EU would make the most of the opportunities offered by the online economy. Because of its characteristics, digital services (and, more generally, the economic transformation that comes with digitisation) have the potential to accelerate and deepen market integration, benefitting EU citizens in the process. The Digital Single Market Strategy,[117] announced in 2015, sketched a number of legislative proposals spanning several areas, including e-commerce, media services and telecommunications. One of the overarching themes of the initiative was the elimination of national barriers hindering cross-border trade in goods and services. For instance, the Commission noted that rules on parcel delivery and on online sales could prevent or make it more difficult for businesses and consumers to purchase, online, goods and services from other Member States.[118]

The authority singled out geo-blocking[119] as a major obstacle to market integration in the digital arena. Geo-blocking restricts the accessibility of websites from certain locations, thereby affecting service providers' ability to offer their online content across borders. This practice, the Commission argued, perpetuates the fragmentation of the internal market and reduces consumer choice.[120] One of the concrete consequences of geo-blocking is that it may prevent end-users from enjoying the content of their choice as they travel to other Member States (for instance, end-users may not be able to access the streaming service to which they subscribe when they spend their holidays abroad). Legislating to remove geo-blocking and to enable the portability of online subscriptions could make a tangible contribution to EU citizens' well-being.[121] In a sense, the initiative

---

[116] European Commission, 'Digital Single Market Strategy: European Commission agrees areas for action' IP/15/4653 (Brussels, 25 March 2015).

[117] European Commission, 'A Digital Single Market Strategy for Europe' COM(2015) 192 final.

[118] Ibid, Section 2.1 and 2.2.

[119] Ibid, Section 2.3. The Commission defines geo-blocking in the Strategy as referring 'to practices used for commercial reasons by online sellers that result in the denial of access to websites based in other Member States'.

[120] Ibid: 'By limiting consumer opportunities and choice, geo-blocking is a significant cause of consumer dissatisfaction and of fragmentation of the Internal Market'.

[121] Margrethe Vestager, 'Competition policy for the Digital Single Market: Focus on e-commerce' (Bundeskartellamt International Conference on Competition, Bonn, 26 March 2015): 'I, for one, cannot understand why I can watch my favourite Danish channels on my tablet in Copenhagen – a service I paid for – but I can't when I am in Brussels'.

was comparable in symbolism to the elimination of roaming charges for users of mobile telecommunications services.[122]

The Commission did not fail to acknowledge in its strategy document that there may be legitimate reasons why content producers engage in geo-blocking strategies. In some instances, the practice is implemented to ensure compliance with regulatory obligations. For instance, there may be legislation in place prohibiting the sale of drugs or dangerous substances across borders.[123] In other cases, however, geo-blocking is put in place to engage in market segmentation and price discrimination. In relation to the latter instances (which were described as 'unjustified geo-blocking), the Commission originally proposed a blanket ban on the practice.[124] In parallel with the announcement of its Digital Single Market Strategy, moreover, the authority launched a sector inquiry[125] into e-commerce to explore the scope and potential for competition law enforcement to ease cross-border trade. Geo-blocking featured prominently in the Preliminary Report accompanying the launch of the investigation.[126]

Intellectual property legislation was (and remains) a major obstacle to the realisation of the Commission's Digital Single Market vision and the one area where reliance on geo-blocking is both legitimate and integral to the system. When the exploitation of copyright-protected content is at stake, geo-blocking is often nothing more than the very manifestation of regulation at work. In particular, an online provider that engages in geo-blocking may not be doing anything other than sticking to the terms of its licensing agreement. Failing to do so (that is, showing protected content outside the territory covered by the licence) may amount to a breach of copyright. This may be true, in particular, where the right of communication to the public is at stake.[127] In such an instance, the freedom to provide services within the meaning of Article 56 TFEU[128] does not supersede intellectual property. This point dates back to *Coditel I*.[129] In that case, the Court ruled that an exclusive licensee may prevent every communication to the public in

---

[122] Regulation (EU) 2022/612 of the European Parliament and of the Council of 6 April 2022 on roaming on public mobile communications networks within the Union (recast) [2002] OJ L115/1.

[123] Digital Single Market Strategy (n 117), Section 2.3.

[124] Ibid: 'However, in many cases online geo-blocking is not justified. These unjustified practices should be expressly prohibited so that EU consumers and businesses can take full advantage of the single market in terms of choice and lower prices'.

[125] European Commission, 'Preliminary Report on the E-commerce Sector Inquiry' SWD(2016) 312 final.

[126] Ibid, in particular paras 389–397 and 745–775.

[127] Article 3 of Directive 2001/29/EC of the European Parliament and of the Council of 22 May 2001 on the harmonisation of certain aspects of copyright and related rights in the information society [2001] OJ L167/10.

[128] In accordance with Article 56 TFEU 'restrictions on freedom to provide services within the Union shall be prohibited in respect of nationals of Member States who are established in a Member State other than that of the person for whom the services are intended'.

[129] Case 62/79 *SA Compagnie générale pour la diffusion de la télévision, Coditel, and others v Ciné Vog Films and others*, EU:C:1982:334.

the territory covered by the agreement without breaching the Treaty's fundamental freedoms.[130] The licensee's ability to authorise or prohibit any communication to the public comprises transmissions that have been duly licensed by the right holder to third parties in other Member States.

As a consequence of *Coditel I*, content producers can, and do, engage in market segmentation (including by means of geo-blocking). By the same token, fully realising the Commission's vision – that is, creating a space where licensees compete with one another across borders or, alternatively, one in which an EU-wide licensee offers a single set of services within the Union – necessitates legislative changes. Such changes, aimed at favouring the freedom to provide services and cross-border competition, can be achieved by amending intellectual property regimes. The so-called 'country of origin' principle is an effective legal device to attain this goal. This principle creates, in effect, a legal fiction: it provides that, as a matter of law, the communication to the public of copyright-protected content takes place only in the Member State in which the communication originates (and thus irrespective of where it is received). Accordingly, even though the broadcast would be accessible across borders, it will be deemed to occur exclusively in the country where the licence has been obtained. Once the principle is introduced, it becomes possible for licensees to compete across borders without breaching the terms of their respective agreements.

The 'country of origin' principle featured in the SatCab Directive,[131] which harmonised certain aspects related to the transmission of copyright-protected content. At the time of the adoption of this legislation (early 1990s), satellite broadcasting was a promising technology: just like online streaming decades later, it had the potential to inject cross-border competition and favour the emergence of a pan-European audiovisual market. The EU legislature sought to make the most of this technology by introducing the 'country of uplink' rule (which is a technology-specific expression of the 'country of origin' principle). Pursuant to Article 1(2)(b) of the SatCab Directive, the broadcast via satellite (that is, the act of communication to the public) 'occurs solely in the Member State where, under the control and responsibility of the broadcasting organization, the programme-carrying signals are introduced into an uninterrupted chain of communication leading to the satellite and down towards the earth'.[132]

Where the 'country of origin' principle is introduced, the balance between intellectual property and the free movement of services changes. Under the

---

[130] Ibid, para 15.
[131] Council Directive 93/83/EEC of 27 September 1993 on the coordination of certain rules concerning copyright and rights related to copyright applicable to satellite broadcasting and cable retransmission [1993] OJ L248/15.
[132] Ibid, Article 1(2)(b): 'The act of communication to the public by satellite occurs solely in the Member State where, under the control and responsibility of the broadcasting organization, the programme-carrying signals are introduced into an uninterrupted chain of communication leading to the satellite and down towards the earth'.

Coditel I doctrine, as explained above, the former prevails. Once the 'country of origin' principle is introduced, the latter does. This so because it enables lawful cross-border competition. The Court confirmed this point explicitly in *Murphy*.[133] In this judgment, the ECJ held that national legislation prohibiting the import and sale of decoding devices acquired in another Member State amounts to an infringement of Article 56 TFEU.[134] The Court distinguished the facts at stake in the case from *Coditel I*. In the latter, the cross-border communication to the public took place without the authorisation of the licensor; therefore, it amounted to a copyright infringement. Under the SatCab Directive, by contrast, the transmission via satellite is deemed to take place only in the 'country of uplink' and therefore occurs with the consent of the licensor irrespective of where it is received.[135]

The *Murphy* judgment is illuminating for an additional reason. It exposed the implications, for right holders and licensees, of the introduction of the 'country of origin' principle. Once the principle is introduced via legislation, the territorial exclusivity enjoyed by licensees is no longer airtight (as it would be under the *Coditel I* doctrine). To a greater or lesser extent, the said licensees must accept competition from broadcasters based in other territories. The loss of airtight territorial protection has consequences for licensees' willingness to pay for content and, by the same token, for the level of remuneration received by licensors creating the said content.[136] According to the Court, however, these considerations do not justify the segmentation of the internal market along national borders. In this regard, the ECJ noted that copyright holders are entitled to receive 'appropriate remuneration for each use of the protected subject-matter', as opposed to the 'highest possible remuneration'.[137]

Because favouring market integration via the 'country of origin' principle comes at the expense of right holders' ability to maximise the remuneration they receive for their content, Member States have proved reluctant to harmonise copyright legislation by replicating the logic of the SatCab Directive.[138] This reluctance was manifested in the context of a consultation launched by the Commission in August 2015. As noted by the authority in the report that followed, there was a 'strong call for caution' by Member States vis-a-vis any initiative aimed at expanding the scope

---

[133] Joined Cases C-403/08 and C-429/08 *Football Association Premier League Ltd and Others v QC Leisure and Others and Karen Murphy v Media Protection Services Ltd*, EU:C:2011:631.

[134] Ibid, para 89.

[135] Ibid, para 119: 'However, those statements were made in a context which is not comparable to that of the main proceedings. In the case which led to the judgment in Coditel I, the cable television broadcasting companies communicated a work to the public without having, in the Member State of the place of origin of that communication, an authorisation from the right holders concerned and without having paid remuneration to them'.

[136] For an economic analysis, see Gregor Langus, Damien Neven and Sophie Poukens, *Economic Analysis of the Territoriality of the Making Available Right in the EU* (Charles River Associates for DG Markt 2014).

[137] *Murphy* (n 133), para 108.

[138] Pablo Ibáñez Colomo, 'Copyright and the Digital Single Market: geo-blocking is here to stay (or so it seems)' (*Chillin'Competition*, 4 May 2016).

of the 'country of origin' principle to the provision of content via the Internet.[139] Unsurprisingly, right holders and major licensees (including leading broadcasters and pay-TV providers) were also opposed to the measure.

Ultimately, the legislation that would follow the Digital Single Market Strategy was less ambitious than the one originally envisioned by the Commission. Instead of a complete overhaul of the copyright regime allowing for unrestricted competition between online service providers across borders, the EU legislature finally settled for a relatively modest amendment. The European Parliament and the Council agreed on the so-called Portability Regulation,[140] which was designed to ensure that end-users can access subscriptions to copyright-protected content while travelling abroad within the EU (that is, while they are 'temporarily present'[141] in another Member State). In such circumstances (and only in such circumstances), the 'country of origin' principle would apply.[142] In 2020, the Commission issued a Report reviewing the geo-blocking initiatives adopted as part of the Digital Single Market Strategy.[143] The document discussed the convenience of adopting more ambitious legislation in the area of copyright but noted that there was little appetite among stakeholders.[144]

4.2. The Pay-TV Investigation

In parallel to the consultations exploring the convenience of introducing the 'country of origin' principle in copyright legislation, the Commission initiated an Article 101 TFEU investigation overlapping in substance with the Digital Single Market Strategy. As noted above, this dual approach is not fundamentally different from that followed by the authority in the energy sector (and was considered at length in Chapter 6). In July 2015 (just two months after the launch of the Digital Single Market Strategy and the Sector Inquiry into e-commerce), the Commission sent a Statement of Objections to Sky UK (a pay-TV operator) and the six Hollywood major studios.[145] The ambition of this investigation ('*Cross-border access to pay-TV*' and, hereinafter, '*Pay-TV*') was to achieve, by means of

---

[139] Ibid.

[140] Regulation (EU) 2017/1128 of the European Parliament and of the Council of 14 June 2017 on cross-border portability of online content services in the internal market [2017] OJ L168/1.

[141] Ibid, Article 3(1): 'The provider of an online content service provided against payment of money shall enable a subscriber who is temporarily present in a Member State to access and use the online content service in the same manner as in the Member State of residence, including by providing access to the same content, on the same range and number of devices, for the same number of users and with the same range of functionalities'.

[142] Ibid, Article 4.

[143] European Commission, 'Report from the Commission on the first short-term review of the Geo-blocking Regulation' COM(2020) 766 final.

[144] Ibid, 11.

[145] European Commission, 'Antitrust: Commission sends Statement of Objections on cross-border provision of pay-TV services available in UK and Ireland' IP/15/5432 (Brussels, 23 July 2015).

competition law enforcement, the sort of changes that the potential reform of the copyright regime could attain.

The Commission took issue with some of the clauses inserted in the licensing agreements concluded between Sky UK and the Hollywood major studios. More precisely, it raised concerns about the territorial restrictions limiting the pay-TV operator's ability to offer the licensed content, both via the Internet and satellite, in territories other than the ones covered by the agreement (UK and Ireland).[146] As a result of these limitations (which include geo-blocking), Sky UK would not be able to respond to unsolicited requests from end-users based in other Member States. The agreements, in other words, would be restricting what is known as 'passive selling' (that is, transactions where the end-user takes the initiative and the seller responds to an unsolicited request).[147] In a similar vein, the Commission expressed concerns about the fact that the agreements would be denying third-party licensees the ability to offer their services in UK and Ireland.

The theory underpinning the case is interesting in that it seeks to extend to the online provision of copyright-protected content the principles that apply to distribution agreements, on the one hand, and satellite transmissions, on the other. To begin with, the distinction between active and passive selling is borrowed from the Vertical Block Exemption Regulation[148] and the Guidelines on vertical restraints,[149] where it was first introduced. In relation to distribution agreements, the Commission's policy has long been grounded on the principle that passive sales should be allowed if the agreement is to benefit from the block exemption.[150] Prior to the *Pay-TV* case, however, there were no precedents of the application the active/passive divide in a context that does not involve the distribution[151] or the production[152] of goods or services.

---

[146] Ibid: 'The Commission's investigation, which was opened in January 2014, identified clauses in licensing agreements between the six film studios and Sky UK which require Sky UK to block access to films through its online pay-TV services (so-called "geo-blocking") or through its satellite pay-TV services to consumers outside its licensed territory (UK and Ireland)'.

[147] Ibid: 'The Commission's preliminary view as set out in the Statement of Objections is that such clauses restrict Sky UK's ability to accept unsolicited requests for its pay-TV services from consumers located abroad, i.e. from consumers located in Member States where Sky UK is not actively promoting or advertising its services (so-called "passive sales")'.

[148] See Article 1(1)(m) of Commission Regulation (EU) 2022/720 of 10 May 2022 on the application of Article 101(3) of the Treaty on the Functioning of the European Union to categories of vertical agreements and concerted practices [2022] OJ L134/4, which defines 'passive sales', as 'sales made in response to unsolicited requests from individual customers, including delivery of goods or services to the customer, without the sale having been initiated by actively targeting the particular customer, customer group or territory, and including sales resulting from participating in public procurement or responding to private invitations to tender'.

[149] Guidelines on vertical restraints [2022] OJ C248/1.

[150] See Article 4 of the Vertical Block Exemption Regulation (n 148).

[151] As in the context of vertical restraints.

[152] See the Commission Regulation (EU) No 316/2014 of 21 March 2014 on the application of Article 101(3) of the Treaty on the Functioning of the European Union to categories of technology transfer agreements [2014] OJ L93/17, which also rely on the active/passive divide and the scope of which is confined to the licensing of technology for the 'production of contract products' (see Article 1(1)(c)). See also the Guidelines on technology transfer agreements (n 75), paras 58–66.

Second, the press release announcing the Statement of Objections also suggests that the case was premised on the assumption that the *Murphy* judgment, described above, is also applicable to the provision of content via the Internet. It is not immediately obvious to reconcile this position with the differences in the legal regime that applies to, respectively, online and satellite transmissions. Pursuant to the 'country of origin' principle, the latter, at stake in *Murphy*, are deemed to occur only in the territory in which the licensee is based, even if its broadcasts can be accessed across the EU. When it comes to the Internet, by contrast, the transmission of content via the Internet outside the territory covered by the licence would amount to a copyright infringement. This is so because a communication to the public that occurs online is subject to the 'country of destination' principle.[153] As a result, the licensee needs the authorisation of the licensor in every Member State in which it is received (and not just the 'country of origin').

Against this background, it is not clear that the contentious clauses limiting Sky UK's ability to provide content via the Internet restrict competition that would otherwise have existed. To the extent that the 'country of destination' principle applies, and to the extent that Sky UK did not have a licence in territories other than the UK and Ireland, contractual clauses restricting its ability to offer content online elsewhere in the EU did not prohibit anything that would otherwise have been lawful. Cross-border competition (or, rather, the absence thereof) would have been the same with and without the clauses. Even if the agreement had not required the geo-blocking of content by Sky UK, the copyright regime would have prevented the firm from providing its services across the Channel. In these circumstances, it is not clear that the agreements can be said to restrict competition, whether by object or effect. What would be restricting competition is the intellectual property system, instead.

These conclusions are in line with the *Coditel II* judgment,[154] which was delivered immediately after the first instalment of the saga. In the second *Coditel* ruling, the Court held that a territorial licence granting the exclusive right to authorise or prohibit any communication to the public in a given Member State does not amount, in and of itself, to a breach of Article 101(1) TFEU, whether by object or effect.[155] This is so even when the licence provides for absolute territorial protection, which is in principle a no-no in the EU competition law system.[156] As noted by the Court in *Coditel II*, the ability to 'require fees' for every communication to the public is 'part of the essential function of copyright'.[157] Therefore, if an exclusive territorial licence is found to restrict competition, it will not be simply because

---

[153] For a discussion, see Pablo Ibáñez Colomo, 'Copyright and the EU Digital Single Market Strategy', in Roger D Blair, and D Daniel Sokol (eds), *Handbook of Antitrust, Intellectual Property and High Technology* (Cambridge University Press 2017).
[154] Case 262/81 *Coditel SA, Compagnie générale pour la diffusion de la télévision, and others v Ciné-Vog Films SA and others*, EU:C:1982:334.
[155] Ibid, para 15.
[156] *Consten-Grundig* (n 5).
[157] *Coditel II* (n 154), para 12.

the licensee is insulated from competition. As noted by the Court, it is necessary to show that there are additional factors at play, such as the length of the agreement, which may be deemed excessive[158] or the fact that it raises 'artificial and unjustifiable' barriers to entry in the relevant market.[159]

The Commission's unprecedented interpretation of Article 101(1) TFEU in *Pay-TV* was never fully laid out in an infringement decision. The Hollywood major studios accepted to change their licensing agreements to address the concerns expressed in the Statement of Objections. Following this move, the Commission closed its investigation with a set of commitments decisions. These proactive measures had the object and effect of altering, in practice, the reach and operation of the copyright regime. The first firm to modify its commercial practices was Paramount (in 2016),[160] followed by the other major studios and Sky in 2018.[161] The preliminary assessment sketched in the various commitments decisions explains that the Commission had concluded, prima facie, that the agreements were restrictive of competition by object insofar as they limited Sky's ability to respond to unsolicited offers from end-users based in other Member States and insofar as they required the studios to impose similar duties on other licensees.[162]

The overarching idea underpinning the decisions is that the clauses requiring Sky to block access to its content from outside the territory covered by the licence (and, similarly, those requiring studios that other licensees be subject to the same restraints) are 'additional obligations' (within the meaning of *Murphy*[163]) that go beyond a mere exclusive territorial licence. To the extent that they are, the Commission argued, they would restrict, by their very nature, Article 101(1) TFEU.[164] The succinct analysis found in the preliminary assessment failed to engage with the fundamental issue discussed above, which is the fact that providing content, online, outside of the territories covered by Sky UK's licence would not be a form of lawful competition. The Commission merely claimed that there were no factors pertaining to the relevant economic and legal context that would call into question the prima facie finding of a 'by object' restriction.[165]

The commitments decision issued in relation to Paramount was annulled on appeal by the Court in 2020.[166] Given the nature of these decisions, the judgment did not, and could not, rule on whether the Commission's interpretation of Article 101(1) TFEU, including the *Coditel II* judgment, was correct. The ECJ

---

[158] Ibid, para 19.
[159] Ibid.
[160] *Cross-border access to pay-TV* (Case AT.40023) Commission Decision of 26 July 2016.
[161] European Commission, 'Antitrust: Commission accepts commitments by Disney, NBCUniversal, Sony Pictures, Warner Bros. and Sky on cross-border pay-TV services' IP/19/1590 (Brussels, 7 March 2019).
[162] *Paramount* (n 160), para 46.
[163] *Murphy* (n 133), para 141.
[164] *Paramount* (n 160), para 39.
[165] Ibid, para 49.
[166] Case C-132/19 P *Groupe Canal + v Commission*, EU:C:2020:1007.

merely took the view that the Commission did not err in law by raising competition concerns about the contentious clauses, which, in light of the relevant case law, may be regarded as restrictive of competition by object.[167] Any decision 'definitively' establishing an infringement of Article 101(1) TFEU would necessitate, as clarified by the Court in the judgment, a 'full examination'[168] of the relevant economic and legal context, and in particular of the copyright regime.

4.3. The Implications of the Commitments for Third Parties: The Appeal Judgment

One of the most notable aspects of the commitments offered by Sky UK and the studios – and the one that makes it stand apart from the cases discussed in the preceding chapter – is that it had a significant impact on the position of third parties. Unlike cases such as *German Electricity Balancing Market*, the proactive changes introduced to the firms' licensing practices negatively affected other players in the market. By committing not to fulfilling their contractual obligations, and by accepting not to take action to ensure that licensees' obligations would be honoured, studios inevitably harmed the value of the exclusive rights acquired by broadcasters based in other Member States. Even though these third parties would not have been involved in the proceedings, they had to accept, as a *fait accompli*, that the territorial exclusivity would no longer be airtight (at the very least de facto, if not de iure).

The major advantage of geo-blocking, from the perspective of both right holders and licensees, is that it significantly reduces the costs of monitoring and ensuring compliance with the copyright regime (and with the terms of the licensing agreement). Such costs would be significantly increased once Sky UK is no longer bound by a duty to block access to its services when accessed from outside the UK and Ireland. It may become prohibitively difficult for a licensee based in another Member States to make sure that Sky UK is not providing content in breach of its exclusive territorial rights. Even if the licensee is able to detect a copyright breach, the commitments decision may make it difficult, if not impossible, for it to seek relief before a national court. One should consider, in this regard, that national courts are bound by a duty of sincere cooperation with the EU institutions.[169] Pursuant to Article 16(1) of Regulation 1/2003, the uniform application of EU competition law demands that Member States' judges do not take decisions that run counter to the Commission's administrative action.[170]

---

[167] Ibid, para 54.
[168] Ibid.
[169] Case C-344/98 *Masterfoods Ltd v HB Ice Cream Ltd*, EU:C:2000:689.
[170] Article 16(1) of Council Regulation (EC) No 1/2003 of 16 December 2002 on the implementation of the rules on competition laid down in Articles 81 and 82 of the Treaty [2003] OJ L1/1.

This background makes it easy to understand why Canal+, a French pay-TV operator and licensee of the Hollywood major studios, brought an action for annulment against the decision making the commitments offered by Paramount binding upon it.[171] The central argument brought by Canal+ is twofold. On the one hand, it claimed that its rights had been affected by a commitments decision in which it was not involved.[172] On the other, it explained that, by requiring Paramount not to oppose the provision of content outside the territory covered by Sky UK's licence (that is, by favouring cross-border competition over territorial exclusivity), the Commission would be affecting the position of content producers (in particular EU producers).[173] As explained above, it is inevitable that, once the protection given to licensees is no longer airtight, the remuneration received by copyright holders is negatively affected. Taken together, these two arguments amount to claiming that the commitments decision had altered the strength of copyright protection in the context of a competition law investigation.[174]

In its 2018 first instance judgment, the General Court dismissed the challenge brought by Canal+.[175] A significant fraction of the ruling is devoted to whether the Commission had erred in law by raising concerns about the potential anticompetitive object of the licensing agreement and about whether the conditions laid down in Article 101(3) TFEU were, if a restriction were established, fulfilled.[176] On the fundamental consequences of the decision (the *de facto* alteration of the substance of the right of communication to the public), the General Court denied that the commitments offered by Paramount affected the right of third parties (such as Canal+ itself). More precisely, it argued that the said third parties would not be precluded from seeking relief before a national judge.[177] Remedies before domestic courts may include, inter alia, the adoption of interim measures.[178]

The Court set aside the General Court judgment and annulled the Commission decision in its 2020 appeal ruling.[179] The ECJ rejected all grounds of appeal except for the fourth one, which focused on the consequences of the Article 9 decision for other undertakings. In this regard, it held that the Commission, when evaluating

---

[171] Case T-873/16 *Groupe Canal + v Commission*, EU:T:2018:904.
[172] Case C-132/19 P *Canal +* (n 166), para 88.
[173] Ibid, paras 89–90.
[174] This is another argument (unsuccessfully) invoked by Canal+ in the proceedings. More precisely, the firm claimed that the proceedings were an attempt to harmonise copyright through the back door. Ibid, para 22 ('Groupe Canal +, supported by EFADs and UPC, essentially claims that by rejecting its arguments that the adoption of the contested decision constitutes a misuse of powers – in that it allowed the Commission to obtain, on the pretext of its intention to halt anticompetitive practices, something which the European Parliament had refused to grant it, namely the end of territorial exclusivity in the cinema sector for the whole of the EEA – the General Court erred in law and failed to fulfil its obligation to state reasons').
[175] Case T-873/16 *Canal +* (n 171).
[176] Ibid, paras 29–75.
[177] Ibid, para 116.
[178] Ibid.
[179] Case C-132/19 P *Canal +* (n 166).

the proportionality of the commitments, must pay attention to their impact on third parties' rights, and in particular on whether they render such rights 'meaningless'.[180] In the specific circumstances of the case, the Court noted that there was little dispute that administrative action had interfered with Canal+'s contractual freedom, without it being involved in the proceedings at any stage.[181] Moreover, the fact that Paramount accepted not to honour some of its obligations vis-à-vis Canal+ would mean that the latter's rights would be affected.[182]

Crucially, the Court disagreed with the first instance ruling with regard to the possibility for Canal+ (and indeed any other third party suffering the negative consequences of the commitments offered by Paramount) to seek relief before national courts. Contrary to what was claimed by the General Court, the ECJ concludes that legal certainty demands that judges from Member States do not issue rulings contradicting a decision issued or contemplated by the Commission.[183] National courts would not be in a position to declare that the contentious agreements do not infringe Article 101(1) TFEU or that they fulfil the conditions set out in Article 101(3) TFEU.[184] By the same token, the ECJ concludes, third parties could not 'adequately and effectively' remedy the Commission's failure to evaluate the proportionality of the commitments.[185]

4.4. The Limits of Competition Law as a Harmonisation Tool

Chapter 6 showed the potential of competition law enforcement to mimic economic regulation, whether as a means to strengthen the effects of an existing regime or to rectify it. The *Pay-TV* investigation, by contrast, exposes its shortcomings. To begin with, it provides a concrete example of the sort of outcomes that cannot be attained by means of proactive enforcement. 'Policy-driven' action by means of commitments decisions presents several advantages from the perspective of an authority, including the flexibility and the ability to secure far-reaching intervention. What *Canal+* reveals, however, is that these decisions may not be an adequate instrument to change a system of property, and this includes the copyright regime. To the extent that it impacts on third parties, altering the nature of the rights and/or the reach of protection may not be possible by means of negotiated procedures.

Commitments may be effective in cases like *German Electricity Balancing Market* and *ENI*, which do not have spill-over effects on other firms. By contrast, the aftermath of *Canal+* suggests that this route is unlikely to be practical where

---

[180] Ibid, paras 106 and 127.
[181] Ibid, para 107.
[182] Ibid.
[183] Ibid, paras 109–110.
[184] Ibid, para 113.
[185] Ibid, para 115.

the case deals with intellectual property rights. Following the Court's ruling in the case, it is inevitable to conclude that the Commission would only have achieved the desired policy outcomes (cross-border competition between pay-TV operators) by securing commitments from every single one of the licensees based within the EU (and, by the same token, from the Hollywood major studios with every one of these licensees). As a result, the benefits that one can expect from Article 9 procedures (such as expedient enforcement and a more effective use of resources) would dissipate. Intervention could become as cumbersome, at the very least, as under Article 7 (which necessitates a formal finding of infringement).

Against this background, the Commission's reaction following the appeal judgment in *Canal+* is relatively unusual. However, it is not difficult to rationalise. Instead of reopening the proceedings and adopting a new set of decisions respecting the principles set out by the Court (either by fully involving third-party licensees in the procedure or by expanding the scope of the investigation to other firms), the authority decided to withdraw the commitment decisions involving the studios and Sky UK and to no longer pursue the case as a matter of priority.[186] The Commission signalled that the changes that had already been introduced by the studios were sufficient to dissipate any concerns. In other words, the authority accepted assurances provided in the absence of any formal route and, by the same token, the reality that fundamental changes to licensing practices by means of Article 101 TFEU enforcement was unlikely to be successful.

In subsequent cases dealing with the priorities of the Digital Single Market Strategy, the Commission focused on other geo-blocking cases that were less ambitious, in the sense that they did not question the operation of the intellectual property system. The string of cases that followed *Pay-TV* focused on agreements limiting distributors' ability to sell products across borders. Thus, in *Guess*, the Commission took issue with some clauses restricting the resale of goods via the Internet.[187] In *Character Merchandise*, it focused on a set of contractual provisions limiting distributors' ability to resell licensed merchandise across borders. Unlike the *Pay-TV* investigation, this case did not concern the right of communication to the public, which is not subject to the exhaustion doctrine.[188] *Character Merchandise*[189] concerned, instead, the right of distribution, which is deemed exhausted once the good is put on the market by the right holder or with its consent.[190] Once exhausted, intellectual property rights could not be invoked to limit or prohibit cross-border trade. By the same token, they cannot be said to restrict competition that would otherwise have existed. Finally, in *Video Games*,[191] the Commission took action against an online distributor and five publishers

---

[186] *Cross-border access to pay-TV* (Case AT.40023) Commission Decision of 31 March 2021.
[187] *Guess* (Case AT.40428) Commission Decision of 17 December 2018.
[188] Article 3(3) of Directive 2001/29 (n 127).
[189] *Character merchandise* (Case AT.40432) Commission Decision of 9 July 2019.
[190] Article 4(2) of Directive 2001/29 (n 127).
[191] European Commission, 'Antitrust: Commission fines Valve and five publishers of PC video games € 7.8 million for "geo-blocking" practices' IP/21/170 (Brussels, 20 January 2021).

of video games in a context in which intellectual property rights could not be invoked, for the simple reason that the online distributor had been given a worldwide licence.

5. Conclusions

The three case studies discussed in this Chapter show the extent to which the Commission's attitude vis-à-vis intellectual property has changed over the past 20 years. The cautious approach that the authority took in 2004, when it was informed of the reverse payment settlements that Lundbeck had concluded with a number of generic manufacturers gave way, over the following decade, to vigorous enforcement. Cases involving the exercise of intellectual property were prioritised and, at various stages, represented a significant fraction of its activity. As part of the recalibration of its policy, the Commission developed new ad hoc doctrines (such as the expansion of the range of 'exceptional circumstances' within the meaning of *Magill* and *IMS Health*). In some instances, this new, non-deferential attitude resulted in the de facto amendment of the copyright regimes (or at least an attempt to do so).

For the purposes of the overall themes addressed in this book, the Chapter is useful in that it exposes the institutional limits that competition law faces when engaged in proactive intervention. The Section devoted to standards shows that the sort of technical issues that the monitoring of SEPs demands (such as solving patent disputes and ruling on whether licensing takes place on FRAND terms) would not be adequately addressed via the enforcement of Articles 101 and 102 TFEU. It is not surprising that, as is true of digital markets, the 'expectation of regulation' has ultimately led to a formal proposal to regulate the matter at the EUIPO level. Section 4, in turn, shows that the commitments route, which is suited to bringing some practices to an end, cannot be the mechanism through which a whole system of property is amended. By definition, a bilateral negotiation between a firm and the Commission cannot empty the rights of a third party of their substance.

The analysis in this Chapter provides an additional insight. The Court's interpretation of Articles 101 and 102 TFEU is not an obstacle to the EU competition law enforcement in relation to intellectual property rights. This said, the ECJ's approach is in several respects more nuanced than that favoured by the Commission. In *Motorola*, for instance, the authority took the view that it is presumptively abusive for a dominant SEP holder to seek an injunction. In *Lundbeck*, it interpreted the notion of potential competition in a relatively expansive manner, which (at least in one of the versions advanced in the decision) is not fully in line with *Generics*. Finally, the Court ruling in *Canal+* resulted in the Commission abandoning the attempts to favour, via competition law enforcement, the cross-border communication to the public of copyright-protected works. These examples suggests that the limits to the new EU competition law may not be exclusively come from the institutional constraints that authorities faced, but from the legal boundaries defined by the Court.

8

Digital Markets

1. Competition Law in Digital Markets: Product Design and Business Models

1.1. *Google Shopping* and *Google Android*: A Turning Point in Policy-making

The decisions in *Google Shopping*[1] and *Android*[2] marked a turning point in the European Commission's (hereinafter, the 'Commission') policy. First, they signalled the reorientation of the authority's resources towards digital markets. In the years that followed, the Commission opened a string of investigations in the sector, including against Google itself.[3] Second, the two decisions represent a change in approach towards cases involving the administration of proactive obligations. Chapters 6 and 7 show that, until *Google Shopping* was adopted, this form of intervention relied, by and large, on commitments decisions.[4] Negotiated procedures dominated proactive enforcement, which often resulted in the fundamental restructuring of markets. In *Google Shopping* and *Android*, by contrast, the Commission chose to adopt an infringement decision formally establishing a breach of Article 102 TFEU. Proactive intervention, after these cases, is no longer the privileged province of commitments or settlements.[5] Infringement decisions allowed the authority to impose – record-setting – fines, thereby marking the shift in strategy.

The nature and consequences of proactive enforcement in both *Google Shopping* and *Android* are also worthy of discussion. Intervention in the first of

---

[1] *Google – Google Search (Shopping)* (Case AT.39740) Commission Decision of 27 June 2017.
[2] *Google Android* (Case AT.40099) Commission Decision of 18 July 2018.
[3] *Google Search (AdSense)* (Case AT.40411) Commission Decision of 20 March 2019; and European Commission, 'Antitrust: Commission opens investigation into possible anticompetitive conduct by Google in the online advertising technology sector' IP/21/3143 (Brussels, 22 June 2021).
[4] Article 9 of Council Regulation (EC) No 1/2003 of 16 December 2002 on the implementation of the rules on competition laid down in Articles 81 and 82 of the Treaty [2003] OJ L1/1. See Chapter 1 for an extensive discussion of the features of this instrument.
[5] An interesting interim period was exemplified by *ARA Foreclosure* (Case AT.39759) Commission Decision of 20 September 2016, which was formally an infringement decision but was the result of a settlement between the Commission and the firm.

these cases led, in effect, to the redesign of Google's search engine. Prior to the decision, the premium space at the top of the results page (the so-called Shopping Unit) was reserved to the firm's own shopping service. Google's affiliate was the only one to be displayed in rich format (Google Shopping's results were accompanied with pictures and additional information). Following intervention, access to the Shopping Unit is open to third-party comparison-shopping sites on non-discriminatory terms and conditions. The search engine was redesigned so that access to this premium space would be decided in the context of an auction. Intervention in the second case is remarkable in that it amounted to challenging the core of the firm's monetisation strategy, which revolved around the joint licensing, at a nominal prize of zero, of applications. The Commission sought to create a level playing field between Google's and rivals' applications. The firm's mobile ecosystem was redesigned to this effect.

The remedies required in the two cases show that the Commission does not hesitate to interfere with and, where necessary, refine, the operation of digital markets and ecosystems. Accordingly, the authority may, by means of Article 102 TFEU enforcement, rectify central aspects relating to the design and monetisation of online platforms. Such aspects include decisions about which segments within an ecosystem are open to third parties and which are closed to rivalry; about the terms and conditions under which operators deal with third parties; and about the appropriate degree of vertical and/or horizontal integration. One cannot assume as given that competition policy would regulate such issues. This is so not just because the administration of proactive remedies is generally complex and demanding for authorities. One should take into account, in addition, the peculiarities of digital markets. These are fast-moving activities where the effective implementation of remedies presupposes a degree of expertise and a commitment in terms of resources that goes beyond what proactive intervention typically demands.

1.2. Self-preferencing in *Google Shopping*

The *Google Shopping* case has a long procedural history in the EU, dating back to 2010.[6] At the origin of this investigation there is the firm's redesign of its flagship product, started in 2007. Universal Search – as it is known – amounted, in essence, to the integration of a variety of Google's services into its search engine. For instance, the results page now displays Google Maps alongside links to other websites. Similarly, the search engine may display a song's lyrics or a YouTube video whenever end-users look up the name of a song, and the league standings when they search for a particular sports championship. The addition of features to the results page represents an objective improvement relative to Google's primitive

---

[6] European Commission, 'Antitrust: Commission probes allegations of antitrust violations by Google' IP/20/1624 (Brussels, 30 November 2010).

search engine design, which exclusively displayed links to other websites. However, it led to complaints from third parties competing with the firm on adjacent segments. It is not difficult to rationalise these reactions. As a result of Universal Search, traffic that might otherwise have gone to an online travel agency or to a newspaper stays within – or is redirected through – the search engine, thereby affecting third parties' ability to generate (among others) advertising revenue and potentially leading to the leveraging of Google's market power from search to neighbouring activities.

Third-party complaints relating to the potential effects of Universal Search on their ability to compete and stay in business were evaluated on both sides of the Atlantic. In January 2013, the US Federal Trade Commission decided to close its investigation without raising concerns about the 'search bias' dimension of the probe.[7] The Statement issued suggests that the US agency was cautious not to interfere with the design of a search engine, even if it amounted to the favouring of Google's own services. The implicit legal test is that the integration of features in a complex product is not anticompetitive unless it has no explanation other than an exclusionary one (that is, unless it has an anticompetitive object). Accordingly, the mere fact that the design changes are a plausible means to improve the quality of a product and/or consumer experience would be sufficient, according to the 2013 Statement, to rule out antitrust liability.[8]

The Commission would only adopt its decision in *Google Shopping* in June 2017,[9] following two attempts to reach a negotiated outcome and after narrowing down the investigation to shopping services alone. The authority concluded that the firm had abused its dominant position by engaging in a self-preferencing strategy. This strategy was understood to have two components. First, the Commission found that the firm had sought to favour its affiliate, Google Shopping. As pointed out above, the firm's own service was the only one to be prominently displayed in the Shopping Unit. Other sites, by contrast, could only aspire to feature as generic search results (and thus would never be displayed in rich format). Second, the Commission claimed that rivals were subject to demotion by the search engine. This system of penalties, however, did not apply to Google Shopping.

The authority found in its decision that the conduct departed from legitimate competition on the merits insofar as it led to the diversion of traffic (away from

---

[7] *In the Matter of Google Inc.* (File Number 111-0163 FTC) Statement of the Federal Trade Commission of 3 January 2013.

[8] Ibid: 'A key issue for the Commission was to determine whether Google changed its search results primarily to exclude actual or potential competitors and inhibit the competitive process, or on the other hand, to improve the quality of its search product and the overall user experience. The totality of the evidence indicates that, in the main, Google adopted the design changes that the Commission investigated to improve the quality of its search results, and that any negative impact on actual or potential competitors was incidental to that purpose'.

[9] *Google Shopping* (n 1).

third-party price comparison-shopping sites and towards Google Shopping), which in turn was found to have, or be capable of having, anticompetitive effects.[10] According to the Commission, the effects of traffic diversion would be manifested in two markets. First, the practice would lead to the leveraging of Google's dominant position to the relevant markets for comparison shopping services.[11] Second, the decision argues, it would strengthen the firm's pre-existing position on the markets for general search services.[12] The authority concluded that this impact would occur both in the short term (in the form of high prices for direct and indirect customers)[13] and in the long term (through reduced incentives to innovate).[14]

The *Google Shopping* decision is based on the premise that there is nothing special or unique about cases challenging the design of a product. The starting point diverges, in this regard, from the FTC's. The Commission noted that the case law does not suggest that improvements to a product are presumptively pro-competitive or that, as valid expressions of competition on the merits, escape Article 102 TFEU (at least so prima facie).[15] The decision treated the strategy as any other one having the effect of extending a dominant position to a neighbouring market.[16] According to the Commission, leveraging conduct such as the one at stake in the case is a 'well-established, independent, form of abuse falling outside the scope of competition on the merits'.[17] The decision suggests that this practice is caught by Article 102 TFEU when it has, or is capable of having, anticompetitive effects.

The finding of infringement was assorted with a fine in excess of €2.42 billion[18] and with a remedy. The approach that the Commission took to the latter is notable in that it did not prescribe a specific obligation and did not dictate the way in which Google had to redesign its search engine. Instead, the authority required the firm to abide by a non-discrimination principle when displaying search results. Accordingly, it was for Google to decide the specific way in which it would be bringing the infringement to an end. For instance, it could have decided to discontinue its price-comparison service and/or the Shopping Unit that it reserved to its affiliate. Alternatively, the firm could have decided to sell Google Shopping to a third party, following which all comparison-shopping services could have been subject to the same treatment. The Commission's principles-based approach created some uncertainty long after the adoption of the decision and raised a number of issues that will be discussed hereinafter.

---

[10] Ibid, para 341.
[11] Ibid, paras 591–607.
[12] Ibid, paras 641–643.
[13] Ibid, paras 593–594.
[14] Ibid, para 595.
[15] Ibid, para 652.
[16] Ibid, para 334: 'Article 102 of the Treaty and Article 54 of the EEA Agreement prohibit not only practices by an undertaking in a dominant position which tend to strengthen that position, but also the conduct of an undertaking with a dominant position in a given market that tends to extend that position to a neighbouring but separate market by distorting competition […]'.
[17] Ibid, para 649.
[18] Ibid, Article 2.

In its November 2021 decision, the General Court (hereinafter, the 'GC' or the 'first-instance court') delivered the first instance judgment in the case.[19] The challenge brought by Google against the decision was by and large dismissed. Only a minor point, pertaining to the evaluation of the impact of the strategy on the markets for general search services, was annulled.[20] The central aspects of the decision were found to rely on a correct interpretation of Article 102 TFEU. This is true, in particular, of the framework applied to evaluate the lawfulness of the self-preferencing strategy. In this regard, the GC dismissed claims by Google that the legality of its behaviour had to be assessed in light of the conditions set out in *Bronner* and that, in particular, the Commission would have had to establish that access to the Shopping Unit is indispensable within the meaning of that case law.[21] This central aspect is addressed at length below. The GC judgment was appealed.[22] At the time of writing, the Court of Justice (hereinafter, the 'Court', or the 'ECJ') was yet to deliver its judgment.

1.3. Tying and Non-compete in *Google Android*

The *Android* decision was adopted by the Commission the following year, in July 2018.[23] The case concerned Google's strategy in relation to its mobile ecosystem, which revolves around its Android operating system. From the outset, the ecosystem was designed to be a relatively open one, which contrasts with Apple's model. Android's openness is manifested in a number of ways. It is manifested, first, in a greater degree of modularity across all segments of the value chain. Unlike Apple's iOS, the Android operating system is licensed to any willing third party. Second, would-be licensees have the choice between two levels of access to the operating system. The first option is to exploit the 'bare bones' operating system, which is licensed for free and on an open-source basis.[24] Amazon, for instance, built Fire OS around an Android core.[25] The second option for licensees is to gain access to Google's version of the Android ecosystem. Under this second option, licensees would be able to exploit not only the operating system but also a suite of proprietary applications and services,[26] including an app store (Google Play), the Chrome web browser and the search application.

---

[19] Case T-612/17 *Google LLC and Alphabet, Inc. v Commission*, EU:T:2021:763.
[20] Ibid, para 458.
[21] Ibid, paras 212–249.
[22] Case C-48/22 P *Google LLC and Alphabet, Inc. v Commission*, pending.
[23] *Android* (n 2).
[24] Ibid, para 124: 'Google makes the source code of Android available for free via the Android Open Source Project ("AOSP") and under an open source licence ("AOSP licence"). This means that anybody can access the AOSP source code and create modified versions of it (so-called "Android forks"). These were major selling points to get OEMs and MNOs to join the OHA'.
[25] Ibid, paras 1092–1105.
[26] These are hereinafter referred to as 'applications' as shorthand.

Competition Law in Digital Markets: Product Design and Business Models   237

Figures 8.1.1 and 8.1.2 Two options to access Android

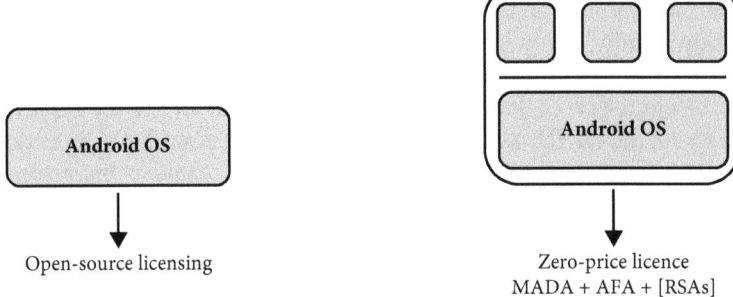

These two manifestations of Android's relative openness are a source of challenges that firms running relatively closed ecosystems, including Apple, do not face. These challenges are both of a dual technical and economic nature. One of the advantages of a relatively closed ecosystem is that the operator can tightly control every level of the value chain. The more open an ecosystem (and, similarly, the more it relies on third parties), the greater the risk that it becomes fragmented. For instance, applications may not be available on every single device; alternatively, the user experience may vary from one device to the other, thereby raising concerns about the reliability of affiliated products and services. In the same vein, the bad quality of the devices produced by some third-party licensees may negatively affect the reputation of the ecosystem as a whole. From an economic perspective, moreover, a relatively open ecosystem may demand specific responses to the risk of opportunistic conduct by some participants within the ecosystem. These challenges arise frequently in similar scenarios, including in the context of vertical restraints.[27]

The Anti-Fragmentation Agreement (hereinafter, the 'AFA'), one of the three contentious issues in the Android case, was a response to these concerns. As mentioned above, Google gives would-be licensees a choice between receiving a licence comprising the 'bare bones' operating system and Google's version of it. Where third parties chose the latter, they were required to comply, at the time of the case, with a series of obligations aimed at preventing the fragmentation of the ecosystem and ensuring the compatibility of their devices.[28] The Commission took issue with the fact that the AFA limited third-party licensees' ability to develop alternative, Android-based, mobile ecosystems (the so-called Android 'forks').[29] The AFA provided for what is, in effect, a non-compete obligation. Accordingly, as soon as a manufacturer opted to rely on Google's ecosystem, it was no longer

---

[27] Guidelines on vertical restraints [2022] OJ C248/1, para 16.
[28] Ibid, paras 157–171.
[29] Ibid, para 124. The decision defines 'Android forks' as 'modified versions of Android' based on the operating system licensed on an open-source basis.

able to exploit Android-based alternatives to it. In other words, those benefitting from the value generated by Google, would not be in a position to develop rival ecosystems built around an Android 'fork'.

The third manifestation of the relative openness of the Android ecosystem is the most relevant for the discussions that follow. Google's ecosystem can be said to be open also in the sense that both the operating system and/or the applications licensed on top of it were made available to any willing third party at a nominal prize of zero. This aspect of Google's licensing strategy explains the firm's business model. Instead of monetising its assets by means of licensing fees (as many software companies do), the firm relied on advertising. As a result, its ability to monetise its assets depended on making its revenue-generating applications widely available. In this sense, the firm's business model is not fundamentally different from that of a free-to-air television station. Just like the latter, Google's strategy depends on reaching as many eyeballs as possible.

The analogy with the activities of free-to-air television channels is also useful to understand the rationale behind some of the contentious clauses in the case. Pursuant to Google's Mobile Application Distribution Agreement (hereinafter, 'MADA'), the zero-prize licensing by Google of its applications was made conditional upon mobile manufacturers pre-installing a suite of its features and services.[30] Put differently, the MADA did not allow the said manufacturers to cherry-pick which of Google's applications were going to be available on their devices. Instead, they were required to pre-instal, along other applications, those generating the thrust of Google's revenues, namely the web browser (Chrome) and Search. Just like a free-to-air television station bundles content and advertising for monetisation purposes, the firm tied access to its ecosystem to the licensing of revenue-generating services. This analogy is imperfect in one sense. The MADA does not prohibit the pre-installation of rival products and services; it merely required the whole basic Google suite to feature from the outset.

In its July 2018 decision, the Commission found that both the AFA[31] and the MADA[32] amount to an abuse of a dominant position. The two practices were treated by the authority as forms of tying, whether implicitly or explicitly. The latter was deemed comparable to one of the practices at stake in *Microsoft I*.[33] The AFA, in turn, was understood to involve the imposition of conditions unrelated to the subject of the licensing agreement.[34] The wording used by the Commission is reminiscent of the letter of Article 102(d) TFEU.[35] In addition, the authority

---

[30] Ibid, paras 172–191.
[31] Ibid, paras 1019–1191.
[32] Ibid, paras 741–1010.
[33] *Microsoft* (Case COMP/C-3/37.792) Commission Decision of 24 May 2004; confirmed in Case T-201/04 *Microsoft Corporation v Commission*, EU:T:2007:289.
[34] *Android* (n 2), paras 1019–1030.
[35] Article 102(d) TFEU refers to 'making the conclusion of contracts subject to acceptance by the other parties of supplementary obligations which, by their nature or according to commercial usage, have no connection with the subject of such contracts'.

took issue with another aspect of Google's licensing practices, the so-called revenue-sharing agreements (hereinafter, 'RSAs').[36] The various iterations of the RSAs concluded by the firm sought to provide financial incentives (that is, shared advertising revenues) for the exclusive pre-installation of Google's search services in licensees' devices.[37] The Commission treated them as exclusivity payments within the meaning of the relevant case law.[38]

The decision did not find that any of the three practices was presumptively abusive. Instead, the Commission considered that they were in breach of Article 102 TFEU only insofar as they were capable of restricting competition.[39] As far as the MADA was concerned, the exclusionary effects would result, first, from the leveraging of Google's dominant position on the market for Android app stores to the national markets for general search services;[40] and, second, from the leveraging of Google's dominant position on the latter markets to the market for ('non OS-specific') web browsers.[41] In relation to the AFA, second, the decision appears to imply that Google exploited its market power on the markets for general search and app stores to preserve the position of the Android ecosystem (the decision refers to rival versions as a 'competitive threat to Google'). Finally, the RSAs were deemed capable of strengthening Google's position on the national markets for general search services.[42] Only the analysis concerning the latter was annulled by the GC in its September 2022 judgment.[43] At the time of writing, the appeal judgment was pending.[44]

2. When Competition Law Interferes with Product Design and Business Models

2.1. Competition Law and the Inner Workings of Firms: How Products are Made

Google Shopping and *Android* differ from the majority of competition law cases. This is so because the two relate to how products are *made*, as opposed to how they are *sold*. Competition law is assumed to be – and most of the time is – about how

---

[36] *Android* (n 2), paras 1188–1336.
[37] Ibid, para 1192.
[38] Ibid, paras 1195–1205.
[39] Ibid, paras 732–733.
[40] Ibid, paras 773–876.
[41] Ibid, paras 896–992.
[42] Ibid, para 1206.
[43] Case T-604/18 *Google LLC and Alphabet, Inc. v Commission*, EU:T:2022:541.
[44] Case C-738/22 P *Google LLC and Alphabet, Inc. v Commission*, pending.

firms deal with third parties: the clauses they include in a distribution agreement, the conditions under which they license a technology or the terms of cooperation with a rival. The inner workings of firms – what one might term the 'black box'[45] – are scrutinised far less often, in relative terms. For instance, competition law rarely questions whether a firm should exploit a technology in-house, as opposed to licensing to third parties. Similarly, competition law avoids second-guessing whether a firm should rely on selective distribution (which is less restrictive of distributors' freedom of action), instead of franchising (which tends to place stricter limits on what resellers can do).

2.1.1. Product Design, Integration and Modularity

For the purposes of the analysis that follows, product design refers to decisions pertaining to the quality of a product and to the features incorporated in it. A firm, when designing a product, must decide which features, and how many, to include. Such decisions comprise the following three. To begin with, the firm must figure out the range of vertically or horizontally-related features that are incorporated in a complex product. Second, it must make choices pertaining to the way rival features developed by third parties are treated. More precisely, the decision in this sense is whether to go for a 'closed' model (only the firm's choice of features is integrated in the complex product) or an 'open' one (that is, make the product modular by permitting the integration of third-party rival features). A final, related decision, is whether the complex product is allowed to work (or interoperate) with complementary goods or services.

Figure 8.2 Product design and the level of horizontal and vertical integration

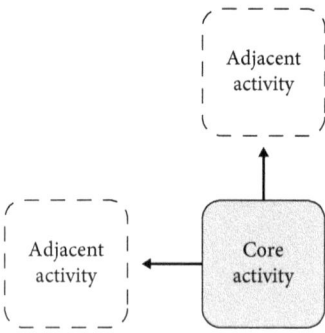

---

[45] Harold Demsetz, 'The Firm in Economic Theory: A Quiet Revolution' (1997) 87 American Economic Review: Papers & Proceedings 426. For a specific application to competition law, see Florence Thépot, *The Interaction Between Competition Law and Corporate Governance: Opening the 'Black Box'* (Cambridge University Press 2019).

When Competition Law Interferes with Product Design and Business Models 241

Figures 8.3.1 and 8.3.2 Product design and the choice between closed and open (modular) layers

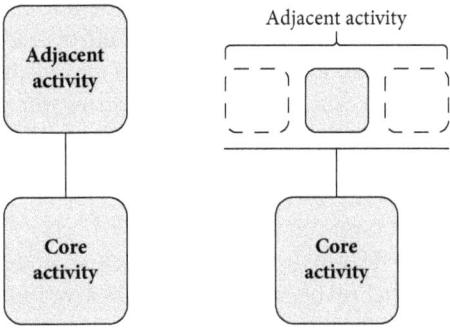

Figure 8.4 Product design and interoperability

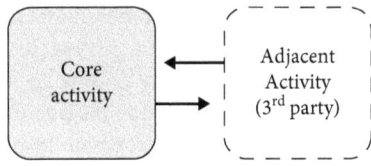

These ideas are perhaps better illustrated by reference to a concrete example. Think of a car, which is a quintessentially complex product. A manufacturer must decide whether the vehicle will incorporate such features as a navigation device, an audio system and air conditioning. In addition, it must ponder whether to accommodate multiple third-party features (an 'open' or 'modular' model) or only its own (that is, a 'closed' model). The question, in other words, is whether to allow end-users to mix-and-match features or whether a single choice is presented to them. To mention an example, cars are sometimes manufactured (or at least they used to be) to allow drivers to include the radio device of their choice. As time passed, however, it became increasingly common for automobiles to come equipped with an embedded audio system that end-users cannot replace. Third, and finally, interoperability issues may also be relevant. For instance, the car manufacturer must decide whether to design its product so that it can work with third-party mobile operating systems.

2.1.2. Business Models and Monetisation Strategies

The notion of business model, in turn, refers to the core of the strategy that a firm follows to monetise its assets. It is useful to think about this question along two main dimensions. First, the monetisation strategy depends on the degree of (vertical and horizontal) integration chosen by the firm. For instance, a firm holding a patent over a technology must decide whether to exploit this asset by vertically integrating downstream or whether, instead, to rely on licensing. An undertaking that has developed a successful restaurant formula faces a similar choice. It may decide to expand its business by opening new owned and operated branches or may decide, instead, to capture the value generated by its formula by relying on third-party franchisees. These two examples concern instances where the monetisation decision revolves around whether to vertically integrate. Horizontal integration may also be relevant for these purposes. The combination of two complements, for instance, may allow a firm to recoup its investments by means of, inter alia, product design.

The latter point is also relevant in relation to a second dimension of the notion of business model. Where a firm operates as a two-sided (or multi-sided) platform, its ability to remain on the market depends on whether it can attract and keep on board two (or more) categories of customers. For instance, a newspaper will have to develop a business model that appeals both to advertisers and readers; a card payment system, one that works for both merchants and consumers. In such scenarios, the platform operator will have to identify which categories of customers to charge, and how much to each. It may choose to rely on a monetisation strategy that depends on payments from one side (as free-to-air television stations do) or from two or more side (as many newspapers do insofar as they charge both readers and advertisers).

2.2. Why Cases Dealing with Product Design and Business Model Issues are Different

2.2.1. Overview

There is a difference between cases dealing with how products are sold and those addressing the way they are made (including product design and business model-related issues). This claim is not an abstract one. It is manifested in several concrete ways, which are relevant from a substantive and an institutional standpoint. The analysis that follows focuses on four main aspects. First, embedding various features in a complex product and, similarly, vertical and horizontal integration, may lead to pro-competitive gains that are not manifested where a case concerns how products are sold. Second, the pro- and potentially anticompetitive dimensions of a design or a monetisation choice are often inextricably linked. Third (and in the same vein), alternative design and/ or monetisation strategies do not necessarily result in more competition (and may well lead to reduced competition). Absent formal regulation, finally, interfering with how products are made invariably demands the administration of complex, proactive remedies.

2.2.2. The Integration of Features and Activities Leads to Pro-competitive Gains

The integration of features in a single, complex product may lead to pro-competitive gains that do not and cannot materialise when a practice deals with the way products are sold. This is the fundamental difference between product design and contractual tying. It is true that both instances can be rationalised on pro-competitive grounds. The potential of contractual tying to lead to efficiency gains, for instance, has been abundantly discussed in the literature.[46] What matters, for the purposes of the discussion that follows, is that the integration of features in a single complex product can be pro-competitive in ways that a contractual tie-in is not and cannot be. When two or more of these features become amalgamated by means of product design, their interaction can be beneficial in a number of distinct ways. For instance, the products can be tailored to work better with one another: one complementary feature could be redesigned so that it meets exactly the needs of another one.

Some concrete examples can illustrate this idea. Consider the integration of cameras in smartphones, which has become widespread. This practice is a source of benefits that would not have materialised if the two products had been sold together (as a contractual tie-in or bundle). For instance, the integration of the camera within the device makes it easier for the user to manipulate the image (including by editing it) and seamlessly share it with her contacts. Consider also the example of the integration of a mapping service and a search engine. Embedding a map in a results page makes it easier for end-users to find an address (in the sense that they may be able to find their destination faster and more effectively). It may also make it possible for the two services to interact in ways that might not have been possible. In particular, end-users may be able to identify on the map the results that appear on the page and, conversely, find information on the results page about the places they identify on the map.

2.2.3. The Pro- and Anticompetitive Potential of Practices are Intertwined

One needs to consider not only that the integration of features in a single, complex product is a source of sui generis pro-competitive gains, but also that the potentially beneficial and potentially anticompetitive dimensions are usually two sides of the same coin. They are intertwined in the sense that a design choice may have restrictive effects for the very same reason that it is beneficial for competition. Again, some examples help illustrate this idea effectively. Consider the merger between Intel and McAfee, authorised with conditions in 2011.[47] This transaction

---

[46] For a summary of this literature, see Robert O'Donoghue and Jorge Padilla, *The Law and Economics of Article 102 TFEU* (3rd edn, Hart Publishing 2020) 701–703.
[47] *Intel/McAfee* (Case No COMP/M.5984) Commission Decision of 26 January 2011.

placed the Commission in a difficult position. On the one hand, the expected efficiency gains from the transaction (that is, the integration of Intel's hardware and McAfee's security solutions) were the very source of the potential concerns to which it gave rise. As noted in the decision, embedding anti-virus software in the chips would have enhanced the security of Intel's hardware.[48] On the other hand (and precisely because integrating the two features would represent such an improvement), it had the potential to restrict competition. It is not surprising, in this sense, that McAfee's rivals feared that the new, improved product design could drive them out of the market. There would be little point in acquiring security solutions separately from Intel's hardware once the latter comes equipped with the former[49] (just like there is little point in purchasing a digital camera once smartphones are sold with them).

The *Android* case also shows how the competitive impact of a business model may be closely intertwined with the pro-competitive gains that result from it. As discussed above, Google's strategy in relation to mobile devices is based on making its operating system and applications as widely available as possible. The GC in its judgment did not question that this relatively open ecosystem creates new opportunities for the firm's rivals on the very markets concerned by the investigation (including the markets for search and web browsers).[50] Google's strategy allowed for the substantial rise in the take-up of smartphones, access to which was greatly expanded as a result (thereby benefitting competitors). On the other hand, the very monetisation mechanisms pursued by the firm (and, in particular, the MADA and the AFA, both described above), and which are inseparable from its overall, pro-competitive strategy, limit the freedom of action of its customers (and may thus constrain in some respects rivals' ability to compete with it).

Even if it is accepted that the pro-competitive and the restrictive dimensions of a product design or a business model are inextricably linked, one could argue that an alternative design or monetisation mechanisms could improve the conditions of competition. To the extent that this is the case, intervention would be desirable. The key point to note, for the discussion that follows, is that this is not necessarily true. One cannot assume as given, or even presume, that the 'but for' world would have allowed for more competition. In fact, alternative designs and monetisation strategies may well reduce competition. It is sufficient to compare, in this regard, the models underpinning, respectively, the Android and the Apple ecosystems. The fact that the former is relatively open is explained by a business model that allows for more modularity. If the monetisation strategy behind this business model is found to be anticompetitive, intervention may well reduce rivals' chances to compete, if the new business model relies on a relatively closed ecosystem.

---

[48] Ibid, para 332.
[49] Ibid, paras 203–210.
[50] Case T-604/18 *Android* (n 43), paras 587–596.

2.2.4. The Administration of the Remedies is Distinctly Complex

For the reasons discussed above, the administration of remedies in product design and business model cases is distinctly complex. The fact that the pro- and anti-competitive dimensions of the design and monetisation decisions are so closely intertwined means that a reactive remedy (that is, a negative obligation ordering the firm to cease its conduct) would come at the price of eliminating the pro-competitive gains resulting from the practice. If, for instance, a dominant undertaking were ordered to remove features from a complex product, it would be required, in essence, to produce an inferior good or service (for instance, hardware without embedded security features, or a search engine without a mapping and a shopping service). It would be difficult to justify a choice of remedy requiring a firm to decrease the quality of a product in the name of the protection of the competitive process.

It seems inevitable, against this background, that intervention second-guessing how products are made will be proactive in nature if it is to be effective and compatible with the aims of competition law. Positive obligations interfering with the design of a product or with a business model are, as already explained at length, particularly challenging for competition authorities. Experience in the context of digital markets shows that efforts in this sense may fail altogether. *Microsoft I* is a case in point. In essence, the Commission ordered the dominant undertaking to offer a redesigned version of its operating system.[51] Subsequent developments revealed that there was no demand for this variation of Windows.[52] There is a chance, second, that the alternative remedy makes end-users worse off. Banning a monetisation strategy based on the sale of advertising, for instance, may mean relying on subscriptions. As a result, consumers would be charged for goods or services that were available at a nominal prize of zero prior to intervention.

One should bear in mind, finally, that remedial action may alter the balance between static and dynamic competition, and not necessarily towards the optimum. There is a risk, more precisely, that the former is promoted at the expense of the latter. If, for instance, a firm is prevented from engaging in a particular monetisation strategy so as to accommodate rivals (or place them on a level playing field), the remedy may well intensify rivalry in the short term. To the extent that it limits the ability of the firm to capture the value generated by its assets, on the other hand, it may have a negative impact on its incentives to invest and

---

[51] Article 6(a) of *Microsoft I* (n 33): 'Microsoft Corporation shall, within 90 days of the date of notification of this Decision, offer a full-functioning version of the Windows Client PC Operating System which does not incorporate Windows Media Player; Microsoft Corporation retains the right to offer a bundle of the Windows Client PC Operating System and Windows Media Player'.

[52] 'EU ruling on Microsoft "flawed"' *BBC News* (London, 24 April 2006), which echoes a point made during the hearing. One of Microsoft's lawyers explained that '"[a]s of today no PC maker has shipped a version of XPN […] not a single one" said […] Jean-Francois Bellis, noting that such companies accounted for nine out of 10 sales of Windows. As for the rest, stores ordered 1,787 copies of XPN among 35m copies of Windows, giving it an order ratio of 0.005%, he said'.

innovate. As a result, the obligations could have the effect of reducing competition in the long run. The same can be said regarding remedial action aimed at redesigning a product. If an authority mandates changes aimed at injecting modularity into a given segment, the measure may, in effect, amount to a duty to share revenues with rivals.

3. How EU Competition Law Deals with Product Design and Business Model Issues

3.1. Background

As explained by the Commission in *Google Shopping*, there is no case law applying specifically to product design (to which one may add business models, which have not been addressed as such, either). This fact does not mean, however, that the Court has not considered the issues underlying such scenarios. It is possible to distil a number of principles from the case law. First, the Court confines to 'exceptional circumstances' the instances where the legal order interferes with a firm's right to property and/or with its contractual freedom. Second, it has consistently held that competition, for the purposes of the application of Articles 101 and 102 TFEU, means competition that would have existed in the absence of the contentious practice. As a result, third, some practices are deemed presumptively lawful, and others may be deemed to fall outside the scope of the relevant prohibition following a case-by-case assessment.

3.2. Product Design, Business Models and the 'Exceptional Circumstances' Doctrine

The *Bronner* and *Magill* lines of case law have already been discussed in the preceding two chapters and this, from a variety of angles. The most relevant for the purposes of this discussion are captured in *Slovak Telekom*, which clarified the instances in which the 'exceptional circumstances' doctrine applies. As explained in Chapter 6, evidence of indispensability is required where intervention would involve mandating a firm to deal with third parties with which it has chosen not to deal.[53] Conversely, this high bar would not be relevant where the firm voluntarily chooses to deal with rivals or is subject to a regulatory obligation to do so. The rationale behind this case law has also been discussed in the preceding chapters. The Court justified the 'exceptional circumstances' doctrine on two grounds.

---

[53] Case C-165/19 P *Slovak Telekom, a.s. v Commission*, EU:C:2021:239. See Chapter 6 for a more extensive analysis.

A duty to deal interferes with fundamental rights;[54] in addition, it may negatively affect firms' incentives to invest and innovate.[55]

It is not difficult to see how and why this case law sheds light where product design and/or business models are at stake. Requiring a firm to share its intellectual property amounts, in essence, to asking it to change its business model (from one reliant on the sale of the end product to one based on the licensing of the upstream input). Similarly, ordering a firm to tweak the design of a product will often involve a duty to deal. Suppose that a firm operating an ecosystem is required to inject modularity at a level of the value chain that the firm had chosen to keep for itself. By necessity, opening up the segment will involve setting up an access regime. This is true, for instance, of the system implemented by Google in the aftermath of the *Google Shopping* case (where access to the premium space was shared with third parties) and the Google *Android* case (where the operating system was redesigned so that competing web browsers would feature on a level playing field).

More importantly, the very reasons why access obligations are confined to exceptional circumstances overlap significantly with the peculiarities of cases dealing with product design and business model issues. As explained by Advocate General Jacobs in *Bronner* (subsequently cited by the Court in *Slovak Telekom*), the Court is cautious before imposing a duty to deal on a firm due to the impact this obligation might have on the existing balance between static and dynamic competition.[56] Where such delicate balance is at stake (and where intervention would take the form of an access remedy), the indispensability condition appears to act as a filter limiting the instances in which Article 102 TFEU comes into play. This case law appears to suggest that interfering with the design of a product and/or with a business model should be confined to circumstances where the obstacles to competition are insurmountable. Absent such circumstances, the Court seems to refrain from upsetting the existing balance.

3.3. Restrictions of Competition against the Relevant Counterfactual

3.3.1. Pro- and Anticompetitive Effects against the Counterfactual

As discussed above, product design and business model cases often involve the use of practices that have the potential to both promote and restrict competition. What is more, the practice under consideration may well restrict competition

---

[54] Ibid, para 46.
[55] Ibid, para 47.
[56] Opinion of Advocate General Jacobs in Case C-7/97 *Oscar Bronner GmbH & Co. KG v Mediaprint Zeitungs- und Zeitschriftenverlag GmbH & Co. KG and others*, EU:C:1998:264. See also *Slovak Telekom* (n 53), para 47, cited above.

248 *Digital Markets*

for the very same reasons that it promotes it. Evaluating, in such circumstances, whether or not it amounts to an infringement may be a challenge for a court or authority. It would be necessary to disentangle the pro- and the anticompetitive dimensions and determine which of the two weighs more than the other. The exercise is particularly complex when establishing a prima facie infringement. Since the pro- and anticompetitive aspects of the practice are so closely intertwined, how is it possible to show that it restricts competition (at least in principle)? What is the benchmark against which the restriction is established?

The question, in other words, is that of which counterfactual is administered when assessing the impact of a practice. The Court has consistently held that an infringement is to be established in light of the conditions of competition that would have prevailed in the absence of the practice.[57] In other words, the assessment of the economic and legal context considers the reality of the market with and without the conduct. If it appears that the latter does not affect (or even improves) the conditions of competition, it does not amount to an infringement.[58] If it does, it might violate Articles 101 and/or 102 TFEU. The need to consider the counterfactual has a number of implications. To begin with, any actual or potential anticompetitive effects must be 'attributable' to the practice for them to be considered in the analysis.[59] An authority or claimant must show, in other words, a causal link between the contentious behaviour and the impact allegedly resulting from it. If the counterfactual reveals that the same effects would have happened in the absence of the practice, there would be no infringement.

A second implication of the counterfactual is the need to consider both the ex ante and ex post dimensions of competition. Simply put, an authority or claimant cannot take the (existing) pro-competitive benefits of an activity for granted and assume as self-evident that they would have existed in the absence of some contentious restraints. In other words, one cannot simply take issue with the latter and ignore how they relate to the relevant pro-competitive gains. If it turns out that the pro- and anticompetitive dimensions of a practice are so inextricably linked that the former cannot realistically exist (and would not have realistically existed) without the other, the practice in question does not amount to an infringement, whether by object or effect. The same is true if the 'but for' scenario absent the contentious restraints is one that allows for less, not more, competition.

---

[57] Case 56/65 *Société Technique Minière*, EU:C:1966:38, 250; Case C-7/95 *John Deere Ltd v Commission*, EU:C:1998:256, para 76; Case C-238/05 *Asnef-Equifax, Servicios de Información sobre Solvencia y Crédito, SL and Administración del Estado v Asociación de Usuarios de Servicios Bancarios*, EU:C:2006:734, para 49; Case C-307/18 *Generics (UK) Ltd and Others v Competition and Markets Authority*, EU:C:2020:52, para 116.

[58] See in particular Case 42/84 *Remia BV and others v Commission*, EU:C:1985:327; Joined Cases T-374/94, T-375/94, T-384/94 and T-388/94 *European Night Services Ltd and others v Commission*, EU:T:1998:198; and Case C-228/18 *Gazdasági Versenyhivatal v Budapest Bank Nyrt. and others*, EU:C:2020:265.

[59] Case C-23/14 *Post Danmark A/S v Konkurrencerådet*, EU:C:2015:651, para 47.

Consider the practice at stake in *Nungesser*,[60] discussed in Chapter 4. The Commission had concluded in its decision that a set of territorial restraints accepted by the licensor restricted competition within the meaning of Article 101(1) TFEU.[61] The Court, by contrast, took into account not only the novelty of the licensed technology, which had been the result of substantial research and development efforts, but also the risk linked to its exploitation in its new territory. In such circumstances, it concluded that one could not assume, without more, that the pro-competitive aspects of the restraints (such as the dissemination of a new technology in another Member State) would have happened in their absence. The counterfactual, in other words, may well be one where no licensing would have occurred. Thus, there would have been less, not more, competition. Accordingly, the said restraints were found to fall outside the scope of Article 101(1) TFEU in the relevant economic and legal context.[62]

The 'exceptional circumstances' doctrine, discussed above, provides another helpful illustration of how the pro-competitive aspects of a practice influence the analysis. If only the ex post dimension of competition were considered, every refusal to deal would be necessarily abusive under Article 102 TFEU. By definition, any such refusal limits access by rivals to an input or infrastructure and thus affects their ability to compete. One could be tempted to argue, that, absent the practice, there would be more, not less, competition. The picture changes once the ex ante dimension is considered, that is, once firms' incentives to invest and innovate are taken into account. In line with what has been explained, one cannot assume as given that the relevant input or infrastructure would have been developed if the firm had been required to deal with third parties. Put differently, the pro-competitive aspects of the practice (that is, the development of the input or infrastructure) are inextricably linked to the alleged, ex post, restriction.

3.3.2. *The Operation of the Counterfactual in Practice*

The Court has developed a number of techniques to integrate the above considerations in its analysis. There are, to begin with, some practices that are deemed lawful prima facie and thus fall outside the scope of Article 101(1) TFEU. The legal status of these practices is based on the presumption that their positive and negative dimensions are so inextricably linked that any ex post restraints are objectively necessary to attain the pro-competitive goals that derive from them. The legal treatment of franchising agreements and selective distribution agreements stands out in this regard. These two distribution methods limit distributors' freedom of action in several ways. In both instances, suppliers will introduce, inter alia, contractual devices aimed at preserving their brand image and the uniformity

---

[60] Case 268/78 *L.C. Nungesser KG and Kurt Eisele v Commission*, EU:C:1982:211.
[61] *Breeders' rights – maize seed* (Case IV/28.824) Commission Decision of 21 September 1978.
[62] *Nungesser* (n 60), para 58.

of end-users' experience. In *Metro I*[63] (in relation to selective distribution) and *Pronuptia*[64] (in relation to franchising) the Court explained that these contractual devices are indispensable for the pro-competitive gains deriving from both distribution methods to be attained. To the extent that this is the case, they escape the prohibition altogether.

The second technique developed by the Court has been discussed at length above. As already pointed out, the 'exceptional circumstances' doctrine can be aptly described as a legal filter (or a 'quasi-legality' test, if one prefers) that limits the instances in which Article 102 TFEU interferes with firms' right to property and which is aimed at preserving firms' incentives to invest and innovate. The strict conditions set out in *Bronner* and *Magill* are an acknowledgement that appropriability is a precondition for dynamic competition to occur. Finally, the third technique is nothing more than the case-by-case evaluation of the conditions of competition that would have prevailed in the absence of the practice. An example in this sense is provided by the *Nungesser* case, discussed above. This third technique has a substantive and a procedural dimension. From a substantive standpoint, it means that the negative effects cannot be considered in isolation from the economic and legal context. From a procedural standpoint, it means that the arguments submitted by the parties in this sense will have to be considered.[65]

4. Pro-competitive Gains and Competition on the Merits

4.1. Pro-competitive Gains, Prima Facie Legality and Competition on the Merits

As discussed above, the Commission rejected in its *Google Shopping* decision the idea that the design of a product should be deemed presumptively lawful. It rejected, accordingly, the first of the legal techniques discussed in the preceding section, and, by the same token, departed from the approach favoured by the FTC in its 2013 Statement. According to the Commission, a product improvement should be subject to a case-by-case assessment of its effects. The decision suggests that there is nothing special about these cases justifying a different legal treatment. This question was raised again in the context of the challenge against the decision before the GC. In two of its pleas, Google argued that, as a product improvement, the addition of features to its search engine should be deemed a

---

[63] Case 26/76 *Metro SB-Großmärkte GmbH & Co. KG v Commission*, EU:C:1977:167.
[64] Case 161/84 *Pronuptia de Paris GmbH v Pronuptia de Paris Irmgard Schillgallis*, EU:C:1986:41.
[65] Joined Cases C-403/08 and C-429/08 *Football Association Premier League Ltd and Others v QC Leisure and Others and Karen Murphy v Media Protection Services Ltd*, EU:C:2011:631, para 143; Case C-413/14 P *Intel Corp. v Commission*, EU:C:2017:700, para 138; and *Generics* (n 57), para 103.

legitimate expression of competition on the merits and, as such, should fall outside the scope of Article 102 TFEU.[66]

The GC could have easily dismissed this argument without examining whether Google's product is a legitimate form of competition on the merits. A cursory look at the case law suggests that Article 102 TFEU frequently applies to behaviour that is, at least in principle, a normal manifestation of competition. For instance, a refusal to license an intellectual property right[67] or standardised rebate scheme[68] are known to be a source of pro-competitive gains and, as such, valid manifestations of healthy rivalry. One should bear in mind, in this regard, that dominant firms have a 'special responsibility' not to impair 'genuine, undistorted competition'.[69] Accordingly, behaviour that would otherwise have been normal, unproblematic and, more to the point, lawful competition on the merits, can be prohibited precisely because it is implemented by an undertaking with a substantial degree of market power.

Summing up, the applicable case law suggests that Google's argument was not compelling. The fact that a practice is an expression of competition on the merits does not insulate a firm from the application of Article 102 TFEU. It does not mean, either, that the behaviour is necessarily presumptively lawful under the provision. As discussed in the preceding section, the legal tests that apply to expressions of normal rivalry range from the presumptively unlawful (as is true of exclusive dealing and loyalty rebates[70]) to the presumptively lawful (as is true of clauses that are necessary for the operation of a selective distribution system and a franchise). The question, as discussed in the preceding section, is not so much whether a practice is potentially pro-competitive as how such pro-competitive gains are integrated in the legal test.

In its first-instance judgment, however, the GC did not simply dismiss as irrelevant arguments to the effect that the integration of features in Google's search engine is an expression of competition on the merits. It explained at length why the self-preferencing strategy at stake in the case was inherently anticompetitive irrespective of its effects. It departed, in this regard, from the Commission's analysis. According to the latter, Google's conduct was not a manifestation of normal competition only insofar as it was capable of having an anticompetitive impact. The decision, in other words, appeared to equate competition on the merits and exclusionary effects. The former issue was subsumed in the former. The GC, while not dismissing this approach (in fact, it expressly held that it the Commission did not err in law by following it[71]), addressed the two issues independently of one another.

---

[66] Case T-612/17 *Google Shopping* (n 19), paras 120–127.
[67] As in Case C-418/01 *IMS Health GmbH & Co. OHG v NDC Health GmbH & Co. KG*, EU:C:2004:257.
[68] As in *Post Danmark II* (n 59).
[69] Case 322/81 *NV Nederlandsche Banden Industrie Michelin v Commission*, EU:C:1983:313, para 57.
[70] *Intel* (n 65), para 137.
[71] Case T-612/17 *Google Shopping* (n 19), para 173.

The GC concluded that the dominant firm's conduct was not an expression of competition on the merits insofar as it involved 'a certain form of abnormality'.[72] The first-instance court reached this conclusion based on the fact that Google's search engine has a 'universal vocation', that is, it is an infrastructure conceived to display results from any website on the Internet. According to the GC, this aspiration towards openness is at odds with the self-preferencing of its own search results. In this sense, the judgment distinguishes an open infrastructure such as a search engine, the value of which depends on generating traffic to (affiliated or third-party) websites, from other infrastructures that an integrated firm chooses to keep for itself, such as those at stake in cases like *Magill*, *IMS Health* and *Bronner* (to which the indirectly refers in the judgment).[73]

The first-instance court goes as far as to claim that the inconsistency between the practice and the said 'universal vocation' of the search engine is 'not necessarily rational'.[74] According to the judgment, the rational strategy for Google would be to display the most relevant results in its engine, irrespective of where they originate. Only such conduct would enable it to recoup its investments and exploit the economies of scale and network effects so as to reach a 'critical mass'.[75] These arguments appear to imply that Google's self-preferencing strategy is only possible because it enjoys a dominant position. In other words, the practice would depart from legitimate competition on the merits because only a firm with substantial market power would be able to afford it. Were it not for the fact that Google can behave independently of rivals and customers, the behaviour would be irrational, according to this view.

The conclusion that Google's conduct is irrational would be reinforced, according to the GC, by the fact that the firm changed its conduct. As mentioned above, Google introduced additional features to the search engine in 2007. As far as its comparison-shopping service is concerned, moreover, the first-instance judgment appears to take issue with the fact that its original incarnation was not given any sort of special treatment. According to the GC (which echoes in this regard the Commission decision[76]) only following the failure of this original version

---

[72] Ibid, para 176: 'It must be observed in that regard that, given the universal vocation of Google's general search engine, which, as is apparent from recital 12 of the contested decision, is designed to index results containing any possible content, the promotion on Google's general results pages of one type of specialised result – its own – over the specialised results of competitors involves a certain form of abnormality'.

[73] Ibid, para 177: 'The infrastructure at issue, namely Google's general results pages which generate traffic to other websites, including those of competing comparison shopping services, is, in principle, open, which distinguishes it from other infrastructures referred to in the case-law, consisting of tangible or intangible assets (press distribution systems or intellectual property rights, respectively) whose value depends on the proprietor's ability to retain exclusive use of them'.

[74] Ibid, para 178: '[…] for a search engine, limiting the scope of its results to its own entails an element of risk and is not necessarily rational, save in a situation, as in the present case, where the dominance and barriers to entry are such that no market entry within a sufficiently short period of time is possible in response to that limitation of internet users' choice'.

[75] Ibid.

[76] *Android* (n 1), para 343.

(named Froogle) did the dominant firm engage in its self-preferencing strategy.[77] In this regard, the judgment appears to place particular emphasis on the fact that the said strategy was a two-pronged one, that is, it involved not only the favouring of the firm's activities but also the demotion of competing ones.[78]

4.2. Analysis

The GC's assessment of Google's self-preferencing conduct is notable in several respects. There are some ideas underpinning the analysis that are worth discussing at some length. It is not unprecedented for the EU courts to evaluate whether a given line of conduct is rational or irrational. The difference between the first-instance judgment and the relevant case law is methodological in nature. Consider *AKZO*, which is the leading case on the question. In that case, the Court ruled that pricing below average variable is in principle an irrational strategy for a firm to pursue, in the sense that it makes no sense for a firm to engage in it if it is not for exclusionary purposes.[79] As discussed in Chapter 7, a similar approach is followed in the context of Article 101 TFEU. In *Generics*, for instance, the Court introduced a framework aimed at ascertaining whether the pay-for-delay strategy can be rationalised other than as a means to restrict competition.[80]

In *Google Shopping*, by contrast, the GC did not evaluate the conduct based on whether it could be explained on pro-competitive grounds. Nowhere in the judgment is it claimed that the firm is sacrificing profits with the aim of leveraging its dominant position to an adjacent market. Similarly, the GC did not contemplate potential pro-competitive explanations for the behaviour. Instead, it claimed that self-preferencing is abnormal based on the sole fact that it is at odds with the conduct it expects a search engine to adopt. The judgment suggests in several passages that self-preferencing could only be implemented because Google enjoyed a dominant position on a market characterised by high barriers to entry. The implicit assumption is that, in an effectively competitive market, Google would not have been able to afford this strategy.

Crucially, the GC does not provide any evidence – theoretical or empirical – to substantiate its claims. In particular, the first-instance court provides no evidence

---

[77] Case T-612/17 *Google Shopping* (n 19), para 184.
[78] Ibid, para 187: 'First, it should be pointed out that Google's arguments are based on the incorrect premiss that the conduct at issue consists solely in the special display and positioning of Product Universals and Shopping Units, when in fact that conduct consists in the combination of two practices: the promotion of specialised results from Google's comparison shopping service and the simultaneous demotion of results from competing comparison services by adjustment algorithms. It must be noted in that regard that Google does not describe the demotion on its general results pages of competing comparison shopping services, but not of its own, as a 'quality improvement' that would characterise competition on the merits'.
[79] Case C-62/86 *AKZO Chemie BV v Commission* EU:C:1991:286, para 71.
[80] *Generics* (n 57), para 89.

supporting its core assumption, which is that Google could only afford self-preferencing because it is 'ultra-dominant'.[81] More generally, the GC's reliance on intuitive, informal economic analysis is one of the most remarkable aspects of the judgment. When examined through expert lenses, the potential limits and flaws in this sort of reasoning become readily apparent. Some economists noted, in the aftermath of the judgment, that hybrid commercial strategies – partially based on the neutral display of results and partially based on specialised services – are pervasive, and not necessarily the province of online platforms and/or of 'ultra-dominant' players protected by high barriers to entry.[82] It is sufficient to think, in this regard, of supermarket chains, which rarely enjoy substantial market power within the meaning of Article 102 TFEU, and which often act simultaneously as resellers of third-party products while favouring their own brands.[83]

In a different vein, the GC appears to present a change in a monetisation strategy as potentially problematic or questionable in and of itself. At the very least, the fact that a firm decides to alter its business model is deemed to be an aspect that reinforces a finding that a practice is not an expression of competition on the merits. It is not clear how this idea can be reconciled with the available expertise, as captured in the relevant body of case law and administrative practice. It appears, first, that firms change their business model (for instance, by vertically integrating, or by resorting to franchisees) even when they do not enjoy a dominant position. Second, nothing in the case law and related administrative practice suggests that it is prima facie problematic for a firm to do so. The Non-Horizontal Merger Guidelines,[84] for instance, do not prejudge a firm's motivation to expand to a vertically or a horizontally-related market. Similarly, nothing in *Metro I* and *Pronuptia*, discussed above, suggests that the decision to change a monetisation strategy plays a role when evaluating the legality of a practice.

5. The Indispensability Condition in Digital Markets

5.1. Background

One of the conclusions to draw from the analysis above is that infringements in cases dealing with the design of products and with business models are likely to necessitate the administration of proactive remedies, in particular access duties.

---

[81] Case T-612/17 *Google Shopping* (n 19), para 180.
[82] Patrice Bougette, Axel Gautier and Frédéric Marty, 'Business Models and Incentives: For an Effects-Based Approach of Self-Preferencing?' (2022) 13 Journal of European Competition Law & Practice 136.
[83] *Streetmap.EU Ltd v Google Inc. & Ors* [2016] EWHC 253 (Ch), para 60. For a discussion, see Ariel Ezrachi, 'Unchallenged Market Power? The Tale of Supermarkets, Private Labels and Competition Law' (2010) 33 World Competition 257.
[84] Guidelines on the assessment of non-horizontal mergers under the Council Regulation on the control of concentrations between undertakings [2008] OJ C265/6.

It is therefore inevitable that debates around the appropriate scope of the *Bronner* case law arise in this context. On the one hand, it makes sense for online platform operators to insist that their design or monetisation decisions can only amount to an infringement if it can be shown that access by rivals to the relevant segment is indispensable within the meaning of the 'exceptional circumstances' doctrine. On the other hand, it is not any less natural for authorities and claimants to argue that the practice differs from the one at stake in *Bronner* and *Magill* and therefore that the strict conditions laid down in the two judgments would not be applicable. In particular, the indispensability requirement is a substantial obstacle to policy-making.

Debates around the appropriate scope of the *Bronner* case law are central to the *Google Shopping* case. In essence, the terms of these debates can be summarised as revolving around whether the 'exceptional circumstances' doctrine should be defined by reference to formal considerations or substantive ones instead. Under a formalistic understanding of the relevant case law, there are two central factors in the analysis: what the Commission formally requires in its decision, first; and whether the factual scenario is identical to the one at stake in *Bronner* (that is, whether there is a request for access and a refusal). Under a substantive interpretation of the doctrine, on the other hand, the relevant question is whether remedial intervention in the case would amount, in effect, to a duty to start dealing with third parties with which the firm had chosen not to deal.

The judgments discussed above suggest that the substantive approach is arguably the one that best captures the essence of existing case law. In particular, *Slovak Telekom* places an emphasis on substance, not form. The relevant consideration, according to this judgment, appears to be whether intervention would interfere with a firm's right to property and its freedom of contract. Other issues, such as the external manifestation of the conduct, were not given any weight. This orthodoxy, however, was questioned by the Commission, and then by the GC, in *Google Shopping*. Both embraced a formalistic approach that reduces the scope of application of the 'exceptional circumstances' doctrine and which, by the same token, expands the range of scenarios in which access remedies can be imposed.

5.2. Indispensability in the Commission decision in *Google Shopping*

5.2.1. *The Commission's Approach in* Google Shopping

As pointed out above, the Commission dismissed as unfounded Google's view that its behaviour could only be abusive if there were evidence that access to Shopping Unit is indispensable for rival comparison-shopping services to compete.[85] This

---

[85] *Google Shopping* (n 1), para 648.

claim was summarily dismissed in the decision on three main grounds. First (and this is a point that has already been mentioned), the Commission argued that the *Bronner* test was not relevant in the case insofar as the practice under consideration was a form of leveraging, which, in the authority's view, constitutes a 'well-established, independent, form of abuse falling outside the scope of competition on the merits'.[86] Second, the Commission distinguished self-preferencing from a refusal to deal on grounds that the latter is a 'passive' behaviour, whereas favouring one's affiliate (and, similarly, demoting rival services) was active instead.[87]

The third argument dismissing the applicability of the 'exceptional circumstances' doctrine deserves to be discussed at greater length. The Commission argued that *Bronner* is not relevant where bringing an infringement to an end does not involve imposing a duty to deal on the dominant undertaking or, to quote the case law cited in the decision, 'transfer an asset or enter into agreements with persons with whom it has not chosen to contract'.[88] In this regard, the decision noted that Google was required to cease the conduct, but did not specify how. The Commission embraced a 'principles-based' approach to the remedy and merely required the firm to display its search results in accordance with a duty of non-discrimination. To the extent that such duty does not formally impose a duty to deal with rivals, the argument goes, the 'exceptional circumstances' doctrine would not be the applicable benchmark.

5.2.2. Analysis

It is difficult to see how the Commission's first two arguments are relevant when ascertaining the relevance of the *Bronner* case law. The first argument appears to claim, in essence, that, as a form of leveraging, the behaviour would be different from a refusal to deal. This position seems to conflate the applicable legal test with the mechanism through which anticompetitive effects are manifested. Contrary to what the passage suggests, leveraging, more than a doctrine, simply describes an instance where a dominant position is extended from one market to a neighbouring one. Crucially, leveraging conduct is not subject to a single, overarching, legal test. In some cases involving the extension of a dominant position to an adjacent market (including – just to mention one – the refusal to deal aspects of *Microsoft I*), indispensability was a condition to establish an abuse. In other cases (including the tying aspects of the latter case), it was not. In fact, indispensability was an element of the legal test in some of the leveraging cases mentioned by the Commission in support of its conclusions. This is true, in particular, of *CBEM-Télémarketing*.[89]

---

[86] Ibid, para 649.
[87] Ibid, para 650.
[88] Ibid, para 651. On this point, the Commission cites Case C-552/03 P *Unilever Bestfoods (Ireland) Ltd v Commission*, EU:C:2006:607, para 137.
[89] Case 311/84 *Centre belge d'études de marché – Télémarketing (CBEM) v SA Compagnie luxembourgeoise de télédiffusion (CLT) and Information publicité Benelux (IPB)*, EU:C:1985:394, para 26.

According to the second argument, the 'exceptional circumstances' doctrine would only be applicable where the conduct is 'passive' in nature. Leaving aside the difficulty of meaningfully distinguishing, in practice, between active and passive behaviour, the case law provides abundant examples showing that indispensability may be an element of the legal test in both circumstances. One needs to look no further than *CBEM- Télémarketing* to find one such example. The facts of that case were not fundamentally different from those at stake in *Google Shopping*. The allegedly dominant firm in that dispute did not just passively refuse to deal with a rival on an adjacent market, but took active steps to remove a competitive constraint. As in *Commercial Solvents*,[90] it brought the contractual relationship to an end, and actively sought to attract customers away from its rivals, once it had decided to extend to an adjacent activity.[91]

The third argument is interesting in that it suggests that, at least superficially, the Commission embraces the substantive approach to the definition of the scope of the 'exceptional circumstances' doctrine. It does so, however, in a sui generis manner. Instead of ascertaining whether intervention in the case would involve, in effect, imposing a positive duty to deal with third parties, the authority appears to argue that the *Bronner* case law is only applicable where the decision expressly requires a firm to do so. The applicability of the doctrine, in other words, is made contingent on what the authority formally orders in its decision. This interpretation of the case law is far from uncontroversial. The fundamental issue with the approach advocated in the decision is that it would give the Commission the discretion to decide when the indispensability condition is applicable in a case and when it is not. Put differently, this interpretation would turn an issue of law into one of discretion, in the sense that it would be left for an authority to decide when a legal doctrine is applicable.

To illustrate this idea, it is sufficient to think of a factual scenario identical to the one at stake in *Bronner* (and thus one which unquestionably falls within the scope of the 'exceptional circumstances' doctrine). In its preliminary reference in *Bronner*, the Court implied that the relevant infrastructure was not indispensable and therefore that the refusal to share it with a rival was not abusive.[92] If the approach advocated by the Commission in *Google Shopping* were followed, the authority – any competition authority – would be able to circumvent the indispensability condition in a *Bronner*-like case (and, indeed, any other case) merely by requiring the dominant firm to bring the infringement to an end without specifying how. The Commission would be able to expand its policy space simply by following a principles-based approach to enforcement.

---

[90] Joined Cases 6 and 7/73 *Istituto Chemioterapico Italiano S.p.A. and Commercial Solvents Corporation v Commission*, EU:C:1974:18.

[91] *CBEM-Télémarketing* (n 89), para 5, where the Court explains the behaviour, and clarifying that the allegedly dominant firm had actively decided to replace CBEM in the telemarketing segment. The conduct was not a mere refusal to deal.

[92] Case C-7/97 *Oscar Bronner GmbH & Co. KG v Mediaprint Zeitungs- und Zeitschriftenverlag GmbH & Co. KG and others*, EU:C:1998:569, paras 42–46.

5.3. Indispensability in the GC Judgment in *Google Shopping*

5.3.1. *The GC's Analysis in* Google Shopping

The GC advanced three lines of arguments to dismiss the idea that the self-preferencing strategy at stake in *Google Shopping* should be examined in light of the 'exceptional circumstances' test. First, it suggests that Google's search engine (and, more precisely, its general results page) has characteristics 'akin' to those of an essential facility and therefore that it may well be indispensable within the meaning of *Bronner*.[93] In its analysis of the case law, the GC appears to imply, following a cursory analysis, that the conditions set out in that judgment may well be fulfilled in *Google Shopping* (even though the Commission never argued that they were in its decision). This may be the case, according to the judgment, for two reasons. In the first place, it may not be easy to duplicate Google's search engine in an 'economically viable manner'. In the second place, the GC emphasises the fact that rival comparison-shopping services lack a 'viable alternative', in terms of traffic, to Google' general results.

Second, the GC embraces a formalistic understanding of the conditions set out in *Bronner*. According to this interpretation, indispensability would only be relevant where the factual scenario is identical to that at stake in that case. For the *Bronner* case law to be relevant in a case, the GC holds, one must identify a 'request' and a 'refusal' that follows it.[94] In the absence of a formal refusal, the 'exceptional circumstances' doctrine would not apply. Even though the GC accepts that *Google Shopping* is, in essence, an access case,[95] it does not consider that the indispensability condition is necessarily the benchmark against which the lawfulness of the self-preferencing strategy is to be assessed. The judgment advances two main reasons in this regard. In the first place, the GC notes that there are other cases dealing with access – including *Slovak Telekom* and *TeliaSonera*[96] – where the indispensability condition was not found to be relevant. In the second place, the GC argues that the behaviour at stake in *Google Shopping* differs from a refusal, in the sense that it is an instance of exclusionary discrimination.[97]

Third, and finally, the *Google Shopping* judgment claims that not every case that involves requiring a firm to deal with rivals is necessarily subject to the 'exceptional circumstances' doctrine. In this regard, the GC takes the view that '[t]here can be no automatic link between the criteria for the legal classification of the

---

[93] Case T-612/17 *Google Shopping* (n 19), para 224: 'It must be noted that Google's general results page has characteristics akin to those of an essential facility [...], inasmuch as there is currently no actual or potential substitute available that would enable it to be replaced in an economically viable manner on the market [...]'.
[94] Ibid, para 232.
[95] Ibid, para 229 ('[...] the practices at issue, as Google maintains, are not unrelated to the issue of access [...]').
[96] Case C-52/09 *Konkurrensverket v TeliaSonera Sverige AB*, EU:C:2011:83.
[97] Case T-612/17 *Google Shopping* (n 19), para 237.

abuse and the corrective measures enabling it to be remedied'.[98] The judgment appears to attribute particular importance to the fact that there was not a single line of conduct but a combination of a promotion of the firm's own services and the demotion of rival ones.[99] The fact that the latter would be an independent line of conduct, adding to the refusal to give access to the rich format features would rule out the application of the refusal to deal line of case law. In the GC's view, the existence of a second discriminatory practice would mean that the analogy with *Bronner* is imperfect.[100]

5.3.2. Analysis

The GC judgment is notable, to begin with, because it tentatively applies the *Bronner* doctrine to the facts of the case. The Commission never sought to argue that the firm's general results page (and, similarly, the Shopping Unit) is indispensable. What is more, the very information provided by the authority suggest that this strict condition is not met.[101] In spite of these factors, the judgment engages at some length with the question. The interpretation of the 'exceptional circumstances' doctrine advanced by the GC is not wholly uncontroversial (or, if one prefers, not fully orthodox). In particular, the fact that duplicating a particular infrastructure would be too costly does not necessarily mean that it is indispensable within the meaning of *Bronner*. The relevant question, under this case law, is whether actual or potential rivals can compete on the adjacent market without having access to the infrastructure. If there are ways around it, even if less advantageous, the indispensability condition would not be fulfilled.[102]

Second, the formalistic approach to the scope of the 'exceptional circumstances' doctrine does not seem to be supported by the relevant case law. As already pointed out, the Commission decision itself conceded that the indispensability condition would apply where intervention would involve mandating a duty to deal with third parties. More interesting is the third line of argument raised to justify departing from the *Bronner* case law. In essence, the GC seemed to argue that evidence of indispensability would not be required insofar as there was an additional practice involved in the case, namely the demotion of rivals when displaying the results. It is not immediately obvious to see how this argument is relevant when deciding the scope of the 'exceptional circumstances' doctrine. The fact that there might have been an additional abuse in *Bronner* does not say anything about the applicability of the indispensability condition. It simply says that the additional abuse may or may not, have required the imposition of an access duty.

---

[98] Ibid, para 244.
[99] Ibid, para 245.
[100] Ibid.
[101] *Google Shopping* (n 1), para 540. Table 24, included in this section of the decision, shows that there are other ways, even if less advantageous, for comparison-shopping services to reach end-users.
[102] *Bronner* (n 92), para 43.

260   Digital Markets

6. The Assessment of Anticompetitive Effects in Digital Markets

6.1. Background

Proving anticompetitive effects in *Google Shopping* and *Android* presented two main challenges for the Commission. First, and in line with the discussion above, establishing the counterfactual was not an obvious task in either of the two cases. In *Android*, the potential restrictive effects of the MADA (in particular) and the AFA were intimately linked to the pro-competitive gains resulting from them. As a result, the latter could not be taken for granted – or assumed to have existed – in the absence of the former. In both cases, second, showing a causal link between the practices and any actual or potential effects was not any easier. Would potential exclusion be attributable to the practice or to the popularity (or superior quality) of the dominant firm's services instead? A close reading of the two decisions (and the accompanying judgments) reveals that the very meaning of the notion of effect was at stake: if an effect is more than a mere competitive disadvantage, what is it, exactly? Or, put differently: when is a competitive effect important enough to trigger the application of Articles 101 and 102 TFEU?

6.2. The Evaluation of the Counterfactual

6.2.1. The Ex Ante and Ex Post Dimensions of the Counterfactual in Android

It is not necessary to explain at length, again, how the pro- and the potentially restrictive aspects of the MADA and the AFA are intertwined. It has already been mentioned that the MADA is, in essence, the core mechanism that allows for the monetisation of Google's assets. As is well known, the firm makes the overwhelming majority of its revenues from advertising, and its business model matches this reality. By requiring the pre-installation of search-related applications, the firm generates the requisite resources to monetise its assets. Arguably, this strategy is the very device that allows for the known pro-competitive benefits of its model (wider access to smartphones, increased opportunities for competitors, modularity) to occur. This background raises a number of questions. As explained in the decision, Google followed this business model since the very early days of the ecosystem.[103] One central question is therefore whether one can assume, without more, that the pro-competitive gains deriving from the MADA would have

---

[103] *Android* (n 2), para 189. As noted by the Commission, the first licensing providing for the MADA was signed in 2009.

The Assessment of Anticompetitive Effects in Digital Markets 261

existed in its absence. A second question, in the same vein, is whether an alternative monetisation strategy would have allowed for more or less competition. A third question has to do with the allocation of the burden of proof between the authority and the firm.

Similar issues arise in the context of the AFA. As already discussed, this behaviour can be equated, in essence, to a non-compete obligation. Google allows rivals to benefit from its ecosystem on the condition that they do not develop competing Android-based ecosystems. Arguably, it is a mechanism to fight opportunistic conduct by licensees, who might be tempted to benefit from Google's efforts while undermining them. From this perspective, the AFA does not come across as fundamentally different from the clauses imposed in the context of a franchising agreement. As is true of the latter, their objective purpose is to appropriate the value generated by the system and to avoid free-riding. To the extent that non-competition obligations are objectively necessary for the franchising agreement to exist in the first place, they would not restrict competition. The question, against this background, is how the counterfactual is to be treated in relation to the AFA.

Neither the Commission nor the GC engaged with these questions, which remain unanswered at the time of writing. The authority, in its decision, advanced several arguments. First, it claimed that its analysis did not concern the MADA as a whole, and only took issue with certain aspects requiring the pre-installation of some applications.[104] Second, the Commission took the view that it would not be required to show whether, absent the practice, there would have been more or less competition, but simply whether or not the behaviour is capable of restricting competition.[105] This said, it points out that it evaluated, at least in some respects, the conditions of competition that would have existed in the absence of the practice.[106] Crucially, the authority expresses the view that it was not required to evaluate the practice since its inception, but only since 2011 (that is, from the moment Google became dominant on the relevant markets covered by the decision).[107]

This line of reasoning, displayed in several passages of the decision, assumes, implicitly, that the pro-competitive aspects of the monetisation strategy would have existed even in the absence of the contentious practice (and, similarly, that they would have existed under an alternative monetisation strategy). In particular, the Commission argues that it is sufficient to consider, in isolation, the observable ex post restrictions independently of the pro-competitive gains to which they are (or may be) related. The decision is explicit about these assumptions in the passages devoted to the objective justifications advanced by Google. The authority suggests

---

[104] *Android* (n 2), para 871.
[105] Ibid, para 872.
[106] Ibid, para 873: '[…] when assessing the capability of the tying of the Google Search app with the Play Store to restrict competition on the national markets for general search services, the Commission has inter alia analysed whether there could have been greater competition on those markets, absent the tying […]'.
[107] Ibid, para 876.

that alternative monetisation strategies (and, in particular, the Play Store and the data generated by its mobile operations) would have been sufficient to support the creation and the maintenance of the Android ecosystem.[108] More importantly, it appears to claim that the burden of proving that, absent the practice, there would have been less, not more, competition, lies with the dominant firm, as opposed to the authority.

The first-instance ruling does not engage with the intertwinement of the ex ante and ex post dimensions of competition. In a brief passage, the GC merely notes – echoing the Commission – that the decision did not challenge the MADA as a whole, but some of the contractual conditions relating to the pre-installation of some applications.[109] On the other hand, it acknowledged (as much as the Commission itself) that Google's business model (and, more precisely, the 'the open and free licensing system'[110]) is a source of pro-competitive gains.[111] However, the GC failed to engage with the fundamental question, which has to do with the link between the restrictive aspects of the business and the pro-competitive gains resulting from it (and, more generally, whether, in light of the counterfactual, the former increase, rather than decrease, competition). Instead, the GC appears to assume that the pre-installation conditions could be disentangled from the business model as a whole and treated independently of it.[112]

6.2.2. *The Definition of the Counterfactual in* Google Shopping

The evaluation of the counterfactual demands, first and foremost, that the reality of the market with and without the market be considered. This is, at the very least, what the Court has spelled out in its Article 101 TFEU case law since the early days.[113] The question of whether it is necessary to consider the 'but for' world when assessing the actual or potential impact of a practice was raised in *Google Shopping*. As summarised by the GC in its judgment, the firm claimed that, in the absence of the contentious strategy, the traffic would not have differed from that observed following its implementation.[114] Google relied, in this regard, on experimental data (including a comparison between jurisdictions where Universal Search had been implemented and those where it had not) in support of its claim.[115]

---

[108] Ibid, para 996.
[109] Case T-604/18 *Android* (n 43), para 590.
[110] Ibid, para 594.
[111] Ibid, para 592.
[112] Ibid, para 594: 'It is those pre-installation conditions of the MADA, and not more generally the open and free licensing system sought by Google with the OEM signatories to that agreement, that constitute the conduct at issue'.
[113] *Société Technique Minière* (n 57), 250: 'The competition in question must be understood within the actual context in which it would occur in the absence of the agreement in dispute […]'.
[114] Case T-612/17 *Google Shopping* (n 19), para 362.
[115] Ibid, para 364.

The GC, however, rejected these arguments. Some of the arguments are specific to the points raised by Google. These have to do with the fact that the firm had only invoked the counterfactual in relation to one aspect of the self-preferencing strategy (the favouring of its own service).[116] Other arguments, however, are general in nature and appear to dismiss the relevance of the counterfactual assessment in the context of Article 102 TFEU. The GC objected to the need or pertinence of considering the 'but for' scenario for two reasons. First, it claimed that doing so may be 'an arbitrary or even impossible exercise' where there were no other markets with similar characteristics.[117] Second, it takes the view that requiring the Commission to establish the counterfactual would amount, in effect, to demanding evidence of the actual effects of the practice (as opposed to potential effects).[118]

If the Court were to accept these arguments, the inevitable result would be the fragmentation of EU competition law. The notion of effects would have a different meaning under Articles 101 and 102 TFEU. In the same vein, the methodology to carry out the assessment of the restrictive impact of a practice would change from one provision to the other. One should consider, in particular, that Article 101 TFEU is concerned both with actual and potential effects.[119] In spite of this fact, it has been clear, from the outset, that a restriction of competition can only be established in light of the conditions of competition that would have prevailed in the absence of the agreement.[120] It is not obvious to see why what is true in the context of Article 101 TFEU would not be true in the context of Article 102 TFEU. More generally, it is difficult to see the relationship between the temporal dimension of the assessment (that is, the divide between actual and potential effects) and the need to examine the counterfactual.

6.3. The Meaning of Effects

Both *Google Shopping* and *Android* have revealed the uncertainty that remains, in the context of Article 102 TFEU, about the exact meaning of the notion of anticompetitive effects. On the one hand, there seems to be little doubt that a competitive disadvantage and/or a limitation of a firm's freedom of action is not enough to trigger the prohibition. The framework laid down by the Court in cases

---

[116] Ibid, para 372.
[117] Ibid, para 377.
[118] Ibid, para 378. The GC argued that the Commission 'cannot be required, either spontaneously or in response to a counterfactual analysis put forward by the undertaking being challenged, systematically to establish a counterfactual scenario in the sense referred to above' insofar as it would 'oblige it to demonstrate that the conduct at issue had actual effects, which, as will be noted in more detail in paragraphs 441 and 442 below in the examination of the first part of Google's fourth plea, is not required in the case of an abuse of a dominant position […]'.
[119] *Generics* (n 57), para 117.
[120] Ibid, para 120. See also *Société Technique Minière* (n 57), 250.

like *Post Danmark I*[121] and *MEO*[122] suggests that something else – namely a negative impact on rivals' ability and incentive to exercise competitive pressure – is necessary. In *Post Danmark I*, for instance, the Court noted that, even though the dominant firm's rivals temporarily lost some customers as a result of the practice, they remained on the market and were able to win them back.[123] As a result, the Court concluded that the behaviour failed to display anticompetitive effects.

In both *Google Shopping* and *Android*, the Commission sought to establish at length how the contentious practices placed rivals at a competitive disadvantage. In the first, the decision meticulously seeks to show how, as a result of the behaviour, Google Shopping gained traffic from the general search results at the expense of third-party comparison-shopping services.[124] What is more, this traffic was deemed to represent a large proportion of the traffic to the rival websites. In *Android*, and just to mention the MADA aspects of the case as an illustration, the Commission explained at length how the pre-installation of Google's proprietary applications led to a 'status quo bias' that placed rivals at a disadvantage.[125] What is more, the authority argued that it would not be possible to uninstall the revenue-generating applications (that is, Search[126] and Chrome[127]).

Such evidence of a competitive disadvantage, even if established to the requisite legal standard, would not be sufficient to show an anticompetitive effect within the meaning of Article 102 TFEU. Consider, first, the factual aspects of *Google Shopping*. An analysis of the decision shows that the diversion of the traffic generated by Google's general search results and, similarly, the fact that such traffic is important for them does not necessarily mean that rival comparison-shopping services' ability and/or incentive to compete was negatively affected. It is sufficient to consider, in this regard, the figures provided in the *Google Shopping* decision. Indeed, the Commission's own analysis reveals that the overall traffic received by Google's rival comparison-shopping sites during the implementation of the practice increased in most cases.[128] In some instances, the traffic by rival sites more than doubled, if not tripled.[129]

---

[121] Case C-209/10 *Post Danmark A/S v Konkurrencerådet*, EU:C:2012:172.
[122] Case C-525/16 *MEO – Serviços de Comunicações e Multimédia SA v Autoridade da Concorrência*, EU:C:2018:270.
[123] *Post Danmark I* (n 121), para 39: '[…] it is worth noting that it appears from the documents before the Court that Forbruger-Kontakt managed to maintain its distribution network despite losing the volume of mail related to the three customers involved and managed, in 2007, to win back the Coop group's custom and, since then, that of the Spar group'.
[124] *Google Shopping* (n 1), paras 462–588.
[125] *Android* (n 2), paras 781–782.
[126] Ibid, paras 801–803.
[127] Ibid, paras 913–915.
[128] *Google Shopping* (n 1), para 540.
[129] Ibid, Table 24. The Table shows that the traffic received by one of the rivals went from 106,950,217 visits in 2011 to 234,308,088 visits in 2016 (thereby more than doubling the traffic during the relevant period) and from 387,817,001 in 2011 to 744,503,251 in the case of another one.

The *Android* case raised equally complex issues. To begin with, pre-installation provides, arguably, a relatively mild competitive advantage, in the sense that it does not limit end-users' ability to access rival applications in other ways (including via downloading). It differs, in this sense, from an exclusivity requirement and from the typical tying scenario. One should note, in this regard, that Google did not prevent the pre-installation of other applications in devices taking part in its ecosystem. Accordingly, any competitive advantage available to the firm's services was also available, at least in principle, to third parties. As discussed in the decision, Samsung chose to pre-instal its proprietary web browser in its mobile phones.[130] The contractual obligation also differs from a requirement to set the relevant applications as default. In fact (and this point is also addressed in the decision), end-users could set competing applications as default.[131]

What is unclear from the two decisions is the question of when a competitive disadvantage is deemed sufficient for it to give rise to an anticompetitive effect. In *Google Shopping*, the Commission appears to equate one and the other. More precisely, the decision is based on the assumption that, by showing the diversion of traffic resulting from self-preferencing, it is providing evidence of an anticompetitive effect to the requisite legal standard. The competitive advantage identified in the decision is deemed to be, at least potentially, a source of exclusionary effects.[132] The fact, mentioned above, that traffic in some instances doubled or even tripled, or the fact, pointed out by Google, that the Commission had failed to identify a single comparison-shopping site excluded, would not be relevant considerations.[133] According to the authority, the number of rival services could potentially be greater absent the practice.[134]

In *Android*, the Commission placed an emphasis on the fact that the 'status quo bias' deriving from the pre-installation of Google's own applications would not be offset by any alternative methods of accessing rival services.[135] In the same vein, the authority appeared to claim that the pre-installation of third-party applications, which was not precluded by the MADA itself, was more theoretical than real. This is so, according to the Commission, because of the limited benefits that might result from the duplication of functionalities and due to transaction costs that come with such duplication. In a different vein, the decision suggests that the pre-installation of additional software might potentially impact user experience.[136] Finally, it notes that the MADA, while not prohibiting the pre-installation of rival applications, would in any event prevent rivals from featuring, on an exclusive basis, on Google Android phones.[137]

---

[130] *Android* (n 2), para 901.
[131] Ibid, paras 914–915.
[132] Ibid, paras 858–866 and 969–982.
[133] *Google Shopping* (n 1), para 601.
[134] Ibid, para 603.
[135] *Android* (n 2), paras 804–834 and 947–963.
[136] Ibid, paras 827–829 and 926.
[137] Ibid, para 830.

The GC failed to shed much light on the difference between competitive advantage and anticompetitive effects. The judgment came close to suggesting that evidence of a competitive disadvantage can be sufficient, in and of itself, to establish an anticompetitive effect. Crucially, the first-instance court dismissed arguments concerning the alleged absence of a link between the evolution of market shares and the competitive disadvantage that might result from the MADA. In principle, rivals' decline could be explained by other factors, including the superior quality or popularity of Google's applications.[138] In this regard, however, the GC implies that it would be enough to establish that the observed evolution of market shares might be – even if it is not – at least partly attributable to the practice (or, to use the vocabulary found in the judgment, to the disruption of the competitive process coming from the behaviour).[139]

7. The Administration of Principles-based Remedies in Digital Markets

The Commission did not prescribe a particular remedy in either *Google Shopping* or *Android*. Instead, it ordered the firm to bring the infringement to an end and to respect a high-level principle. In the first of the cases Google was required to abide, as already explained, by a broad duty of non-discrimination. In *Android*, the firm was ordered, inter alia, to refrain from requiring the pre-installation of Google Search and/or Google Chrome when licensing, respectively, Google Play and Google Search.[140] In addition, the remedies package provided for obligations pertaining to the AFA dimensions of the case. More precisely, the firm was asked to refrain from asking device manufacturers to accept non-compete obligations preventing them from producing the so-called incompatible Android 'forks'.[141] Again, Google was just ordered to bring the infringement to an end, without specifying how.[142]

If one considers the *Microsoft I* precedent, discussed above, the potential advantages of following a 'principles-based' approach to the remedy need not be discussed at length. The firm subject to the investigation is the one that controls the operation of the 'black box' and is thus better placed to identify the appropriate manner to change, proactively, the design of its product and/or its business model. On the other hand, an infringement decision within the meaning of Article 7 does not come across as the most obvious context within which to embrace such an

---

[138] Google's arguments to this effect are summarised in para 838 of the same decision.
[139] Case T-604/18 *Android* (n 43), para 575: '[…] the Commission was not required to determine precisely whether those usage shares could be explained not only by pre-installation – as it believes – but also, or rather, by the superior quality claimed by Google […]'.
[140] *Android* (n 2), paras 1394–1396.
[141] Ibid, paras 1398–1400.
[142] Ibid, paras 1407–1410.

approach to remedial intervention. If anything, the *Google Shopping* and *Android* cases showed that the institutional apparatus enshrined in Regulation 1/2003 was neither designed nor equipped to deal with proactive policy-making.

The main reason why intervention under Article 7 does not seem suited to dealing with proactive remedies relates to the fact that it provides for no mechanism like the one enshrined in Article 9 of Regulation 1/2003. As seen in Chapter 1 (in addition to Chapters 6 and 7), commitments are made binding upon firms once the latter specify how they intend to modify their behaviour (and, sometimes, their very structure) to address the concerns identified. Under Article 7, by contrast, there is no procedural avenue allowing the Commission to express that the implementation of the remedies brings the infringement effectively to an end. It is implicitly assumed in Regulation 1/2003 that the decision is sufficiently specific about the nature and scope of the measures that the firm is required to adopt. As the *Microsoft* saga shows, the only mechanism available to the Commission is to open proceedings for failure to comply with the decision.[143]

As a result of this reality, the system is not adequately equipped to address the mismatch that might arise between the principles laid down in the decision and the interpretation of these principles by firms. Several consequences follow. First, uncertainty might remain about whether the undertaking has brought the infringement effectively to an end. The decision might remain in limbo long after it has been adopted. The lack of clarity about compliance with the terms of the decision is problematic both from the perspective of the undertaking (which faces the prospect of a subsequent penalty if its interpretation of the remedy turns out to be incorrect[144]) and that of the Commission (which has to deal with third-party complaints). A second consequence of this institutional reality is that any negotiations between the authority and the firms take place informally, outside any legal framework, which makes it impossible to get a sense of the nature of the discussions and to ensure that the measures ultimately adopted remain proportionate.

It makes sense to mention some of the most salient aspects of the aftermath of *Google Shopping* and *Android* to illustrate these ideas. The precise implementation of the remedy in the first of these cases was the result of a process during which the search engine was redesigned several times. As explained above, Google opened the premium space in its search engine page to third parties. In the initial iteration of the remedy, Google Shopping and rival comparison-shopping sites competed on non-discriminatory terms and conditions for access to slots in the Shopping Unit.[145] These slots display links, in rich format, to merchants' sites using the relevant comparison-shopping service. Google subsequently tweaked the design of

---

[143] Case T-167/08 *Microsoft Corp. v Commission*, EU:T:2012:323.

[144] Suffice it to mention, again, the example of the *Microsoft* saga. See European Commission, 'Antitrust: Commission imposes € 899 million penalty on Microsoft for non-compliance with March 2004 Decision' IP/08/318 (Brussels, 27 February 2008).

[145] For a description of the remedy, see Thomas Graf and Henry Mostyn, 'Do We Need to Regulate Equal Treatment? The Google Shopping Case and the Implications of its Equal Treatment Principle for New Legislative Initiatives' (2020) 11 Journal of European Competition Law & Practice 561.

its search engine to give end-users an alternative. This alteration added a second tab on the Shopping Unit. This second tab provides links to comparison-shopping sites (as opposed to merchants' sites).[146]

The implementation of these measures was followed by the Commission. Pursuant to the terms of the decision, Google was required to inform the authority of the means by which it intended to bring the infringement effectively to an end,[147] and was given 90 days to do so.[148] As already pointed out, however, there is no mechanism to declare the conformity of Google's design changes with the requirements of the decision. In fact, the decision is explicit about the fact that statements from the authority (or the absence thereof) were not to be interpreted as an endorsement of the measures chosen by the firm. As a result, the issue of compliance remains in limbo. It is not surprising, against this background, that third-party complainants (and their legal advisors) have been regularly claiming, to this day, that Google has never complained with the remedy,[149] thereby contributing to the legal uncertainty.

Intervention in a case like *Android* puts competition authorities in a difficult position. Changing the monetisation strategy of a firm does not necessarily lead to better outcomes for end-users, and, more generally, does not necessarily improve the conditions of competition relative to the counterfactual. If a firm is prevented from monetising its assets by means of advertising, it may decide to start charging device manufacturers for the licensing of its applications, with the consequences that inevitably follow. In the wake of the *Android* decision, Google changed its business model. More precisely, it announced that it would be licensing its suite of applications (other than the web browsers and the search application, which would be offered separately) in exchange for a fee.[150] In addition, it further tweaked its business model by replicating the commitments offered in *Microsoft II*.[151] Thus, Google's ecosystem was redesigned to present end-users with 'choice screen' that allows them to pick their preferred provider.[152]

---

[146] Ibid.
[147] *Google Shopping* (n 1), para 702.
[148] Ibid, para 701.
[149] Thomas Hoppner, 'Google's (Non-) Compliance with the EU Shopping Decision' (2020), available at https://ssrn.com/abstract=3700748; and Philip Marsden, 'Google Shopping for the Empress's New Clothes –When a Remedy Isn't a Remedy (and How to Fix it)' (2020) 11 Journal of European Competition Law & Practice 553.
[150] Simon Van Dorpe, 'Google to start charging a licensing fee after EU Android ruling' *Politico* (Brussels, 16 October 2018). See also Hiroshi Lockheimer, 'Complying with the EC's Android decision' (*The Keyword*, 16 October 2018), available at https://blog.google/around-the-globe/google-europe/complying-ecs-android-decision/.
[151] Paul Gennai, 'Presenting search app and browser options to Android users in Europe' (*The Keyword*, 18 April 2019), available at https://www.blog.google/around-the-globe/google-europe/presenting-search-app-and-browser-options-android-users-europe/.
[152] The remedy went through several iterations following its implementation. See in this sense Paul Gennai, 'An update on Android for search providers in Europe' (*The Keyword*, 2 August 2019), available at https://www.blog.google/around-the-globe/google-europe/update-android-search-providers-europe/; and Oliver Bethell, 'Changes to the Android Choice Screen in Europe (*The Keyword*, 8 June 2021), available at https://blog.google/around-the-globe/google-europe/changes-android-choice-screen-europe/.

8. Conclusions

8.1. Expansion and Fragmentation

The enforcement of Articles 101 and 102 TFEU in digital markets tells a story of expansion and fragmentation. The Commission, in line with its ambitions across the board, has decidedly sought to expand the policy arena in two ways. To begin with, the authority treats cases interfering with product design and business models just like any other investigation. It sees no difference, from a policy-making perspective, between cases addressing how products are sold and those dealing with how they are made. Thus, the fact that intervention would involve altering the features of a product (which will typically involve imposing a duty to deal with rivals) or requiring a firm to change its monetisation strategy does not warrant any deference. The complexities associated with the administration of proactive remedies, which became apparent in both *Google Shopping* and *Android*, are equally immaterial in this regard.

The Commission has enlarged the policy arena in a second way: by embracing a restrictive understanding of the *Bronner* case law. According to its reinterpretation of the 'exceptional circumstances' doctrine, indispensability would only be an element of the legal test where the authority formally requires a firm to deal with third parties with which it has chosen not to deal. This approach to *Bronner* gives the Commission, in effect, the discretion to decide when the 'exceptional circumstances' are applicable and when they are not, thereby reducing the legal constraints on administrative action. The GC did not object to the expansion of the authority's policy space at the expense of the 'exceptional circumstances' doctrine. If anything, it widened the scope for agency discretion. It did so by embracing a formalistic understanding of *Bronner*, whereby the latter judgment is only relevant where the exact same factual scenario is at stake (that is, one where there is a request, followed by a refusal to deal).

An inevitable side-effect of the expansion of the Commission's policy space appears to be the fragmentation of the EU competition law system. The authority's reasoning in both *Google Shopping* and *Android* seems grounded, at least in part, on the idea that the analytical framework varies between Articles 101 and 102 TFEU. In particular, the two decisions appear to take the view that the case law pertaining to the evaluation of the counterfactual does not apply to the second of these provisions. In *Android*, for instance, the Commission assumes that the restrictive aspects of the ecosystem can be considered in isolation from its pro-competitive dimension. Similarly, it suggests that the evaluation of the economic and legal context, which is central to the identification of restrictions under Article 101(1) TFEU, is not to be undertaken under Article 102 TFEU (or at least not to a similar extent, or at the same stage of the analysis). It remains to be seen, at the time of writing, whether the Court will accept this form of legal fragmentation.

8.2. Remedial Intervention

Google Shopping and *Android* expose, perhaps more eloquently than the decisions discussed in the preceding two chapters, the limits of proactive enforcement under Regulation 1/2003. Unlike the cases addressed in Chapter 6, remedial action followed the adoption of an infringement decision. Unlike the intervention in relation to standard-essential patents, the duties imposed were not a mere tweak at the margin, but a central modification of Google's product design and business models. The legal uncertainty that followed – the question of whether the firm has brought the infringement effectively to an end remains unanswered – has shown, above all, that the system did not anticipate and, more importantly, was not designed to handle proactive remedies in a systematic and sustained manner. In the absence of a regulatory apparatus supporting enforcement – like the energy and telecommunications regimes – the application of Articles 101 and 102 TFEU can only meet the 'expectation of regulation' on a temporary and precarious basis.

The adoption of the Digital Markets Act (hereinafter, the 'DMA') in the years that followed the *Google Shopping* and *Android* decisions will relieve the pressure off the competition law system and open the door to a – more sustainable – relationship between the sector-specific regime and Articles 101 and 102 TFEU. Along the lines of what has been suggested in Chapter 3, the frontier between competition law and regulation may no longer be easy to identify. The extent of the blending of both systems may well go beyond a gap-filling role. The Commission has not ceased to enforce Articles 101 and 102 TFEU in relation to the activities falling firmly within the scope of the DMA. For instance, it accepted commitments offered by Amazon concerning the use of the non-public data generated by its marketplace.[153] Similarly, it has continued to investigate the terms and conditions imposed by Apple on application developers.[154] Given the relatively rigid legislative technique on which the DMA relies, it is not difficult to imagine competition law enforcement paving the way for the expansion of the scope of sector-specific regulation.

---

[153] *Amazon Marketplace* (Case AT.40462) and *Amazon Buy Box* (Case AT.40703) Commission Decision of 20 December 2022.

[154] European Commission, 'Antitrust: Commission sends Statement of Objections to Apple on App Store rules for music streaming providers' IP/21/2061 (Brussels, 30 April 2021).

Conclusions

1. The New EU Competition Law in a Changing Landscape

1.1. Changes in the Institutional Landscape

The evolution of enforcement since the adoption of Regulation 1/2003[1] is consistent with the original ambitions of the legislature. The institutional landscape was designed to give the European Commission (hereinafter, the 'Commission') greater leeway to decide the cases and areas on which to concentrate its efforts. It did so in two main ways: by reducing some of the institutional burdens that constrained its discretion under the former framework[2] and by empowering national courts and authorities to enforce Articles 101 and 102 TFEU. The Commission has exercised its renewed jurisdiction in the manner one would expect from an authority placed at the top of a decentralised system. It has focused on what it considers to be the most egregious ('detection-deterrence') and the most demanding ('market-shaping') breaches. The 'missing-middle' (labelled 'market-protecting'), which had kept the authority busy during the formative years, is now the province, by and large, of soft law instruments (at least at the Union level).

The cases discussed at length in Part II provide a detailed and concrete illustration of the ways the original vision of the legislature has come to be realised. They show how ambitious (or, more precisely, 'market-shaping') EU competition policy has progressively become over the past two decades. The Commission fundamentally restructured energy markets following its Sector Inquiry into the industry.[3] As explained at length in Chapter 6, *Swedish Interconnectors* resulted in the root-and-branch reshaping of transmission activities in that Member State.[4] *German Electricity Balancing Market*, in turn, led to the structural break-up of an electricity incumbent.[5] Some of the cases analysed in Chapter 7 reveal a

---

[1] Council Regulation (EC) No 1/2003 of 16 December 2002 on the implementation of the rules on competition laid down in Articles 81 and 82 of the Treaty [2003] OJ L1/1.
[2] Regulation No 17: First Regulation implementing Articles 85 and 86 of the Treaty [1962] OJ 13/204.
[3] European Commission, 'Inquiry pursuant to Article 17 of Regulation (EC) No 1/2003 into the European gas and electricity sectors (Final Report)' COM(2006) 851 final, paras 18–20 and 35–37.
[4] *Swedish Interconnectors* (Case 39351) Commission Decision of 14 April 2010.
[5] *German Electricity Wholesale Market* (Case COMP/39388) and *German Electricity Balancing Market* (Case COMP/39389), Commission Decision of 26 November 2008.

similar degree of ambition. The objective behind *Cross-border access to pay-TV*, for instance, was to alter in fundamental ways the operation of copyright regimes so as to enable intra-brand competition between licensees.[6] If anything, the shift in focus towards digital platforms, addressed in Chapter 8 in light of the *Google* saga,[7] suggests that the move towards 'market-shaping' enforcement has gained momentum.

This book also shows the central role that legal instruments play in the advancement of an authority's policy goals. Generally speaking, the Commission has prioritised outcomes over the clarification of issues of law (at least so in relation to its decision-making activity). During the first decade of enforcement under Regulation 1/2003, this attitude is exemplified, above all, by its reliance on commitments decisions. This instrument, which allows the authority to reach a negotiated solution without formally establishing an infringement, has been so pivotal to some developments that it is inseparable from them. This is true, in particular, of enforcement in the energy sector, addressed in Chapter 6. The Commission managed to fundamentally restructure the electricity and gas industries mostly without ruling on whether Articles 101 and 102 TFEU had been breached. Over time, and in particular once enforcement efforts shifted to digital markets, the balance between infringement and commitments decisions changed in favour of the former. During the second decade, the amount and scale of fines in 'law-intensive' cases became a reliable (and very noticeable) indicator of the Commission's priorities.

1.2. Changes in the Intellectual Landscape

It is difficult to make sense of the transformation of EU competition policy without considering shifts in the intellectual landscape. Regulation 1/2003 was adopted when the 'more economics-based approach' to enforcement was about to reach its peak. As discussed in Chapter 2, this understanding of the discipline favours a relatively modest role for Articles 101 and 102 TFEU. It is an approach that is wary of enforcement errors (in particular on the side of over-enforcement) and of the impact of intervention on long-term incentives to invest and innovate. The two distinct manifestations of this philosophy are, first, the emphasis on the need to evaluate, case-by-case, the actual or potential impact of practices and, second, the focus on efficiency as the overarching benchmark guiding action.

Over the past decade, the 'more economics-based approach' came increasingly under attack. The loss of influence of this philosophy of enforcement is attributable to changes in the perceptions of what makes intervention legitimate. The anxieties

---

[6] *Cross-border access to pay-TV* (Case AT.40023) Commission Decision of 26 July 2016.
[7] *Google – Google Search (Shopping)* (Case AT.39740) Commission Decision of 27 June 2017; *Google Android* (Case AT.40099) Commission Decision of 18 July 2018; *Google Search (AdSense)* (Case AT.40411) Commission Decision of 20 March 2019; and European Commission, 'Antitrust: Commission opens investigation into possible anticompetitive conduct by Google in the online advertising technology sector' IP/21/3143 (Brussels, 22 June 2021).

that accompanied the rise of Big Tech had a marked impact on stakeholders' priorities in this regard. Within many constituencies, EU competition policy is no longer judged based on whether the analysis underpinning intervention is clean, predictable and grounded on the mainstream consensus. What counts, in the changing economic climate, is whether Articles 101 and 102 TFEU can address the concerns raised and enact the desired changes to the operation of markets. The emerging approach is concerned less with underenforcement and more with the effectiveness of policy-making. Similarly, it does not feel constrained or limited by efficiency considerations alone. Redistribution, in particular, has come to be seen as a desirable goal of intervention in and of itself.

1.3. Consequences of the Changing Landscapes: Expansion, Fragmentation, Blending

Changes in the institutional and intellectual landscapes have had three main consequences. The first can be termed expansion. It refers to the progressive broadening of the Commission's leeway to attain the desired policy outcomes. Expansion has been manifested in the interpretation of Articles 101 and 102 TFEU and, more generally, in the various ways in which the boundaries of intervention under both provisions have been tested. The second phenomenon is fragmentation. It seems almost inevitable that, when enforcement is driven by policy, inconsistencies emerge within and across provisions, and between sectors. The final phenomenon relates to the relationship with regulation. As the scope of Articles 101 and 102 TFEU expands, the dividing lines between competition law and sector-specific regimes become blurred, to the point that it is difficult – or futile – to draw the line between one and the other.

2. Expansion

2.1. The Expansion of Legal Doctrines that Broaden the Commission's Policy Space

The phenomenon of expansion is manifested, first, in the interpretation of legal doctrines by the Commission. In a number of instances, the authority has explored the outer limits of existing case law. This point became apparent, just to mention one area of enforcement, in Chapter 6. The string of commitments decisions in the energy sector was premised on a new understanding of the 'exceptional circumstances' doctrine enshrined in *Bronner*.[8] The most remarkable feature of

---

[8] Case C-7/97 *Oscar Bronner GmbH & Co. KG v Mediaprint Zeitungs- und Zeitschriftenverlag GmbH & Co. KG and others*, EU:C:1998:569.

this reinterpretation of the case law is the idea that firms that control an indispensable input or infrastructure have a duty not just to share it with third parties, but to ensure that the input or infrastructure in question has enough capacity to accommodate rivals.[9] A duty to deal, in other words, was transformed into a duty to expand capacity to meet other firms' requests. More generally, the decisions discussed in Chapter 6 hinted at the idea that vertically-integrated dominant firms are under a duty not to discriminate against non-integrated rivals. This novel idea would feature again in the *Google* saga.

2.2. The Restrictive Reading of Legal Doctrines that Limit the Commission's Policy Space

The phenomenon of expansion has also been manifested in a relatively restrictive interpretation of the legal doctrines with the greatest potential to constrain the scope for policy intervention. Given the nature of 'market-shaping' enforcement, it is inevitable that the 'exceptional circumstances' doctrine is a frequent stumbling block potentially jeopardising the Commission's ability to engage in proactive decision-making. Unsurprisingly, the authority has construed the *Bronner* case law in a manner that confines its scope of application to the specific circumstances of that case. In *Google Shopping*,[10] for instance, it argued that the applicability of the 'exceptional circumstances' doctrine depends on whether the decision formally requires a firm to deal with rivals with which it has chosen not to deal. This interpretation of the case law gives the Commission, in effect, the discretion to decide when the indispensability condition is applicable and when it is not.

2.3. The Link between the Infringement and the Obligations

An additional way in which the phenomenon of expansion has been manifested is in the lack of proportion that can be observed, in certain instances, between the (established or alleged) infringement and the obligations aimed at bringing it to an end. In some of the cases discussed in Chapter 6, in particular, it is not entirely clear whether the obligations imposed on the firms were necessary to address the concerns identified by the Commission. In *German Electricity Balancing Market*, for instance, there are reasons to wonder whether the structural separation was required to deal with the conflict of interest resulting from vertical integration (in light, among other things, of the legislation adopted in the wake of the decision). In other cases, the link between the alleged infringement and the commitments offered is not immediately obvious to establish.

---

[9] *ENI* (Case COMP/39.315) Commission Decision of 29 September 2010.
[10] *Google Shopping* (n 7).

In *BEH Electricity*,[11] arguably the most obvious example, the firm did not just cease its conduct; it accepted to alter the operation of the relevant market in fundamental ways by setting up a power exchange that replaced bilateral trading.

2.4. Challenging Market Structures, as Opposed to Behaviours?

The most persistent limit to the expansion of the Commission's policy space is the need to identify a behavioural trigger allowing for intervention under either Article 101 or 102 TFEU. In the absence of an agreement or – as far as potentially abusive conduct is concerned – a unilateral practice by a dominant undertaking, these two provisions cannot apply. Articles 101 and 102 TFEU were both designed to tackle conduct having the object or effect of restricting competition. They were never conceived as tools to reshape industries or to inject rivalry. For instance, dominance is not prohibited as such. However, some of the cases discussed in the preceding chapters come close to questioning market structures themselves, as opposed to a (concerted or unilateral) behaviour. In other cases, the mismatch between the alleged infringement and the obligations imposed suggests that the point of intervention was not so much to bring a conduct to an end as to alter the operation of the relevant market.

It is sufficient to think, in this regard, of the expansion of the 'exceptional circumstances' doctrine, discussed above. The idea that dominant firms are under a duty to expand capacity to accommodate third parties ultimately questions the existing market structure, as opposed to a refusal to deal (or indeed, any other potentially abusive practice). The same can be said, turning to the issues discussed in Chapter 7, about the *Cross-border access to pay-TV* case. Challenging behaviour that does not go beyond the scope of the copyright regime amounts, in essence, to challenging the very market structure created by the intellectual property system. It should be reminded, in this regard, that the contentious clauses in the licensing agreements identified by the Commission did not restrict competition any more than the operation of copyright did.

3. Fragmentation

3.1. Fragmentation between Provisions

Fragmentation comes across as an inevitable by-product of 'policy-driven' enforcement. When the emphasis is placed on the outcomes sought, some friction in the

---

[11] *BEH Electricity* (Case AT.39767) Commission Decision of 10 December 2015.

interpretation of provisions is bound to arise. The *Google* saga exemplifies how fragmentation in the interpretation of, respectively, Articles 101 and 102 TFEU might emerge. As far as Article 101(1) TFEU is concerned, the Court of Justice has made it consistently clear, from the very early days, that a restriction of competition must be established in light of the relevant economic and legal context, and this, by taking into account the conditions of competition that would have existed in the absence of the practice. One of the immediate consequences of this long-standing doctrine is that the actual or potential effects of an agreement are to be established against the relevant counterfactual.

In both *Google Shopping* and *Android*, however, the General Court seemingly held that what is true in the context of Article 101 TFEU is not necessarily true under Article 102 TFEU. In the judgment delivered in the first of the cases, to begin with, it went as far as to hold that requiring the Commission to establish the relevant counterfactual would be tantamount to requiring it to provide evidence of actual – as opposed to potential – anticompetitive effects. In *Android*, in turn, the General Court suggested that it is possible to evaluate the restrictive aspects of a particular practice in isolation from the pro-competitive gains that might result from it, and thus irrespective of whether the former are objectively necessary to realise the latter (or, more generally, irrespective of the conditions of competition that would have prevailed in their absence).

3.2. Sectoral Fragmentation

It would be reasonable to argue that some of the transformations summarised in these conclusions are not universal and that are best understood as responses to the specificities of the relevant sector and the particular circumstances in which the cases were decided. There is little doubt, in this sense, that the investigations discussed in Chapter 6 arose in the very sui generis context of the liberalisation of EU energy and telecommunications markets and against the background of the Commission's efforts to inject competition by means of legislative harmonisation. One may also claim, equally convincingly, that the *Google* saga – and the string of decisions in the digital sector that followed – is no less exceptional. These are, after all, activities with a marked tendency towards concentration. Accordingly, the development or the adaptation of some legal doctrines is arguably to be expected (and, some may even argue, desirable).

There may be some truth in the above observations. To the extent that there is, it raises a separate concern, which is the sectoral fragmentation of the EU competition law system. Instead of a body of case law and administrative practice applying uniformly across markets and industries, the flavour of the discipline and the intensity and frequency of intervention may vary slightly depending on the activity to which it applies. There would be no one EU competition law, but a multiplicity of sectoral iterations thereof. For instance, the conditions under which access obligations are imposed may be relaxed in digital markets, on account of the peculiar features of the industry. The same may be true of recently liberalised industries, as a means to support the efforts to open the sector to competition. In other segments, however, the conditions may be stricter, and *Bronner* may remain the law of the land.

It is not difficult to see how legal uncertainty might result from the fragmentation of the legal landscape along sectoral borders. In such a divided landscape, the existing body of case law may not necessarily provide a reliable indication of the outcome of intervention. There may always be special circumstances pertaining to the industry under consideration that might justify a different interpretation of Articles 101 and 102 TFEU. Over time, competing legal doctrines with different implications may emerge. For instance, some precedents may suggest that a firm may have a duty to expand capacity if it controls an essential facility; others may suggest the opposite. The fragmented legal universe may eventually change the way one thinks about competition law matters altogether: the discipline may be organised around industries and/or issues, just like Part II is.

4. Blending with Economic Regulation

Chapter 3 explains how competition law occasionally applies as a safety net that makes up for the flaws and imperfections of economic regulation. There may be instances where the sectoral regime works imperfectly and where an alternative enforcement avenue is necessary to ensure that its objectives are attained. On the other hand, Chapter 6 concluded that the safety net analogy probably does not fully capture the reality of the interaction between competition law and economic regulation. The relationship between both has grown to become symbiotic in nature. It is symbiotic in the sense that some aspects of competition law enforcement can only be explained by the overlap with a regulatory apparatus, and, conversely, also in the sense that the success of sector-specific regulation depends, at least in part, on the application of Articles 101 and 102 TFEU. Looking back at the preceding chapters, it seems that blending is, arguably, the expression that captures best the deepening interaction and interdependence between the two systems.

With the rise of proactive enforcement, and with the Commission exploring the boundaries of Articles 101 and 102 TFEU, competition law has been effectively mimicking sector-specific regimes. Conversely, economic regulation replicates the substance and, in some respects, the operation of competition law. The Digital Markets Act,[12] the central provisions of which can be aptly described as a codification of (completed, contemplated and ongoing) Article 101 and 102 TFEU

---

[12] Regulation (EU) 2022/1925 of the European Parliament and of the Council of 14 September 2022 on contestable and fair markets in the digital sector and amending Directives (EU) 2019/1937 and (EU) 2020/1828 (Digital Markets Act) [2022] OJ L265/1.

investigations, is the legal development that captures this idea well. Against this background, any attempt to draw a precise line between competition law and regulation becomes a difficult and, more importantly, artificial exercise. Competition law, in its current incarnation, can work as regulation; conversely, it would not be inappropriate to treat the Digital Markets Act and other regimes such as the EU Regulatory Framework for electronic communications as forms of (sector-specific) competition law.[13]

5. Epilogue: Towards the Demise of Articles 101 and 102 TFEU?

A look at the evolution of EU competition policy leaves one wondering whether its future lies, or can lie, in Articles 101 and 102 TFEU. The two decades of enforcement since the adoption of Regulation 1/2003 have exposed the limits of these two provisions. As mentioned above, the need to identify a behavioural trigger (whether an agreement or a unilateral practice) precludes unconstrained market restructuring by the Commission. Chapters 6 to 8, in turn, have shown how much the competition law system struggles with the administration of proactive remedies. Such obligations cannot be systematically implemented and sustained in time in the absence of a formal regulatory apparatus supporting intervention. The aftermath of *Google Shopping* and *Android* reveals that Regulation 1/2003 was not designed or equipped to deal with measures aimed at restructuring products and markets. Several years after the adoption of the two decisions, the question of whether the firm had brought the infringement effectively to an end remains unanswered.

Against this background, it is submitted that the approaches and processes set in motion by the rise of the new EU competition law might ultimately lead to the demise of Articles 101 and 102 TFEU. The mismatch between the policy ambitions of the Commission and what can be realistically attained under the two provisions may crystallise in the introduction of a new set of powers that would formally free the authority from existing constraints. Such was exactly the idea behind the 'new competition tool',[14] which would have allowed it to restructure markets without identifying a behavioural trigger and, similarly, without the need to establish an infringement. The absence of effective competition would justify, in and of itself, intervention. At the time of writing, there were no formal plans for the adoption of a new tool. This said, it comes across as the logical endgame of the rise of the sort of 'market-shaping' enforcement that has defined the past two decades.

---

[13] Directive (EU) 2018/1972 of the European Parliament and of the Council of 11 December 2018 establishing the European Electronic Communications Code [2018] OJ L321/36.

[14] Commission, 'Commission launches consultation to seek views on Digital Services Act package' IP/20/962 (Brussels, 2 June 2020) and Commission, 'Antitrust: Commission consults stakeholders on a possible new competition tool' IP/20/977 (Brussels, 2 June 2020).

BIBLIOGRAPHY

Books

Akman P, Brook O and Stylianou K (eds), *Research Handbook on Abuse of Dominance and Monopolization* (Edward Elgar 2023)
Backhouse RE, *The Puzzle of Modern Economics: Science or Ideology?* (Cambridge University Press, 2010)
Baker JB, *The Antitrust Paradigm: Restoring a Competitive Economy* (Harvard University Press)
Baldwin R, *Rules and Government* (Oxford University Press 1987)
——, Cave M and Lodge M (eds), *The Oxford Handbook of Regulation* (Oxford University Press 2010)
——, Cave M and Lodge M, *Understanding Regulation: Theory, Strategy, and Practice* (2nd edn Oxford University Press 2011)
Bently L, Sherman B, Gangjee D and Johnson P, *Intellectual Property Law* (5th edn, Oxford University Press 2018)
——, Sherman B, Gangjee D and Johnson P, *Intellectual Property Law* (6th edn, Oxford University Press 2022)
Blair RD, and Sokol DD (eds), *Handbook of Antitrust, Intellectual Property and High Technology* (Cambridge University Press 2017)
Bohannan C and Hovenkamp H, *Creation without Restraint: Promoting Liberty and Rivalry in Innovation* (Oxford University Press 2012)
Bourgeois J and Waelbroeck D (eds), *Ten years of effects-based approach in EU competition law: State of play and perspectives* (Bruylant 2012)
Burk DL and Lemley MA, *The Patent Crisis and How the Courts Can Solve It* (University of Chicago Press 2009)
Cahill D, *The Modernisation of EU Competition Law Enforcement in the EU* (Cambridge University Press 2004)
Carey P, *Data Protection: A Practical Guide to UK Law* (6th edn, Oxford University Press 2020)
Chang HJ, *Economics: The User's Guide* (Pelican 2014)
—— *Competition Law and Regulation of Technology Markets* (Oxford University Press 2011)
Contreras JL (ed), *The Cambridge Handbook of Technical Standardization Law: Competition, Antitrust, and Patents* (Cambridge University Press 2017)
Craig P, *EU Administrative Law* (3rd edn, Oxford University Press 2019)
Decker C, *Modern Economic Regulation* (Cambridge University Press 2018)
Drexl J, Kerber W and Podszun R, *Competition Policy and the Economic Approach Foundations and Limitations* (Edward Elgar 2011)
Dunne N, *Competition Law and Economic Regulation: Making and Managing Markets* (Cambridge University Press 2015)
Ehlermann CD and Marquis M (eds), *European Competition Law Annual 2007: A Reformed Approach to Article 82 EC* (Hart Publishing 2008)
Glachant JM, Joskow PL and Pollitt MG, *Handbook on Electricity Markets* (Edward Elgar 2021)
Govaere I, *The Use and Abuse of Intellectual Property Rights in European Community Law* (Sweet & Maxwell 1996)
Hamburger P, *Is Administrative Law Unlawful?* (Chicago University Press 2014)

Haskel J and Westlake S, *Restarting the Future: How to Fix the Intangible Economy* (Princeton University Press 2022)
Hayek FA, *New Studies in Philosophy, Politics, Economics and the History of Ideas* (University of Chicago Press 1978)
Ibáñez Colomo P, *The Shaping of EU Competition Law* (Cambridge University Press 2018)
Jackson E, *Law and the Regulation of Medicines* (Hart Publishing 2012)
Jaffe AB, Lerner J and Stern S (eds), *Innovation Policy and the Economy*, vol 1 (MIT Press 2006)
—— and Lerner J, *Innovation and Its Discontents: How Our Broken Patent System is Endangering Innovation and Progress, and What to Do About It* (Princeton University Press 2011)
Johnston A and Block G, *EU Energy Law* (Oxford University Press 2013)
Jones C and Kettlewell WJ (eds), *EU Energy Law*, vol 1 (5th edn, Claeys & Casteels 2020)
Korah V, *An Introductory Guide to EC Competition Law and Practice* (Hart Publishing 2007)
Laffont JJ and Tirole J, *Competition in Telecommunications* (MIT Press 1999)
Landes WM and Posner RA, *The Economic Structure of Intellectual Property Law* (Belknap 2003)
Langus G, Neven D and Poukens S, *Economic Analysis of the Territoriality of the Making Available Right in the EU* (Charles River Associates for DG Markt 2014)
Larouche P, *Competition Law and Regulation in European Telecommunications* (Hart Publishing 2000)
Lerner J and Scott S (eds), *The Rate and Direction of Inventive Activity Revisited* (University of Chicago Press 2012)
Lianos I and Geradin D (eds), *Handbook on European Competition Law: Substantive Aspects* (Edward Elgar 2013)
Lyons B (ed), *Cases in European Competition Policy: The Economic Analysis* (Cambridge University Press 2009)
Mankiw GN and Taylor MP, *Economics* (3rd edn, Cengage 2014)
Marquis M and Monti G (eds), *European Competition Law Annual 2013 – Effective and Legitimate Enforcement of Competition Law* (Hart Publishing 2016)
Motta M, Peitz M and Schweitzer H, *Market Investigations: A New Competition Tool for Europe?* (Cambridge University Press 2021)
Neven D, Papandropoulos P and Seabright P (eds), *Trawling for Minnows: European Competition Policy and Agreements Between Firms* (Centre for Economic Policy Research 1998)
Nikolic I, *Licensing Standard Essential Patents: FRAND and the Internet of Things* (Hart Publishing 2021)
O'Donoghue R and Padilla R, *The Law and Economics of Article 102 TFEU* (2nd edn, Hart Publishing 2013)
—— and Padilla J, *The Law and Economics of Article 102 TFEU* (3rd edn, Hart Publishing 2020)
Pila J and Ohly A (eds), *The Europeanization of Intellectual Property Law: Towards a European Legal Methodology* (Oxford University Press 2013)
Pottage A and Sherman B, *Figures of Invention: A History of Modern Patent Law* (Oxford University Press 2010)
Rosati E, *Originality in EU Copyright Full Harmonization through Case Law* (Elgar 2013)
Sibony AL, *Le juge et le raisonnement économique en droit de la concurrence* (LGDJ 2008)
Thépot F, *The Interaction Between Competition Law and Corporate Governance: Opening the 'Black Box'* (Cambridge University Press 2019)
Waelbroeck M and Frignani A, *Commentaire J. Mégret : le droit de la CE, vol 4. Concurrence* (Éditions de l'Université de Bruxelles 1998)
Wardaugh B, *Competition, Effects and Predictability: Rule of Law and the Economic Approach to Competition* (Hart Publishing 2020)
Weatherill S, *EU Consumer Law and Policy* (2nd edn, Edward Elgar 2013)
Witt AC, *The More Economic Approach to EU Antitrust Law* (Hart Publishing 2016)
Wu T, *The Curse of Bigness: Antitrust in the New Gilded Age* (Columbia Global Reports 2018)

Articles

Ahlborn C, Evans DS and Padilla J, 'The antitrust economics of tying: a farewell to per se illegality' (2004) 49 Antitrust Bulletin 287

Autor D, Dorn D, Katz LF, Patterson C and Reenen JV, 'The Fall of the Labor Share and the Rise of Superstar Firms' (2020) 135 Quarterly Journal of Economics 645

Ayres I and Klemperer P, 'The old Limiting Patentees' Market Power Without Reducing Innovation Incentives: The Perverse Benefits of Uncertainty and Non-Injunctive Remedies' (1999) 97 Michigan Law Review 985

Baker J, 'Taking the Error Out of "Error Cost" Analysis: What's Wrong with Antitrust's Right' (2015) 80 Antitrust Law Journal 1

Bernheim BD and Whinston MD, 'Exclusive Dealing' (1998) 106 Journal of Political Economy 64

Bethell O, 'Changes to the Android Choice Screen in Europe (*The Keyword*, 8 June 2021), available at https://blog.google/around-the-globe/google-europe/changes-android-choice-screen-europe/

Boldrin M and Levine D, 'The Case against Intellectual Property' (2009) 92 American Economic Review 209

Bostoen F, 'Margin Squeeze: Where Competition Law and Sector Regulation Compete' (2016–17) 53 Jura Falconis 3

Botta M, 'Unfair Pricing and Standard Essential Patents' (2020) EUI Working Paper RSCAS 2020/60, available at https://cadmus.eui.eu/

Briones J and Padilla J, 'The Complex Landscape of Oligopolies under EU Competition Policy – Is Collective Dominance Ripe for Guidelines?' (2001) 24 World Competition 307

Cave M, 'Six Degrees of Separation Operational Separation as a Remedy in European Telecommunications Regulation' (2006) 64 Communications & Strategies 89

Chowdhury A and Jenkins H, 'Inference or Evidence? The Uncertain Fate of Patent Settlement Agreements' (2018) 9 Journal of European Competition Law & Practice 449

Clancy M, Geradin D and Lazerow A, 'Reverse-payment patent settlements in the pharmaceutical industry: An analysis of US antitrust law and EU competition law' (2014) 59 Antitrust Bulletin 153

Coates K, 'The Stoppel Abuse' (*21st Century Competition*, 28 October 2013) available at https://www.twentyfirstcenturycompetition.com/2013/10/the-estoppel-abuse/

Coscelli A, Edwards G and Overd A, 'Parallel trade in pharmaceuticals: more harm than good?' (2008) 29 European Competition Law Review 490

de Pablo L and Bayón Fernández N, 'Why the Proposed DMA Might Be Illegal under Article 114 TFEU, and How to Fix It' (2021) 12 Journal of European Competition Law & Practice 576

de Ridder M, 'Market Power and Innovation in the Intangible Economy' (2022), available at http://www.maartenderidder.com/research.html

Demsetz H, 'The Firm in Economic Theory: A Quiet Revolution' (1997) 87 American Economic Review: Papers & Proceedings 426

Dolmans M, 'Sustainable Competition Policy' (2020) 5(4) and 6(1) Competition Law and Policy Debate CLPD

Dunne N, 'Commitment Decisions in EU Competition Law' (2014) 10 Journal of Competition Law & Economics 399

—— 'Between competition law and regulation: hybridized approaches to market control' (2014) 2 Journal of Antitrust Enforcement 225

—— 'Margin squeeze: theory, practice, policy, part I' (2012) 33 European Competition Law Review 29

—— 'Regulating Prices in the European Union' (2018) 37 Yearbook of European Law 344

—— 'From Coercion to Cooperation: Settlements within EU Competition Law' (2019) LSE Legal Studies Working Paper 14/2019

—— 'Fairness and the Challenge of Making Markets Work Better' (2021) 84 Modern Law Review 230

Easterbrook FH, 'Limits of Antitrust' (1984) 63 Texas Law Review 1

Evans DS and Schmalensee R, 'Economic Aspects of Payment Card Systems and Antitrust Policy Toward Joint Ventures' (1995) 63 Antitrust Law Journal 861

Ezrachi A, 'The European Commission Guidance on Article 82 EC – The Way in which Institutional Realities Limit the Potential for Reform' (2009) Oxford Legal Studies Research Paper 27/2009, available at http://ssrn.com/abstract=1463854
—— 'Unchallenged Market Power? The Tale of Supermarkets, Private Labels and Competition Law' (2010) 33 World Competition 257
Farrand B, 'Lobbying and Lawmaking in the European Union: The Development of Copyright Law and the Rejection of the Anti-Counterfeiting Trade Agreement' (2015) 35 Oxford Journal of Legal Studies 487
Fox EM, 'We Protect Competition, You Protect Competitors' (2003) 26 World Competition 149
Galetovic A and Haber S, 'The Fallacies of Patent-Holdup Theory' (2017) 13 Journal of Competition Law & Economics 1
Gennai P, 'Presenting search app and browser options to Android users in Europe' (*The Keyword*, 18 April 2019), available at https://www.blog.google/around-the-globe/google-europe/presenting-search-app-and-browser-options-android-users-europe/
—— 'An update on Android for search providers in Europe' (*The Keyword*, 2 August 2019), available at https://www.blog.google/around-the-globe/google-europe/update-android-search-providers-europe/
Geradin D and O'Donoghue R, 'The Concurrent Application of Competition Law and Regulation: The Case of Margin Squeeze Abuses in the Telecommunications Sector' (2005) GCLC Working Paper No. 04/05
—— 'Refusal to supply and margin squeeze: A discussion of why the 'Telefonica Exceptions' are wrong' (2011) TILEC Discussion Paper 2011-051
Gerbrandy A, 'Solving a Sustainability-Deficit in European Competition Law' (2017) 40 World Competition 539
Goyder J, 'Cet Obscur Objet: Object Restrictions in Vertical Agreements' (2011) 4 Journal of European Competition Law & Practice 327
Graf T and Mostyn H, 'Do We Need to Regulate Equal Treatment? The Google Shopping Case and the Implications of its Equal Treatment Principle for New Legislative Initiatives' (2020) 11 Journal of European Competition Law & Practice 561
Grullon G, Larkin Y and Michaely R, 'Are US Industries Becoming More Concentrated?' (2019) 23 Review of Finance 697
Hagiu A, Teh TH and Wright J, 'Should platforms be allowed to sell on their own marketplaces?' (2022) 53 RAND Journal of Economics 297
Handke C and Towse R, 'Economics of Copyright Collecting Societies' (2007) 38 International Review of Intellectual Property and Competition Law 937
Hawk B, 'System failure: Vertical restraints and EC competition law' (1995) 32 Common Market Law Review 973
Hayek FA, 'The Use of Knowledge in Society' (1945) 35 American Economic Review 519
Hemphill CS and Sampat BN, 'Evergreening, patent challenges, and effective market life in pharmaceuticals' (2012) 31 Journal of Health Economics 327
Holmes S, 'Climate change, sustainability, and competition law' (2020) 8 Journal of Antitrust Enforcement 354
Hoppner T, 'EU Copyright Reform: The Case for a Publisher's Right' (2018) Intellectual Property Quarterly 1
—— 'Google's (Non-) Compliance with the EU Shopping Decision' (2020), available at https://ssrn.com/abstract=3700748
Hovenkamp H, 'Whatever Did Happen to the Antitrust Movement?' (2019) 94 Notre Dame Law Review 58
—— 'Antitrust Error Costs' (2022) 24 University of Pennsylvania Journal of Business Law 293
—— 'The Invention of Antitrust' (2022) 96 Southern California Law Review 131
Ibáñez Colomo P, 'On the application of competition law as regulation: elements for a theory' (2010) 29 Yearbook of European Law 261

—— 'Post Danmark II: The Emergence of a Distinct "Effects-Based" Approach to Article 102 TFEU (2016) 7 Journal of European Competition Law & Practice 113
—— 'Article 101 TFEU and Market Integration' (2016) 12 Journal of Competition Law & Economics 749
—— 'Restrictions on innovation in EU competition law' (2016) 41 European Law Review 201
—— 'Copyright and the Digital Single Market: geo-blocking is here to stay (or so it seems)' (*Chillin' Competition*, 4 May 2016) available at https://chillingcompetition.com/2016/05/04/copyright-and-the-digital-single-market-geo-blocking-is-here-to-stay-or-so-it-seems/
—— 'Indispensability and Abuse of Dominance: From Commercial Solvents to Slovak Telekom and Google Shopping' (2019) 10 Journal of European Competition Law & Practice 532
—— 'Self-Preferencing: Yet Another Epithet in Need of Limiting Principles' (2020) 43 World Competition 417
—— and Kalintiri A, 'The evolution of EU antitrust policy: 1966–2017' (2020) 83 Modern Law Review 321
—— 'The Draft Digital Markets Act: A Legal and Institutional Analysis' (2021) 12 Journal of European Competition Law & Practice 561
—— 'Future-Proof Regulation against the Test of Time: The Evolution of European Telecommunications Regulation' (2022) 42 Oxford Journal of Legal Studies 1170
—— 'Will Article 106 TFEU Case Law Transform EU Competition Law?' (2022) 13 Journal of European Competition Law & Practice 385
Joliet R, 'La notion de pratique concertée et l'arrêt ICI dans une perspective comparative' (1974) 10 Cahiers de droit européen 251
Kallaugher J and Sher B, 'Rebates revisited: anti-competitive effects and exclusionary abuse under Article 82' (2004) 25 European Competition Law Review 263
Katz ML and Shapiro C, 'Systems Competition and Network Effects' (1994) 8 Journal of Economic Perspectives 93
Khan L, 'The New Brandeis Movement: America's Antimonopoly Debate' (2018) 9 Journal of European Competition Law & Practice 131
Korah V, 'EEC Competition Policy – Legal Form or Economic Efficiency' (1986) 39 Current Legal Problems 85
Laffont JJ and Tirole J, 'The Politics of Government Decision-Making: A Theory of Regulatory Capture' (1991) 106 Quarterly Journal of Economics 1089
Lang JT, 'Mandating Access: The Principles and the Problems in Intellectual Property and Competition Policy' (2004) 15 European Business Law Review 1087
Larouche P, 'Contrasting Legal Solutions and the Comparability of EU and U.S. Experiences' (2006) TILEC Discussion Paper No. 2006-028, available at https://ssrn.com/abstract=943615
Lemley MA, 'Intellectual Property Rights and Standard-Setting Organizations' (2002) 90 California Law Review 1889
—— 'A New Balance between IP and Antitrust' (2007) 13 Southwestern Journal of Law and Trade in the Americas 237
—— and Shapiro C, 'Patent Holdup and Royalty Stacking' (2007) 85 Texas Law Review 1991
—— 'Ignoring Patents' (2008) Michigan State Law Review 19
—— 'Industry-Specific Antitrust Policy for Innovation' (2011) Columbia Business Law Review 637
—— 'Can the Patent Office Be Fixed?' (2011) 15 Marquette Intellectual Property Review 295
—— 'The Surprising Resilience of the Patent System' (2016) 95 Texas Law Review 1
Leyden A and Dolmans M, 'The Google Commitments: Now with a Cherry on Top' (2014) 5 Journal of European Competition Law & Practice 253
Lianos I, 'Competition Law and Intellectual Property Rights: Is the Property Rights' Approach Right?' (2006) 8 Cambridge Yearbook of European Law 153
—— 'Some Reflections on the Question of the Goals of EU Competition Law' (2013) CLES Working Paper Series 3/2013, available at https://ssrn.com/abstract=2235875
Lockheimer H, 'Complying with the EC's Android decision' (*The Keyword*, 16 October 2018), available at https://blog.google/around-the-globe/google-europe/complying-ecs-android-decision/

Marquis M and Rousseva E, 'Hell Freezes Over: A Climate Change for Assessing Exclusionary Conduct Under Article 102 TFEU' (2013) 4 Journal of European Competition Law & Practice 32

Marsden P, 'Google Shopping for the Empress's New Clothes –When a Remedy Isn't a Remedy (and How to Fix it)' (2020) 11 Journal of European Competition Law & Practice 553

Melamed AD and Petit N, 'The Misguided Assault on the Consumer Welfare Standard in the Age of Platform Markets' (2019) 54 Review of Industrial 741

Monti G, 'Managing the Intersection of Utilities Regulation and EC Competition Law' (2008) LSE Law, Society and Economy Working Papers 8/2008, available at https://ssrn.com/abstract=1273615

—— 'Article 82 EC: What Future for the Effects-Based Approach?' (2010) 1 Journal of European Competition Law & Practice 2

Nihoul P, 'The Ruling of the General Court in Intel: Towards the End of an Effect-based Approach in European Competition Law?' (2014) 5 Journal of European Competition Law & Practice 521

Odudu O, 'The Wider Concerns of Competition Law' (2010) 30 Oxford Journal of Legal Studies 599

Petit N, 'The Judgment of the EU Court of Justice in Intel and the Rule of Reason in Abuse of Dominance Cases' (2018) 43 European Law Review 728

Rato M and English M, 'An Assessment of Injunctions, Patents, and Standards Following the Court of Justice's Huawei/ZTE Ruling' (2016) 7 Journal of European Competition Law & Practice 103

Rey P and Venit JS, 'Parallel trade and pharmaceuticals: a policy in search of itself' (2004) 29 European Law Review 153

Ritter C, 'How Far Can the Commission Go When Imposing Remedies for Antitrust Infringements?' (2016) 7 Journal of European Competition Law & Practice 587

Röller LH and Buigues PA, 'The Office of the Chief Competition Economist at the European Commission' (May 2005)

Rosati E, 'Five Considerations for the Transposition and Application of Article 17 of the DSM Directive' (2021) 16 Journal of Intellectual Property Law & Practice 265

Rubin EL, 'Law and Legislation in the Administrative State' (1989) 89 Columbia Law Review 369

Schellingerhout R and Cavicchi P, 'Patent ambush in standard-setting: the Commission accepts commitments from Rambus to lower memory chip royalty rates' (2010) 1 Competition Policy Newsletter 32

Schmidt VA, 'Democracy and Legitimacy in the European Union Revisited: Input, Output and "Throughput,"' (2013) 61 Political Studies 2

Shapiro C, 'Antitrust: What Went Wrong and How to Fix It' (2021) 35 (3) Antitrust 33

Sidak JG and Teece DJ, 'Dynamic Competition in Antitrust Law' (2009) 5 Journal of Competition Law & Economics 581

Steinbaum M and Stucke ME, 'The Effective Competition Standard' (2020) 87 University of Chicago Law Review 595

Stigler GJ, 'The theory of economic regulation' (1971) 2 Bell Journal of Economics and Management Science 3

Thambisetty S, McMahon A, McDonagh L, Kang HY and Dutfield G, 'Addressing Vaccine Inequity During the COVID-19 Pandemic: The TRIPS Intellectual Property Waiver Proposal and Beyond' (2022) 81 Cambridge Law Journal 384

Turner D, 'The Definition of Agreement Under the Sherman Act: Conscious Parallelism and Refusals to Deal' (1962) 75 Harvard Law Review 655

Waelbroeck D, 'Michelin II: A Per Se Rule Against Rebates by Dominant Companies?' (2005) 1 Journal of Competition Law & Economics 149

Whish R, 'Reflections on Regulation 1/2003, declarations of inapplicability and informal guidance' (2022) 2 Concurrences 2

Wils WPJ, 'Settlements of EU Antitrust Investigations: Commitment Decisions Under Article 9 of Regulation No 1/2003' (2006) 29(3) World Competition: Law and Economics Review 345

—— 'Ten Years of Regulation 1/2003: A Retrospective' (2013) 4 Journal of European Competition Law & Practice 293

—— 'The judgment of the EU General Court in Intel and the so-called 'more economic approach' to abuse of dominance' (2014) 37 World Competition 405

—— 'Ten Years of Commitment Decisions Under Article 9 of Regulation 1/2003: Too Much of a Good Thing?' (2015) Concurrences Journal 6th International Conference 'New frontiers of antitrust' (Paris, 15 June 2015)

Witt AC, 'The enforcement of Article 101 TFEU: What has happened to the effects analysis?' (2018) 55 Common Market Law Review 417

Zenger H, 'Loyalty Rebates and the Competitive Process' (2012) 8 Journal of Competition Law & Economics 717

Other Sources

EU Press Releases

Commission, 'Antitrust: Commission ensures carmakers give independent garages access to repair information' IP/07/1332 (Brussels, 14 September 2007)

Commission, 'Antitrust: Commission initiates formal proceedings against Qualcomm' MEMO/07/389 (Brussels, 1 October 2007)

Commission, 'Antitrust: Commission imposes € 899 million penalty on Microsoft for non-compliance with March 2004 Decision' IP/08/318 (Brussels, 27 February 2008)

Commission, 'Antitrust: Commission probes allegations of antitrust violations by Google' IP/20/1624 (Brussels, 30 November 2010)

Commission, 'Antitrust: Commission seeks feedback on commitments offered by Google to address competition concerns' IP/13/371 (Brussels, 25 April 2013)

Commission, 'Antitrust: Commission fines Lundbeck and other pharma companies for delaying market entry of generic medicines' IP/13/563 (Brussels, 19 June 2013)

Commission, 'Digital Single Market Strategy: European Commission agrees areas for action' IP/15/4653 (Brussels, 25 March 2015)

Commission, 'Antitrust: Commission sends Statement of Objections on cross-border provision of pay-TV services available in UK and Ireland' IP/15/5432 (Brussels, 23 July 2015)

Commission, 'Antitrust: Commission accepts commitments by Disney, NBCUniversal, Sony Pictures, Warner Bros. and Sky on cross-border pay-TV services' IP/19/1590 (Brussels, 7 March 2019)

Commission, 'Commission launches consultation to seek views on Digital Services Act package' IP/20/962 (Brussels, 2 June 2020)

Commission, 'Antitrust: Commission consults stakeholders on a possible new competition tool' IP/20/977 (Brussels, 2 June 2020)

Commission, 'Antitrust: Commission sends Statement of Objections to Amazon for the use of non-public independent seller data and opens second investigation into its e-commerce business practices' IP/20/2077 (Brussels, 10 November 2020)

Commission, 'Antitrust: Commission fines Valve and five publishers of PC video games € 7.8 million for "geo-blocking" practices' IP/21/170 (Brussels, 20 January 2021)

Commission, 'Antitrust: Commission sends Statement of Objections to Apple on App Store rules for music streaming providers' IP/21/2061 (Brussels, 30 April 2021)

Commission, 'Antitrust: Commission opens investigation into possible anticompetitive conduct by Google in the online advertising technology sector' IP/21/3143 (Brussels, 22 June 2021)

Commission, 'Competition: Second EU-US Joint Technology Competition Policy Dialogue consolidates international cooperation on competition policy and enforcement in technology sector' IP/22/6167 (Brussels, 13 October 2022)

Commission, 'Antitrust: Commission accepts commitments by Amazon barring it from using marketplace seller data, and ensuring equal access to Buy Box and Prime' IP/22/7777 (Brussels, 20 December 2022)

Commission, 'Antitrust: Commission sends Statement of Objections to Apple clarifying concerns over App Store rules for music streaming providers' IP/23/1217 (Brussels, 23 February 2023)

Commission, 'Antitrust: Commission announces Guidelines on exclusionary abuses and amends Guidance on enforcement priorities' IP/23/1911 (Brussels, 27 March 2023)

EU Comfort Letters

Commission, 'Comfort letter: coordination in the pharmaceutical industry to increase production and to improve supply of urgently needed critical hospital medicines to treat COVID-19 patients' (Brussels, 8 April 2020)

Commission, 'Comfort letter: cooperation at a Matchmaking Event – Towards COVID-19 vaccines upscale production' (Brussels, 25 March 2021)

Official Reports and Documents

Badea A, Bankov M, Da Costa G, Elías Cabrera J, Marenz S, O'Connor K, Rousseva E, Theiss J, Usai A, Vasileiou S, Winterstein A and Zedler M, 'Competition Policy in Support of Europe's Green Ambition' Competition Policy Brief (September 2021) https://ec.europa.eu/competition-policy/publications_en

Crémer J, de Montjoye YA and Schweitzer H, 'Competition Policy for the Digital Era' Special Advisors' Report (2019) https://ec.europa.eu/competition/publications/reports/kd0419345enn.pdf

Digital Competition Expert Panel (led by Jason Furman), 'Unlocking digital competition: Report of the Digital Competition Expert Panel' (2019), available at http://www.gov.uk/government/publications

EAGCP, 'An economic approach to Article 82' (July 2005), available at http://ec.europa.eu/dgs/competition/economist/eagcp_july_21_05.pdf

Federal Trade Commission, 'FTC Sues Drug Companies for Unlawfully Conspiring to Delay the Sale of Generic AndroGel Until 2015' (Washington DC, 2 February 2009)

Federal Trade Commission, 'In the Matter of Google Inc.' (File Number 111-0163 FTC) Statement of the Federal Trade Commission of 3 January 2013

McCallum L, Bernaerts I, Kadar M, Holzwarth J, Kovo D, Lagrue M, Leduc E, Manigrassi L, Ramos JM, Pereira Alves I, Pozzato V and Stamou P, 'A dynamic and workable effects-based approach to abuse of dominance' Competition Policy Brief (March 2023), available at https://ec.europa.eu/competition-policy/publications_en

Monopolkommission, 'Recommendations for an effective and efficient Digital Markets Act' Special Report 82 (2021)

OECD, 'Competition issues concerning news media and digital platforms' (2021) OECD Competition Committee Discussion Paper, available at https://www.oecd.org/daf/competition/competition-issues-in-news-media-and-digital-platforms.htm

—— 'Relationship between regulators and competition authorities' DAFFE/CLP(99)8

Oldale A and Padilla J, 'From state monopoly to the "investment ladder": competition policy and the NRF', in Swedish Competition Authority, The Pros and Cons of Antitrust in Deregulated Markets (2004)

Stigler Committee on Digital Platforms: Final Report (2019), available at https://www.chicagobooth.edu/-/media/research/stigler/pdfs/digital-platforms---committee-report---stigler-center.pdf

Newspaper Articles

―――― 'EU ruling on Microsoft "flawed"' BBC News (London, 24 April 2006)
Aranze J, 'Guersent: EU considering new chief tech officer role to assist antitrust cases' *Global Competition Review* (London, 15 June 2022)
Dave P, 'Genius Media, The Nation sue Google in advertising antitrust lawsuit' *Reuters* (Oakland, 17 December 2020)
Gibbs S, 'Getty Images files antitrust complaint against Google' *The Guardian* (London, 27 April 2016)
Van Dorpe S, 'Google to start charging a licensing fee after EU Android ruling' *Politico* (Brussels, 16 October 2018)
Yun Chee F, 'Daimler to pay Nokia patent fees, ending German legal spat' *Reuters* (Brussels, 1 June 2021)

Speeches

Laitenberger J, 'Accuracy and administrability go hand in hand' (CRA Conference, Brussels, 12 December 2017
Monti M, 'EU Competition Policy' (Fordham Annual Conference on International Antitrust Law and Policy, New York, 31 October 2002)
Vestager M, 'Competition policy for the Digital Single Market: Focus on e-commerce' (Bundeskartellamt International Conference on Competition, Bonn, 26 March 2015)

Other

'DVD Read-Only Disk File System Specifications' ECMA Technical Report TR/71 (February 1998)
USB 2.0 Specification, available at https://www.usb.org/document-library/usb-20-specification
Technical Specifications and Technical Reports for a 5G based 3GPP system', available at https://portal.3gpp.org/

INDEX

A
access
  bottleneck segments   84, 159, 163
  competition law provisions   92
  digital markets   135–136, 138–139, 145
  indispensable infrastructure   35, 141, 146, 158–159, 173–175, 179, 274
  infrastructure, to   188, 274, 275
  intellectual property access rights   92, 94, 105, 108, 114–115, 117, 122, 223–231
  network industries   84, 159, 161, 163
  product redesign   247, 254–259, 266–270
  regulation   84, 92, 159, 163
  self-preferencing *See* self-preferencing conduct
  soft law instruments   161
Actavis   209, 210
Ahlborn, C and Padilla, J   50
airline sector
  commitments decisions   29
  market-shaping enforcement   25
Airtours   48–50
AKZO   181
Alrosa   163, 186
appropriability principle
  Digital Markets Act   143–147
  intellectual property   101, 102–103, 106–108, 109, 110, 115–116, 118, 120–123
as efficient competitor test
  Brussels Consensus   55, 56, 64
  margin squeeze cases   157–158
  more economics-based approach   49–50, 59, 60, 64, 157–158
AstraZeneca
  regulatory gaming   89, 207
automobile sector
  commitments decisions   29
  market-shaping enforcement   25–26

B
Baltic Rail   189
BAT *(Toltecs-Dorcet)*
  intellectual property   115
  trade mark delimitation agreements   211

BEH Electricity   176, 183, 184–185, 188–189, 275
Big Tech *See also* **digital markets; Digital Markets Act; dominant position**
  competition law investigations   97
  competition policy towards   8, 66–68, 273
  data harvesting and use   67, 123, 126, 127, 134–135, 136–137
  digital gatekeepers   124, 126, 127, 129
  exclusionary/exploitative conduct   133–135
  fines imposed   30–31, 232–239
  growth   1, 8
  interoperability obligation   127, 136–137, 142
  market concentrations/power   36–37, 65, 66–68, 70
  new consensus approach   69–70
  policy focus on   14
  regulation   97
  search engines   90, 123, 138–139, 146
Birss J   205
blanket prohibitions
  cartels   53
  more economics-based approach   53
Block Exemption Regulations
  ex-ante intervention   80
  power to issue   160
  purpose   18, 34
  Vertical   49
bottleneck segments
  access obligations   84, 159, 163
  Bronner doctrine   158–159, 163
  digital markets   36–37, 41, 98
  divestiture   92, 159, 160
  energy sector   158–159, 162
  market-shaping enforcement   26, 35, 158–159
  network industries   91, 158
  ownership unbundling   162, 171
  proactive measures   36–37, 41, 91, 92
  regulatory obligations   75, 76, 82–83, 84, 158–159
  telecommunications sector   36, 41, 158–159
bpost   79, 172
Brandeis J   65
Breyer J   209

British Airways   47–48, 57, 60
Bronner doctrine   84, 105, 141–142, 172–173, 175, 187, 188, 202–203, 236, 246–247, 250, 252, 255–259, 269, 273–274
   bottleneck segments   158–159, 163
   indispensability condition   255–259, 274
   intellectual property rights   105, 117
   margin squeeze conduct   164–165, 167, 168–172
   market-shaping enforcement   22, 158–159, 163, 180, 187
Brussels Consensus
   case-by-case approach   53, 55, 56, 63, 72, 141, 143, 147, 272
   decline   62–68
   as efficient competitor test   49–50, 55, 56, 60, 64, 68
   emergence   50–51, 66
   exclusionary behaviour, focus on   47–50, 53–55, 60–61, 66–69, 133
   goals   56
   good administration principle   61
   implementation of principles   51, 55–56
   input legitimacy   51–52, 56
   legitimacy of enforcement under   51–52, 56
   predictability, value placed on   8, 50, 52, 66, 69
   principles of intervention under   52–55
   proxies   56
   public interest, intervention must serve   52
   theory of harm principle   54–55, 58, 63
   throughput legitimacy   51, 56
Budapest Bank   59, 62
burden of proof *See* **proof**

C
Canal+   228–230, 231
capacity hoarding   172–173, 175
cartels
   allocative inefficiency   53, 59
   blanket prohibitions   53
   detection and deterrence   14, 16–17, 21, 34
   fines in cartel cases   30
   industrial-era competition law   33, 34
   policy towards   13–14, 21, 47
Cartes Bancaires   58–59
CBEM-Télémarketing   256–257
CDS – Information Market   22
Centrafarm v Sterling Drug   113
CEZ   183
Character Merchandise   230
Chief Competition Economist   50

climate change
   effect on attitudes   66–67
Coditel I
   freedom to provide services   220–222
Coditel II
   selective distribution system   103, 113, 114, 225–227
comfort letters
   limited use   28
   no entitlement to   37
Commercial Solvents   80, 257
Commission *See* **European Commission**
commitments decisions
   advantages   86–87
   Alrosa   163, 186
   behaviour and commitments, link   183–185
   Cross-border access to pay-TV   226–231
   effect   28, 86–87
   intellectual property   197, 226–231
   introduction   160
   law-intensive cases   29, 38
   market integration concerns   177, 179–181
   market restructuring   183–186, 188
   negotiation   29
   policy-driven enforcement   28–29, 38, 143, 229
   proactive enforcement   232, 267
   proportionality   163, 183, 185–186, 229
   role   29, 38, 162–163
competition
   appropriability of benefits   101, 102–103, 106–108
   contestability principle   106–108, 110, 117–118
   counterfactual, analysis against   55, 117, 218, 247–250, 260–263, 268, 276
   on the merits   47, 54, 181, 213, 216, 234–235, 250–254, 256
   restriction   59
   static and dynamic   103–106, 121, 122, 143–147, 245
competition authorities
   enforcement by *See* **enforcement**
   limits of   4–5
   market-shaping by *See* **market-shaping enforcement**
   monitoring role   19
   priorities   20
   variable role   13–15, 16, 17, 19–20, 21, 41
competition law
   advantages over economic regulation   83, 86

attaining objectives of another
    regime   82–83
auxiliary role   82–85
case-by-case approach   53, 55, 56, 59, 61,
    63, 72, 80, 108–110, 141, 143, 147,
    197, 246, 250, 272
competition policy and   8, 13
conduct increasing competition   116–117
contextual approach   108–110
copyright harmonisation   219–231
differing policy options   13–15
dynamic competition   103–106, 147
economic regulation, interaction with *See*
    economic regulation
enforcement *See* enforcement
existence/exercise divide   111–112
expectation of regulation, used in   76, 82,
    97–99, 195, 231, 270
flexibility   79, 81, 86, 91, 97
fragmentation   273, 275–277
gap-filling role   82, 86–91, 122–123, 154, 195
horizontal scope   86
hybridisation   148
incentivising investment   106, 110, 272
industrial era, development during   31–34
innovation, enabling   104–107, 117, 123,
    147, 272
intangible property *See* intangible property;
    intellectual property
law-driven enforcement, decline   7, 26–31, 40
legal certainty   4, 20, 26, 99, 229
market power, controlling   104–105, 106
more economics-based approach *See* more
    economics-based approach
new product condition   109
objective   80–81, 84–85
overlaps with regulation   73–79, 82, 91–97
perpetual change   1
policy-making through   3–4, 8
positive obligations   19, 36, 80, 141, 245
potential demise   147–148
presumptively abusive conduct   203, 204, 231
presumptively lawful   210, 246, 249, 250–251
presumptively unlawful   70, 72, 81, 141,
    176, 251
pro-competitive practices   116–117
proportionality of intervention   81, 183–187
proscriptive intervention   80
protection of competition as aim   80–81,
    84–85
rectifying regulation   82, 91–97, 154, 160,
    189, 195
Regulation 1/2003 *See* Regulation 1/2003
remedial interventions   3, 81, 99, 181–182
remedies *See* remedies
restrictions by object and by effect   57–59,
    60–61, 62, 72, 226
rivalry, static competition and   104, 122
safety net, acting as   82–85, 153–154, 164,
    166, 170, 191, 277
sectoral fragmentation   188, 190–191, 273,
    276–277
sector liberalisations   153–155
Société Technique Minière   116
testing boundaries of   8, 41, 85, 181–187,
    195–197
traditional understanding of   2, 31–34
trends in case law   57
competition policy
Big Tech, towards   14, 66–68
Brussels Consensus *See* Brussels Consensus
cartels, towards   13–14, 16–17
Commission Guidelines   39–40, 161
Commission's discretion   29, 37–38
competition law and   8, 13
competition law institutions and   4–5
exclusionary abuses   49, 68–69, 201
expansion of Commission leeway   37–38,
    273–275
implementation   13
input legitimacy   51–52, 56
legitimacy shift   128
market-protection   17–18, 19, 20, 34, 40,
    84–85
market-shaping *See* market-shaping
    enforcement
more economics-based approach *See* more
    economics-based approach
new consensus *See* new consensus
outcome legitimacy   68–70, 128, 130–131, 273
perpetual transformation   1
policy-driven enforcement   26–31, 40–41, 229
policy-making through law   3–4, 8
recalibration under Regulation 1/2003   6–9,
    20–21
redistribution as goal   273
soft law instruments   39–40, 160–162
Special Advisers' Report   70, 71
throughput legitimacy   51, 56
trade-enabling   17, 19, 20, 33–34, 40
variables   13–15
concentration
Big Tech   36–37, 65, 66–68, 70–71
coordinated effects   49

neo-Brandeisians 65
tendency towards 34–35, 276
conditional rebate schemes
  British Airways 47–48
  case-by-case analysis 48
  Hoffmann-La Roche 48
  Michelin II 47–48, 61
  potential benefits 53
Consten-Grundig 111
consumer welfare principle
  more economics-based approach 52, 55, 56, 64, 65, 68
  neo-Brandeisians 65–66
  new consensus 69, 71
Container Shipping 23
contestability principle
  Digital Markets Act 125–126, 127, 132, 135–139, 143–147
  intangible property 106–108, 110, 115–116, 117–118, 120–121
Continental Can 182
contract, freedom of 47, 169, 202, 203, 229, 246, 255
cooperation agreements
  sustainability goals 40
copyright *See* **intellectual property**
Coty 102
country of destination principle 225
country of origin principle 95, 221–223, 225
country of uplink rule 221–222
Court of Justice of European Union (CJEU) 15–16
Cross-border access to pay-TV
  copyright harmonisation 223–231
  intellectual property 122, 223–231
  market-shaping enforcement 23, 275
cross-border trade
  country of destination principle 225
  country of origin principle 95, 221–223, 225
  country of uplink rule 221–222
  Digital Single Market Strategy 219
  geo-blocking 219–231
  intellectual property rights 95, 194, 195, 219–231
  market integration 175, 176–179
  Murphy 222, 225, 226
  Portability Regulation 223
  price discrimination 220
  SatCab Directive 95, 221–222
  Sector Inquiry into e-commerce 220, 223
  trade-enabling enforcement 17, 19, 20, 34, 40

D
DE-DK Interconnector 176
democracy, competition law and 65
Deutsche Telekom
  competition law intervention 78–79, 191
  margin squeeze 157–158, 167–172
  market structure 156
digital markets *See also* **Big Tech; Digital Markets Act**
  access obligations 135–136, 138–139, 145
  anticompetitive effects, proving 260–266
  bottleneck segments 36–37, 41, 98
  competition law 3, 76–77, 97, 123
  competition policy towards 66–71
  contestability principle 125–126, 127, 132, 135–139, 143–147
  counterfactual, analysis against 247–250, 260–263, 268, 269, 276
  country of destination principle 225
  country of origin principle 95, 221–223, 225
  country of uplink rule 221–222
  cross-border trade 219
  data harvesting and use 67, 123, 126, 127, 134–135
  dominant position *See* dominant position
  enforcing competition law in 14, 25
  exceptional circumstances doctrine 246–247, 249, 250, 254–259, 269
  exclusionary/exploitative conduct 67–68, 133–135
  expectation of regulation 76–77, 270
  fairness principle 125–126, 127, 139–140
  freedom to provide services 220–221
  gatekeepers 124, 126, 127, 129
  geo-blocking 219–231
  Google Android 24, 37, 98, 99, 142, 232–233, 236–239, 244, 265, 276
  Google Shopping 24, 25, 37, 98, 99, 126, 142–143, 232–236, 246, 255–259, 276
  indispensability condition 236, 246–247, 250, 254–259, 274
  infringement decisions 232–239, 266–268
  innovation, enabling 123, 144, 145, 147
  integrated features 243–244, 245
  Intel and McAfee merger 243–244
  Internet of Things 206
  interoperability and integration 240–241
  interoperability obligation 127, 136–137, 142
  market integration 219
  market intervention 14–15
  market power 36–37, 135–140

market-shaping enforcement   25, 26, 36–37,
    135–140, 232–239, 255–259
market structure   36–37, 66–68
Microsoft I   120, 123, 146, 238, 245, 256, 266
Microsoft II   268
monopolies/quasi-monopolies   36–37, 65,
    66–68, 70–71, 136–137
more economics-based approach   133–134
network effects   36, 136–137
new consensus approach   69–71, 72
opening up ecosystems   135, 137–138, 141,
    233–241
presumptively lawful   246, 249, 250–251
presumptively unlawful   251
principles-based remedies   235, 256, 257,
    266–268
product redesign and business models   23–24,
    37, 232–250, 254–259, 266–270
SatCab Directive   95, 221–222
search engines   90, 123, 138–139, 146
Sector Inquiry into e-commerce   220, 223
segmentation   221–222
self-preferencing conduct   126, 135, 139,
    145, 232–236, 250–254, 256–259,
    263, 265
single market *See* Digital Single Market
    Strategy
Special Advisers' Report   70, 71, 72
standard development   194, 195, 198–206
status quo bias   139, 264, 265
tying   236–239, 256, 265
value chain   66–67, 127, 132, 135–139
value gap for content creators   89–90
Digital Markets Act
    access obligations   135–136, 138–139, 145
    adoption   72, 76–77, 97, 124–125, 270
    advertising space, fairness provisions   140
    alternative dispute settlement
        mechanism   140
    applicability of the regime   131
    appropriability, increasing   143–147
    burden of intervention   129–130, 141, 143
    Commission's leeway   130–133
    competition law compared   124–128,
        146–147
    competition law enforcement   141
    compliance, focus on   132, 141, 143
    compliance function   130
    contestability principle   125–126, 127, 132,
        135–139, 143–147
    data harvesting and use   126, 127, 134–135,
        136–137

data sharing   135, 141, 146
dynamic competition   143–147
enforcement   126, 132, 140–143
ex-ante intervention   147
exclusionary/exploitative conduct   135, 140
fairness principle   125–126, 127, 132, 135,
    139–140, 144, 146
flexibility   146
FRAND conditions   144
gatekeeper, designation as   126, 127,
    129–130, 131, 132
gatekeepers' burden of intervention   129–130,
    141, 143
gatekeepers' core segments   135, 136–138
generally   3, 124–125
hybrid nature   124–128
implementing acts   132, 141, 142, 143
innovation, enabling   144, 145, 147
intellectual property regulation compared   146
interoperability obligation   127, 136–137, 142
investigatory and monitoring powers   126
judicial review of decisions   132–133
legitimacy shift   128, 130–131
litigation disincentivised   143
market restructuring   135–140, 143, 144
negotiated outcomes   143, 189
network effects   136–137
objectives   125–126, 127, 131, 135
obligations under   149–150
obligation to deal   141, 256
opening up ecosystems   135, 137–138, 141,
    233–241
outcome-driven policy-making   127–128,
    130–133, 147
policy-driven enforcement   127–128
proactive enforcement   127, 140–143,
    269–270, 277–278
procedural factors   132
promotion of competition   135–139
refusal to deal   141–142, 256–258, 269
restructuring value chains   127, 132,
    135–139
returns to scale/scope   136–137
reverse merger control   125
role of Commission   129–130
search engines   127, 138–139, 146
self-preferencing conduct   126, 135, 139,
    145, 233–236, 250–254, 256–259,
    263, 265
sideloading   137–138, 145
status quo bias   139, 264, 265
structural separation of gatekeeper   143

294 Index

target companies   127–128
third-party applications/app stores   137–138, 139, 145
Digital Single Market Strategy
copyright   219–223
creation   219
intellectual property legislation   220, 230
intellectual property value gap   90
market integration   219
discrimination
Google Shopping   37, 98, 99, 233–236, 256, 266, 274
vertically-integrated dominant firms   188, 274
divestiture
bottleneck segments   92, 159, 160
market-shaping enforcement   19, 24, 92, 159, 160, 179, 182
power to require   92
dominant position *See also* **market power**
abuse of   83, 85, 105, 108, 234–236
Airtours   48–50
AKZO   181
behaviour triggering intervention   3, 188
BEH Electricity   183, 184–185, 188–189, 275
Big Tech   65, 66–68, 70–71
breach of sector-specific regulation   76
British Airways   60
capacity allocation   175
challenging   41, 275
collective dominance   184
competition law approach   85, 275
constructive refusal to deal   82–83, 141–142
contextual approach   108
exceptional circumstances doctrine   105, 107, 112, 115, 116, 141–142, 187, 196, 201–204, 231, 275
exclusionary conduct   49–50, 87
GDF foreclosure   173–175, 179, 180
German Electricity Balancing Market   177–178, 179, 180, 181, 185–186, 229, 274
German Electricity Wholesale Market   183–184
Google Android   236–239
Google Shopping   233–236, 254
inferred infringement   60
injunctions as abuse of   200, 201–204
intellectual property   87, 105, 201–203
Magill doctrine   105, 120
market integration and   176–181, 183–185
pricing and   181
sharing infrastructure   188, 274, 275
Slovak Telekom   83, 105, 141

special responsibility   181, 251
strategic underinvestment   159, 163, 172–175, 188
Dunne, N   148

E
Economic Advisory Group on Competition Policy   50
economic regulation
access regulations   84, 159, 163
advantages of competition law   83, 86
auxiliary role of competition law   82–85
bottleneck segments   75, 76, 82–83, 158–159
competition law and, generally   126–127, 153–154, 188, 191, 270, 273, 277–278
competition law as instrument of   81–82
competition law used to rectify   82, 91–97, 154, 160, 189, 195
Digital Markets Act *See* Digital Markets Act
divergences from competition law   79–81, 84–85
gap-filling role of competition law   82, 86–91, 154
industry capture   83–84
intellectual property   74–75, 78, 79, 87–90
interaction with competition law   8–9, 73–91, 93–94, 147–148
intervention in expectation of regulation   76, 82, 97–99
intervention under competition law   78–79
market power   74, 84–85
market structure   74, 156–157
network industries   75
objective   80–81, 84–85
overlaps with competition law   73–79, 82, 91–97
positive obligations   80
prescriptive intervention   80
promotion of competition   81, 84–85
safety net, competition law as   82–85, 153–154, 164, 166, 170, 191, 277
sector-specific   3, 76, 82–84, 93, 155–159
efficiency principle
allocative inefficiency   53, 54, 55, 59
Brussels Consensus   55, 56, 64, 68
as efficient competitor test   49–50, 55, 56, 64, 68
more economics-based approach   49–50, 52–54, 59, 64, 68
new consensus   71
Post Danmark I   60
Servizio Elettrico Nazionale   60

electronic communications *See also*
        network industries
    Electronic Communications Code   185, 186
    Regulatory Framework   127
emerging consensus *See* **new consensus**
energy sector
    access regulations   84, 159, 163
    BEH Electricity   176, 183, 184–185,
        188–189, 275
    bottleneck segment   158–159, 162
    capacity hoarding   172–173, 175
    CEZ   183
    commitments decisions   29, 160, 162–163, 188
    competition law   3, 83, 153–193
    competition law rectifying regulation   154,
        160, 189
    cross-border trade   176–177
    DE-DK Interconnector   176
    Energy Sector Inquiry   160, 161–162, 176, 177
    ENI   24, 159, 173–175, 179, 180–181, 183,
        188, 229
    expectation of regulation   97
    gap-filling role of competition law   154
    Gazprom   176
    GDF foreclosure   173–175, 179, 180, 186–187
    generally   75, 80
    German Electricity Balancing Market   177–178,
        179, 180, 181, 183, 185–186, 229, 274
    *German Electricity Wholesale
        Market*   183–184
    liberalisation   153–155, 157–158, 159, 163
    market integration   175–179
    market restructuring   181–187, 188–190
    market-shaping enforcement   14–15, 25, 26,
        84–85, 158–159
    market structure   156
    more economics-based approach   155,
        157–158
    promotion of competition   84–85, 154, 160
    regulation, interaction with competition
        law   155–159
    Romanian Gas Interconnectors   187
    safety net, competition law as   153–154,
        164, 166, 170, 191
    sector-specific regulation   155, 158, 159
    strategic underinvestment   159, 163,
        172–175, 188
    Swedish Interconnectors   23, 178–179, 180, 187
    Third Energy Package   153, 161, 185
enforcement
    alternative enforcement actors   37, 38
    behavioural remedies   3, 6, 16, 19, 24,
        186–187

behavioural triggers for intervention   3,
    130–131, 188, 275
Brussels Consensus   51–52, 56
cartels, against   14, 21, 33
case-by-case approach   53, 55, 56, 59, 61,
    63, 72, 80, 91, 108–110, 141, 143, 147,
    246, 250
cross-border trade   17, 19, 20
detection-deterrence   16–17, 19, 20–21,
    33–34, 40–41
digital markets   14, 25
Digital Markets Act   126, 132, 140–143
establishing infringement   3
European Commission powers   2
fact-intensive investigations   14, 15, 30
fines   30–31, 232–239
industrial-era competition law   31–35
input legitimacy   51–52, 56
inter-brand or intra-brand
    competition   15–16
law-driven, decline   7, 26–31, 40
law-intensive   15, 38, 39, 187
legitimacy   8, 51–52, 56, 68–70
market-protecting   17–18, 19, 20, 34, 39–40
market-shaping *See* market-shaping
    enforcement
more economics-based approach   51–52,
    56, 70
national courts and authorities, by   37, 38
new consensus approach   69–71, 72
outcome legitimacy   68–70, 128,
    130–131, 273
overenforcement, tolerance of   70, 72
policy-driven *See* policy-driven enforcement
proactive   15, 16, 18–19, 21–24, 40–41,
    79–80, 95, 127, 140–143, 232–239,
    242, 267, 269–270, 277–278
reactive   15, 16, 17, 19
regulated markets   155–159
Regulation 1/2003, effect   271–272
remedial action   3, 16, 19, 99, 166, 169–172,
    181–182, 245
remedies *See* remedies
testing boundaries of law   41, 181,
    195–197
throughput legitimacy   51, 56
trade-enabling   17, 19, 20, 33–34, 40
traditional, limits of   34–35
underenforcement, avoidance   70–71
ENI   24, 159, 173–175, 179, 180–181, 183, 185,
    188, 229
equal treatment principle
    Google Shopping   37, 98, 99, 233–236

Index

Erauw-Jacquery 114
European Commission
  alternative enforcement actors 37, 38
  authority and powers 2, 37, 38, 160
  Digital Markets Act 129–133
  discretion to shape policy 29, 37–38
  Guidance Paper on exclusionary abuses 7, 8, 49, 59, 61, 68–69, 165, 167
  Guidelines 39–40, 161
  priorities 39
  variable role 19–20, 21, 38, 41
ex-ante interventions
  Block Exemption Regulations 80
  case-by-case enforcement 80
  competition law 79–80
  Digital Markets Act 147
  intellectual property 147
  soft law instruments 80
exceptional circumstances doctrine *See also* **indispensability condition**
  applicability 274
  Bronner See Bronner doctrine
  digital markets 246–247, 249, 250, 254–259, 269
  expansion 273–275
  Google Shopping 236, 255–259, 269, 274
  intellectual property 105, 107, 112, 115, 116, 141–142, 187, 196, 201–204, 231
  Magill and *IMS Health* 105, 111, 115, 141, 164, 196, 202, 231, 250, 255
  market-shaping enforcement 274, 275
  product redesign and business models 246–247, 254–259, 269
  Slovak Telekom 141, 168–170, 171–172, 202, 246, 247, 255, 258
exclusionary/exploitative conduct
  action against 35
  Big Tech 133–135
  Brussels Consensus 47–50, 53–55, 60–61, 66–69, 133
  Commission Guidelines 7, 49, 68–69
  competition law 119
  conditional rebate schemes 50, 55
  digital markets 67–68, 133–135
  Digital Markets Act 135, 140
  dominant position, creating 87
  as efficient competitor test 49–50, 56, 59, 60, 64, 68
  evaluation 55, 59–61, 133
  Google Android 236–239
  Google Shopping 233–236, 251–253, 258, 265
  intellectual property 87, 119
  ITT Promedia 201, 202
  margin squeeze 158
  more economics-based approach 47–50, 53–55, 60–61, 66–69, 133
  Post Danmark I 60
  potentially exclusionary 50, 53–54, 135
  traditional enforcement against 32, 35
  tying 53–54, 66, 98, 236–239
exclusive dealing, enforcement against 34
exploitative conduct *See* **exclusionary/ exploitative conduct**

F

fair, reasonable and non-discriminatory (FRAND) conditions
  Digital Markets Act 144
  intellectual property 22, 95, 199–200, 202, 205, 206, 231
  market-shaping goal 21–22
fairness principle
  Digital Markets Act 125–126, 127, 132, 135, 139–140, 144, 146
  new consensus 71
FA Premier League 22
field-of-use restrictions 102
financial services
  market-shaping enforcement 25
fines
  cartel cases 30
  digital market cases 30–31, 232–239
  Google Shopping 30–31, 232, 235–236
  infringement decisions 232–239
  law-intensive cases 30
  policy choices, expressing 30–31
  settlement reducing 30
franchising agreements 240, 249–250, 251
  intangible property 103, 117

G

Gazprom 176
GDF foreclosure 173–175, 179, 180, 186–187
Generics 71
  intellectual property rights 111–112, 231
  restriction by object 58, 62
  reverse payment settlements 217–218
geo-blocking 219–231
German Electricity Balancing Market 24, 159, 177–178, 179, 180, 181, 183, 185–186, 229, 274
German Electricity Wholesale Market 183–184
goodwill
  intangible property 102

Google Android
  anticompetitive effects, proving   260–266, 276
  counterfactual, establishing   260–262, 268, 269, 276
  market-shaping enforcement   24, 37, 98, 99, 142, 232–233, 236–239, 269–270
  principles-based remedy   266–268
  product redesign and business model   24, 37, 233, 236–239, 244, 247, 266–270
  status quo bias   264, 265
  tying   236–239, 265
Google Shopping
  anticompetitive effects, proving   260–266, 276
  counterfactual, establishing   260, 262–263, 269, 276
  dominant position   233–236, 254
  exceptional circumstances doctrine   236, 255–259, 269, 274
  exclusionary/exploitative conduct   126, 233–236, 251–253, 255–259, 265
  fines imposed   30–31, 232, 235–236
  indispensability condition   255–259
  market-shaping enforcement   24, 25, 37, 126, 142–143, 233–236, 269–270
  non-discrimination duty   37, 98, 99, 233–236, 256, 266, 274
  product redesign and business model   24, 37, 233–236, 246, 247, 250–251, 254, 266–270
  self-preferencing conduct   232–236, 250–254, 256–259, 265
Guess   230

H
Hoffmann-La Roche   48
horizontal cooperation agreements
  Commission Guidelines   39, 40
Huawei   204–206

I
IBM–Maintenance Services   22
IMS Health   147, 252
  exceptional circumstances doctrine   105, 111, 115, 141–142, 164, 196, 202, 231, 250, 255
  margin squeeze conduct   164
  market-shaping enforcement   22
  refusal to licence intellectual property   105, 108, 120, 123
inapplicability, finding of
  adoption   28
  no entitlement to   37

indispensability condition *See also* **exceptional circumstances doctrine**
  Bronner   255–259, 274
  CBEM-Télémarketing   256–257
  digital markets   236, 246–247, 250, 254–259
  Google Shopping   236, 255–259
  indispensable infrastructure   35, 141, 146, 158–159, 173–175, 179, 274
  intellectual property, access to   108, 114–115
  margin squeeze conduct   164, 166–170, 172–175, 179
  product redesign   247, 250, 254–259, 269
industry capture   83–84
infringement
  digital market decisions   232–239, 266–268
  establishing   3
  intervention triggered by   3, 130–131, 188, 275
injunctions
  intellectual property   200, 201–204
intangible property *See also* **intellectual property**
  appropriability of benefits   101, 102–103, 106–108, 109, 110, 115–116, 118, 120–123
  Coditel II   103, 113, 114, 225–227
  competition law and   75, 100–123
  contestability principle   106–108, 110, 115–116, 117–118, 120–121
  Coty   102
  deferential approach to   111–123, 195, 231
  existence/exercise divide in competition law   111–112
  field-of-use restrictions   102
  franchising agreements   103, 117
  goodwill   102
  growing importance   1
  incentivising investment in   101, 106, 110
  intervention, scope for   112–115
  licensing   102–103, 105–106, 108–109, 115
  non-rival in use   100, 103
  Pronuptia   103, 117, 250
  public goods   100
  Remia   102
  risk of underinvestment   100–101
  selective distribution systems   102–103
  unprotected   101–102
  value, preservation   101–103
Intel   61–62, 64, 71
intellectual property *See also* **intangible property**
  access rights   92, 94, 105, 115, 117

Index

appropriability of benefits   101, 102–103, 106–108, 109, 110, 115–116, 118, 120–123
BAT (Toltecs-Dorcet)   115, 211
Bronner   105, 117
Canal+   228–230, 231
CDS – Information Market   22
Centrafarm v Sterling Drug   113
Character Merchandise   230
Coditel I   220–222
Coditel II   103, 113, 114, 225–227
collecting societies   35
commitments decisions   197, 226–231
competition law and   8–9, 75, 78, 79, 81, 87–90, 91, 92, 94–95, 103–110, 194, 195–197
Consten-Grundig   111
contestability principle   106–108, 110, 115–116, 117–118, 120–121
copyright harmonisation   219–231
country of destination principle   225
country of origin principle   95, 221–223, 225
country of uplink rule   221–222
Cross-border access to pay-TV   23, 122, 223–231
cross-border nature   95, 194, 195, 219–231
cross-border trade   95, 194, 195, 219–231
deferential approach to   111–123, 195, 231
Digital Markets Act compared   146
Digital Single Market Strategy   90, 219–223
domestic regimes   194, 222
dominant position, right creating   87, 105
duty to disclose   102, 107
dynamic competition   104–105
Erauw-Jacquery   114
EUIPO, proposed   206, 231
ex-ante intervention   147
exceptional circumstances doctrine   105, 107, 112, 115, 116, 141–142, 187, 196, 201–204, 231, 246–247
exclusionary/exploitative conduct   87, 119
exhausted rights   101, 112, 113–114, 121, 230
existence/exercise divide in competition law   111–112
expectation of regulation   195, 231
field-of-use restrictions   102
franchising agreements   103, 117
FRAND conditions   95, 199–200, 202, 205, 206, 231
freedom of contract   47, 169, 202–203, 229, 246, 255
gap-filling role of competition law   87–90, 91, 122–123, 195

Generics   111–112, 217–218, 231
geo-blocking   219–231
geographic reach of rights   95
Guess   230
Huawei   204–206
IMS Health   105, 108, 115, 120, 123
incentivising investment in   101, 106, 107, 109, 110, 121
inflexibility of regulations   87, 94, 109, 110, 146, 194
injunctions as abuse of dominance   200, 201–204
innovation, incentivising and enabling   81, 87, 94, 104–107, 110, 117, 123, 147, 194, 207
intervention, across-the-board   108–110
intervention, scope for   112–115
ITT Promedia   201, 202
Landgericht Düsseldorf   206
licensing   102–103, 105–106, 108–109, 113–114, 120–121
Magill doctrine   105, 111, 115, 116, 120
malaise with and within   118–119, 194–197
market integration   195
market power, controlling   104–105, 106
market segmentation   221–222
market-shaping enforcement   22, 23, 25, 195, 196
market structure   275
Microsoft I   120, 123, 238, 256, 266
Microsoft II   268
Motorola   203–204, 231
Nokia v Daimler   206
non-rival in use   100, 103
Nungesser   106, 107, 109, 117, 249, 250
originality, threshold of   111
patent ambushing   200
patent evergreening   89, 208
patent holdup theory   89, 200
patent thicket   88, 195
pharmaceutical sector See pharmaceutical sector
Portability Regulation   223
prioritisation   231
process patents   111–112
protection, qualification for   109–112, 114–115, 117–118
Protégé International   201
public goods   100
refusal to licence   105, 115, 120–121, 147
regulation   74–75, 79, 81, 87–90, 92, 94–95
regulatory gaming   89, 207–209
rights   74–75, 101–102, 110, 112–115, 196

right to property and 169, 202–203, 246, 250, 255
risk of underinvestment 100–101
Samsung 203–204
SatCab Directive 95, 221–222
scope of patent 113–114
selective distribution systems 102–103
short- and long-term competition 74–75, 78, 92, 95
standard development 194, 195, 198–206
standard development organisations 88–89, 198–205
standard essential patents 23, 194, 195, 196–197, 200–206, 231
static and dynamic competition 103–106, 121, 122
territorial licensing restrictions 102, 106, 113–114, 249
time-limited rights 101–102, 104, 107–108, 109, 111–112
trade-offs where rights awarded 101–102
trade secrets 102
unprotected 101–102
Unwired Planet 205
value, preservation 101–103
value gap for content creators 89–90
Video Games 230–231
Windsurfing 114
inter-brand competition
cartels *See* cartels
enforcement against 15–16
Internet of Things 206
interventions
behavioural triggers 3, 130–131, 188, 275
Brussels Consensus 52–55
digital markets 14–15, 129–130, 140
ex-ante 79–80
expectation of regulation, in 76, 82, 97–99, 270
intellectual property 108–110, 112–115
market-shaping enforcement 14–15, 19, 20, 24
more economics-based approach 52–55
new consensus 70–71
prescriptive 80
proportionality of 81, 183–187
proscriptive 80
remedial 3, 16, 19, 81, 84–85, 99, 166, 169–172, 181–182, 245
shift in burden of 129–130, 141, 143
structural 14–15, 19, 20, 24
intra-brand competition
CJEU decisions 15–16
enforcement against 15–16

investment, incentivising
capacity hoarding 172–173, 175
competition law 106, 110
intellectual property 100–101, 106, 107, 109, 110, 121
more economics-based approach 272
public goods 92, 101
strategic underinvestment 159, 163, 172–175
ITT Promedia 201

J
Jacobs AG 105, 117, 169–170
judicial review 71
Article 9 decisions 29
Digital Markets Act decisions 132–133

K
Khan, L 66
Korah, V 46

L
Landgericht Düsseldorf 206
Larouche, P 171
law-intensive investigations
exclusionary impact 158
legal certainty
case-by-case approach and 63
competition law 4, 20, 26, 99, 229
lex specialis doctrine 78
sectoral fragmentation resulting in 191, 277
Lemley, MA and Shapiro, C 119
***lex specialis* doctrine** 78
linkLine 165
Lundbeck 209, 210, 215–216, 217, 218, 231

M
Magill 147, 252
dominant position 105, 172–173
exceptional circumstances doctrine 105, 111, 115, 141–142, 164, 196, 202, 231, 250, 255
intellectual property rights 105, 111, 115, 116, 120
market-shaping enforcement 22
market squeeze conduct 164
margin squeeze conduct
abusive 55, 60–61, 82–83, 157–158, 163–170
Bronner doctrine 164–165, 167, 168–172
concept, generally 1
constructive refusal to deal 164–166

300   Index

Deutsche Telekom   157–158, 167–172
   as efficient competitor principle   157–158
   Guidance Paper on exclusionary
      abuses   165, 167
   IMS Health   164
   indispensability condition   164, 166–170, 172
   linkLine   165
   Slovak Telekom   168–172
   Telefónica   166, 168
   TeliaSonera   167, 168–172
market investigations
   UK competition law   72, 125
market power *See also* **dominant position**
   Big Tech   36–37, 65, 66–68, 70, 135–140
   competition law, generally   104–105, 106
   digital markets   36–37, 135–140
   economic regulation   74, 84–85
   Electronic Communications Code   185, 186
   exceptional circumstances doctrine   105, 107, 112, 115, 116, 141–142, 187, 196, 201–204, 231
   Google Shopping   232–236
   intellectual property   104–105, 106
   monopolies *See* monopolies
   neo-Brandeisians   65
   remedial interventions   84–85
   strategic underinvestment   159, 163, 172–175, 188
   vertical restraints and   49
market processes
   industrial era competition law   33–35
market-protection measures
   Block Exemption Regulations   18, 34, 49, 160
   decline   40
   enforcement   17–18, 19, 20, 34
   industrial-era competition law   33–35
   objective of competition law   84–85
   soft law instruments   39–40, 160–162
market-shaping enforcement
   aims   19, 26, 35
   airline sector   25
   automobile sector   25–26
   behavioural obligations   186–187
   bottleneck segments *See* bottleneck segments
   boundaries of law and policy-making   41, 85, 181–187
   Bronner   22, 158–159, 163, 180, 187
   business model alteration   23–24, 37, 232–250, 254, 266
   case law   41
   CDS – Information Market   22
   clustering around sectors   25–26
   Commission Guidelines   39–40

Commission's role   21, 41
commitments decisions *See* commitments decisions
Container Shipping   23
Cross-border access to pay-TV   23, 275
digital markets   25, 26, 36–37, 135–140, 232–239, 255–259
divestiture   19, 24, 92, 159, 160, 179, 182
energy sector   25, 26
ENI   24, 159, 173–175, 179, 180–181, 183, 188, 229
EU competition policy   21, 278
exceptional circumstances doctrine   274, 275
FA Premier League   22
financial services   25
FRAND conditions   21–22, 199–200
German Electricity Balancing Market   24, 159, 177–178, 179, 180, 181, 183, 185–186, 229, 274
Google Android   24, 37, 98, 99, 142, 232–233, 236–239, 244
Google Shopping   24, 25, 30–31, 37, 98, 99, 126, 142–143, 232–236, 255–259
IBM–Maintenance Services   22
IMS Health   22
intellectual property   22, 23, 25, 195, 196
Magill   22
market integration   175–179, 195, 219
market restructuring   24, 135–140, 143, 158–159, 181–187, 188–190, 196, 232, 275
monitoring by authority   19
negotiated procedures   143, 189, 232
network industries   175–179
obligation to deal   22, 24, 141, 256
positive obligations   19, 36, 80, 141, 245
proactive nature   18–19, 21–24, 40–41, 140–143, 277–278
proactive obligations   42–47, 232–239, 242, 267, 269–270
product redesign and business models   23–24, 37, 232–250, 254–259, 266–270
proportionality   274–275
regulated terms and conditions   22
Regulation 1/2003   21, 22, 160
remedial action   181–182
remedies   24
rise of   6, 13–15, 21, 35, 36–37, 40
risks for enforcing authority   19, 20
Romanian Gas Interconnectors   187
sector-specific measures and   36
single-buyer rule   22
structural interventions   14–15, 19, 20, 24, 182

supply/purchase terms and conditions   22, 24
Swedish Interconnectors   23, 178–179, 180, 187
unintended consequences   19
value chains, restructuring   22, 132, 135–139
vertically-integrated firms   21, 23–24
market squeeze conduct
  Magill   164
  remedial interventions   166, 169–172
market structure
  bottleneck segments See bottleneck segments
  challenging   81, 275
  competition and   3, 84–85
  competition law objective   85
  concentration, tendency towards   34–35, 276
  Deutsche Telekom   156
  economic regulation   74, 84–85, 156–157
  industrial era   31–35
  intellectual property   275
  monopolies See monopolies
  oligopolistic   32–33, 34
  preservation   85
  remedial action, triggering   84–85, 182, 275
  restructuring   24, 135–140, 143, 158–159, 181–187, 188
  sector-specific regulation   156–157
  Slovak Telekom   156
  TeliaSonera   156
  workable competition   32
MasterCard   98–99
Mazák AG   165, 166, 167
medicines See **pharmaceutical sector**
mergers
  Airtours   48–50
  Commission Guidelines   49
  concentration, tendency towards   34–35
  coordinated effects, leading to   49
  monopoly, creating   34–35
  TFEU Articles 101 and 102   3
Metro I   250, 254
Michelin II   47–48, 57, 61
Microsoft I   120, 123, 146, 238, 245, 256, 266
Microsoft II   268
monopolies
  Big Tech   36–37, 65, 66–68, 70–71, 136–137
  bottleneck segments   35, 36, 41
  exploitative conduct   35
  intellectual property   78
  intellectual property collecting societies   35
  neo-Brandeisians   65
  network effects   136–137
  Post Danmark I   34, 57, 60
  tendency towards concentration   34–35

more economics-based approach
  allocative efficiency   53, 54, 55
  anticompetitive effects, assessment   52–61, 68, 71
  Brussels Consensus   50–56, 61
  Budapest Bank   59, 62
  burden of proof   58
  Cartes Bancaires   58–59
  case-by-case approach   53, 55, 56, 59, 61, 63, 72, 141, 143, 147, 272
  case law   56–57
  consumer welfare principle   52, 55, 56, 64, 65, 68
  digital markets   133–134
  efficiency principle   52–54, 60, 64, 68
  as efficient competitor test   49–50, 56, 59, 60, 64, 68, 157–158
  exclusionary conduct   47–50, 53–55, 60–61, 66–69, 133
  Generics   58, 62, 71
  good administration principle   61
  implementation of principles   51, 55–56
  innovation, incentivising   272
  input legitimacy   51–52, 56
  Intel   61–62, 64, 71
  investment, incentivising   272
  legitimacy of enforcement   51–52, 56, 70
  liberalised industries   157–158
  margin squeeze   157–158
  Post Danmark I   60
  Post Danmark II   60
  principles of intervention   52–55
  procedural devices   61–62
  public interest, intervention must serve   52
  purpose   46–47, 56
  Regulation 1/2003   272
  restrictions by object and by effect   57–59, 60–61, 62, 72, 226
  rise and decline   3, 7–8, 13–14, 46–50, 62–68, 155, 272–273
  Servizio Elettrico Nazionale   60
  theory of harm principle   54–55, 58, 63
  throughput legitimacy   51, 56
  vertical restraints, treatment of   47, 49
Motorola   203–204, 231
Motta, M   47
Murphy   222, 225, 226

N
national courts and authorities
  Commission Guidelines   39–40
  Commission intervention   38

302 Index

enforcement by 37, 38
soft law instruments and 39–40
negative clearance decisions
Regulation 17 27–28
negative obligations
industrial-era competition law 33–35
neo-Brandeisian School 65–66
network effects
digital markets 36
Digital Markets Act 136–137
payment systems 98–99
network industries
access regulations 84, 159, 161, 163
Baltic Rail 189
bottleneck segments 91, 158–159
capacity hoarding 172–173, 175
digital *See* Big Tech; digital markets; Digital Markets Act
dominant position 172, 188
energy sector *See* energy sector
gap-filling role of competition law 90–91, 122–123
indispensable infrastructure 35, 141, 146, 158–159, 173–175, 179, 274
industry capture 83–84
liberalisation 1, 83–84, 91, 93–94, 153–155
market integration 175–179
market restructuring 181–187, 188–190
policy focus on 14
promotion of competition 160
regulation 75, 83–84, 90–91
search engines 90, 123, 138–139, 146
sharing infrastructure 188, 274
strategic underinvestment 159, 163, 172–175, 188
telecommunications *See* telecommunications sector
value gap for content creators 89–90
Neven, D et al 47
new consensus
burden of proof 71
consumer welfare principle 69, 71
digital markets 69–71, 72
Digital Markets Act 147–148
effective enforcement valued 69
efficiency considerations 71
enforcement policy 69–71, 72
fairness principle 71
goals 72
Guidance Paper on exclusionary abuses 7, 8, 49, 59, 61, 68–69, 165, 167
implementation, emphasis on 19, 36, 71–72, 140, 141, 148

judicial review and 71
objectives 8, 69–70
output legitimacy 69–70, 72, 273
overenforcement, tolerance of 70, 72
presumptive prohibitions 70, 72, 141, 176
principles of intervention 70–71
procedural devices 71
redistribution as goal 273
shift from process to outcomes 68–70, 128, 130–131, 147–148, 273
Special Advisers' Report 70, 71, 72
underenforcement, avoidance 70–71
Nokia v Daimler 206
Nungesser 106, 107, 109, 117, 249, 250

O
online platforms
competition law investigations 97–99
Digital Markets Act *See* Digital Markets Act
ownership unbundling 162, 171

P
passive selling 224
patents *See* **intellectual property**
pay-for-delay settlements
reverse payment 209
payment systems
competition between 98–99
MasterCard 98–99
network effects 98
per se infringements 53
pharmaceutical sector
AstraZeneca 89, 207
at risk entry by generic manufacturers 208, 215–218
BAT (Toltecs-Dorcet) 115, 211
blockbuster drugs 207
contentious patents 196
exclusive rights 207–209
Generics 217–218, 231
innovation, incentivising and enabling 207
intellectual property system 89, 102, 111–112, 194, 195, 196
Lundbeck 209, 210, 215–216, 217, 218, 231
originator companies 207
out-of-court settlements 208–209, 210–211
patent evergreening 89, 208
pay-for-delay settlements 209, 210–218
potential competitors, assessment 211–212, 214, 215–216
process patents 111–112
regulation 73, 207
regulatory gaming 89, 207–209

reverse payment settlements 209,
210–218, 231
secondary patents 208, 215–216
Supplementary Protection Certificates 207
trade mark delimitation agreements 211
policy-driven enforcement
Commission Guidelines 39–40
commitments decisions 28–29, 38, 143, 229
Digital Markets Act 127–128, 130–131
expansion of Commission leeway 37–38,
273–275
fines 30–31, 232–239
fragmentation resulting from 273, 275–277
outcome-driven policy-making 127–128,
130–131, 147–148, 273
proactive obligations 41–47, 232–239, 242,
267, 269–270, 277–278
product redesign and business models 23–24,
37, 232–250, 254–259, 266–270
redistribution as goal 273
settlements 29–30
shift to 37–38, 40–41
Portability Regulation 223
positive obligations
market-shaping enforcement 19, 36, 80,
141, 245
Post Danmark I 34, 57, 60
Post Danmark II 34, 60, 264
predictability and consistency
value placed on 8, 50, 52, 66, 69
presumptively abusive 203, 204, 231
presumptively lawful 210, 246, 249,
250–251
presumptively unlawful 70, 72, 81,
141, 176, 251
pricing
AKZO 181
cross-border trade 220
dominant position and 181
predatory 34
price discrimination 176, 220
price fixing 53, 59
Pronuptia 103, 117, 250, 254
proof
more economics-based approach 58
new consensus 71
restrictions by object and by effect 57–59
property, right to
intellectual property 169, 202–203, 246,
250, 255
product redesign and business model 246
proportionality requirements
Alrosa 163, 186

commitments decisions 163, 183,
185–186, 229
generally 81, 163
structural interventions 183–187
public goods *See also* **intangible property;**
intellectual property
appropriability of benefits resulting
from 101
incentivising investment in 92, 101
risk of underinvestment 100–101

R
refusal to deal
constructive, margin squeeze as 164–166
Digital Markets Act 141–142, 256, 269
self-preferencing conduct
distinguished 256–258
regulation *See* **economic regulation**
Regulation 17 2, 21, 26, 38
Regulation 1/2003
adoption 272
aims 37–38
Article 7 30
Article 9 28, 29, 38
Article 10 28
changes introduced by 37–38, 147, 160,
271–273
Commission leeway to shape policy 37–38,
273–275
commitments decisions 160, 267
competition policy, recalibration 6–9,
20–21
decentralising ambition 2
enforcement, generally 2
market-shaping enforcement 21, 22, 278
more economics-based approach 272
negotiated procedures, rise of 143
remedial action 181–182
sector inquiries 160, 161
regulatory gaming 89, 207
remedies
access requirements 92, 159
behavioural 3, 6, 16, 19, 24, 186–187
business model alteration 23–24, 37,
232–250, 254, 266–268
commitments decisions *See* commitments
decisions
divestiture 19, 24, 92, 159, 160, 179, 182
infringement decisions 232–239, 266–268
liberalised industries 159
market restructuring 24, 135–140, 143,
158–159, 181–187, 188
negative obligations 33–35, 245

304 Index

negotiated procedures   143, 189, 232
obligation to deal   22, 24, 141, 256
positive obligations   19, 36, 80, 141, 245
product redesign   23–24, 37, 232–250,
    254–259, 266–270
proportionality   81, 163, 183–187
remedial interventions   3, 16, 19, 81, 84–85,
    99, 166, 169–172, 181–182, 245
settlements *See* settlements
structural   3, 6, 16, 19, 24, 182
supply/purchase terms and conditions   22, 24
Remia   102
reverse payment settlements
economic and legal context   210
meaning   1, 209
pharmaceutical sector   209, 210–218, 231
United States   209
Roberts J   165
Romanian Gas Interconnectors   187

S
Samsung   203–204
SatCab Directive   95, 221–222
Saugmandsgaard Øe AG   169, 170
sector-specific measures
market-shaping enforcement and   36
selective distribution systems   103, 113, 114,
    225–227, 240, 249–250, 251
self-preferencing conduct
Digital Markets Act   126, 135, 139, 145,
    250–254, 256, 258, 263, 265
Google Shopping   233–236, 250–254,
    256–259, 265
refusal to deal distinguished   256–258
services, freedom to provide   220–221
Servizio Elettrico Nazionale   60
settlements   29–30
Shapiro, C   106–107
Sibony, A-L   56
single-buyer rule
FA Premier League   22
Slovak Telekom   191
abuse of dominant position   83, 105, 141
exceptional circumstances doctrine   141,
    168–170, 171–172, 202, 246, 247,
    255, 258
margin squeeze conduct   168–172
market structure   156
Société Technique Minière   116
soft law instruments
advantages   87
Commission Guidelines   39–40, 161
ex-ante interventions   80

generally   160–162
rise   39–40
standard development agreements   87
Special Advisers' Report   70, 71, 72
status quo bias
digital markets   139, 264, 265
sustainability
cooperation agreements   40
Swedish Interconnectors   23, 178–179,
    180, 187

T
technology transfer agreements
Commission Guidelines   39
telecommunications sector
access regulations   84, 159, 161, 163
bottleneck segment   36, 41, 92, 158–159
capacity hoarding   172–173, 175
commitments decisions   160, 162–163, 188
competition law   3, 75, 77, 78–79, 80,
    82–83, 153–193
competition law rectifying regulation   154,
    160, 189
Deutsche Telekom   78–79, 156, 157–158,
    167–172, 191
expectation of regulation   97
gap-filling role of competition law   154
Guidelines   161
investment incentive   92
liberalisation   153–155, 157–158, 159, 163
market intervention   14–15, 84–85,
    158–159, 188
market restructuring   181–187, 188–190
market structure   156–157
more economics-based approach   155,
    157–158
Notice on access agreements   161
objectives   80
promotion of competition   84–85, 92, 160
regulation and competition law,
    interaction   3, 155–159
safety net, competition law as   153–154,
    164, 166, 170, 191
sector inquiries   160
sector-specific regulation   155, 158, 159
Slovak Telekom   83, 105, 141, 156, 168–172,
    191, 255
strategic underinvestment   159, 163,
    172–175, 188
Telefónica   166, 168
TeliaSonera   156
Telefónica   166, 168
TeliaSonera   156, 167, 168–172, 202, 258

territorial licensing restrictions   102, 106, 113–114, 249
TFEU Articles 101 and   102
   application   1, 2, 3
   decentralised application   38, 39
   intervention, behavioural triggers   3
   potential demise   147–148, 278
   restrictions by object and by effect   56–59
   use to attain objectives of another regime   82–83
Tournier   35
trade-enabling enforcement
   cross-border trade   17, 19, 20, 33–34
   decline   40
   industrial-era competition law   34
trade marks *See* intellectual property
trade secret
   unprotected   102
tying
   digital markets   256
   efficiency gains   53–54, 243
   exclusionary/exploitative conduct   53–54, 66, 98, 236–239
   Google Android   236–239, 265
   market dominance   98
   Microsoft I   120, 238, 256, 266
   potential benefits   53–54, 243
Type I errors (false positives)   53, 66, 67, 70
Type II errors   70

U
underinvestment
   intellectual property   100–101
   strategic   159, 163, 172–175, 188
United Brands
   market integration   176

United Kingdom
   market investigations   72, 125
United States
   neo-Brandeisian School   65–66
   price squeeze conduct   165
   reverse payment settlements   209
Unwired Planet   205

V
value chains
   allocation of rents across   66
   digital markets   66–67, 127, 132, 135–139
   market-shaping conditions   22, 135–139
Van den Bergh Foods   48
vertically-integrated firms
   market-shaping conditions   21, 23–24
   non-discrimination   188, 274
   strategic underinvestment   159, 163, 172–175, 188
vertical restraints
   Commission Guidelines   39
   context, importance   47
   degree of market power, consideration   49
   more economics-based approach   47, 49
Vestager, Commissioner   66
Video Games   230–231

W
Wils, W   63
Windsurfing
   scope of patent   114
workable competition
   industrial-era competition law   32

Z
Zenger, H and Walker, M   54